# BOMB

# *BOMB*

## The Author
## Interviews

## Edited by
## Betsy Sussler

Published by
Soho Press, Inc.
853 Broadway
New York, NY 10003

Designed by
Everything Studio

Library of Congress Cataloging-in-Publication Data is available.

ISBN 978-1-61695-379-9
eISBN 978-1-61695-380-5

Printed in Canada

10 9 8 7 6 5 4 3 2 1

# CONTENTS

# Foreword
# by Betsy Sussler

These spirited dialogues are intimate and provocative because they are created between authors—playful and probing, they draw revelations from the experience of writing. They have taken place over lunch, in bars and homes, as recorded interviews or as epistolary exchanges via email and fax. They are intellectual explorations that range over life, influence, inspiration, craftsmanship, and the ineffable mysteries that transform the act of writing into a work of art. As discourse, they include you, the reader, in their making and in the interpretation of meaning. Welcome.

Betsy Sussler, Cofounder, Editor-in-Chief, *BOMB*

# Introduction
# by Francine Prose

Imagine eavesdropping on a conversation in which the writer whose work you most admire speaks honestly, openly, and articulately about how a book—or a sentence—gets written. Imagine an interview that touches on everything a favorite writer has read and thought about literature, about the craft of writing, about art, music, inspiration, revision—and the temptations of procrastination. Imagine that all these subjects have been collected and distilled into a leisurely, thoughtful, intimate dialogue about the most important things in a writer's life.

That is just the kind of conversation collected in this anthology culled from the interviews that *BOMB Magazine* has published over the last decades, a collection that will come as a revelation to readers—and to writers at every stage of their career. In these pages, we overhear authors talking to their peers, to people they respect, trying to make sense of the mystery that occurs when they sit down at their desks.

Here we can listen to Roberto Bolaño describe his enthusiasm for the stories of Edgar Allen Poe and the novels of Philip K. Dick, ponder how much of his work is autobiographical, and explain what interests him in fiction: "The form, the rhythm, the plot." The great Somalian novelist Nuruddin Farah discusses the differences between his early and late drafts. Lydia Davis considers how much she knows, from the beginning, about what's going to happen in one of her stories or novels.

Paula Fox reflects on the relation in her work between fearlessness and innocence. Jonathan Franzen speaks, with astonishing frankness, about the ways in which his family experience found its way into *The Corrections*. Maryse Condé recounts how she reimagined Emily Brontë's *Wuthering Heights* as a Caribbean novel. Jeffrey Eugenides takes on post-modernism and describes the challenge of sustaining the original impulse that led him to write *Middlesex*.

Sapphire addresses the question of mortality: how her awareness of the fact that "one day I'll be dead" spurs her determination not to waste time. And Lore Segal shares the advice she gives her writing students: "The one thing you can rely on in any situation is that the feelings you're going to have are not the ones you think you're supposed to have. Look and see what's really going on."

In these conversations, writers recall how they started writing a certain novel or story; they remember the various stages of the process; they willingly tell us what a character really signifies, what a plot turn represents. They explain what they were trying to do and say. They expound on the importance of the well-made sentence, on cadence and rhythm, on the challenge of creating characters and moving plots along, on the ways in which they have learned to deal in their work with the problems of time and space. And they are willing to get down to the nitty-gritty: editing, revision, dealing with an agent or publisher, literary prizes, the demands and obligations of "a writer's life."

Of course, reading the conversations collected in this anthology might give you a strange idea about how writers talk. Asked to account for themselves, from their earliest encounters with Dick and Jane to the moment when the first copy of their first published book arrived in the mail, they respond with concise, compressed, compact replies. On the subject of their literary influences, they say provocative and original things. Ben Lerner speaks movingly about his admiration for John Ashbery, Jennifer Egan cites Cervantes, Sterne—and *The Sopranos*. Geoff Dyer reminds us of the benefits of reading history and of watching the films of Andrei Tarkovsky.

And the most amazing thing is: they never sound stupid, never repeat themselves, never stammer or mumble unintelligibly. They always seem to have a smart and readily comprehensible answer. And they have no problem saying what they mean!

Reader, I have a surprise for you. Writers don't talk that way. No one, or practically no one, talks that way. Like everyone else, maybe more than everyone else, writers stutter, stumble, correct themselves, and say plenty of stupid things. They claim that they have no idea why they wrote what they did. Asked to name their favorite writers, they can't think of a one.

But this is how they sound when we read them in *BOMB Magazine*: articulate, truthful, open, funny, honest, touching, and consistently informative. Speaking for publication in *BOMB*, writers think harder than they normally do. They search their memories and their pasts, they try to come up with something that may be interesting or even helpful to their readers and to other writers. The raw material of these conversations has been distilled, compressed, edited—and the editor's job has been made easier by the fact that the material is itself better than normal conversation. Because these are *BOMB* conversations.

That is why we need *BOMB Magazine*, and why we have come to so treasure and enjoy it over the years. And why we—and you—need this book.

*BOMB* gives us conversation distilled into dream conversation, talk that transcends talk, thought that digs beneath transient impressions to get at the essence, the meaning, the purpose, the experience of the writing process. There is something to be remembered and learned from every one of the conversations gathered here. Read them for pleasure, for entertainment, for insight, and for clues to the mystery—to the hard labor and the profound satisfactions—of what writers do.

# BOMB

BOMB 96 — SUMMER 2006

# Chris Abani
# and Colm Tóibín

CHRIS ABANI  was born in Afikpo, Nigeria, in 1966. He is the author of several volumes of fiction and poetry, including the novels *GraceLand* and *The Virgin of Flames*. He is the recipient of a Guggenheim Fellowship, the Hemingway/PEN Prize, the PEN Beyond Margins Award, the Hurston Wright Award, and a Lannan Literary Fellowship, among many honors. He is currently a Board of Trustees Professor of English at Northwestern University. He lives in Chicago.

COLM TÓIBÍN  was born in Enniscorthy, Ireland, in 1955. He is the author of several novels, including *The Blackwater Lightship*; *The Master*, winner of the *Los Angeles Times* Book Prize; *Brooklyn*, winner of the Costa Book Award; and *The Testament of Mary*, as well as two story collections. Twice shortlisted for the Man Booker Prize, Tóibín lives in Dublin and New York and currently serves as Irene and Sidney B. Silverman Professor of the Humanities in the Department of English and Comparative Literature at Columbia University.

COLM TÓIBÍN  There are very few obvious connections between Ireland and Nigeria, other than the heritage we received from Her Majesty's government over the years. In Ireland, we haven't struck oil yet. Nonetheless, there's an astonishing passage in Chinua Achebe's book *The Trouble with Nigeria* that connects the two countries. Achebe is in Dublin, and he's watching a ceremonial event that the Irish government has organized. And he notices that the president of Ireland, Patrick J. Hillery—he was the president of Ireland from 1976 to 1990—sidles into the room, just moves into a public event with no obvious security, with no obvious sense of pomp, no medals, no uniform; he just walks into the room, greets a few people and sits down. And Achebe thinks that's an astonishing idea, and it stays in his mind. Of course, for us, that is the Irish, it was an aspect of the sheer dullness of Patrick J. Hillery that nobody wanted to kill him, or mob him. If you were a novelist in the society, you had trouble, because although the conflagration of Northern Ireland was happening just two hours away, it did not impinge on this world. To try to create fiction in this world created certain difficulties. But for Achebe, of course, this was to be envied. In some ways, the same difficulty arises for novelists operating in a theater of war as for novelists in a theater of dullness. The simple business of the sentence and the paragraph—the substance of fiction—in war or in peace seems to me not to be a particularly different task, no matter what the society. But the task you faced, where your president did not sidle into rooms unguarded, nonetheless created a different problem for you than Patrick J. Hillery did for me. Is that correct?

CHRIS ABANI  I like that. I would agree. It creates the problem of how to write an interior, somewhat quiet yet still important novel about people in that culture when the external theater seems so much more alluring, urgent even. But there is the problem, the obvious becomes the trap, and precisely because it is obvious it is considered important, so the rendering of the culture, of life in that culture, as art, is often not the measure. But to go back to the connections between Nigeria and Ireland, for me, on a personal level, a familial level almost, but also at the level of being Igbo, these connections go deep because much of the education of Igbos in Nigeria was from Irish priests and missionaries, directly in Catholic schools and through the Church, but also in the form of scholarships to Irish universities. In fact my father was at the University of Cork in the early 1950s and is still known around Cork as that bloody black idiot speeding down the middle of the road, causing pedestrians to flee either way. The Irish missionaries were different in Nigeria from, say, the Scottish or the Protestants. There was a quietness, almost an apology, in the way they were supposed to be "civilizing" us, partly because culturally there was so much in common that they would often want to defend the indigenous culture. They were the only ones who stayed during the Biafran Civil War—these incredible nuns and priests put themselves between the soldiers and the guns. They made a strong impression on people like my father. That quiet elegance continues even to today in Ireland, not just in the area of government, but also in the way that the literature is produced. I remember doing a reading in Dublin with Seamus Heaney. This guy shuffles into the room in a shabby jacket, sits down next to me. He's drinking a Guinness. I had just come offstage and he's like, "That was rather nice." I was like, "Who is this strange man?" Not out loud, of course. Then they announce, "Nobel prize winner Seamus Heaney." I'm looking for Seamus, and this guy says, "Hold my Guinness." It was him! We all went to his house afterward, all these young poets sitting around on the floor. This notion that art is available to everyone and there is no hierarchy has a quiet elegance too. I see that in your writing, and I wonder if that is more your tradition?

CT There are two traditions in Ireland. One is that you want to write a book that will change books forever, that will have its reader contained within the book. Those books have made a difference all over the world— for example, *Ulysses*, the work of Beckett, Flann O'Brien's *At Swim-Two-Birds*—in that they take on the entire business of language itself, consciousness itself, and create a new way of working with them. But as the Republic of Ireland settled down, there was an older tradition that could be worked on, which came from song, fundamentally, and also from prayer. It tended toward melancholy, which often worked best in the short story; it tended to use unadorned sentences, and be very respectful to rhythms and to the idea of a book itself. The master of this, who died last month, was the Irish writer John McGahern. What we don't have in Ireland is a novel that describes the disintegration of Gaelic society and its replacement with English-speaking society. We don't have a *Things Fall Apart*. We don't have a novel from which everything must take its bearings, that seems to catch history at a certain point and deal with it using a sense of fable, but also making it almost like a song, almost simple, immensely moving, as well as complex, but that could be read by everyone all over the world. Is Achebe's *Things Fall Apart* as important a book in Nigeria as it has been for people outside Nigeria?

CA Well, yes and no. I was going to ask you about *Ulysses* and Dublin. We both seem drawn to re-render cities that other writers have inhabited, but we can talk about that later. *Things Fall Apart* has more import, I think, as a political moment and has caused me to question if there is a Nigerian novel and what shape it should take. As beautiful as Achebe's book is, it seems to me that it didn't come from an aesthetic engagement, but rather a political one, written in response to Joyce Cary's *Mister Johnson*. It is a response to colonialism. Whereas Amos Tutuola, who comes before him, and even Cyprian Ekwensi, seem to be engaged with their own imagination, their own aesthetic. There are two schools of writing in Nigeria: Tutuola, Fagunwa, Okara, Soyinka, Okri and Oyeyemi and then Achebe, Aluko, Okpewho, Iyayi, Atta and Adichie. Habila and myself, I think, occupy a form somewhere between these two.

CT Tutuola's *The Palm-Wine Drinkard* is written getting everything there is in the oral culture, and playing with it.

CA Playing with it in this new form, which is the written form.

CT And it is totally alert to the possibilities of bringing a modernist aesthetic into a society that has had an oral culture.

CA Completely, and at the same time being aware of the political moment. It is very subversive. Achebe has set up a difficult thing to follow, the representational approach to Nigerian literature; we have to perform the culture to other people. I would much prefer to be like Joyce and Tutuola.

CT Yes, but Joyce comes in two guises: the author of *Dubliners*, which for anyone working to create a simple moment, seen and understood, offers a poetic zeal and beauty. To the aura surrounding, say, defeat or poverty— *Dubliners* does that. Whereas *Ulysses* breaks the possibility of anyone doing that again. But then you can never contain those two traditions. For example, in—what's the name of the later Achebe novel that has a wonderful woman character that Nadine Gordimer called "the best female character yet created by an African writer"?

CA *Arrow of God*?

CT No, the later one.

CA *A Man of the People*?

CT No, the later one.

CA *Anthills of the Savanna*!

CT  Yes! As an aesthetic achievement, that woman's presence in the book—I know that she has a role in politics, but for example, when she talks about the taste of sperm in her mouth and how she feels about that, that's got nothing to do with Nigerian politics, but it's a wonderful moment.

CA  It depends on whose sperm it is.

CT  Irrespective of whose sperm it is, you feel that the way it's described—sorry, I picked a good example—that could be in any country, anywhere. That novel is full of extremely interesting perceptions about people, about men and women, her voice especially. Am I right about that?

CA  You're absolutely right, but that's part of the beauty, the tragedy of political insurgency. It's not until his fourth novel that Achebe continues the experiment with form and voice begun in *Arrow of God*. But Gabriel Okara had done this already in *The Voice*. That's what happens in political contexts where literature takes on this role. I wouldn't be able to write if Achebe hadn't written. So it's not a criticism. His generation's privileging of the political moment has created a space for the Nigerian novel that allows my generation to enter and start to talk about the aesthetic moment.

CT  You've written recently about [Wole] Soyinka. How important has he been?

CA  You can't talk about Nigeria in any context without Soyinka. The country comes to birth in Soyinka's imagination. There's no political moment, no nationalistic moment that he doesn't have some involvement in. Purely as a voice of conscience, he's been the one constant. In Nigeria we have 250 ethnicities that are engaged in the often violent moments of self-determination. Soyinka is one of a few people able to occupy that duality that's required if Nigeria is to find itself. And you see that in his plays and novels as well. His work begins to achieve a universalism that has often led to criticisms over authenticity because he doesn't privilege folklore. For him myth and mythology exist only in terms of what they can do for the aesthetic moment, the way it did for the Greeks and the Romans. For me as a writer he is the most influential, both as a voice of conscience, but also in terms of aesthetic rigor and framework.

CT  Compared to *Things Fall Apart*, I never liked *The Interpreters*. It seems to me very dull indeed. Is that just an outsider's view? Maybe Soyinka's theater is his best work.

**CA** Theater is his best work, but I do think it is an outsider's view. In many ways *Things Fall Apart* performs a certain reassuring expectation of Africa. This means that most writers within my generation are resisting that performance. I am in fact lucky to get any kind of exposure because all my work is about resisting that performance. This new storytelling is a difficult balance.

**CT** Yes, but it seems to me that you've taken both. In *GraceLand* you're certainly alert to what Tutuola has done, in terms of your repetitions and style. But also there are pure pieces of nineteenth-century Russian realism, which both Achebe and Soyinka have worked with. So you're actually bringing the two forms together in order to dramatize what is quite a difficult public life for quite a fragile consciousness, your protagonist, Elvis. You're conscious of using both?

**CA** Very, but more conscious of actually taking directly from the Russians. There are references in the book—the books that Elvis is reading—that talk about the way the book is made. I read Dostoyevsky very early—ten, twelve years old—and became sucked into that ridiculous existential melancholy that thirteen-year-old boys feel, but haven't earned. Dickens, too. It's a colonial education, and so I had those references. Soyinka and Tutuola have been much more influential than Achebe in terms of my actual writing style. But in terms of how you build a worldview, Achebe has been more important, how you integrate what is essentially an Igbo cosmology into a very modern, contemporary, twenty-first-century novel. There are all of those things, but James Baldwin also plays into this.

**CT** As does Ralph Ellison's *Invisible Man*. I think that with every novel, there's this shadow novel: the novel that should have been and that was in my head at first, that was set in a much more public place. For example, I was in Spain when Franco died. I was at all the demonstrations. There was always a novel to be written. But when I went to write the novel, it was about those earlier years when there was nothing much happening. The Henry James book really should have been a novel about Oscar Wilde, which would have been much more exciting, funnier, more glamorous and sadder in the end. I was also conscious in *GraceLand* that there are things you are leaving out; the war is mentioned only in passing. It must have been tempting to have done a very big war novel, written the novel of the Biafran war.

**CA** Do you get that?

**CT** Of course, of course I do: "Where is the novel of Northern Ireland? Where is the novel of the civil rights movement? Where is the novel of the IRA?" Well, why don't you write it? (*laughter*)

**CA** It's funny, because when I was reading *The Master*—the beautiful opening scene with James's play, when Wilde is mentioned—I can see that temptation. Yes, it is tempting, but *GraceLand* was doing the very reverse of that; it was trying to be both minute and epic, which is a contradiction in terms. Here's a book that's dealing with a whole generation—my generation—of Nigerians, and our coming of age and our notion of the country's coming of age. So it sprawls all over the place, but it had to follow this single consciousness if it was going to bear through with any degree of resonance. Otherwise it would veer too easily into the polemic. *GraceLand* is like a manifesto: I wanted to talk about gender, sexuality, the performance of masculinity, and how that is always associated with violence, the terrain of which is the female body within Nigeria; all of those spaces of silence that exist in Nigerian literature and are not privileged in the way that the easily political is privileged. *Abigail* comes out of that, as does a book I wrote about a boy soldier. They're both novellas. They're small and minute because I'm afraid of that easy political grandstanding. I'm looking for a more effective way of discussing both the political and human. I've returned more and more to Baldwin, because Baldwin is always about the quiet human moment. He never shied away from race, from the civil rights movement. He never shied away from dealing with issues of sexuality. Being ten and reading *Another Country*, in a very homophobic culture, I realized that for James the only aberration in the world is the absence of love. And what's even more perverse is the giving up on the search for love, which is that melancholic voice that carries us in the quiet moments. That's what I want to return to. You too have this quietness at the heart of your work. Your writing is elegant, it's sparse—*Blackwater Lightship*, for example—and where the hell do you get these beautiful titles from? For you, is the more distilled voice the better voice? Do you like it more in this sense?

**CT** There's a lot of fear involved, that you're going to mess up the sentence, so you leave it short. It arises from having to struggle enormously just to get the thing down. I have no natural ability, I don't think. I have colleagues in Ireland who have a real natural ability—almost like having a natural singing voice—where you can write anything. I don't have that at all. So it always comes from fear, I think.

**CA** It's funny you should say that. Do you know Dermot Healy's work?

**CT**  He has a natural ability to just do anything with words.

**CA**  But he says the same thing! He says that he's terrified. *A Goat's Song* took him ten years and it's a beautiful book. Do you think that it's just that Irish writers are better writers precisely because they feel that they're not?

**CT**  I think that in societies like yours and mine, mothers realize: if my son can read and write, it'll be a way out of poverty. Reading and writing have a special sacred aura around them. You do not take them for granted. Because of the broken traditions and loose connections in our countries, what we write about also has its own rules and regulations. If you read your two books together, *GraceLand* and *Abigail*, there's always dislocation, the dead father or the dead mother. You could say that *Ulysses* is about a man whose father committed suicide, whose son died, and whose wife is having an affair with somebody else, walking in a city to meet someone whose mother has died. And you'll say, "Ah, this must be an Irish novel!" I don't know how I would write a novel—this might sound like a joke but I mean it—with two parents who would be alive at the end of the book. Your two most recent novels are about someone whose mother has died and who's a ghostly presence in both of the books.

**CA**  Yes. But everything in Nigeria is about haunting. It's about ghosts. The dead are everywhere, and just won't stay dead. In my Igbo culture, dead parents used to be buried in the middle of the living room and not in cemeteries. So in this way the dead are always there, to guide us, to teach us. I grew up around domestic graves and you couldn't have a drink without offering them libation. So the dead informed everything that the living did. They are in many ways our way of mediating self and history, partly because there's a real existential loss at the heart of what it means to be Nigerian, because three or four hundred years ago much of the culture was interrupted when the Portuguese arrived and began to deal in enslavement. What happens is that from that time on, Nigerian culture begins to cede itself to the invader, to this invasion of otherness. So even now in Nigeria, when we talk about "our culture," there's a certain Victorianness about what we think our culture is, which actually comes from Victorian England's colonial presence. It's that way in which all of our "selves" are built around ghosts, and sadly, mostly violent ghosts, malevolent ghosts. In *GraceLand* and *Becoming Abigail*, the mothers are dead and in a new book, *The Virgin of Flames*, the father's dead. So the body of becoming is often an absence made more present by its haunting, by the ectoplasmic residue. In my books, the dead return as text, as skin (diaries and maps), as inscriptions that act as the medium, the way to visit the ghostly places of self and yet return safely. So much of the ectoplasm of these ghosts is patriarchy and masculinity. My work asks if it is possible, if this absence, this malevolent place, can enfold and nurture and be reclaimed through prose and poetry, to turn into possibility. For me it's alchemy.

CT Who is Percival Everett? He gets acknowledged in both of your books.

CA He's an amazing African American writer who has been a huge presence for me. I started out as a genre writer, writing thrillers, and couldn't find a way to blend all that with the literary. He really brought things together for me. He has helped me solve one of the core challenges for contemporary African writers: how to occupy the spaces of imagination when the political moment is either inadequate or has exhausted itself. This is an interesting moment for Nigerian writers. We now have a more global moment, diasporas where even when you're in Nigeria you're on your BlackBerry all the time. There are none of the usual places of engagement anymore. We have to find new topographies for our imagination.

CT One of the ways that you have tried to solve this, by its very implication in *GraceLand*, even by the title—and this is something that Ireland and Nigeria have in common, that both societies were ready to let America wash over them in every way. For example, there is no such thing as Irish capital. If Irish people have money, they put it in a bank or they buy more houses, but they wouldn't ever invest in something that might make or lose money. There's no tradition of that. Irish people adore American country music. If you're a writer, you love Hemingway, Scott Fitzgerald. We see ourselves in certain ways as an aspect of America, and we are happy for that to continue, despite the fact that there was very little support for the current American regime in Ireland. There are images throughout *GraceLand*—it isn't overplayed. There's the relationship between Nigeria and Portugal, Nigeria and Britain, Nigeria and its own internal disputes, and all that almost pales in comparison with this new one, which is Nigeria and America.

CA In many ways it's always been a concern of Nigerian literature, the engagement with the Western voice. But it has always been seen as the bogeyman coming in to erase the existing culture. But I was more interested in *GraceLand* in the moments of possibility. Rather than its being a limitation, its being subversion too as well as possibility. Here's a Nigerian kid named Elvis, putting on whiteface to imitate a white guy who imitated black people, ridiculing the notions of race and ownership of art. I think my argument, or my belief, is that ultimately art in any form—literature, music, even cinema—offers dialogue. Once dialogue is introduced, the subversive element comes in. And so it can be transmuted into something else. America exports itself to Nigeria in this way, and Nigeria digests it and then exports itself back to America in a completely different way. A lot of things come from that conversation: possibility rather than limitation; something beautiful.

CT *GraceLand* is one of those books—I would love to have seen you writing it. To have known if it was day or night, the room, how many words per day. There are books like that, where you would love to see the thing being created. Could you give us some idea?

CA It was written in America, on a laptop, mostly in Starbucks, which seems appropriate. It was written very frenetically in nine months. I got obsessed with it. I was writing 16-hour days. The real difficulty was writing the fractured language. My tendency is to make everything beautiful. But I wanted to capture that cityscape. You were in the Lannan House, right?

CT No, I was never in Lannan. I was in Yaddo.

CA I thought you were in Marfa, Texas?

CT No, no. If you know them, do tell them I'd like to come.

CA A train went by Marfa at three o'clock in the morning, and it had the most melancholic whistle. But this is a town where the cemetery is segregated, still. So, to be there working on my new novel, *The Virgin of Flames*, in a place where the sky blends with the landscape and it looks like you're caught in a glass bubble with all that contradiction was quite the gift. That's where I wrote *Becoming Abigail*—in three weeks. I wanted to ask you how you write, how you make the work you make. I'm very intrigued, because each of your books is very different. But at the core of everything—like this Henry James book, *The Master*, is this notion of exile: this separation, this displacement, this melancholy and loss. How do you infuse all of that into the sparsest sentences? How do you write?

CT I wonder—and to ask you if this is true about you—if the first five or six books you read at a certain age matter to you more than any number of experiences? Or tend to merge with those experiences? And that they become your style, those books. Or a DNA in you, a magnet in you hits a magnet in them. Certainly, reading *The Sun Also Rises* in Tramore on the beach, when I was sixteen or seventeen, I was amazed. The hero being in Paris and going to Spain, having a whale of a time in Spain. But he was always separate from the others. I did all that, I did all that that happens in that book, after reading it. I didn't like the bullfighting thing; it wasn't my scene. Instead, I went to Catalonia. I was always there, watching the others, like the guy in book. And at the same age—I'm talking 1971 or '72—Penguin had published Sartre's trilogy, and it was being read by serious people. It's not read now. And *Guernica* was on the cover of the Penguin edition. It was everywhere you went. I didn't know anything about his philosophy—I still have no interest in his philosophy—but reading the first two books of his trilogy made an enormous difference to me. And then coming through those two books to Camus, to *The Outsider*. I ended up living like that. I didn't murder anybody, but nonetheless, those books didn't just affect the way I wrote, but they affected the way I lived. Notice that I'm not mentioning any Irish books, because in those years, the censors had been lifted and every book was coming in from the outside and the last thing you wanted to read was about Ireland. I read them later, but at that age those American and French books really hit me. Those books were what mattered, nothing else since of either reading or experience has mattered in any way like that.

CA I want to ask you about being Catholic or growing up in a Catholic household. I grew up very Catholic. I grew up going to a seminary and being kicked out, several times actually, for heresy. There's something about being Catholic that seems that you existentially displace all the time—it's almost like joy is a foreign country, and when you travel to it, you take all this flagellation. I'm talking about me here. I wanted to ask you if that informs any of the work you do?

CT Catholicism didn't affect me very much, other than that the rituals were both interesting and boring. I was an altar boy. I find it very hard to create a Catholic character. Maybe if they banned it I would start wanting it. But I suppose there is an elephant in the room, which is the matter of being gay. That did make a very big difference. At the moment I'm in the Castro in San Francisco, where every single person is gay. Which is most disconcerting because where I am in my head, there's no one gay guy for a hundred miles on all sides. Obviously, the business of holding a secret like that, which I did for years, affects you. It happens in Henry James. The best James books are where there's a secret and if told, it will be explosive. That is what interested me so much about James at the beginning, both personally and as a writer.

**CA** To answer the question that I actually asked you about influence: for me it's a lot of Marvel and DC comics. Silver Surfer: all of my melancholy comes from the Silver Surfer. As a child, there were these books that they shouldn't have allowed children to read, these little comic books from England called the *Commando* series, about the Second World War. There was a particular one called *Darkie's Mob* that sort of stayed with me. It is all of the ways in which the English, completely unaware, celebrate their own racism. I play with sexuality in all my books. There's an ambiguity to all my characters. In *The Virgin of Flames*, the protagonist wants to be a woman. I write my characters from the inside out. There's no spectacle to it, so of course the first question is, Where is your body in relationship to this text? That always fascinates me. Before I wrote this book about this guy who wants to be a woman—I had always prided myself on, while being straight, being not homophobic at all. Until I wrote a scene where the character is finally about to make love to a transsexual stripper but realizes that that's not what he wants. In fact, he wants to occupy the stripper's position. And you have that whole *Crying Game* moment, but instead of the penis revelation being the thing, it's the penis disappearance. So this transsexual stripper is teaching this guy how to disappear his penis, so that he could wear a G-string were he to perform as a stripper. I researched it on the Internet. My girlfriend at the time read what I had written and said, "This reads like a manual." The rest of the book was beautiful but then it's, "Okay, over here we have the penis." I really had to go there, so I hired someone who performs as a woman. I said, "Okay, show me how to do this."

**CT** Do you have his number? (*laughter*)

**CA** I wanted to ask you, did coming out change your interaction with the text or with readership or with editorship or all of this?

**CT** Yeah. For me, writing down the opening section of *The Story of the Night* and publishing it, was a very big moment. It was like what you were describing, except I realized I was going to go on being it, even if I stopped writing about it. It was like writing down the truth, which is something we should all be very suspicious of. And the question then is that of putting the truth genie back in the bottle. I would like a rest from either being gay, gay, gay or being Irish, Irish, Irish. Some other thing you could be—French, maybe, or very old, or clean-living—I might try. Obviously, being a woman would be terrific. I did it in my first novel so I suppose I cannot do it again. I wish there were more categories. I suppose there will be in time.

# Kathy Acker
# and Mark Magill

KATHY ACKER  (1947–1997) was born in New York City. She was a novelist, performance artist, playwright and essayist. Her books include *Blood and Guts in High School*, *Great Expectations*, *Empire of the Senseless*, *Don Quixote*, and numerous other works. She taught, among other places, at the San Francisco Art Institute; the University of California, San Diego; and the California Institute of Arts.

MARK MAGILL  was born in New York City in 1952. He is the author of *Meditation and the Art of Beekeeping* and *Why Is the Buddha Smiling?* He has served on the board of advisors of *Tricycle: The Buddhist Review*. He is also a filmmaker whose work is part of the permanent collection of the Museum of Modern Art. He lives in New York City.

**1. When were you born?**

1947.

**2. Age?**

35.

**3. Where were you born?**

NYC.

**4. Name of parents:**

Something Lehmann and Claire Weill.

**5. Why were you born? a.) Plan b.) Accident c.) Neither**

My mother was scared to have an abortion.

**6. Any brothers or sisters?**

One half-sister.

**7. Parents' professions:**

Mother—none. I never knew my father. His family owned Wildroot Cream Oil among other properties (no sobriety here).

**8. Last employment:**

Full or partial? Partial (and ended), oh, *Artforum* (*laughter*) (just to make trouble). Full, selling cookies in a now defunct bakery off St. Mark's Place.

**9. Last book read:**

Oh, *Story of Irene*. [A French pornographic novel]

**10. Last film seen:**

*King of Comedy.*

**11. Favorite book:**

Too schizzy and changeable to have anything permanent.

**12. Favorite film:**

The film that Jap guy did of *Story of O* and *Return to the Chateau*—something like *The Fruits of Passion*.

**13. Political party:**

I belong to some party; I forgot what. Oh, the Writer's Union, 'cause Jeffrey Weinstein's my friend. I belong to friendship and destruction (sentimental shit).

**14. Favorite recording artist:**

That Egyptian woman who just died about a year ago.

**15. Favorite artist:**

Jackson Pollock.

**16. Occupation:**

Writer or not . . . not occupied.

**17. Position desired:**

At times dead. I've been fighting against that one. Otherwise, enough money to buy clothes.

**18. World outlook:** (circle one) a.) Pessimistic b.) Optimistic c.) Zen-like detachment d.) Manic confusion

Enough money to buy clothes.

**19. Do you regularly abstain from any of the following: a.) Red meat b.) Sugar c.) Boiled vegetables d.) Pizza e.) Hard liquor f.) Coffee g.) Herbal tea h.) Black bean sauce i.) Shellfish j.) Potatoes k.) Chef salad l.) Hot sauce**

**20. How often do you bathe?** (circle one) Daily 5 4 3 2 1 times per week.

No one's allowed in my house.

**21. Do you brush your teeth after every meal?**

Fuck you.

**22. Do you have any large outstanding debts?**

I don't owe no one nothing.

**23. Does free will exist?**

What else is this about? I'm no superstar shit and never will be. If anything, I'm what happens after death, which is writing.

**24. If you were forced to take sides in a dinner table discussion, which of the following world views would you support? a.) Freudian psychology b.) Marxist economics c.) Mechanistic determinism d.) Probability and chance e.) Judeo-Christian dogma f.) Buddhist duality g.) Structuralism h.) Situationalism i.) Positionalism j.) Ayn Rand individualism k.) Trotskyism l.) Anarchism m.) Socialism n.) Liberalism o.) Nihilism p.) Existentialism q.) Educated skepticism r.) Other (please explain)**

Oh yeah—honey it's all there. Yuck, yuck. I'll do what I have to for the particular moment. Being an intellectual, I uphold guerrilla warfare.

**25. You are sharing a piece of pie after dinner. There is only one bite left. Do you: a.) Take it b.) Wait for the other person to take it c.) Offer it to the other person d.) Offer to split it e.) Split it and take half no matter how small**

I don't eat sugar.

**26. Are you basically: a.) Shy b.) Outgoing c.) Indifferent**

A human is a reflection of and reflects all phenomena. That is, a human who has made her or himself active (what pretentious bullshit).

**27. Are you subject to deep and inexplicable depression?**

Absolutely.

**28. Do you talk to yourself?**

I live alone, dummy. It's hard to get pleasure these days.

**29. Is your memory: a.) Exceptional b.) Good c.) Normal d.) Bad e.) Senile**

Let's compare a pencil to a vagina.

**30. Where would you most like to be right now?**

With you-know-who's cock in me.

**31. Who would you most like to be? Contemporary personality:**

His fuck.

**Historical personality:**

History doesn't exist.

**32. Favorite fashion designer:**

Azalea. But I can't afford his shit. You want to give me some?

**33. Favorite animal:**

Male.

**34. Do you have any pets?**

Yeah, sometimes.

**35. Do you have any house plants?**

I never raise the shades.

**36. What is your bedtime?**

When I fall asleep over my books and stuffed animals.

**37. What time do you get up?**

When I get angry at myself for thinking too much about this guy I went to sleep with.

**38. Who is the most famous person you ever met?**

I don't even know who's famous anymore. I guess Warhol is. He once took my photo at the Keith Haring Fun Gallery opening, but I never met him.

**39. Do you have a driver's license?**

No way.

**40. Have you ever been arrested?**

Oh yeah.

**41. Are you a registered voter?**

Oh no.

**42. Next of kin?**

[no response]

**43. Do you have any existing medical conditions for which you are currently receiving medication or are under a doctor's care?**

Oh yeah. No, I hate doctors. They kill even faster than me. I hate them worse than I hate society.

**44. Are you subject to fainting or dizzy spells?**

Yes, in the spring when I get hot.

**45. Why do you feel you are qualified to give this interview?**

I want to fuck you, Mark. Do you want to fuck me? But not as much as I want to fuck __.

**46. Is there a history of mental illness in your family?**

What's the question? My mother went cuckoo (from loneliness? Does anyone go cuckoo from anything?). My father murdered someone supposedly for trespassing on his yacht.

**47. Do you believe in God?**

[no response]

**48. Do you like to travel?**

I like to fuck. Don't put this in *BOMB*. I'm just horny, hee hee.

**49. What is your favorite pastime or hobby?**

Listening to records.

**50. Educational history:**

Lots. I had to fight against it for years.

**51. Are you for or against the integration of schools through busing?**

You've got to be kidding. I'm against the integration of the USA government in my life.

**52. What political figure (living or dead) do you admire most?**

I don't admire anyone. Now and then, art. Then my friends.

**53. Do you think the Thirteenth Amendment should be abolished?**

What's the Thirteenth Amendment?

**54. Do you think there should be a Palestinian homeland?**

Yeah, I'm a good Jew.

**55. If so, where?**

In my cunt.

**56. Do you believe in the right to own private property?**

Yes, only people. Not private property, living people.

**57. Do you believe in the right of inherited wealth?**

Yeah. I was born with me. I'm okay. No one touches me. Money's a fake.

**58. Do you think there should be socialized health care in this country?**

There should be all the food and medicine you need (though doctors stink so much, maybe it's better to kill them). Luxury, fun, etc. everywhere all the time.

**59. Do you believe in mandatory long term prison sentences for those convicted of violent crime?**

Generalities are unanswerable and stupid language.

**60. Do you believe in trial by jury?**

I don't like judgment. Frivolity should take the place of judgments. Females know best.

**61. Do you think there will be thermonuclear war (limited or unlimited) in the next 20 years?**

There is a worse war now. The war now is at least partly a language war. What else is writing (now) about?

**62. Should there be an income tax or laissez-faire economies?**

Should there be suicide or murder?

**63. Should the city of New York maintain a police department? If not, would you willingly give up your private property to the poor?**

I'll give my cunt to . . . (sober up, cunt. This is *serious*).

**64. Do you believe in the value of Vitamin C?**

Yes. I'm a believer.

**65. What's your sign?**

I do voodoo. I am Legba and Grassi (the child). This is serious, even more than sex.

*Note: Legba is the god of words who permits Grassi, the child-spirit, to speak through Kathy.*

**66. Do you hum along or tap your foot to popular tunes?**

"Popular" tunes are about half my mind.

**67. Have you ever been treated for alcohol or drug abuse?**

No way.

**68. What's your favorite lipstick?**

Red. My mom used it. Looks like cunt color after fucking.

**69. Have you ever been to a baseball game?**

I am really hooked on this fascination with machoism.

**70. Have you ever been married?**

Twice.

**71. What is your marital status now? a.) Married b.) Single c.) Divorced d.) Separated e.) Other**

Fucked up. Give me a divorce, Gordon.

**72. What is your current legal status? a.) Guilty b.) Innocent**

No registered anything. As I said, I have trouble enough just not wanting to be dead.

**73. What was your last major purchase?**

Who gives a shit. When you buy, you don't buy; you give away. Everyone's got everything all backwards. This money shit's about giving away.

**74. Do you own a tape recorder?**

No.

**75. Do you own a camera?**

No.

**76. Have you ever taken a photograph?**

No.

**77. What is your regular newspaper?**

None. *TV Guide.*

**78. What is your favorite food?**

Opium.

**79. Have you ever had a near death experience?**

Yes. Three times. Maybe more.

**80. Have you ever seen a ghost?**

Yes. Once.

**81. Have you ever been psychoanalyzed?**

This is control shit and makes me angry.

**82. Have you ever played poker?**

Of course.

# Martin Amis
# and Patrick McGrath

MARTIN AMIS was born in Swansea, Wales, in 1949. He is the author of numerous works of fiction, including the novels *Money*, *London Fields*, and *Lionel Asbo: State of England*, as well as *Time's Arrow* and *Yellow Dog*, both of which were listed for the Booker Prize. His memoir *Experience* received the James Tait Black Memorial Prize. He lives in Brooklyn, New York.

PATRICK MCGRATH was born in London, England, in 1950. He is the author of eight novels, including *Spider* and *Asylum*. A graduate of Stonyhurst College, England, he has been shortlisted for the Whitbread and Costa Book Awards, and he won the Premio Flaiano Prize in Italy for his novel *Martha Peake*. He lives in New York City.

**PATRICK MCGRATH**  I'd like to quote something you wrote about London in *Money*. John Self is speaking and he says, "Blasted, totaled, broken-winded, shot-faced London, doing time under sodden skies." But when he mentions New York, he has a somewhat more affectionate attitude, I think. He speaks of America as being "a vigorous mongrel."

**MARTIN AMIS**  Yes, that's all slightly ironic. I think *Money* makes a break from the English tradition of sending a foreigner abroad in that (a) John Self is half American, and (b) as a consequence cannot be scandalized by America. You know the usual *Pooterish* Englishman who goes abroad in English novels and is taken aback by everything. Well, not a bit of that in John Self. He completely accepts America on its own terms and is perfectly at home with it. A bit shocked at some things, like taxi meters on ambulances. Personally, I love New York. I did find though that my attitude changed overnight when I went there with my wife and child. I just thought, "Well, it's a great place to be by yourself but when you've got your personal tribe with you, it's hard to relax." Everyone's windmilling around in this neurotic state. Some are just not up to it and are coming apart at the seams. When you stroll alone down the streets of New York, you take this on as part of the deal. But when you're wheeling someone that's four months old, it's rather more of an undertaking. It was actually in Cape Cod that I really fell out of love with America, even as I was experiencing it at its best. My wife's American and we were staying at her father's shack in Cape Cod. Provincial America can be wonderful. But then the child got ill. We got out the yellow pages— I'd seen these little greed parlors all over the place, these sort of drive-in health studios or whatever they are. We rang round to all of them and none of them would let us bring him in because it was a weekend and they were all golfing. You realize they're not doctors at all, they're people who hold the health concession on that little bit of the island. Health entrepreneurs is what they are. The baby was in a terrible state and we were in a terrible state. The next day we drove to New York, with him in a bad way. True, once you're in New York, it's a bit better; it costs a lot of money, as it does in Cape Cod, but at least it's there. I think that explains the poor morale of ordinary Americans. On that particular trip I was researching a long piece on AIDS that I wrote. It was being reinforced in me all the time, that when something bad happens to you in America it's a double disaster because they always clean you out financially. That's a terrible aid to neurosis.

**PM**  You'd finished *Money* by this point.

MA Yes. In fact, *Money* was coming out. I'd noticed it before but it had never really struck me. You feel things so much more fearfully through your children. You take your own chances but when there's a child . . . it's the only developed country in the world, apart from South Africa, that doesn't offer a pretty good health safety net to its citizens and they don't seem to think that's odd. Have you heard about Joseph Heller's book about his illness?

PM Yes.

MA There were 250 pages of this stuff without it occurring to anyone that it's a grotesque system to promote. It cost terrible anxiety to Joseph Heller. One of his premiums had run out through sheer inadvertence. If he had just paid one $20 premium he would have had another $40,000 in coverage. He minds about that but he doesn't mind about the system. We all know that illness is very tied up with how your morale is generally and here you are getting charged for every Kleenex. Of course Reagan is another reason for looking askance at America at the moment.

PM The only tenderness and kindness John Self receives is in New York. In London he's treated pretty consistently with duplicity and brutality—by his lover, his supposed father, his stepbrother . . .

MA Even by me. Even by the Martin Amis character.

PM Even by you.

MA Yeah, he's more at home there. I didn't follow all the implications of that. Although he does say at one point that if you're completely ruined in New York, people just think you're European and artistic—like when he goes to address that meeting of the moneymen in some hotel. He opens his mouth to start giving his spiel about how successful the film is going to be, and he starts making a noise that reminds him of trying to squeeze the last bits of tomato sauce out of a plastic tube. It's a terrible wheezing sound. And he sort of staggers into the bathroom and explodes and has to be helped into the Autocrat (the limo). At which point he says, "I don't think I did myself any harm. They probably just think I'm a bit of a genius." The reason he feels at home in New York is because of class, I suppose. There are people in England who do terribly well and even lead quite a patrician life, ride to hounds and have a very good collection of first editions and a good wine cellar, for whom every second of their lives is completely poisoned by the thought of their inferiority in class matters. John Self would never have felt okay in England but he might just have pulled it off with himself in America.

PM In much of your work we find a contest between a suave upper-class decadent and an uppity yob, with no middle class in sight. And it seems the yobs are winning. There's a lovely scene in *Money* where John Self and his partners go out to lunch in a good restaurant. There's a respectable couple at a nearby table—

MA Backing off with napkins round their necks.

PM There's no hope. They're driven out as the lads get on with spraying champagne at each other—

MA —and singing "We are the Champions". . .

PM —and then falling into perplexed silence when the menus arrive.

MA Yes, as if over examination scripts. I think that's a characteristic of mine, to leave out the middle class. Either a weakness or a shortcoming or at any rate an empty space. It's really because I don't seem to be interested in the norm so much as the extremes. It's something you begin to notice after you've written about three or four books. You look at the book you're writing and it's the same sort of thing. The novel I'm currently writing has a nuke background, but it's the same old story. There's a Dickensian lout who works as a cheat in London. That's his job.

PM He's a cheat?

MA Yeah. And there's a remnant of the upper classes who's sitting very uneasily on a pile of the dirtiest money there is. I mean, all money is dirty if you go back far enough. Someone in a sweatshop somewhere. And there's this girl that they're clashing over. So I think I'll probably go on writing like that right until the end. With regard to the upper-class figure, I think the idea of having confidence is in the margin of all my books: and being on top of things is finally identified in *Money* as being a cry for help. Confidence is an entirely inappropriate response to the sort of world we live in. But I think, too, that my imagination is very much rooted in the shuffling, unattractive figure.

**PM** John Self winds up as a tramp, though there's the possibility that he will rise again.

**MA** Yes, he gets a foothold just before the last gulch. I regard that as, in fact, my happiest ending so far.

**PM** In the sense that John Self has a moral career and that there is a faint, tentative hope for him?

**MA** Yes.

**PM** That it will continue.

**MA** Also that it did him a lot of good to be deprived of money. Which is the great fear of the world of money. And in fact, he bursts out of the novel in the end.

**PM** Yes, he's all in italics.

**MA** He was really meant to die but in fact he clawed his way out of the novel. John Self . . . One of the ways I manage this business of having a doltish narrator and yet writing at full steam is a quite simple device which I realized Saul Bellow was using in *Henderson the Rain King*. Henderson has the most elaborate and poetic thoughts, but every time he opens his mouth to speak, it's drivel. So everything in quoted speech is faintly embarrassing and tongue-tied, but the thoughts are allowed full justice.

**PM** There's a moment when John Self marvels at the rewards of a relationship with a mature and graceful woman. He says: "It seems that all you've got to do to them is be nice, and candid, and faithful, and you get all this. What a deal." Is that the zenith of his moral career?

**MA** (*laughter*) Yes. He's limited by thinking that everything is a deal. And he's flummoxed because she doesn't seem to want anything from him, he thinks it's sick that all she wants is friendship; she hasn't got any designs on him. I think it's all a bit hedged with irony. It's fairly clear that he doesn't know what he's missing out on. So there is a dormant morality. And, in fact, he never actually gets away with anything really bad. For instance when he attempts to rape his girlfriend Selina. It's meant to be fairly horrible in a comic way, but after the first attempt he calms down and apologizes. Then there's a line break and a new paragraph; and he says: "Then I tried to rape her again." Not learning from mistakes is one thing, but it's fairly carefully fixed that his attempts at real wrongdoing always rebound on him very quickly.

**PM** Do you think this is why he's likable? Because otherwise he's a big, fat, ugly, greedy, violent man and there's no real reason to like him apart from the fact that he does fail and is victimized.

**MA** I never had any doubts about him of course. I always adored him. I was pretty surprised that in America, particularly—America is not noted for a sense of irony—they had absolutely no trouble with him. But one or two reviewers in London, even intelligent reviewers, said that it is really very depressing, which I couldn't understand because I thought the book erred on the side of mad exuberance really. He's not very nice, it's true, but he's certainly generous, and he wants to get rid of all this money that he's somehow got hold of. He gives money away in the street. He's capable of generous thoughts. I think Updike said a good thing about this. He said it's very mysterious what we like and don't like in fictional characters. And he said what we like in the end, I suspect, is life. If they've got that, it doesn't matter. There's a bit of Nabokov that's very good on this too. He says that actually you don't punish villains, you certainly don't anymore, you show them wiggling a matchstick in a profitable nostril, you show them as ridiculous, and that's much better than portraying them as tiptoeing conspirators.

**PM** You've written plenty of unlikable villains, though.

**MA** I'm not sure how likable the one I'm doing at the moment is. Not very, would be my answer. One of the funny things that's happening in literature is that the genres are getting a bit distorted. Now it seems clear to me that I'm basically a comic writer. The shape of my novels are all comic, or anticomic, but certainly not anything else, not tragic or even satirical. Whereas the butts of eighteenth- or nineteenth-century comedy were pedantry and pretension, particularly pretension, now the butts of comedy are criminals, wrongdoers. Dickens wouldn't be comic about his villains, for instance, and Jane Austen always gets very earnest when talking about villainy. The comic novel now seems to have gone into spaces formerly occupied by other sorts of writing, such as the melodrama; and nasty types are just laughed at. Though I think you can make everything very clear with style. *Lolita* is a very good example—you can see Nabokov really searching for the worst possible thing you can do to someone, and there's absolutely no ambiguity about that, even though the style gloats about everything.

**PM** You're clearly fascinated with transgressors. Why is this?

**MA** I don't know. The novel I'm writing at the moment is about a murder and it's not a whodunnit, it's a who'll-do-it, because the female character is that rare and possibly non-existent type of woman, a murderee—she arranges her own murder.

**PM** Consciously and deliberately?

**MA** Consciously and deliberately, yeah. It has to happen on a particular night. I think, in my case, and maybe this is terrible laxity but what puzzles me is not my characters doing it, it's why I make them do it. Someone wrote a thesis about me, I don't think there are many, but she wrote asking if she could talk to me about it, and the title was so good I said sure. It was, *Victimization in the Novels of Martin Amis*. And I thought, Jesus, man, she's ripped the hard covers off me! And there is something in that. I wonder what I'm up to that I must arrange these things. What does it mean morally? Is one accountable for it? Because it's so clear to me that it's not happening, that it's my invention, and that perhaps I don't really consider what the characters are up to. Again, maybe it's the impacting and compacting, the whole process. How dare I do it?, is the way I feel. And then you have this very troublesome analogy, the equivalence of the writer and the godlike figure, in that they are entirely on a par. In *Other People*, the narrator is the murderer, and the writer and the murderer are equivalent in that each has the power to knock Amy Hide off. Then, in this next novel, where there is a nuclear crisis going on, with the same old snap of my fingers I can have that happen too.

**PM** You played a game of chess with John Self at the end of *Money*, and it was a very close game really. It was an exquisite game and he lost only because he had the last move.

**MA** The chess game is parallel to the tennis game that occurs earlier in the book. Self is physically humiliated by Fielding and then mentally humiliated by me, as it were. What I enjoyed about putting myself in the book was that it was still John Self narrating. So, while Martin Amis was spouting off about the accountability of the author in fiction, and so on, John Self would be thinking about his toothache or his car. I do think that John Self is a representative figure and I don't want to say the *id* or anything like that. But he's who you are when you think no one is looking. And the great, the horrible joke of the novel is that there's always someone looking.

He is never just being a monster of sloth in his flat. And in a sense the novel is a suicide note in which he's offering this information.

PM Yes, the bathroom Self. And his sins are to a large extent bathroom sins. His carnality and his excess are very private sins, aren't they? Victimless sins for the most part.

MA Naturally, masturbatory. The element of lone gratification is bluntly stressed, as he says, in all his hobbies. And the drinking and the eating end up as bathroom events. He says at one point, "What did I do last night? I never meant me any harm." He is the victim of all his crimes.

PM Do you think he'll return in your work?

MA I don't think so. It's not entirely impossible. Something would have to come along that only he could narrate, for instance. You keep thinking you've come to the end of a certain vein. When I wrote *Other People*, which is the odd one out among my books, everyone said, "He's finally got all that adolescent nonsense behind him, let's see how he does now." And then straight back, in *much* more detail than ever, in *Money*. I don't think many writers have an awful lot of versatility. There are these amazing virtuosos like Anthony Burgess, but even then virtuosity becomes the thing.

PM One motive that recurs again and again is the mortality of the body—the rotting, the decaying, the baldness, the toothaches and so on.

MA Hefty reminders of corporeal nature. I'm always amazed by how successfully we do in fact banish all that from daily discourse. We all have our little dramas in the bathroom most days. Something's not quite right. You can see the way a certain bit is going. And we've all got our back pains and our knee aches and so on, and yet people can spend the whole day together and it's never mentioned—everyone's got their little cargo of health anxieties, their little cargo of entropy. I wonder why I've gone on about it so much because it's only in the last year or two that every time you bend over, your age seems to come all at once. I play tennis a lot and suddenly instead of adding to your vigor, playing tennis subtracts from your vigor. So some evenings you're sitting around thinking, "Oh, I feel really good today. Wonder why that is?" And then you realize it's because you didn't play tennis. It's a one way street really. In John Updike's new novel, he says it's rather depressing when you realize that, genetically speaking, we deliver our mail very early in the day. The rest is hanging around . . . my father is certainly making that subject his own. There's a chap in his new novel that's so fat he has to clip his toenails in the garden. There's no way around it. With a mirror in the garden. But I think actually I really like decay because it's just comic. And again, it's an attack on dignity and competence.

**PM** Are you close to finishing a new book?

**MA** I've in fact finished a new book. Just handed it in. I wrote five short stories on the trot, which is more than I'd ever done before, and although it wasn't clear to me at once, they all turned out to be about the same thing, nuclear weapons. So I wrote a long introduction about nuclear weapons, and to my surprise it was a book. It clearly was. I'm also halfway through a novel, which has been going on for a couple of years now. Also set slightly in the future and with a nuclear theme or background. One of the things that struck me while writing the introduction to the stories is actually how difficult nuclear weapons are to write about. As evidenced by the fact that the major writers of a generation ago who lived through the strange metamorphosis between a non-nuclear and a nuclear world, who were there when it all changed, didn't, on the whole, write about it. With some hefty exceptions. In the end one attributes that to the power of the subject in that it couldn't be taken in all at once. It resisted being written about, perhaps until the generation who had lived their whole lives under them came of age. It's the one evolutionary thing that I'm absolutely clear has happened in this century. Post-1945 life is completely different from everything that came before it. We are like no other people in history. We somehow got ourselves on this great wobbling ladder thousands and thousands of feet above the ground. The thing is, how do you get down? Rung by rung? Or do you say the ladder was never there? And it is all so grotesque and fantastic that it's tempting to say that the ladder is just an illusion. These things are completely unusable. That's where the insane hubris comes in—the fact that you think you can enslave this cosmic force. It's clear instantly that we have become enslaved by it.

**PM** How do you write about this without becoming didactic?

**MA** Exactly. Well, the introduction to this book, for instance, is quite long, and it is didactic, even though I don't ever come out and say what I think should be done about it, although I do have some ideas brewing. That's why I think what you write about has to be partly accidental. And it was in my case. I feel the nuclear scene is a background that sneaks up on you as a writer. A background that insidiously foregrounds itself by the time the story or the novel is done. I don't think you can address it head on. If you try and look at it between the eyes, all you can say really is that you love your family, and what is this monstrous novelty you must consider? And I don't think you can get very far with that. One of the things, one of the handles on it, I believe, is that human beings and, in fact, humanity, have already been very gravely altered by the threat, by the possibility, by the change in the evolutionary pathway nuclear weapons represent. I think nukes are responsible for a very great many modern defamations, things that make you reel back from tabloid newspapers—"What the hell is *that* all about?"— some raping of a ninety-year-old woman. Our ideas about what it is to be human are much changed by it already. It's a very good point that Jonathan Schell makes in *The Fate of the Earth* when he says there won't be any experience of nuclear war. All it will be is different kinds of death. And it will take place in a world without discourse anyway. So this is nuclear war. What we're having *now* is nuclear war. Because it's the anticipation of it, that's the only kind of experience that anyone's going to get . . . It's not a bad war so far. There's plenty of stuff in the fridge I suppose. But psychologically, psychically, it's happening now.

PM Are you moving away from that concern with individual morality that's present in the last few books? That concern with the venality, the corruption that comes in a character like John Self from simply choosing to do the bad thing when he knows he could do otherwise. Does that get dwarfed as you deal with nuclear issues?

MA Yes, I think it's bound to. But then nuclear weapons are at heart a moral area. One of the things about writing about nuclear weapons is that I suspect I've been writing about them all along.

PM How so?

MA Well, people ask me—I've never asked myself—why do you see the world as being such a grotesque, venal, sordid place? I can now say, "Well, that's one of the reasons." For example, you can't believe in a central authority that's sitting round making plans for fifty million dead. Once that's happening, then morality just tumbles right down from the top. If at the top morality is so unreal, then this is going to have a pyramid effect right on down. Of course, there's a danger of submitting to one idea and explaining everything in terms of it. But for the time being, it works as worldview. Aligned to this world view is the entropy business. People ask me, "Do you really think the world is getting worse?" I came up with a perfectly good paragraph-sized explanation as to why the world always seems worse even if it isn't. Which is that clearly, demonstrably, even if the world is not getting worse all the time, it's getting less innocent. It's getting more beaten up, raddled, older. Everything it's been through before . . . You know, people say, "It seemed just as bad in the nineteenth century." Yes, well maybe it did, but we've had all that now. We've suffered all that and now we're suffering all this. And every day there's more, we take on more. The world is like a human being. And there's a scientific name for it, which is entropy—everything tends towards disorder. From an ordered state to a disordered state.

PM So you would say that the past was probably a bit less bad than the present because we hadn't quite got so far.

MA It was less bad, yes. I think it was a lot less bad five hundred years ago. Less bad things had been done. I look at it as an aggregate really.

PM Evil accumulates?

MA Evil takes it out of you. Evil's always been winning.

PM Why should evil keep on winning?

MA Perhaps because the brain is partly reptilian. I have a rather schmaltzy notion of human potentiality which is, in fact, embodied in literature.

PM How do you mean?

MA It's a commonplace that literature evolves in a certain way but it doesn't improve. It just stays there. It's a model. I think literature has not just been about, but embodies: the best. The best that humans can do.

PM The best moral thought?

MA The best moral thought. The representation of humanity at the crest of itself. Something like that. In fact, I've never understood why the idea of literature as religion was demolished so quickly. It seems to me that would be a tenable way of looking at it. It's a constant, making something out of the present and the past at the same time. Certainly an elitist thing, there's no question about that. But it's an elite open to everyone.

PM Do you see it decaying alongside everything else?

MA Literature? No. I mean, they say the novel is dead. Well, try and stop people writing novels. Or poems. There's no stopping people. I suppose it's conceivable that no one will know how to spell in fifty years' time, but not while the books are still there. You don't need a structure. The autodidact is omnipresent in fiction.

# Roberto Bolaño and Carmen Boullosa

ROBERTO BOLAÑO (1953–2003) was born in Santiago, Chile, and lived in Chile, Mexico, and Spain. He was the author of numerous books, including *The Savage Detectives*, for which he won the Rómulo Gallegos Prize; *By Night in Chile*; and *2666*, for which he posthumously won the National Book Critics Circle Award. *The New York Times* described him as "the most significant Latin American literary voice of his generation."

CARMEN BOULLOSA was born in Mexico City in 1954. She is the author of over a dozen novels, including *They're Cows, We're Pigs* and *Leaving Tabasco*. She has won the Café Gijón Novel Prize and the Premio Xavier Villaurrutia and has been translated into several languages. Boullosa has taught at Georgetown University, Columbia University, and New York University, and is currently a Distinguished Lecturer at City College of New York.

*Translated by Margaret Carson.*

**CARMEN BOULLOSA**  In Latin America, there are two literary traditions that the average reader tends to regard as antithetical, opposite—or frankly, antagonistic: the fantastic—Adolfo Bioy Casares, the best of Cortázar, and the realist—Vargas Llosa, Teresa de la Parra. Hallowed tradition tells us that the southern part of Latin America is home to the fantastic, while the northern part is the center of realism. In my opinion, you reap the benefits of both: your novels and narratives are inventions—the fantastic—and a sharp, critical reflection of reality—realist. And if I follow this reasoning, I would add that this is because you have lived on the two geographic edges of Latin America, Chile and Mexico. You grew up on both edges. Do you object to this idea, or does it appeal to you? To be honest, I find it somewhat illuminating, but it also leaves me dissatisfied: the best, the greatest writers (including Bioy Casares and his antithesis, Vargas Llosa) always draw from these two traditions. Yet from the standpoint of the English-speaking North, there's a tendency to pigeonhole Latin American literature within only one tradition.

**ROBERTO BOLAÑO**  I thought the realists came from the south (by that, I mean the countries in the Southern Cone), and writers of the fantastic came from the middle and northern parts of Latin America—if you pay attention to these compartmentalizations, which you should never, under any circumstances, take seriously. twentieth-century Latin American literature has followed the impulses of imitation and rejection, and may continue to do so for some time in the twenty-first century. As a general rule, human beings either imitate or reject the great monuments, never the small, nearly invisible treasures. We have very few writers who have cultivated the fantastic in the strictest sense—perhaps none, because among other reasons, economic underdevelopment doesn't allow subgenres to flourish. Underdevelopment only allows for great works of literature. Lesser works, in this monotonous or apocalyptic landscape, are an unattainable luxury. Of course, it doesn't follow that our literature is full of great works—quite the contrary. At first the writer aspires to meet these expectations, but then reality—the same reality that has fostered these aspirations—works to stunt the final product. I think there are only two countries with an authentic literary tradition that have at times managed to escape this destiny—Argentina and Mexico. As to my writing, I don't know what to say. I suppose it's realist. I'd like to be a writer of the fantastic, like Philip K. Dick, although as time passes and I get older, Dick seems more and more realist to me. Deep down—and I think you'll agree with me—the question doesn't lie in the distinction of realist/ fantastic but in language and structures, in ways of seeing. I had no idea that you liked Teresa de la Parra so much. When I was in Venezuela people spoke a lot about her. Of course, I've never read her.

CB  Teresa de la Parra is one of the greatest women writers, or greatest writers, and when you read her you'll agree. Your answer completely supports the idea that the electricity surging through the Latin American literary world is fairly haphazard. I wouldn't say it's weak, because suddenly it gives off sparks that ignite from one end of the continent to the other, but only every now and then. But we don't entirely agree on what I consider to be the canon. All divisions are arbitrary, of course. When I thought about the south (the Southern Cone and Argentina), I thought about Cortázar, Silvina Ocampo's delirious stories, Bioy Casares, and Borges (when you're dealing with authors like these, rankings don't matter: there is no "number one," they're all equally important authors), and I thought about that short, blurry novel by María Luisa Bombal, *House of Mist* (whose fame was perhaps more the result of scandal—she killed her ex-lover). I would place Vargas Llosa and the great de la Parra in the northern camp. But then things become complicated, because as you move even further north you find Juan Rulfo, and Elena Garro with *Un hogar sólido* and *Los recuerdos del porvenir*. All divisions are arbitrary: there is no realism without fantasy, and vice versa.

In your stories and novels, and perhaps also in your poems, the reader can detect the settling of scores (as well as homages paid), which are important building blocks in your narrative structure. I don't mean that your novels are written in code, but the key to your narrative chemistry may lie in the way you blend hate and love in the events you recount. How does Roberto Bolaño, the master chemist, work?

RB  I don't believe there are any more scores settled in my writing than in the pages of any other author's books. I'll insist at the risk of sounding pedantic (which I probably am, in any case), that when I write the only thing that interests me is the writing itself; that is, the form, the rhythm, the plot. I laugh at some attitudes, at some people, at certain activities and matters of importance, simply because when you're faced with such nonsense, by such inflated egos, you have no choice but to laugh. All literature, in a certain sense, is political. I mean, first, it's a reflection on politics, and second, it's also a political program. The former alludes to reality—to the nightmare or benevolent dream that we call reality—which ends, in both cases, with death and the obliteration not only of literature, but of time. The latter refers to the small bits and pieces that survive, that persist; and to reason. Although we know, of course, that in the human scale of things, persistence is an illusion and reason is only a fragile railing that keeps us from plunging into the abyss. But don't pay any attention to what I just said. I suppose one writes out of sensitivity, that's all. And why do you write? You'd better not tell me—I'm sure your answer will be more eloquent and convincing than mine.

CB  Right, I'm not going to tell you, and not because my answer would be any more convincing. But I must say that if there is some reason why I don't write, it's out of sensitivity. For me, writing means immersing myself in a war zone, slicing up bellies, contending with the remains of cadavers, then attempting to keep the combat field intact, still alive. And what you call "settling scores" seems much fiercer to me in your work than in that of many other Latin American writers.

In the eyes of this reader, your laughter is much more than a gesture; it's far more corrosive—it's a demolition job. In your books, the inner workings of the novel proceed in the classic manner: a fable, a fiction draws the reader in and at the same time makes him or her an accomplice in pulling apart the events in the background that you, the novelist, are narrating with extreme fidelity. But let's leave that for now. No one who has read you could doubt your faith in writing. It's the first thing that attracts the reader. Anyone who wants to find something other than writing in a book—for example, a sense of belonging, or being a member of a certain club or fellowship—will find no satisfaction in your novels or stories. And when I read you, I don't look for history, the retelling of a more or less recent period in some corner of the world. Few writers engage the reader as well as you do with concrete scenes that could be inert, static passages in the hands of "realist" authors. If you belong to a tradition, what would you call it? Where are the roots of your genealogical tree, and in which direction do its branches grow?

RB  The truth is, I don't believe all that much in writing. Starting with my own. Being a writer is pleasant—no, *pleasant* isn't the word—it's an activity that has its share of amusing moments, but I know of other things that are even more amusing, amusing in the same way that literature is for me. Holding up banks, for example. Or directing movies. Or being a gigolo. Or being a child again and playing on a more or less apocalyptic soccer team. Unfortunately, the child grows up, the bank robber is killed, the director runs out of money, the gigolo gets sick and then there's no other choice but to write. For me, the word *writing* is the exact opposite of the word *waiting*. Instead of waiting, there is writing. Well, I'm probably wrong—it's possible that writing is another form of waiting, of delaying things. I'd like to think otherwise. But, as I said, I'm probably wrong. As to my idea of a canon, I don't know, it's like everyone else's—I'm almost embarrassed to tell you, it's so obvious: Francisco de Aldana, Jorge Manrique, Cervantes, the chroniclers of the Indies, Sor Juana Inés de la Cruz, Fray Servando Teresa de Mier, Pedro Henríquez Ureña, Rubén Darío, Alfonso Reyes, Borges, just to name a few and without going beyond the realm of the Spanish language. Of course, I'd love to claim a literary past, a tradition, a very brief one, made up of only two or three writers (and maybe one single book), a dazzling tradition prone to amnesia, but on the one hand, I'm much too modest about my work and on the other, I've read too much (and too many books have made me happy) to indulge in such a ridiculous notion.

CB  Doesn't it seem arbitrary to name as your literary ancestors authors who wrote exclusively in Spanish? Do you include yourself in the Hispanic tradition, in a separate current from other languages? If a large part of Latin American literature (especially prose) is engaged in a dialogue with other traditions, I would say this is doubly true in your case.

RB  I named authors who wrote in Spanish in order to limit the canon. Needless to say, I'm not one of those nationalist monsters who only reads what his native country produces. I'm interested in French literature, in Pascal, who could foresee his death, and in his struggle against melancholy, which to me seems more admirable now than ever before. Or the utopian naiveté of Fourier. And all the prose, typically anonymous, of courtly writers (some Mannerists and some anatomists) that somehow leads to the endless caverns of the Marquis de Sade. I'm also interested in American literature of the 1880s, especially Twain and Melville, and the poetry of Emily Dickinson and Whitman. As a teenager, I went through a phase when I only read Poe. Basically, I'm interested in Western literature, and I'm fairly familiar with all of it.

CB  You only read Poe? I think there was a very contagious Poe virus going around in our generation—he was our idol, and I can easily see you as an infected teenager. But I'm imagining you as a poet, and I want to turn to your narratives. Do you choose the plot, or does the plot chase after you? How do you choose—or how does the plot choose you? And if neither is true, then what happens? Pinochet's adviser on Marxism, the highly respected Chilean literary critic you baptize Sebastián Urrutia Lacroix, a priest and member of the Opus Dei, or the healer who practices Mesmerism, or the teenage poets known as the Savage Detectives—all these characters of yours have an historical counterpart. Why is that?

RB  Yes, plots are a strange matter. I believe, even though there may be many exceptions, that at a certain moment a story chooses you and won't leave you in peace. Fortunately, that's not so important—the form, the structure, always belong to you, and without form or structure there's no book, or at least in most cases that's what happens. Let's say the story and the plot arise by chance, that they belong to the realm of chance, that is, chaos, disorder, or to a realm that's in constant turmoil (some call it apocalyptic). Form, on the other hand, is a choice made through intelligence, cunning, and silence, all the weapons used by Ulysses in his battle against death. Form seeks an artifice; the story seeks a precipice. Or to use a metaphor from the Chilean countryside (a bad one, as you'll see): It's not that I don't like precipices, but I prefer to see them from a bridge.

CB Women writers are constantly annoyed by this question, but I can't help inflicting it on you—if only because after being asked it so many times, I regard it as an inevitable, though unpleasant ritual: How much autobiographical material is there in your work? To what extent is it a self-portrait?

RB A self-portrait? Not much. A self-portrait requires a certain kind of ego, a willingness to look at yourself over and over again, a manifest interest in what you are or have been. Literature is full of autobiographies, some very good, but self-portraits tend to be very bad, including self-portraits in poetry, which at first would seem to be a more suitable genre for self-portraiture than prose. Is my work autobiographical? In a sense, how could it not be? Every work, including the epic, is in some way autobiographical. In the *Iliad* we consider the destiny of two alliances, of a city, of two armies, but we also consider the destiny of Achilles and Priam and Hector, and all these characters, these individual voices, reflect the voice, the solitude, of the author.

CB When we were young poets, teenagers, and shared the same city (Mexico City in the '70s), you were the leader of a group of poets, the Infrarealists, which you've mythologized in your novel, *Los detectives salvajes*. Tell us a little about what poetry meant for the Infrarealists, about the Mexico City of the Infrarealists.

RB Infrarealism was a kind of *Dada á la Mexicana*. At one point there were many people, not only poets, but also painters and especially loafers and hangers-on, who considered themselves Infrarealists. Actually there were only two members, Mario Santiago and me. We both went to Europe in 1977. One night, in Rosellón, France, at the Port Vendres train station (which is very close to Perpignan), after having suffered a few disastrous adventures, we decided that the movement, such as it was, had come to an end.

CB Maybe it ended for you, but it remained vividly alive in our memories. Both of you were the terrors of the literary world. Back then I was part of a solemn, serious crowd—my world was so disjointed and shapeless that I needed something secure to hold on to. I liked the ceremonial nature of poetry readings and receptions, those absurd events full of rituals that I more or less adhered to, and you were the disrupters of these gatherings. Before my first poetry reading in Gandhi Bookstore, way back in 1974, I prayed to God—not that I really believed in God, but I needed someone to call upon—and begged: Please, don't let the Infrarealists come. I was terrified to read in public, but the anxiety that arose from my shyness was nothing compared to the panic I felt at the thought that I'd be ridiculed: halfway through the reading, the Infras might burst in and call me an idiot. You were there to convince the literary world that we shouldn't take ourselves so seriously over work that wasn't legitimately serious—and that with poetry (to contradict your Chilean saying) the precise point was to throw yourself off a precipice. But let me return to Bolaño and his work. You specialize in narratives—I can't imagine anyone calling your novels "lyrical"—and yet you're also a poet, an active poet. How do you reconcile the two?

RB Nicanor Parra says that the best novels are written in meter. And Harold Bloom says that the best poetry of the twentieth century is written in prose. I agree with both. But on the other hand I find it difficult to consider myself an active poet. My understanding is that an active poet is someone who writes poems. I sent my most recent ones to you and I'm afraid they're terrible, although of course, out of kindness and consideration, you lied. I don't know. There's something about poetry. Whatever the case, the important thing is to keep reading it. That's more important than writing it, don't you think? The truth is, reading is always more important than writing.

# Guillermo Cabrera Infante and Oscar Hijuelos

GUILLERMO CABRERA INFANTE (1929–2005) was born in Cuba and went into exile in London in 1965. He was a film critic, essayist, journalist, translator, and writer. His novels include *Tres Tristes Tigres* (*Three Sad Tigers*), which was nominated for a Prix Formentor; *View of Dawn in the Tropics*; and *Infante's Inferno*.

OSCAR HIJUELOS (1951–2013) was born in New York City. He was the author of several novels, including *The Mambo Kings Play Songs of Love*, which was adapted into a movie and a musical; *Our House in the Last World*, winner of the Rome Prize; and *Dark Duke*. He was the winner of the 1990 Pulitzer Prize for Fiction, the Ingram Merrill Foundation Award, and the Hispanic Heritage Award for Literature. He was Professor and Writer-in-Residence at Duke University.

**OSCAR HIJUELOS**  When you were a child in Cuba what were your first exposures to the notion of narrative?

**GUILLERMO CABRERA INFANTE**  As a child I was exposed to the narratives of the movies. But the funnies (or *monitos* as they were called; in Havana we called them *muñequitos*) were as important—if not more so. The radio came later, where I heard a series of episodes or comedy programs. I was, by the way, the only one of my friends and/or classmates who read the funnies or could tell the difference between the movies and the serials. From the comic books in Havana I learned that a strip could be a trip, as in *The Spirit*, where Will Eisner's heroes were always dressed in blue (blue suits, blue felt hat, blue gloves) and had a sidekick who was a black boy, called Ebony in Cuba as in Ebony Concerto. Serials like *The Three Daredevils of the Red Circle* (the titles are approximations of the Spanish ones) were exercises in waiting for the Coming Attractions. It is rather baffling—at least to me—that there were more thrills in the funnies than in the movies. I taught myself to read by deciphering the inscriptions in the balloons because my father or my mother was fed up with my insistence on instant gratification by translation. They were all, as it should be, forms of popular art more pertinent than literature then.

**OH**  Were you fascinated by the story content of old Cuban songs?

**GI**  Cuban songs, or rather, *boleros*, were more important when the tunes carried a message. I became intrigued about what the lyrics could mean that made people sing almost in unison, *"Voy por la vereda tropical!"* But the first phrase that conveyed any meaning for me, of all things, came from a movie—some sort of appreciation expressed by Paul Muni in *Scarface* every time he encountered something that for him was tempting and therefore meant what I later knew was called class. The phrase, which I learned through repetition, was "Expensive, eh?"—more menacing than a direct threat.

**OH**  Can you remember the first time that you were conscious of seeing your name written, as a child?

**GI**  My name was a source of embarrassment, as my father had the grand idea of giving me the first name at home, of "Junior." In school, Cabrera, my second name became my first. And all because my father was my namesake and nobody was called Guillermo. Within my family I was called Guillermito.

**OH** Did you know any writers and were there books in your house?

**GI** There were books around when I was a boy as my father inherited all the books from my great-uncle, Tío Matías's library; he was sort of an intellectual who wrote in one of my hometown afternoon newspapers called *El Gibareña*, under the nom de plume Sócrates. He was a great influence on my father's life, whom he almost adopted when an awful tragedy made him an orphan. My paternal grandfather killed his wife, Tío Matías's sister, and then he shot himself. My father was only two years old at the time and was raised by his older sister and by my great-grandmother, a terrible tyrant of a woman. It was inevitable that my father would be a communist who in turn made of my mother another communist—though she was educated in a convent. She used to have at home a lithograph of a bleeding Jesus next to a colored photograph of bloody Joseph Stalin! With such knowledge, what forgiveness? My great-grandfather and my great-grandmother on my mother's side were avid readers of at least two national newspapers. A godsend, for those papers had a supplement of funnies on Saturday and Sunday with *Tarzan*, *Smilin' Jack*, and last and not least, *Dick Tracy*, which also appeared during the week but not in color, as the *X-9 Adventures*. I was reading Dashiell Hammett without knowing it. On Sundays there was *Prince Valiant* and the original *Tarzan* in color drawn by the incredible Hogarth, no kin to the English master and illustrator of *Tristram Shandy*. My father had the first byline in the family: he was a columnist and typographer for *El Triunfo*, the other (town) newspaper. He was then also the clandestine responsible for the propaganda of the Communist party—which proved his undoing. Both my father and mother were taken to jail in Santiago de Cuba, and my brother and I were left in the custody of my maternal grandmother. Six months later, they were released for lack of evidence that they were dealing in clandestine propaganda against the Batista regime, then in power for the first time. Nevertheless, two years later they were helping Batista become the legal president—on party orders. That should have been a lesson to them, but it was an unforgettable memory for me. When my father and mother came back from prison, my father was without a job and my mother had to begin working at home as a lace-maker. Two years later we emigrated to Havana, where my father worked as a journalist for *Hoy*, the communist sheet—a legal newspaper with Batista's blessing. The funniest thing is that *Hoy* came on Sundays with Superman as a feature funny based more on Nietzsche than on Marx! I didn't start to write and have a short story published in Cuba's leading weekly magazine until seven years later with my name suffering a sea change as I had to call myself Guillermo C. Infante.

OH  Was there an author, long dead, who you would have liked to meet?

GI  I wanted to meet Cervantes, and I did. My speech of acceptance was, in fact, a dinner date with Don Miguel himself. I could see, from my vantage point, King Juan Carlos of Spain shaking his head in disbelief. (Earlier, he had put around my neck a medal with the writer's effigy.) But the joke was on me. How dare this uncouth Cuban talk to Cervantes himself?

OH  Did you have a favorite movie actor?

GI  For a time I believed that Marlon Brando was the best actor I'd ever seen. But of course my favorite actor had to be the cigar smoking, gun-toting and dangerous Edward G. Robinson. I became a sedulous ape, cigar and all. My moment came during the Barcelona Film Festival when the director sat me next to the former Mrs. Robinson. She asked for it. She said to me: "You remind me of Eddy." And I said, "Who, Eddie Fisher?" She was aghast. Cigars are the best reminders.

OH  As your books are filled with puns and word plays, I am wondering who the first punster in your life might have been?

GI  My English teacher, Emilio González, was a master punster. No sooner had I taken my seat than he was engaging me in a spelling match and asking me to spell or not to expel or be expelled. He also concocted anagrams in Spanish, as when he asked for *la peneta para el patroceto*, meaning a quarter (a *peseta*) for *el patronato* (school fees).

OH  Why is it that while reading *Three Trapped Tigers* I sometimes thought of the writer James M. Cain? Am I imagining that you were intrigued by the more emphatic elements in his work? In any event, what did the works of Cain and other American writers do for you, if anything?

GI  As usual I saw the movie before I read the book. One of the reasons I read it was that I was looking for a gorgeous facsimile of Lana Turner in its pages. But she was not there of course. I admired *Double Identity* (that's how my typewriter spells "indemnity") because of Barbara Stanwyck. To watch her coming downstairs and see first her ankles and then her legs. As she wore an anklet on one of them, it was a lesson not in anatomy, but in eroticism. As you know, an anklet is called an *esclava* in Spanish and I became myself a slave of hers. It was, literally, my first erotic experience in a movie—but not in a moviehouse. At the time I didn't care for directors or actresses—called actors nowadays. I found a new kind of eroticism in other books, other writers. Like Erskine Caldwell with his white trash stories or the Faulkner of *Sanctuary* with wicked Popeye letting Temple Drake have it with a corncob. Yes, Old Cuthbert made me do it: I read *The Wild Palms* before I could spell Yoknapatawpha. Here it was Borges who made me do it. Or rather his translation of *The Wild Palms* with a better title, *Les plameras salvajes*, and a better prose. (Borges would say that I improved the novel by reading it.) After reading *Palms* I searched for all the novels of Faulkner translated into Spanish— or rather into the Argentine idioms that I then retranslated into Cuban. (As you know *God's Little Acre* became *La chacrita de Dios* before I trans-lated *chacrita* as *la finquita* when it really meant *la pequeña parcela*.) Then I discovered Signet Books, where all Faulkner was published in paperback and then Cain came along, not as brutal as Faulkner but more eroticiz-ing. Especially when Cora asks her lover, that is me, the reader, to bite her, to beat her—and I am quoting from a distant memory. But it was all there, on the printed page and it was, like Hugo would have said, "*un frisson nouveau*."

OH Did you, if memory serves me correctly, write movie reviews for *Carteles*, under the pseudonym Cain?

GI I used this pseudonym, among others, because I had been put in prison sometime before for writing and publishing under a spreading synonym a short story with "English profanities"—and here came the judge and fined me with the then extraordinary amount of $250.

OH Having first published in Cuba, at a time when José Lezama Lima and Alejo Carpentier were about, did you know them well? Did you like their work? Were they kindly toward you?

GI Lezama was a literary lion but Carpentier was a cowardly lion. Lezama's prose (I am not qualified to judge his poetry because I don't read poetry) was like an Orphic testament while Alejo Carpentier became, in Cuba under Castro, too much of a commissar to judge him kindly. (But I can say now that *The Lost Steps* is a masterpiece—though a Venezuelan one. At the time Carpentier was a Venezuelan according to his passport and himself.) If Carpentier looked like an alien and talked like an alien it was because he was an alien. He was born, in fact, in Geneva, Switzerland, to a French father and Russian mother. Lezama, on the contrary, was the opposite of a commissar but he ruled over Cuban poetry (my dyslexic eye almost wrote "pottery" instead) from his siege in Trocadero Street as if sitting in his sedan chair between two poles, poetry and prose. Furthermore, he was a good man, Carpentier was not.

**OH** Though Cuban writers like Reinaldo Arenas, Calvert Casey, and Severo Sarduy have passed on, are there any writers from Castro's Cuba who you are friendly with, despite the "adjustments of politics?"

**GI** There are some interesting new writers, all born under the bad sign of Fidel Castro. Among them Zoé Valdés, a little lady with a big hand, and Senel Paz and Abilio Estévez, being homosexuals together—and for that you need a lot of courage, as proven by Senel's short story whose outlook on life dominates all of *Strawberry and Chocolate*. Antón Arrufat and Estévez are now openly writing in Cuba and abroad valedictions of Virgilio Piñera, who was crushed by State Security only because he was homosexual and proud of it. Piñera died in obscurity but now his *Cuentos completos* are published in Spain with a brave introduction by Arrufat and a braver remembrance of his last years in Darkest Cuba by Estévez.

**OH** That you left Cuba in the 1960s (I believe) speaks for itself, but did you have any conversations with El Líder, and at what time of day did you decide that enough was enough?

**GI** I knew Castro when he was not yet Fidel in Havana in 1948. He was then a member of a gangstcroid group called the UIR, without an H. The group was leadered by a brave madman called Emilio Tró, who used to avenge past grievances by shooting his enemies—and then placing a sign over their dead bodies which said, "*La justicia tarda pero llega,*" meaning that his own brand of justice could be slow in coming but it always arrived. Castro was about that time a tall young thug who always dressed in double-breasted suits to better conceal the gun underneath. He was accused of killing his namesake Manolo Castro, no kin, but the black humor of a Castro killing a Castro did not escape many. Later, when he was El Maximo Líder, I collaborated with him in *Revolución* (I was the editor of the literary supplement) when he said in a televised speech, "This Revolution won't be like Saturn," meaning Kronos, "and it won't devour its children." I said loudly, "But it will devour its grandchildren instead." It was pathetic but it was also prophetic. Saying things like that contributed to the banning of the magazine some time later in 1961. Enough was enough when he closed the magazine and announced his Stalinist credo: "With the Revolution everything, against the Revolution nothing." And it was only for him to decide when and who were against or in favor of his Revolution. It took me years to extricate myself because you don't leave your country as if leaving the party—which was over anyway.

# Maryse Condé
# and Rebecca Wolff

MARYSE CONDÉ  was born in Pointe-à-Pitre, Guadeloupe, in 1937 and has lived in Guinea, Ghana, Senegal, France, and the United States. She is the author of numerous books, including, *Windward Heights*, *Tales from the Heart*, *Segu* and *I, Tituba, Black Witch of Salem*, which won the Grand Prix Littéraire de la Femme. A graduate of the Sorbonne in Paris, where she majored in English, Condé has taught at the University of California, Berkeley; UCLA; the Sorbonne; the University of Virginia; and the University of Nanterre. She retired as Professor Emerita of French from Columbia University in 2004.

REBECCA WOLFF  was born in New York City in 1967. She is the author of three collections of poetry, including *Manderley* and *Figment*, and the novel *The Beginners*. For her poetry, she has won the National Poetry Series Award and the Barnard Women Poets Prize. A graduate of the Iowa Writers' Workshop, Wolff is a fellow at the New York State Writers Institute.

**REBECCA WOLFF** *Wuthering Heights* is what is known as a "classic"; I read it at least six times before I was fifteen. What kind of place did it have in your imagination before you retold it?

**MARYSE CONDÉ** There is a strong tradition of what is called literary cannibalism in the Caribbean. A lot of people have done it before me. When I read *Wuthering Heights*, I was fourteen. It was given to me at a prize ceremony for being good in writing. I read the book in September, which is rainy season in the Caribbean. I was lying on my bed in my bedroom, and for me it was an enchantment. I really was transported to wherever Emily Brontë wanted to transport me . . . and then I forgot all about it. I saw it at the cinema after that, by chance—the version with Laurence Olivier. It revived memories of my adolescence, so I read it again and discovered it had a meaning beyond the actual meaning, beyond the meanings the author wanted to give. It was a story you could transplant into any society. I was teaching a few years later and I discovered Jean Rhys, who wrote *Wide Sargasso Sea*, a rewriting of *Jane Eyre*. I thought, It's not so bizarre that I'm attracted to Emily Brontë. Because, in fact, there is something about the Brontë sisters that speaks to Caribbean women, regardless of their color, regardless of their age, regardless of the time they live in. So I decided I was going to rewrite it. But it was at least another five years for me before I really started. Because my husband, who is English, was shocked when I was telling him my vague intention. He did not see the connection between the Caribbean and Brontë's work. It seemed blasphemy to him to rewrite Brontë's masterpiece. So I took another five years to decide—and when I could not help it, I started to write.

RW Blasphemy!

MC But I totally understand. It is such a masterpiece, such a beloved work in England. For example, when we promoted the book in England we went to the Museum at Haworth, where Emily Brontë was born. People came to listen to me but I could see when they were sitting down looking at me, there was a kind of . . . I wouldn't say fear, but a kind of shock. What is she doing to the text? How can she dare touch that text?! I really had to convince them that I did not do any disrespect to Brontë; on the contrary, I was paying homage to her. It seems to me the greatest homage that I pay is to her artistry.

And it is another way of telling people that you should not draw barriers between colors, ideas, et cetera. Everybody says: But why an English novel? Why not a French one? Why not an African one? You see—it's as if you should never cross a barrier, when, in fact, to live is to cross barriers.

RW You said that there is something about the novel that appealed to you, that struck a chord with you. Was it a parallel you saw there?

MC This is difficult to explain. It seems to me that Cathy, by refusing her passion for Razyé, was refusing the most vivid part of herself, which was, maybe, her African heritage. She was trying to look only at white values, the white element of her being. It is a kind of everlasting choice, a choice that everybody is confronted with: Follow your inner impulse, don't look for respectability, money, and so on.

RW It's fascinating that what you're describing as the passion that she doesn't follow is to marry *within* her race. The passion that you, in your personal life, followed, was to marry outside . . .

MC Outside.

RW It's a beautiful parallel. Much has been made already of you, as an activist in the past and in the present, being married to a white European man and living in New York City. You have said, "I did not really choose to marry a European. For twelve years I lived with a man who happened to be European, then we got married." How does one reconcile a position of practical apoliticism—the ways in which our lives and our decisions are guided by events and feelings, not principle—with the kind of political astuteness and caring you have in your work? How does it feel to be a politically engaged writer now, in ridiculous America?

MC That is a long story. I married twice. The first time I was married to an African, a man from Guinea, and there was a confusion for me between the man and the country behind him. Because Guinea was the first African country to say *No!* to General DeGaulle, the first African country to take independence in the French-speaking arena. So I confused a man, love, and marriage with making the revolution. Of course, the marriage did not work at all. It was a failure, and we divorced a few years after. So I was already conscious that marriage is an individual matter—only two persons are concerned, and there is no question of putting on the shoulders of the man you are going to marry all your idealistic views about your country, about your cause. I became very wary of that kind of confusion. So when I met Richard, I was already informed of the mistake I could make. But it was difficult for a politically minded person to pay attention to a white man. For me, he belonged to the enemy, and moreover, I had four children from my first marriage. For them, it was completely impossible to have a white man for a stepdaddy; that is why we refused to marry. We lived together. After having lived together for twelve years we had to accept that we were in love, seriously, and we had to follow the consequences.

I admit now the distinction between the private person, the private things we do, and the political person. For example, I used to believe that if you write, you have to be committed to expressing particular opinions. Now I don't feel that it is necessary. You can be committed in your life and your activities and write novels that do not translate your political activities. Your question is a very sad one. I suppose that now, in 1999, I'm no longer a committed writer because everything that I tried to do failed miserably. I was involved in the African revolution and it failed. I turned to Guadeloupe and we dreamed that Guadeloupe would be liberated, that one day we should be Guadeloupe—a national entity, and now we are part of Europe. We are entering the Common Market. It seems to me that now, you see me in my old age, as somebody who is totally dissatisfied with the course of events, so I can be a nonpolitical writer in America, because America is not political and I'm just like that.

RW Your novel *Windward Heights* embodies exactly that ambivalence about the need to be political and the things that work against it.

MC I cannot prevent myself from thinking about political ideas, political fight, political struggles. But thirty years ago I was convinced that the conclusion of the fight would be positive—that we shall get to liberation, that we shall get to the end of colonialism. Now I know that we have fought sincerely, bravely, and that nothing happened and . . . okay, we have to face it. In a way, for it not to be *too* sad, I still have what I call a cultural political activity. At Columbia, for example, which is such a conservative place, I teach Caribbean literature in French. We speak about politics, about people like Aimé Césaire. I bring so many visitors from the Caribbean who give speeches and conferences. Although I realize that, without a plan, I can't achieve any political agenda . . . On the other hand, I'm trying to remain active. I'm not just sitting in my apartment writing novels and going to the movies.

RW In another interview you said, "Race and color questions have become secondary for me." This led me to wonder, What's primary? If you can say something is secondary, then it means that something else is primary.

MC Yes, but you have to put that declaration into context. Some years ago, when I went to Africa, race was all-important. I was going to Africa because

I was going to meet *my* people, I was going to find my true home. And when I got there, I discovered that, in fact, I had little in common with the people of Guinea, as I was a French Caribbean. So, what I put first is the question of culture. Now that I live in New York, for example, I relate socially mainly with people from the French Caribbean; for example Edwidge Danticat, who is a Haitian writer, is a friend of mine. I see now that culture is the most important thing. And you would be surprised, some of my closest friends are from France. Why? Because of the language. I discovered that language is not something unimportant; in fact, it is essential that you can communicate with somebody in your own language. You will say, "But what about your husband who is English-speaking?" I will say again that it is the exception. The private love affair has nothing to do with theory, or culture, or politics. It is something you cannot explain; it is the exception to the rule. There are some things you have to accept in your life, and to try to reconcile with your other opinions.

RW One of the many things that fascinated me, reading *Windward Heights*, was how the tale had so many different tellers. In the sense that *Wuthering Heights* is a creaky old novel, one of those tales in which you know how the devices are being used—the maidservant begins the tale and retells the story from the present. But she, the servant, is really not a part of the story. She is the servant of the story. Whereas, in *Windward Heights*, the story is picked up by so many different voices; servants, children, who are not central to the story—yet, their stories are told.

MC One day I had a discussion with a friend of mine, a writer from Martinique, and we were wondering what is the most important element if you want to write a Caribbean novel—a novel that somebody will open and say, "Yes, it is coming from the Caribbean." He believed that it was language; that if you could deconstruct French and use a lot of Creole metaphor and images, it would be enough. My feeling was that only by capturing the very structure of the narrative technique could you make a Caribbean novel. You have to find the Caribbean technique of telling a story, a polyphonous technique.

RW Polyphonous?

MC To mix chapters in the first person, chapters in the third person, to mix female and male voices, and especially, mix the people who are supposed to be important—like M. de Linsseuil, who is a master. But in a society like the Caribbean, who knows more than the servants about the construction of society, the details of the society? Nobody ever asks them their opinion, but they are there, they are witnesses; they are the ones who see, they are the ones who arrange everything. Simply, a Caribbean story could not really be told without reference to servants. Don't forget that, after all, as a black person, I descend from the slaves, and the slaves were always silent, forced to be silent. They knew they were the real masters of the island. It was a way of giving voice to my people, who were never given voices before. So, it was an artistic and a political device.

RW It's clear that there are extremely complicated racial politics within the islands, and set hierarchies. These are played out in the novel.

MC Now, in Guadeloupe, we are moving toward an understanding of races, of racism. We understand that we are a plural-ethnic society where black and white, mulatto, Indians, have formed and have given birth to a kind of common society. But not even fifty years ago it was totally different. My mother told me stories about how when she was a child going to school, you could not, as a black girl, sit by an Indian child or by a white child. It was a segregated society. At the time, in Guadeloupe, the color of skin was a marker for everything. It meant your class, your condition, your culture. It was a society based on hate, contempt, on tension. But I suppose it was too difficult, too painful to live in that kind of situation. Little by little, in Guadeloupe and Martinique, we've tried to find a way of settling differences in order to come together. Because after all, the three groups have invented a language, Creole. The three groups have invented a kind of religion, Kimbwa. The three groups have invented so many things in common. The time came when we looked for the end of that state of war. Now, it seems to me, we are going toward peace.

RW In *Windward Heights*, the central love affair is one that becomes a pattern, one that ruins people's lives.

MC Emily Brontë wrote about the love between Cathy and Heathcliff; a young girl and a young man who was a bit of an outcast. Nobody knew where he was from and he had no family. You can take that as a kind of metaphor for the need to accept your love for somebody as coming out of the blue. And that you shouldn't have to leave true love for any social position or situation in your society. The mistake Cathy committed was that she preferred Edgar Linton, who was a well-educated man, and a landed-property man. My Cathy cannot accept being in love with a black or Indian man, somebody with no family, and she decides she is going to climb up into the white society by marrying de Linsseuil. In so doing, she's killing herself.

RW I was thinking a lot about essentialism reading *Windward Heights*. In *Wuthering Heights*, what gives Cathy and Heathcliff this unbreakable bond is their essential sameness. They perceive themselves as having the same soul and arising from the same place in the world. So the mistake is to pull them apart. In *Windward Heights* you've translated the essentialism into a racial characteristic.

MC I wanted to say that I believe in that kind of essentialism. Two people are made for each other. These people can be extremely different—one can be white, one can be black, one can be yellow, or what have you. Cathy and Razyé were made to be together. But instead of living their love to the full expression, Cathy decided to become an important lady, to marry a man who had money, who had land, who used to have slaves, and to climb the social hierarchy of the country. She turned her back on her true love, and of course, that was the end of her. In the pursuit of your private happiness, class and color should not come into consideration.

RW You're really implying the total separation of the political from the personal.

MC I do believe that.

RW And yet, political reality is the only reality of the novel.

MC Yes. I wanted to portray the period of time they were living in. It was fascinating in Brontë that the outside world did not exist. There were the two of them, Cathy and Heathcliff, and nothing around. At the time of my novel, Guadeloupe was full of chaos, noise, fury; it was the emergence of the black people, it was the decline of the white people, of the white majority. You cannot separate the life of an individual from the society he belongs to. That is why I took so much pain to portray their society. The lesson of my book is that Cathy and Razyé, in spite of the political situation around them, should have listened to themselves. Because of their political situation, they could not and so they faced death. They should have been strong enough not to pay attention to all the differences between black and white and all the conflicts around, because it did not matter for them.

RW In *Wuthering Heights*, Heathcliff despises Edgar Linton because he's a passive man who doesn't really have much of a spine or fire, the way that Heathcliff and Cathy do. In *Windward Heights*, Linton's character is translated into Aymeric—a knee-jerk liberal, bleeding-heart white guy whose intentions are good. *He's* the one who climbs the racial barrier to marry Cathy.

MC Because in Guadeloupe there is a tendency to see white people, the *beke*, as we say, as bad, negative characters. Aymeric is a man trapped in a society, a class, an ethnicity, in everything. But he would like to do good. He's trying to be good to his slaves, he fights negative ideas about the blacks. But he remains, whether he likes it or not, a prisoner of his class.

RW I found it amusing that, throughout *Windward Heights*, the male member—to use the term used in the translation—seemed to be a defining characteristic of Razyé and his son: they are these virile, literally well-endowed men . . . and then Aymeric—

MC Had nothing, in fact. But, you know, there is a bit of irony too. When I was writing that, I was playing with the idea that people see the black man that way, as opposed to the way they see the white man. You can use stereotypes in so many ways. Seriously, sometimes. But, a lot of times, I use irony just to make fun. I smile at the readers—of course they don't see it most of the time. There is a bit of a stereotype in the confrontation between Razyé, the black powerful man, the native of the island, with the weak, the mild. A stereotype, yes, but in a way all stereotypes build stories. If you want to build a fascinating story, you have to use some stereotypes.

RW There's this one really priceless quote: "Razyé made an appearance. How can I describe the contrast between the two men? Never had I noticed how the master's nickname suited him so well. He looked like a choirboy who serves at high mass on Sundays or else a lamb that sucks his mama's teat, or a red-eyed twitchy-nosed rabbit in its hutch. As for Razyé, he was a volcano, a hurricane, an earthquake—a nigger stud with his iron spike pointing between his legs." There's a much more frank sexuality, obviously, being discussed.

MC You know there is a kind of proverb in the Caribbean, saying that a black man is an earthquake, a volcano, and so on. In Brontë, the sexuality is always there, but she was too shy to speak of it by name. So it was very enticing for me to bring it out in the open and speak those ideas, which were her ideas—but she was mute about them.

**RW** Basically, Cathy is attracted to Heathcliff and not attracted to Edgar.

**MC** The idea is that in the original novel, Cathy and Heathcliff never made love. And there they were, alone all the time . . .

**RW** Out on the heath . . .

*Your* Cathy says, "Heaven is not for me, I dream of an afterlife where we can express all the emotions and desires we have had to stifle during our lifetime: an afterlife where we would be free at last to be ourselves. Ever since I was little, I've wondered if the Christian religion is not a white-folks religion made for white-folks, whether it's right for us who have African blood in our veins."

**MC** Emily Brontë says that. I think Nelly Dean was telling Brontë's Cathy about heaven and Cathy replied, "I don't want to go there, I don't believe that I'm fit to go to heaven." I just elaborated on that idea. My Cathy doesn't want to go there, she's not interested in heaven, because she believes it's a white man's place.

**RW** It's still fascinating to me that when Cathy says, "Free at last to be myself" in *Wuthering Heights*, she's referring to this humanist, human-nature-type quality that she was purportedly born with, which she shares with Heathcliff. In *Windward Heights*, Cathy speaks of literal bloodlines and racial characteristics as what keeps her out of heaven—where she would, in the end, rather *not* go.

**MC** But that's the humanness that somebody from the Caribbean has. To be part of so many worlds—part of the African world because of the African slaves, part of the European world because of the European education—is a kind of double entendre. You can use that in your own way and give sentences another meaning. I was so pleased when I was doing that work, because it was a game, a kind of perverse but joyful game.

**RW** It seems that you're expressing a certain belief in something essential, something inherent in African blood, in racial distinction. I'm curious to know what you think about white people and white culture's apparent desire to emulate black culture in music and otherwise.

**MC** Why not? Because after all we must communicate, we must exchange. I don't believe that you should only stick to your own culture and legacy. For example, I have a friend who is a Haitian and a well-known musician. His last record was a kind of Brazilian music. Why not? We have to borrow. I did the same thing—I borrowed the idea from Emily Brontë, who, after all, is a white writer.

RW I'm glad you see that as a positive thing.

MC Yes. I do, I do.

RW Speaking about West Indian literature, you have said, "Blacks were always depicted as victims. They were also portrayed as spontaneous, sensitive, and in tune with nature." Now you've written a novel in which there is an essentialism at the heart of its plot. Does this make you a grand ironist?

MC I have a lot of irony all the time in my novels, irony about ideas that are supposed to be set, but I'm always trying to find the reality behind the clichés. It seems to me one of the best clichés we have in the West Indies is the separation, or division between races, and each of us behave according to a set pattern. Yes, there is a lot of irony in it.

RW Are you worried that there will be those who miss the irony?

MC Oh, they certainly will. People don't like irony, especially in the Caribbean. They want a writer to say seriously what she or he believes in. They don't like people to mess around. Give "false" images or "false" ideas. They don't like the writer to joke. So, I mean, if you joke you are bound not to be understood, and not to be liked.

RW And yet you joke.

MC I shall go on joking.

RW *Windward Heights* is a complicated and delicate balance between romantic tragedy—with fate, blood, undying devotion, and, quite literally, magic—and historically accurate political and social struggle in which the characters play out a tragedy of extremely material proportions. You have said, "The very act of writing is supernatural in itself." Thinking also of the presence of *real* magic in your fiction; it is a force not to be dismissed. Is there a struggle within you, as a writer or activist, and as a thinker, between superstition and rationalism? Between a magically real vision of the world and a politically real, or, just an everyday worldly world?

MC Yes, but I don't feel that one must fight. I suppose that if you belong to the Caribbean—meaning that, if you are a creolized person, you have a lot of influences in you. You have the African coming through you because of the science of the magic, the respect for the invisible. But you have been trained by Europeans, so you adopt some of their values. You realize that faith in magical realism is faith in social realism, socialist realism. With all these different influences your inner self is always in a kind of turmoil. You believe in this or that, which seems to contradict another kind of belief, but they can cohabitate in your mind. The words that you are producing are a reflection of all the elements, all the influences that are in you. If you reduce a human being to one single line of thought or opinion, it is petty. Maybe the advantage of being a colonized person is the realization that you have so many things that belong to you: your tradition, something coming from the West, something indigenous to the area where you have been living—you have to blend all that to express yourself. I don't see a fight, I just see a kind of complexity.

RW A negative capability. I am curious about the spiritual aspect of the novel. In *Wuthering Heights*, everything is based on the romantic notion of the soul; Cathy basically withers away and dies, of her own volition. This seems to be very similar to the whole basis of Santería—I don't know if I'm using the correct term.

MC There is an idea in the Caribbean that people who are dead are still with you. Normally the room is full of dead people, close to me, who like to see the way I live now, how I go on with my life. But I cannot see them, I do not have the power, I'm not trained to see them. Some people are trained to see them. Those people belong to what we call Santería, or Kimbwa, or voo-doo, and if I had their services, they could well come in here, and say, "Yes, your mother is sitting there, looking at you." The idea is that we are always trying to be in communication with the souls of the people that we love and who have left us. A very Caribbean idea.

RW And a very *Wuthering Heights* idea.

MC That is one of the reasons why it pleased me so much. Because that idea is a Caribbean idea.

RW Right, and it's an idea about passion, really.

MC When Heathcliff was opening the windows in the captain's room and telling her, "Come, and possess me," Caribbeans find nothing strange in that. We could easily do that. For example, if a girl loses her husband—I have a friend who lost her husband two months ago—she was all the time to the Kimbwa, because he had promised to help her meet her husband again. He never did. He was just taking her money for nothing. But, in fact, there was nothing surprising in the quest. Emily Brontë doesn't know how close she was to the Caribbean imagination.

RW It's interesting, because in the Caribbean tradition, that would be commonplace, but in the English culture . . .

MC The idea that you want to be reunited with somebody after death could be very shocking. I heard *Wuthering Heights* shocked the English readers when it was published.

RW I'm continually surprised at how little mainstream acceptance there is in America of the supernatural.

MC People are afraid. I suppose it is fear. It is much more convenient to believe the world is a closed place. Especially in America, where they don't want to see anything related to death. "Let them be where they are." In the Caribbean there is close communication between the two worlds. Everything is open for us.

RW I'm curious why, in *Windward Heights*, you never provide the closure, as we say, of a real meeting again between—

MC First of all, it would be treason to the original. Secondly, the charm. The charm of the quest is that it has no end. He is all the time looking for her and he cannot find her. If I had found an end, if they met and were reunited, the book would lack poetry and mysticism. It is a gesture that is not finished that speaks more to your imagination. A gesture that is closed is finished.

I was a child when my mother died—I was in France, so I didn't go see her. At that time, it was very difficult to get back to Guadeloupe. Imagine the number of Kimbwa who offered to me, for one thousand francs, two thousand francs, "I shall make you see your mother." And nobody had any success at all. I never found one. So I suppose that maybe I didn't find the best one.

RW When I was in college, and in graduate school—in the early '90s—I was very aware of a tremendous outburst of interest and academic activity around Caribbean women's literature, around any kind of marginalized, oppressed communities. My impression now, living outside the academic world, is that there was a fashion for this kind of literature which has perhaps receded, to a certain extent.

MC I don't think Columbia University has ever been touched by that kind of fashion.

RW Really?

MC The place is—I like it after all—but Columbia is a very white, conservative place. It was, for example, one of the last to have a department of Francophone studies. It is only when I came four years ago that they started to teach Francophone literature here at Columbia.

RW Really.

MC All these ideas of political correctness—I think Columbia is not touched by that at all. What we thought at the beginning, even my students, was that there would be a kind of unity between my Francophone literature classes, and the department of African American studies. I did everything I could to join forces with them, and they were never interested.

RW That's strange, it seems as though it would be a natural alliance.

MC The Caribbean does not interest them; they are interested in their own issues in America—the shooting of Amadou Diallo. Caribbeans are not black enough for them. But we are close to the Pan-African studies program, the Institute for African Studies, we work together a lot. It's normal: African Americans have their own agenda. After all, they are Americans, they are first and foremost Americans, dealing with white Americans.

RW So when you're thinking about what you're going to be working on next, what are you considering?

MC I have written so many serious novels, with a very serious concern, and so on—so my next novel is going to be a kind of fantasy, about a person who is not a human being, who is supposed to be a kind of she-devil, doing all sorts of harm and wrong around herself. Of course there will be a political representation of Guadeloupe because it is set at the beginning of the century, around 1920. I shall have to deal with politics, but mainly, it is a kind of entertainment.

RW Perhaps you are unwilling, or unable, to leave that political context behind.

MC It seems *that* is what is left of my political involvement. I could not write anything—although I write an entertaining fantasy novel—unless it has a certain political significance. I have nothing else to offer that remains important. I could not write something with no meaning. I could not.

RW So, it would be impossible for you to write, say, just a love story.

MC No. It has to be a love story as you would have in *Wuthering Heights*. It is a love story, but has a background of oppression and is political. I could not do something different.

RW Would it be boring to you?

MC Yes. And actually, I'd be ashamed. I'd be ashamed of doing that.

RW Do you think that's some kind of relic? A left-over feeling—

MC Of political commitment? Yes.

RW Once you're committed, you're always committed.

MC After all, the people who taught me how to write, who gave me the desire to become a writer, were politically motivated. They were saying something in the defense of our people, or to enlighten our people, to raise their consciousness, to make people in the world know how unhappy and oppressed they are. The legacies and the lesson—you cannot forget about that.

# Dennis Cooper
# and Benjamin Weissman

DENNIS COOPER was born in Pasadena, California, in 1953 and has lived in Los Angeles, New York, and Paris. He has written or collaborated on over three dozen books, including *The Marbled Swarm*, *The Sluts*, and the George Miles Cycle: *Closer*, *Frisk*, *Try*, *Guide*, and *Period*. In addition to his writing, he is also an editor and artist. Cooper attended Pasadena City College and Pitzer College. He has been nominated for the *Los Angeles Times* Book Prize, and he won the first Ferro-Grumley Award for gay literature and the Lambda Literary Award. His work has been published in seventeen countries.

BENJAMIN WEISSMAN was born in Los Angeles in 1957. He is an artist and a writer. Along with his painting collaborations with people like John McCarthy, he writes for online journals, newspapers, and magazines, and is the author of *Dear Dead Person and Other Stories* and *Headless*. Weissman is a professor at Art Center College of Design and Otis College of Art and Design.

# DENNIS COOPER AND BENJAMIN WEISSMAN

**BENJAMIN WEISSMAN**  You're the funniest writer I've ever read, and that never seems to be mentioned. Occasionally someone will admit there's a comic moment. But I'm blown away. I mean, people sticking their fingers in others' body parts and talking about the temperature.

**DENNIS COOPER**  Obviously no one has sex like that. Maybe if you were a bona fide psychotic. Who's that guy, Robert Berdella? He would kill boys and keep journals during the murders like . . . 8:02 P.M.—Coughed, 8:04 P.M.—Moved his hand.

**BW** You lift material from these kinds of guys?

**DC** I'm fascinated by people who can depersonalize fellow human beings to that degree and decide they're just sources of information. When a surgeon's operating on you, you're just a soft machine, like Burroughs said. The idea of combining that kind of exploration of the body with sex seems useful somehow. Blurring together sex, an art that's passionate and mindless with an act that's completely clinical; it's a way to talk about something that is neither clinical nor sexual. It's sex that's not about sex, if you know what I mean.

**BW**  I think it's funny. It's weird.

**DC**  It's weird but it's not surprising.

**BW**  I mean, you're not a comical writer like Mark Leyner (*My Cousin, My Gastroenterologist*).

**DC**  In my work comedy's like a sedative. It helps readers ease into the material. It's a standard trick, but . . . Well, people don't think the *Friday the 13th* movies are comedies either.

**BW**  Everyone always feels like they have to deal with your subject matter.

**DC**  I hardly think about the material, or not in that way. I write about things that scare the shit out of me, that determines what I write. I feel like I'm a formalist. I think if my work has a problem, it's that it risks being a bit mannered. My books are so constructed. It's odd to me that I'm attacked for my content. How can you attack someone for what they write about? People write about what they write about, and the chips fall where they may.

BW  As tight as *Try* is, there are parts where it goes loose in a way, where nothing's happening, it's almost disappearing.

DC  Yeah. My books always begin with this mulch. I start writing, and I start to get formal ideas, and eventually this skin forms on the writing, and I fuck with it until it's as intricate as I can get it. Sometimes I have elaborate structural plans. *Frisk* was supposed to resemble a dismembered body.

BW  What do you mean, a dismembered body?

DC  I wanted to write a book in which the body of the text would be dismembered, as though the writer had dismembered a novel the way a murderer might dismember a body. That's why it's in those weird, formally dissimilar but linked pieces. Parts where it almost resembles a conventional novel, parts where the book's internal workings and the writer's ideas are sticking out. Altogether it formed a dead, open body ready to be explored by a reader curious about how it came to be. *Try*'s different. It came into focus more gradually. I wanted to write about this real kid I knew named Ziggy. And I wanted to write a novel that would in some way include the energy and formalities of the "queer zines" I was so interested in. I wanted to talk about emotion the way I'd talked about the body. And I was in the middle of worrying terribly about a friend who was very addicted to heroin. So I also wanted to reflect that struggle, how people on heroin become blanks, objects on which to project your fears and interests. And finally, I wanted to write a book that would prove in a complicated way that I'm not an amoral fuck who wants to kill boys. Because I'm not. Anyway, all that might explain why it seems out of control at times. In fact, it's extremely controlled but it obsesses on certain things in a relentless way, which gives it a weird, spaced out quality that I hope is of interest.

BW  So your books are just love stories.

DC  Well, I wanted *Try* to propose a love that had nothing to do with romance or sex. A love that was about friendship. That's an important distinction.

BW  Your books parallel real life. They're dedicated to people who they're partly about.

DC  Right. Even *Frisk* is about my boyfriend of the time, Mark. Or about the relationship between Kevin, who's sort of based on Mark, and Dennis who's based on me, and how the former's interest in Tolkien and sci-fi/fantasy is the same as the latter's interest in murder. They cancel each other out. Kevin's ability to be close to Dennis proves that his horrific fantasies are really benign, like all fantasies. So . . . yeah, I have to write about what I'm going through and who interests me. I know there are writers who pick out plots in advance and then fill in the blanks. I can't imagine what that's like.

BW Writers whose response to a writing "career" is: "I did this coming of age book, and now for my career I have to do that historical hook . . ." And end up wearing a clown outfit when they're not even going to the circus. (*laughter*)

DC Nailed it.

BW Why do you think it's important to write about violence?

DC I write about it as a way to decide not to be violent, as a decision to be a good person, hopefully. Because I do think that killing another person is probably the most profound thing you can do, since people are the only really meaningful things in the world. To stop another person has to be an amazing, overwhelming experience. That's why serial murderers are interesting, because they do that in a methodical, thoughtful way. They hone their craft.

BW Most murderers aren't very analytical.

DC Occasionally you get someone like Dennis Nilsen who's analyzed his acts, but . . . yeah. Why do they do it? The popular explanation that they were abused is so lame and simplistic. That's just solving a riddle to solve a riddle.

BW In the *New York Review of Books* a couple of years ago, someone said certain readers of *Frisk* would enjoy it as pornography.

DC If you were to just read the letter section of *Frisk*, where the character is describing his supposed murders, yeah, you could call it porn, because I was mimicking the style of porn. But the novel is structured such that when you reach that section, you're prepared, hopefully, to question your ability to be aroused. Every section bounces off every other section; they infect each other.

**BW** People could flip to a sex scene in *The Godfather* and say, "You could read this as porn."

**DC** Yeah, well, there you go. (*laughter*)

**BW** How do you find the language for your books? Everything echoes everything else in a particular way. You're able to make the most intense things happen in a single, seemingly nondescript sentence.

**DC** It's a combination of things. The writing has a very strong rhythm. It seems half of what I do is maintain rhythms and fuck with them. I choose words partially based on syllable count and on sound. You don't notice all this reading it necessarily, but it's structured like music. Every sentence length, the way it moves, sounds . . . it's all calculated to create an effect. In *Try*, I was working with a hyper-real version of how I talk or the way inarticulate Californian kids speak. The way you might start to say something clearly then wander, confused, and you'll stall, then you'll take it back and rush forward in a different direction, then step back, and try to sum up your thought . . . all that movement is so beautiful. I try to mimic that a lot, make it recognizable, but brewing it up with a kind of poetry.

**BW** You talk about California speak, critics have this thing about a "California book." Or an "LA book." It's bullshit.

**DC** Yeah, John Rechy, T. Coraghessan Boyle, Charles Bukowski, Kate Braverman, Steve Erickson, Wanda Coleman, Brian Moore . . . what's the commonality? To me one of the strengths of Los Angeles is that it's such a total nothing. Maybe writers out here share a certain kind of odd comedy, but even that's questionable.

**BW** What about contemporary fiction?

**DC** It's in a good state. There's a lot of energy in these pockets, like the Fiction Collective Two scene, where highly experimental writing is going on, then there are great new presses like High Risk. There are some real talented, odd people getting mainstream success: Stephen Wright, Denis Johnson, Mary Gaitskill, and so on. And I see tons of brand new, really brilliant writers coming up.

**BW** So you want to talk about some of your influences?

**DC** Robert Bresson is the biggest one. His films deal with extreme isolation and pain and emotion, but they're so rigorously stylized and composed that they're almost invisible, they're my ideal. Otherwise, you know, Rimbaud, Sade, Blanchot, rock music. Recently, I went back and reread a bunch of psychedelicky books from the late '60s and early '70s by, like, Tom Wolfe, McGuane, Ishmael Reed, Hunter Thompson, and they're terrific. Where for years I'd been thinking they'd be dated and dumb, they're actually really lively and crazed.

**BW** In your writing, you use a lot of different voices. That kind of thing in another writer's hands could just bomb, but you handle it really well.

**DC** Well, all the voices are mine. All the characters are just shards of the fractured me. That's why I sympathize with them all, even the monsters.

**BW** There's this odd humility in your writing.

**DC** Everybody has equal weight. There's a balance of perspectives. They all get their . . . space? Is that what you mean?

**BW** There's an equality to the agony the characters go through.

**DC** To understand something, you have to listen, right? You have to study it clinically. If you reject things as gross, or people as horrible, you'll never understand them. I really want to understand why horrible things happen. And I don't think people are at fault. I think it's something else, I'm not sure why. But everyone in my books gets a chance to gain sympathizers, as far as I can control such things. It's up to the reader. You know . . . what's that saying . . . "Kill 'em all, let God sort 'em out." Let the reader sort them out.

# Lydia Davis
# and Francine Prose

LYDIA DAVIS  was born in Massachusetts in 1947. She is the author of one novel, *The End of the Story*, and several story collections, including *Break It Down* and *Varieties of Disturbance*, which was a finalist for the 2007 National Book Award. She is the recipient of a MacArthur Fellowship, the American Academy of Arts and Letters Award of Merit Medal, and was named a Chevalier of the Order of Arts and Letters by the French government for her fiction and her translations of modern writers, including Maurice Blanchot and Marcel Proust. She is the winner of the 2013 Man Booker International Prize and is currently a Professor and Writer-in-Residence at the University of Albany.

FRANCINE PROSE  was born in Brooklyn, New York, in 1947. She is the author of twenty works of fiction. Her novel *A Changed Man* won the Dayton Literary Peace Prize, and *Blue Angel* was a finalist for the National Book Award. Her nonfiction includes *Anne Frank: The Book, The Life, The Afterlife*, and *Reading Like a Writer*. The recipient of numerous grants and honors, including a Guggenheim Fellowship and a Fulbright Fellowship, Prose is a former president of PEN American Center, and a member of the American Academy of Arts and Letters and the American Academy of Arts and Sciences. She lives in New York City.

**FRANCINE PROSE**  Do you remember learning to read?

**LYDIA DAVIS**  Yes, and my memories of the Dick and Jane books are very happy memories. I *loved* learning the words "look" and "see": "Run, Jane, run. See Jane run." It was so clear and easy and unconfusing and neat. Actually I spent my second grade year in Austria. I had one year of learning to read in English and then I learned to read in German. I still have the German textbooks in which the letters got smaller and smaller as the pages progressed through the book.

**FP**  How sadistic!

**LD**  That's right, very sadistic.

**FP**  Do you think about the rhythms of Dick and Jane?

**LD**  I always liked clarity and simplicity and balance. All rhythms can be seductive. I was attuned to the music of language as well as the music of music. Learning another language when I was seven probably made me hyperconscious of language; also the German language in the classroom was a wall of incomprehensibility around me. Gradually the words began to have meaning. But first I heard the language as rhythm.

**FP**  So do you write for rhythm now?

**LD**  Yes, it's always rhythm. I always hear it in my head.

**FP**  There are lots of books that make me think: I don't care what's in them as long as they're written beautifully.

**LD**  In fact Beckett said somewhere that he didn't care what a text said as long as it was constructed beautifully, or something like that—all of meaning, all of beauty is in the construction.

**FP**  It's rare that people pay attention to that any more. What were your favorite books when you were a kid? Do you remember?

**LD**  A turning point for me was Dos Passos' *Orient Express.* That was one of the first "grown-up" books that made me excited about the language. It was one of the first I wasn't reading for plot. Another was *The Unnamable* by Beckett. I got into that at thirteen.

FP  You read Beckett at thirteen?

LD  Yeah, I didn't read the whole thing.

FP  Where did you find it?

LD  My father was an English professor, and somehow it must have been in the house. It made a very strong impression because it was so different from anything I had read. I opened this book and it said on the first page, "I'm lying here. I've dropped my pencil." Later, in high school, I would go through one novelist after another—Nabokov, Thomas Hardy, George Eliot, Dostoevsky, Joyce—and read everything.

FP  Do you think about Beckett a lot now?

LD  He was very important to me in my early twenties. I studied him. I was really picking apart sentence structures, seeing exactly how he constructed a sentence. Why it worked so beautifully. I suppose I wanted to do it as well as Beckett. So if I was going to do it as well as he did, I had to learn how he did it.

FP  So you knew you wanted to write?

LD  I knew from a very early age—maybe twelve—but the funny thing was that it was more of a burden than a pleasure.

FP  (*laughter*) How prescient.

LD  Right. I knew it would be a lot of hard work. Like a Chinese emperor, the child knowing he's going to grow up to be emperor. He may not really want to, but has no choice in the matter. I wasn't reconciled or really content with the idea until I was in my twenties. As a child, what I really loved was music! I enjoyed writing a story when I had to write one, but what I really sought out was music.

FP  Playing the piano?

LD  Playing the piano, and I loved listening to music. I would listen to a record over and over again. Then I would go out and get the score and listen to the record with the score because I wanted to get as deeply into it as I could. I didn't go into my room and write stories or write a novel the way some kids do. I spent all my time on music.

**FP**  If you had to think of a modern writer . . . who's the closest to music? Beckett and Joyce often seem to be writing more for the music of the language than for content.

**LD**  How about Nabokov? Do you include him?

**FP**  Well Nabokov, yes, he's sort of like Bartók. What was the first thing you wrote, the first thing you thought was really something?

**LD**  I can remember a day when the teacher read aloud my story and also a story by a classmate. I loved her story. I wasn't so fond of mine. So I can say her story was a big influence on me, the first thing that I really remember liking. You know the book *Iron and Silk* where the English teacher asks a class of Chinese students to describe their most memorable experience? One of the students hesitates and hesitates and finally says that his most memorable experience was when his wife went to Beijing and ate duck there. He didn't go. She went, but that was his most memorable experience.

**FP**  I can remember some dreadful little moralistic tales that I wrote in grade school and horrible little love poems in high school.

**LD**  In high school I was more excited by essays because I was discovering how to think things through and come to new thoughts.

**FP**  When did the stories in *Break It Down* start?

**LD**  The earliest ones were written about ten or twelve years before they were published. They were written when I was in France after college. I was having trouble writing a traditional narrative story. There was one long story that I worked on endlessly. Looking back at the notebooks, I realize it took me over two years to finish it, trying another version and another version. In the meantime, I started doing these very short stories to break myself out of the rut of not writing or resisting writing. I told myself: You have to write two tiny stories every day. It didn't matter how silly they were, I just had to finish two one-paragraph stories.

**FP**  This is probably an impossible question, but when you say a story's "not working" or "working," what does that mean?

**LD**  It's flat. It's dull. There were two stories, one called "What Was Interesting."

**FP** Oh, I love that story.

**LD** The other was "The Center of the Story." Both of those didn't work as they were. The core of the story didn't work. I left them alone for a long time. The way I rescued them was to come back and address the question as a part of the story. Why isn't it working? The problem with one of them was that it had no center. The problem with the other was that it just wasn't interesting enough.

**FP** Speaking of "What Was Interesting," why do you think that obsessive love is such an interesting subject? It's not in fact a condition that people find themselves in all the time, or even most of the time. And yet it's always somehow riveting, and a number of the stories in *Break It Down* are about that.

**LD** It's one of the first things we experience when we're changing from being children to being adolescents. One of the signs is that we suddenly start falling in love with a camp counselor or with a teacher. Usually the first objects of our affections are at a distance, rather than someone who falls in love with us in return. Maybe it's so compelling later because of those first experiences.

**FP** There's that dreadful familiarity each time you have those first experiences all over again.

**LD** Obsessive or foiled or frustrated love is very compelling because you don't have control over it. It's the most extreme example of not being able to control another person.

**FP** It also puts you smack up against some unknowable mystery that I think at some points, or for some people, wisely gets turned into religious emotion. It's that sense of the unknowable. In some of the stories in *Break It Down* it's the question: Why is this guy doing this? You might as well be Job asking God why He's done what He's done.

**LD** Right, and I'm not allowed to ask. I can ask, but He won't really tell me. Just as I can strive for grace or perfection but maybe it won't be granted to me.

**FP** Or strive for knowledge. (*pause*) When did you figure out that the self watching the self write was a permissible thing to put in the story? So many of the stories have that element. It's one of the things that gives them dimension and textures and layers.

LD  In *The Unnamable*, Beckett certainly includes the self watching the self write. There's a story within a story. The old man who keeps losing his pencil is trying to tell a story about a strange family whose name I forget—Saposcat or something. I didn't do it for a long time, because everything I read said you don't do that.

FP  You're not supposed to do that.

LD  So even though I got that from Beckett right away, it's as if you have to go through the stages of writing more traditional stories before you can go back to what really spoke to you first.

FP  Right. Here I am trying to write, trying to describe this thing for which there are no words, for which there is no point in writing, which I don't understand the *point* of writing. Before that, there was Flaubert with all those pronouncements about how the writer should be as invisible in the work as God is in creation.

LD  That's why I felt as though I was cheating with "The Center of the Story." I added another layer, and that other dimension or perspective automatically made the stories richer and more interesting. But is that cheating or not?

FP  Why would you think it would be?

LD  I guess this is why: either I should have had that intention from the very beginning, it should have been part and parcel of the whole conception; or the story should have been strong enough to stand on its own, anyway. My slightly uneasy feeling was, couldn't I do that with each story that didn't work? Here's another story coming along with a broken leg. This one is just too slow. How can I speed it up? Ah, here comes another with another problem. I often seem to work in pairs: whatever impulse I have with one story there's enough of that impulse left to do another story.

FP  I was going to ask you about that, if the stories led to other stories or if they were all discrete stories?

LD  They usually don't lead to others, except that as I'm writing, I get a certain level of energy going that makes me more inclined to think of other stories. So in that sense one story will spawn a lot of other beginnings. I got into a strange thing at one point: "How He Is Often Right I & II" ended one way in one version and went off in another direction in another version. I simply didn't know which was better. They seemed like two alternatives. I did publish them as "I & II" in a couple of instances, and then in another instance I combined the two into one. I decided one was weaker and one was stronger. I got very intrigued by that dilemma when I was writing the novel, feeling like I could have done it like this or just as well like that. It's so much more comfortable when you're writing a story and you see there's only one way to go with it, but when you see that there are all these forks in the road and you're not sure you've taken the right one . . .

FP But it's also because the consciousness of the narrator in most of the stories is the consciousness of someone who can see a number of different possible explanations or paths or interpretations.

LD Yes. It's very unnerving. It was very unnerving with the novel not to be sure that this or that decision was right.

FP How far in advance do you know?

LD Know what?

FP What's going to happen with a story or the novel?

LD I hate to say "right from the beginning" because that contradicts every-thing I've ever thought and studied and learned and taught students—that you shouldn't know. But of course in most pieces even if you know, there are a lot of things you don't know that will happen along the way. With the novel I knew roughly what events and what time period I wanted to cover. But in the one-paragraph stories, I didn't know exactly where a certain argu-ment was going to land. But that's a different problem because those are not plotted stories. In a plotted story I might know that X was going to get sick and better again, but in these logical argument stories, I really do have to write them over and over again.

FP You say "logical argument," but it's always a kind of logic that's just tee-tering on the edge of absurdity.

LD Right, it's got to be water-tight logic within an absurd situation or start-ing from an absurd premise.

FP   That's what's thrilling about them. You're reading it and you're absolutely convinced, and it's not until the end that you go, "Huh?"

LD   Yes. I'm thinking of one called "Ethics." I heard on a television program that the idea of "Do unto your neighbor as you would have him do unto you" was the basis for all systems of ethics. Then I realized if I applied it to one person I knew, it wouldn't work because he would really want certain people to be angry and hostile towards him because he was already feeling that way towards them. So I had to work that out.

FP   What is it that you're trying to get to in "What I Feel"?

LD   The revelation that the character has is that her feelings may someday not seem very important to her. Once they're not important, then life is a lot easier. But it's still important to her what she feels, or it still plays a big part in how she reacts to things. I guess what's so hard to get is the very end, that she's comforted both because she realizes "Ah, I am free of this horrible burden of my feelings" and that she realizes "*Someday* I will be free of this horrible burden of my feelings." I still haven't quite got it.

FP   I always think how much of what the Buddha said made perfect sense, and yet is difficult and impossible to follow. Still, it's comforting to think that you *can* get to that point.

LD   Exactly. But I can't even get the last sentence. It's 95 percent there, but not 100 percent. I was still working on it in the copyediting stage. So that really is an example of the thought not being quite there until the writing is there. As long as it's not expressed quite right I haven't brought it to some sort of completion or realization.

FP   So I guess the question is: Do you think about—I don't know how to even put it—the religious states of consciousness?

LD   More and more, I suppose. Maybe because I'm approaching fifty. It seems much more urgent to . . . I have always loved the language of the King James version of the Bible. It's hard not to love that. I was asked to write an essay on the New Testament last year and I did.

FP   What was the essay about?

LD   I wrote about a book written by the Jesus Seminar about what Jesus actually, *probably* said. It's a fascinating work of detective analysis to try to discover what in the Gospels is actually quoting or nearly quoting. They color-code it so that only what's printed in red are the words that Jesus probably spoke. And there are very few, some of the parables and then the word *Abba*, which I love. Aramaic for "father." The word Abba is the only thing he quite certainly said. It's partly my fascination with detective work, but I love the idea of taking this figure who has really been such a problem and trying to put all of the images or the preconceptions and misconceptions to one side and try to get to what the man actually said. You get to one word, *Abba*. Which is also pleasing because of the pattern of the letters, a rhyme scheme in poetry: ABBA.

FP   And also a palindrome.

LD   And the first two letters of the alphabet.

FP   Why is Jesus a problem for you?

LD   The figure of Jesus has been so overlaid with sentimentality. It has served so many political agents. It has been so completely co-opted by certain groups of people.

FP   Also it seems to me that one of the things that you're writing about is how difficult it is to practice the things that the scriptures make sound easy. Kindness, charity, patience—all the virtues. So many of the stories in *Almost No Memory* are about what happens if you actually think about those things for two seconds, or try to put them into practice. It's impossible.

LD   Like a good Christian, which I'm not, I wrestle daily with these problems. How to have more patience, how to love someone.

FP   And the situations for which you need the most patience are precisely the most difficult ones to be patient in.

LD   Right. If it's easy for you to be brave, are you really being brave? If it's easy to be patient, are you really being patient? It may be easier to be brave in a heroic situation than patient in a boring, mundane situation. So you should get more credit for being patient with your two-year-old in the supermarket than you should for saving somebody's life. It's the tedious things that are more difficult.

**FP** I want to go back to the self-watching-the-self-write question. One of the things I like best about writing is that it shuts off the voice of the self when you really get into the work, all those voices, "What are we having for dinner?" or "Why did blah-blah say that to me?" or "How are we going to pay the bills?"—shut up. I think this is one reason I write, because it's the only way I can get some peace and quiet. How does the self watching the self write enter into that equation? Is it also a way out of distraction, or is it just using the distraction?

**LD** It is definitely just as far from the annoying distractions of daily life. I seem to be moving in the direction of less and less fiction and more and more philosophical investigation. But then there's another part of me that says that it would be really very enjoyable to write a straightforward novel in which fictional characters interact in fictional situations. A simply told novel—that would be fun, too.

**FP** In *Break It Down* a number of the narrators wear glasses. Are you nearsighted?

**LD** Definitely. And now I'm bifocal. I probably have an astigmatism, or I'm myopic. I don't know all the technical terms. My father wore trifocals—the ultimate English professor.

**FP** One of the things that I love about the stories is that there's something out of focus that reduces everything to first principles. Only in very few stories does the reader know where the story is taking place—what city—and only in very few stories do the characters have names. Or they have odd generic names like Wife Number One. When I was a kid I didn't wear my glasses for years because I was too vain. And when I first read the stories they recreated that sense of not seeing exactly, but somehow feeling that not seeing is more accurate than seeing.

**LD** When you're not wearing your glasses, all you can see is what is close to you. You can't see the context. You can't see the rest of the room or across the street. I also didn't wear my glasses some of the time out of vanity. I have thought about this because I notice it all the time—that in reading students' work or discussing other peoples' work, I don't have much trouble focusing on detail, word to word, sentence to sentence, but I have to make a major effort to step back from a piece of writing and summarize what its themes are. As a child I resisted knowing much about the outside world—politics, international situations. In college I had only a very vague sense of facts, of distances. I remember being asked in some psychological test how far it is from New York to London, and even though I'd been to Europe at least twice already, I said about 15,000 miles. I was terrible at current events in school. I did well on one assignment which was to take a newspaper article and point out where the reporter was showing bias. Again, that was a close textual analysis.

FP  It was just about language.

LD  I hated history because the events could have come out too many different ways. Whereas I loved math because there was only one way a problem could come out.

FP  And languages?

LD  I was very good at languages. I loved Latin. Latin actually made more sense than French, probably because of the math element again.

FP  I loved Latin, although I hated math. That the two things were related never occurred to me. I loved Latin because of how logical it was, like solving a crossword puzzle. There was an answer, and you got it.

LD  When you're solving the problem of the Latin sentence, there are two things going on: the pleasure of solving the puzzle, but also the emotional satisfaction of finding out what this mysterious thing is. Then there's another pleasure—the pleasure of putting it into English words. I like English best. People assume because I translate French I'm a Francophile, but the fact is I don't like French as much as I like English.

FP  What is it about English?

LD  The plainness. I love the Anglo-Saxon words as opposed to the Latinate. Bread, milk, love, war, peace, cow, dog. The English word "and" seems much more solid, like an apple. Maybe it has to do with those early Dick and Jane books again. Words beginning with "a," "and" and "apple" are somehow healthy. The Spanish "y" is just preposterous. It's weird and strange. (*laughter*)

FP  Does translation help in other ways besides taking up so much of your time?

**LD**  I get a lot of pleasure out of it. I've been doing it for about twenty-five years and it's become even more enjoyable, but I worry that as it becomes more enjoyable maybe I'm becoming a worse translator. I'm worrying about this with the latest text I've been working on, Michel Leiris's *Rules of the Game*, a four volume autobiographical essay. I did the first two volumes and then I started working on the third volume in a sort of blissful state, because I was translating it almost literally rather than reworking a sentence. That's the way I like to translate anyway, keeping, as much as possible, the same word order and the same words. If I could use a cognate of the French word I would. It was like a hand in a glove. But then I began to worry: Have I gone too far? Am I creating a language that is going to read as a stilted difficult language in between French and English?

**FP**  But it does make you more conscious of the words and of the necessity of dithering long enough to find the right word. I always wish my students would understand that one word may actually be *better* than another word, and it's worth the time to get that word no matter how long it takes.

**LD**  That's one thing that I really like about translating—I don't have to think up the next word. I don't have to use my imagination. That's why it's a relaxing thing to do, and at the same time it's a form of writing.

**FP**  Do you take notes on, as they say, real life?

**LD**  If I'm in that really nice awake, alert frame of mind I'll take copious notes. I like to be in that frame of mind because it usually means I'm working on something, but sometimes for months and months at a time I'll just stop writing. Then at other times I write just about everything down.

**FP**  I love when that happens—when everything seems related to what you're writing. It's like everything has a little message that you're being sent that will be useful to you someday. Oh, look at the way that person holds that chicken drumstick!

**LD**  And listen to what they just said. Everything you notice forms a nice sentence. I'm afraid I sometimes take notes on telephone conversations even as they're going on, but I hasten to say only within my own family.

**FP**  Thank God! (*laughter*)

**LD**  My own family—because I've been hearing the way they talk and the sorts of things they say for so long, sometimes I'm thinking more about how they're talking than what they're saying. My family tends to say rather funny things. My mother will refer to "the nicest Republican you could find." My sister will mention a man with three premature nephews. So I am sometimes guilty of what most people would probably think of as how a writer works. People are afraid a writer will take notes on what they're saying or doing and use it as material.

**FP**  I do that, too. I think that my job is to notice the things that you're not supposed to notice. The things that people say that are just supposed to be normal conversation or friendly chat, but that are searingly unkind. I can't stop noticing them. Of course when you put those things in your book no one ever thanks you for it.

**LD**  I have to say, though, that I've never put anything into a story that my mother or sister has said. I have used things that my husband has said. I think it's uncomfortable for people to be written about even when it's very positive, because they feel as if they're being used.

**FP**  Do you think so? I think people are often flattered.

**LD**  One friend was very uncomfortable. Another friend skimmed the story to find all the places she appeared to see if they were okay. Then she settled down and read it again from the beginning. She said it actually had a very good effect on her because at that time she was feeling: What does my life add up to? She's in her forties, and enough decades have gone by so she was feeling a little discouraged. When she saw herself in print and saw all the things that she had said and done and thought, she had a different feeling. Her life did add up to something. She was a real person. Not because she was in the book, but because the book showed her to herself. That was very nice.

**FP**  It also means that on the simplest level somebody's been paying attention or listening, which I think everyone wants. Or at least that's what I try and tell myself when I'm afraid of the other response which is: How dare you invade my privacy and use me?

**LD**  Even though a lot of my friends are writers, I've rarely felt troubled by that, are they going to go home and make a note of our conversation?

**FP**  You're right, it never occurs to me. (*laughter*)

**LD**  It never occurs to me, either. I ought to know better.

**FP**  One of the things about your work—even though I'm not sure what I mean—is if you took Lydia's name off the story, you would still know it's a Lydia Davis story. What do I mean? Maybe you know.

**LD**  Well, I was just writing a letter yesterday to a man who read my novel and wrote about it in exactly the way you would want someone to read a book of yours.

**FP**  Where was this?

**LD**  This was in the *London Review of Books*. Michael Hofmann wrote it. It was smart. It was beautifully written. He saw things I didn't see. He caught everything I would have wanted someone to catch. He called the book a comedy—toward the end of this very serious discussion—which pleased me to no end. What I found interesting was after a couple of months of enjoying this review I began having this uneasy feeling that maybe he just read it the way I would like someone to read it, but that doesn't mean that's what the book was, or is. I really had to face up to the philosophical idea that a book is completed by the reader. Suddenly the book didn't have a single existence anymore. And maybe another review, a short little dismissive review that it also got was just as accurate. I mean that reader saw this negative version of the book which had been my worst fear as I was working on it.

**FP**  If somebody's response is what you intended, it's as if you asked a question and got an answer. The right answer. If no one in the entire universe understood the thing you were trying to do, then maybe you weren't able to do it. But if someone actually got it, as this guy clearly did, then it was *there* to be gotten and someone else just *didn't* get it.

**LD**  Well, that would be nice. But, if he's the only one who got everything, then was it written for only one person?

**FP**  Hardly anyone can read anymore, that's the trouble.

**LD**  That might be one answer. Hofmann used some very nice phrases. Here's the phrase that sprang to mind when you asked how would you know a story was by me—he used the phrase "fussy drone." (*laughter*) What he appreciated was the shapeliness of thought, the shapeliness of structure. He implied that there was a sensuality to the structure of the sentences and the structure of the thought. If all the sensuality is contained in the shapeliness of the grammar or the structure of the sentence then that structure has to be exactly right. The sentence has to be just right and the thought has to be just right because if it isn't, well, it's not as shapely.

# Junot Díaz
# and Edwidge Danticat

JUNOT DÍAZ was born in the Dominican Republic in 1968. He is the author of *Drown; The Brief Wondrous Life of Oscar Wao*, which won the 2008 Pulitzer Prize and the National Book Critics Circle Award; and *This Is How You Lose Her*, a *New York Times* bestseller and National Book Award finalist. He is the recipient of a MacArthur Fellowship, the PEN/Malamud Award, the Dayton Literary Peace Prize, a Guggenheim Fellowship, and a PEN/O. Henry Award. A graduate of Rutgers College, Díaz is currently the fiction editor at Boston Review and the Rudge and Nancy Allen Professor of Writing at the Massachusetts Institute of Technology.

EDWIDGE DANTICAT was born in Haiti in 1969. She is the author of numerous books including *Brother, I'm Dying*, which won the National Book Critics Circle Award and was a National Book Award finalist; *Breath, Eyes, Memory*, an Oprah Book Club selection; *Krik? Krak!*, a National Book Award finalist; *The Farming of Bones*, winner of the American Book Award; *The Dew Breaker*; and *Claire of the Sea Light*. She is the recipient of a MacArthur Fellowship and currently lives in Miami with her husband and daughters.

# JUNOT DÍAZ AND EDWIDGE DANTICAT

**EDWIDGE DANTICAT**  I think most folks would want me to ask you, those of us who've been waiting with bated breath for this book: What the heck took you so long?

**JUNOT DÍAZ**  What, really, can one say? I'm a slow writer. Which is bad enough but given that I'm in a world where it's considered abnormal if a writer *doesn't* produce a book every year or two—it makes me look even worse. Ultimately the novel wouldn't have it any other way. This book wanted X number of years out of my life. Perhaps I could have written a book in a shorter time but it wouldn't have been this book and this was the book I wanted to write. Other reasons? I'm a crazy perfectionist. I suffer from crippling bouts of depression. I write two score pages for every one I keep. I hear this question and want to laugh and cry because there's no answer. What I always want to ask other writers (and what I'll ask you) is how can you write about something so soon after it's happened? What's to be gained by writing about something—say, the death of a father and uncle, as you do in your new book, *Brother, I'm Dying*—when the moment is close?

**ED**  There are several factors for me. The first is that I'm totally compulsive. If something is on my mind, writing-wise, I have to do it and do it in the instant. I have to at least put down a first draft. Otherwise, I am so afraid I will lose it. Like you, I live with the eternal fear that I am not supposed to be doing what I'm doing. Who do I think I am to be writing books and shit, as you might say. So I write when the moment is close so it won't slip away. Writing is also the way I process things and when I am done with a piece I feel a lot closer to understanding the subject.

Now back to you and your brilliant new book, *The Brief Wondrous Life of Oscar Wao*. I knew I had entered a Junot Díaz universe when the book's epigraph had a quote from the *Fantastic Four* and a poem by Derek Walcott, both poignant and immediate windows into the book. *The Fantastic Four* quote is from April 1966, a little bit before you were born. It says, "Of what import are brief, nameless lives . . ." That's not all it says, but that's the gist of it. The Walcott quote ends with "either I'm nobody or I'm a nation." You know I am obsessed with the notion of namelessness and the idea of brief lives and how individuals and nations disrupt and end lives, so *Oscar Wao* was the kind of book I could easily swallow whole. I was preparing to read about this one life, however, this person who is immediately named in the very title of the book and is claimed from namelessness. But I ended up reading about a nation. How did Oscar Wao come to be?

I'm not going to play the autobiographical game too much, but you and he share so many things: you're both writers, sci-fi and fantasy nuts. Does he come from some inner part of you? Or is he wholly a creature of your imagination? Were you once a game master who tried his hand at being a real writer?

**JD** There are, as you and I well know, certain kinds of people that no one wants to build the image of a nation around. Even if these people are in fact the nation itself. Poor dark people are not usually central to a nation's self-conception (except perhaps as a tourist attraction). But in this novel I wanted to start with a different kind of erasure, a smaller one but one that to me felt equally horrible. In the Dominican culture that I know, a character like Oscar was not going to be anyone's notion of the ideal Dominican boy. In the Dominican culture I know, someone like Oscar would not be labeled Dominican, no matter what his actual background was. So that's what really attracted me to him. His compassion, his outré interests, his dearth of traditional masculine markers—these were the things that defined Oscar in my head but that also guaranteed that no one would ever happily connect him to the nation he grew up out of and the nation that I thought he was representative of.

But the character himself, this supernerd. I was a ghetto nerd supreme: a smart kid in a poor-ass community. The thing with me was that I was a nerd embedded in a dictatorial military family where the boys had to fight all the time, where we were smacked around regularly by our father (to toughen us up), where we shot guns every weekend (just in case anything should happen), where you were only a human being if you were an aggressive violent *hombre*. So I was a nerd who had all this "man" training, for lack of a better term. I was a nerd with a special passport that allowed me to hang with the non-nerd boys. So I grew up with this whole group of smart kids of color, was one of them and yet wasn't, and that's how Oscar came to be. Oscar was a composite of all the nerds that I grew up with who didn't have that special reservoir of masculine privilege. Oscar was who I would have been if it had not been for my father or my brother or my own willingness to fight or my own inability to fit into any category easily.

I must have had him in my mind a long time because he emerged, like Athena, almost fully formed out of my skull. His sections of the novel were the easiest for me to compose. It was the rest of it that took years.

**ED** I am utterly intrigued by the idea of *fukú americanus*, "a curse or doom of some kind; specifically the Curse and the Doom of the New World." There are so many examples of this all around us still. In our part of the world, we have not totally recovered from colonialism and even have a new brand of it we're currently dealing with, being so close to the United States.

We see *fukú americanus* just rip through the lives of the characters in this book. Is there any hope of recovery from it?

**JD** Well, the *fukú* has been one of those Dominican concepts that have fascinated me for years. Our island (and a lot of countries around it) has a long tradition of believing in curses. The *fukú* was different in that it was the one curse that explicitly implicated the historical trauma of our creation, as an area, a people. I mean, how crazy is that? A Dominican curse that seems to have its origins in the arrival of the European? In Columbus? Say his name aloud and bad shit will happen to you? For a writer like me—the *fukú* was a narrative dream come true. I'm not the only one: when the Russian poet Yevgeny Yevtushenko visited Santo Domingo and learned about the *fukú* it inspired him to write a book-length poem called—surprise, surprise—"Fuku." (I've read it; it's pretty damn good.)

For me, though, the real issue in the book is not whether or not one can vanquish the *fukú*—but whether or not one can even see it. Acknowledge its existence at a collective level. To be a true witness to who we are as a people and to what has happened to us. That is the essential challenge for the Caribbean nations—who, as you pointed out, have been annihilated by history and yet who've managed to put themselves together in an amazing way. That's why I thought the book was somewhat hopeful at the end. The family still won't openly admit that there's a *fukú*, but they're protecting the final daughter, Isis, from it collectively, and that's close, very close to my dream of us bearing witness to (in Glissant's words) "the past, to which we were subjected, which has not yet emerged as history for us (but that) is however, obsessively present."

**ED** Both Fanon and Glissant discuss the use of language as a manifestation of different types of pains, personal and communal traumas. Glissant talks in his particular context about *délire verbale*, verbal delirium. This book is epic in so many ways, with a canvas as broad as the Americas and beyond. You often talk about the immigration experience as resembling space travel in the sense that you leave one completely different world, get in a steel machine that flies, and suddenly you're a resident of a vastly different planet. Reading this book I felt like I was traveling through time and space. It was delirious and dizzying at times. The range of experience and characters are simply breathtaking. I do see why you needed all this time. You needed these people to reveal themselves to you. You needed time to unravel. Like Oscar you needed to address your own furies and organize your personal pantheon to tell this huge story.

Aside from Octavia Butler, Tananarive Due, and Walter Mosley, I don't read much fantasy and science fiction, but science fiction is an obvious influence, as are comic books. Were there any patterns in these types of narratives that you wanted to follow? Any traditional voices?

JD Praise from my favorite writer who's been writing epics for years? Thank you, Edwidge, thank you.

I've always wanted to write epic books. My favorite books as a kid were all epics. *Watership Down*, *Lord of the Rings*, the Lensmen series. In the DR all my dreams were about a future in the US but in the US all my dreams were about a future . . . elsewhere. And I've definitely been wanting to write science fiction/fantasy, to write genre, to use some of those models to strike out in (for me at least) new directions.

Why this continued commitment to genres? So much of our experience as Caribbean Diasporic peoples, so much of it, exists in silence. How can we talk about our experiences in any way if both our own local culture and the larger global culture don't want to talk about them and actively resist our attempt to create language around them? Well, my strategy was to seek my models at the narrative margins. When I was growing up those were the narratives that most resonated with me and not simply because of the "sense of wonder" or because of the adolescent wish fulfillment that many genre books truck in. It was because these were the narratives that spoke directly to what I had experienced, both personally and historically. The X-Men made a lot of sense to me, because that's what it really felt like to grow up bookish and smart in a poor urban community in central New Jersey. Time travel made sense to me because how else do I explain how I got from Villa Juana, from latrines and no lights, to Parlin, NJ, to MTV and a car in every parking space? Not just describe it but explain the missing emotional cognitive disjunction? I mean, let's be real. Without shit like race and racism, without our lived experience as people of color, the metaphor that drives, say, the X-Men, would not exist! Mutants are a metaphor (among other things) for race, and that's one of the reasons that mutants are so popular in the Marvel Universe and in the Real. I have no problem re-looting the metaphor of the X-Men because I know it's my silenced experience, my erased condition that's the secret fuel that powers this particular fucking fantasy. So if I'm powering the ship, at a lower frequency, I'm going to have a say in how it's used and in what ports of call it stops.

For another example, we have as a community been the victim of a long-term breeding project—I mean, that was one component of slavery: we were systematically bred for hundreds of years—but in mainstream literary fiction nobody's really talking about breeding experiments. If you're looking for language that will help you approach our nigh-unbearable historical experiences you can reach for narratives of the impossible: sci-fi, horror, fantasy, which might not really want to talk about people of color at all but that take what we've experienced (without knowing it) very seriously indeed. Shit, they've been breeding people in sci-fi since its inception (*The Island of Doctor Moreau*) and the metaphors that the genres have established (mostly off the back of our experiences as people of color: the eternal other) can be reclaimed and subverted and expanded in useful ways that help clarify and immediate-ize our own histories, if only for ourselves. To quote Glissant again: this time that was never ours, we must now possess. Because it certainly has no problem possessing us any time it wants.

**ED** There are many footnotes and asides in *The Brief Wondrous Life*. You seem to be purposely addressing your own anxieties about writing through Oscar's. Paradoxically Oscar dreams of being the Dominican James Joyce, at the same time "he saw his entire writing future flash before his eyes; he'd only written one novel worth a damn . . . wouldn't get a chance to write anything better—career over." Were there moments when you worried that you might not write again? Does Junot Díaz, minimalist in *Drown* and definitely Joycean here, dream of being the Dominican James Joyce?

**JD** Edwidge, you'll like this one. The footnotes and the reference to the femme matador in the text are a shout-out to my favorite of Caribbean writers: Patrick Chamoiseau. I read *Texaco* many years ago and it blew my head off. I wanted to write a book with footnotes like that. Hell, I wanted to write a book like *Texaco*.

Vollmann and Danielewski and the postmodern white-boy gang have been deploying footnotes for a while and Cisneros used them in *Caramelo* but nobody, and I mean nobody, has done them like Chamoiseau. As for Joyce: Lola wants Oscar to be the Dominican James Joyce but Oscar just wants to be a Dominican Andre Norton. I'm a Joyce fanatic—the Irish have had a colonial relationship with the English a long, long time and that's one reason they're so useful to immigrant writers of color in the US—but I don't dream of being Joyce any more than I dream of being Jack Kirby. If I dreamed of being any writer I dream of being a Dominican Octavia Butler or a Dominican Samuel Delany. Prolific, brilliant, and impossible. But since this is not a fantasy world: I just want to write four books before I die. For real. And yes: I worry all the time about never writing again. Most of my writer peers write like it's a daily they're producing. I write like it's an organ I'm pulling out of myself. I wish I could do what they do. But you can only be yourself. And for me that means being a dedicated writer who can only write a book a decade if I'm lucky.

**ED**  There are many wonderful writers who started a lot later than you and take their time and have produced an incredible body of work. In my crystal calabash, that's what I see for you.

**JD**  You have the Power so I won't argue. Fingers crossed.

**ED**  In this book, you do tackle a lot of people, including Joyce. Maria Montez is here—cue J.Lo for movie role. Kim Novak, among others. You also address other novels that have been written about the Dominican Republic. Are you responding to some of these books?

**JD**  Yes, guilty as charged. I populated this book with as many side characters as possible. Maria Montez is my favorite bad actress in the world. (Really. Have you seen *Cobra Queen*?) And besides, her name was María Africa Gracia Vidal—how can you hate that? (But I'd rather see Dania Ramirez in the role.) There are also a lot of fake people in the book. Darkseid is my all-time favorite comic book villain and he casts a long, long shadow over the story. His main power? The Omega Effect. That can vaporize a person until he chooses to put them back together again. Now if that's not a basic dictator power I don't know what is. But more than people, fake or real, I tried to stuff as many books as I could into *Oscar Wao*. I mean, shit, even the title refers to Oscar Wilde and *The Short Happy Life of Francis Macomber* simultaneously.

**ED**  Damn, how could I have missed that?

**JD**  What can I tell you? I'm book-obsessed and I wrote about a book-obsessed protagonist. The narrator too: book-obsessed. You better believe that I was fucking with other books written about the Dominican Republic. I mean, have you read *The Feast of the Goat*? Pardon me while I hate, but people jumped on that novel like it was the greatest thing on earth! And you should have seen the Dominican elites fawning over Vargas Llosa. The Great Vargas Llosa has deigned to visit the Dominican Republic! Call me a nationalist slash hater, but Vargas Llosa's take on the Trujillo regime was identical to Crassweller's and Crassweller wrote his biography forty years ago!

**ED**  Uhm . . . have you ever met the great man?

**JD**  Only in the books.

**ED** "What is it with Dictators and Writers anyway?" is one of the questions raised in the book. One of the answers proposed is Salman Rushdie's claim that tyrants and scribblers are natural antagonists, competitors. But this is refuted for the notion that like recognizes like. Writers too are dictators. I find this interesting because a lot of dictators, in Haiti for example, have considered themselves writers. No writer of his time was left alive long enough to be as prolific as François "Papa Doc" Duvalier. Did Trujillo try to write poetry? I remember hearing that. I think dictators want to silence writers because they want to be the only ones speaking.

I think of the poem by Carolyn Forché, where the poet goes to dinner at the dictator's house. After dinner, he spills a bag of human ears on the table while saying something like, *This is for your poetry.* This dictator was trying to take away the power he knew this writer had by attempting to stun her into silence. Still I agree that dictators and writers will be eternally linked in battle. Even when dictators kill or disappear the writers, though, the writers win. In Haiti we have the case of the extraordinary Jacques Stephen Alexis, one of our best writers, who was killed by Papa Doc's henchmen in the 1960s. His work has certainly outlasted Papa Doc's treatises. People have embraced him even more in death than they had in life. Most writers won't sit quietly by while a dictatorship rolls on—though people in today's US seem to be missing the clues—and the dictators know that.

**JD** Yeah, I do have a weird view of both writers and dictators. The dictators we're talking about, Trujillo and Papa Doc (or as I call him in the novel, P. Daddy) both had their writing components. Trujillo wrote the *Foro Público* where he would publicly humiliate his enemies, the discursive *click*, before he followed through with some terminal praxis, the killing *clack*. But I think that this "scribbling" was just a sideline to Trujillo's real writing, which was done on the flesh and psyches of the Dominican people. That tends to be the writing that the Trujillos of the world are truly invested in, and it's the kind of writing that lasts far longer and resonates far deeper than many of its victims would care to admit. I don't think there's a Dominican writer, past or present, who's matched the awful narrative puissance that Trujillo marshaled; his "work" deformed, captured, organized us Dominicans in ways we can barely understand, and this "work" has certainly outlasted his physical existence. (And unless I'm nuts, this writing continues to be more popular than the work of any of the competition—me and my peers included. What I write about the Haitian community moves maybe three people, but what he "wrote" about the Haitian community still moves the fucking pueblo.) If you think about it: Ozymandias would have had more luck if, instead of carving stone, he had carved people. Then he could have lasted—sheesh, almost forever.

I remember that Forché poem! But I read it a little differently. The dictator, perhaps without being conscious of it, by throwing down the ears, is basically saying, *This is how I write: now what you got?* It's an attempt to terrorize, clearly, but it's also implicitly a challenge. I impact, viscerally, collectives—how about you? And if we regular writers can't admit how powerful and tenacious this other form of writing is, I doubt we'll ever be able to counter it.

And maybe I've been to one too many writer's conferences, but I really do believe that writers and dictators are eternal antagonists primarily because yes: like recognizes like. Partially it's Rushdie's point and yours: dictators, no matter from what side of the globe they hail, tend to recognize the power of word magicians, which is why they so thoroughly seek to control, negate, or exterminate the narrative competition. And many writers discern that this is ever the dictator's weak point, like the missing scale on Smaug's underbelly in *The Hobbit*. The more they silence, the more powerful the voice that speaks into that silence becomes.

**ED** Trujillo is a big presence in the book. He is a kind of *fukú* himself. He died before you were born, but are there any firsthand accounts that were passed on to you as a child? People believed he had supernatural powers, just like they thought Haiti's Papa Doc had supernatural powers.

Of course, people like Papa Doc and Trujillo took great pains to foster that perception. Papa Doc used to dress every day like Baron Samedi, the *lwa* or spirit that was guardian of the cemetery. People thought he roamed the streets at night personally looking for them. When he died, my mother said, a strong wind swept down around the earth, probably a protest in hell. This perception of being supermen—there's the sci-fi for you—was crucial to their reign. I guess what I am asking is, what was it about Trujillo, in your opinion, that allowed him to remain in power for so long?

**JD** Like I sort of said earlier: these guys are a lot better at manipulating narratives—in this case traditional folkloric ones—than most folks give them credit for. And believing Trujillo to be a super-being can be a narrative of consolation for a pueblo, but it can also be a useful metaphor to understand what we're really dealing with. I think it's these outsized visions of these dictators that are most accurate about their power and its awful consequences.

I for one will never forget the Trujillo stories I heard while growing up. My father was a police soldier for Balaguer's post-but-pro-Trujillo regime so

I was exposed to a lot of trujillista craziness through him. (One of the scariest moments I had with my dad in Santo Domingo was when he "jokingly" locked me into one of the prison cells in the *cuartel* where he worked. Same cells where the Trujillo regime used to torture its victims. Real swell dad-son moment.)

The fear people had of speaking, really speaking—that's not something I will soon forget, and I wonder if it wasn't what shaped my frankness, my distrust of politeness (its own form of silencing).

**ED** You use the "N-word" liberally in this book, as you have done in the past. There's been renewed discourse on this recently, a renewed sensitivity. Are you concerned about any backlash over the use of the word?

**JD** There's a lot of language in this book that many could find offensive. The N-word is without question one of them. But as I'm always saying: there's a difference between representing a thing and endorsing it. The Yunior narrator feels comfortable using "the N-bomb," but Oscar never would, not for anything, and I think it's important to remember that. What's funny is that this is a conversation that interests the middle class and the upper classes in our communities—but talk to kids where I grew up or where I'm living now and that's not really what's at the top of their priorities. They're wondering why they've been abandoned educationally, politically, culturally—why living in these urban zones is so very bad for your goddamn health.

As an artist and as a person of color who's never had a moment in his life where someone hasn't been actively trying to control my tongue, I'm seriously conflicted about these debates. To keep it short: language has never been a good dog and its free exercise will never provide comfort to cultures of respectability. And I guess I've never really been one for comforting my readers either.

**ED** Recently the *Miami Herald* published two articles. One, that was also run by the Associated Press, about the American embassy having to call out Dominican clubs for denying entry to its black American marines and other embassy staff. The other article was called "Black Denial" and it was about the desire of most Dominicans not to be considered or called black. The piece was extremely controversial, in part because a well-known Dominican intellectual was quoted as saying black women have enormous asses and that no black woman could be considered beautiful in the DR. I was extraordinarily upset by this for reasons I didn't even understand at the moment. But thinking back to the touchy issue of genocide and how it sometimes turns on phenotype, I was heartbroken by these remarks.

In your book one character says, "That's the kind of culture I belong to: people took their child's black complexion as an ill omen." I felt like this great intellectual woman, in spite of herself, belonged to that kind of culture, but people kept saying she did not, but rather was only trying to explain it. Here when I say *culture* I mean the culture of black denial, not necessarily Dominican culture, as I know many black and proud Dominicans. Do we all belong to that black denial culture courtesy of racial supremacy? Even then it's so hard to forgive in our own, because it has wounded us so deeply in the past.

JD  The club thing is endemic. Me and my boys were denied entrance to a club in Santo Domingo and the doormen came right out and said: you and you and you are too black! We filed a lawsuit against the owners and guess what happened? Nada! God bless the Third World! The elites in the DR are as brazen as they are racist as they are cruel and there has yet to be a protracted social action to knock them back.

The black denial article was a slightly different matter—I took umbrage with it for a number of reasons. First off it was another on the same: once again someone pathologizing Dominicans as self-hate machines *par excellence*. For those who don't know: Dominicans are perpetually singled out whenever there's a discussion of self-hatred and black denial. (It's almost like if we talked about Dominican self-hatred we don't have to talk about anybody else's self-hatred.) Mostly because it's easy—owing to some awful peculiarities in Dominican history, our version of "black denial" grates on the Imperial Black sensibilities common throughout the US. Dominicans are easy to single out about the blackness problematic because we make certain issues explicit, *not* because we're alone in having these issues. This can't be emphasized enough. The same author, Frances Robles, later wrote an article on Cuban "black denial" but she went out of her way to historicize it, something she denied her Dominican subjects. (Another note of ridiculousness: how Robles could spend an entire article talking about Dominican self-hatred and never mention the one term that defines all these dysfunctions: white supremacy. Some real blame-the-victim shit.) Robles certainly didn't touch on the fact that Dominicans have historically had to define blackness in the face of the anti-Haitian genocide we inflicted and survived in 1937. You wonder why Dominicans might be a little leery of talking about blackness in the same way as folks in the US or Jamaica do? You'd be amazed how you reconstruct self when there's a machete in your face. That article was so wearying and under-cooked. People who truck in this kind of simplification never deal with the fact (for example) that of all Latino groups in the US, Dominicans have the *highest* rate of identifying themselves as "of African descent." And we're not talking by one or two percentage points, we're talking by a *lot*.

It's not that I'm saying that Dominicans don't have trouble with their African-ness. No one, after all, has a black problem quite like black folks. (Please notice I'm talking about collectives, not individuals; this might seem like sophistry, but it's not.) In *Oscar Wao* I'm deeply interested in (and critical of) this craziness, but instead of insisting that Dominican "black denial" is a pathology unique to Dominicans, I try to foreground the Dominican example in order to explore how general and pernicious this is throughout the African Diaspora. Scarily enough, it's one of the things that "in the darkness binds us." It's one of the great silences of our people—no one really wants to talk about how much of a role anti-black self-hatred has in defining what we call "our cultures." But the Dominican example for me helps unlock the other examples. It's a key, not a lock.

And yes, I do believe we all belong to that culture where a child's dark skin is often taken as a bad omen. Even those of us who don't suffer from this peculiar malaise individually live in communities that do suffer from it, extensively. It's a *fukú* we desperately need a *zafa* for. Problem is, most of us don't want to believe it's even a problem. After our lawsuit in the DR I told our sitting president Leonel Fernández about the incident and he denied that such a thing could happen in the DR. My fucking god.

**ED**  You've just won The American Academy of Letters' Rome fellowship. Before you won, I was reading the new Ralph Ellison biography by Arnold Rampersad, where that fellowship seemed to have been, to put it mildly, a mixed blessing for Ellison. Please read that book before you go. When do you leave for Rome, and what are you going to work on there?

**JD**  I've read the Rampersad biography and it's drop-dead amazing. As far as the Rome Prize is concerned I think I have a sense of what you mean by "mixed blessing." But we'll see. (I'm predisposed to negativity so I'm trying hard to keep my mind open about Europe . . . ) Everyone I've talked to has said it's been an unforgettable experience and I'm hoping this proves to be true for this easily-confused-for-a-North-African brown man.

I leave in September, and while at the Academy I'm hoping to write a chunk of the science fiction novel that I failed to write in the years before *Oscar Wao*. This book was supposed to be a 9/11 novel—not that 9/11, but the other one, which the US inflicted on Latin America (see Pinochet), a shadow 9/11 viewed through an apocalyptic science fiction filter. (Sound crazy enough for you?) The book, *Dark America*, is set in an alternate US where New York City has been destroyed by a psychic terrorist (a plot that was inspired not by the "real" 9/11 or the TV show *Heroes* but by all those damn end-of-the-world books I read as a kid). The book (my very own Dominican *Akira*) deals with the aftermath of this apocalypse. About the survivors and the growing sense that a worse eschaton is in the making. We'll see. I always start with the best intentions and then end up screaming.

**ED** Finally, in spite of Oscar's brief life, the narrator's life—writing-wise—ends on a happy note. Yunior says, "These days I write a lot. From can't see in the morning to can't see at night. Learned a lot from Oscar. I'm a new man, you see, a new man, a new man." Is Junot Díaz a new man?

**JD** Again, I wish. I'm happier, no doubt about it, and less devoured by my fears, but I still have no handle on my talent. I don't know how to make it work. I don't write with any regularity or joy. I fear that it might take me another eleven years to write another book. But I did finish a novel that was threatening to break me, and I finished it in a manner that I feel reflects my hard work, and this finishing has been one of the happiest accomplishments of my life. Through all those years I never did think I would ever finish *Oscar Wao*, so the fact that somewhere inside me I found the strength to do what I thought was impossible . . . it almost makes me believe that one day I *will* be like Yunior: a new man, a new man.

# Geoff Dyer
# and Jonathan Lethem

GEOFF DYER was born in Cheltenham, England, in 1958. He is the author of numerous books, including the novels *Paris Trance* and *Jeff in Venice, Death in Varanasi*; the essay collection *Otherwise Known as the Human Condition*, which won the National Book Critics Circle Award for Criticism; and several genre-defying titles, including *Out of Sheer Rage* and *Zona*. A graduate of Corpus Christi College, Oxford, he is the winner of the E.M. Forster Award from the American Academy of Arts and Letters and the Somerset Maugham Prize and is a Fellow of the Royal Society of Literature. He lives in Venice Beach, California.

JONATHAN LETHEM was born in Brooklyn, New York, in 1964. He is the author of over a dozen works of fiction and nonfiction, including *Gun, with Occasional Music*; *The Fortress of Solitude*; *Chronic City*; *The Ecstasy of Influence*; *Dissident Gardens*; and *Motherless Brooklyn*, which won the National Book Critics Circle Award, the Macallan Gold Dagger for Crime Fiction, and the Salon Book Award. He has served as editor for numerous collections of fiction. In 2005, Lethem received a MacArthur Fellowship. He lives in Brooklyn.

**JONATHAN LETHEM**  When I agreed to play the role of your interviewer in this exchange, I felt that immediate freshening of the spirit I associate with occasions where I'm expected to talk about someone else's work instead of my own. It then immediately occurred to me that despite this momentary reversal, you were much cleverer than I was because you seem to have made that pleasure into much of your life's work—from the jazz book to the Lawrence, the photography, and so on. Of course it leads you around to yourself, but in a much more tolerable way. Was there a point where you became conscious of always wanting there to be a "room" in which you "worked," other artists in between, or amid, you and your writing?

**GEOFF DYER**  Well, first up, how unusual for us to be having an email exchange with proper sentences, punctuation, and uppercase letters rather than the usual typo-riddled notes we've dashed off in the past! The thing is it didn't even occur to me that I could be a normal writer in the sense of "novelist," because I could never think up stories or plots. But I didn't want to just be a straight-down-the-line critic either. I always liked the idea of some kind of creative criticism à la Berger or Barthes. When I have written novels, there's often been some kind of barely submerged critical thing going on—*Paris Trance* or *Jeff in Venice* were versions of, or homages to, other books. I like books that are about other books in some way. In terms of well-being or psychological health, certainly I'm extremely happy when I set out, either for an article or a book, to read and learn everything I can about a given person or subject, to completely immerse myself in it. I feel, at that point, that I have a purpose. When it comes to actually *writing* a book, that excitement and well-being would soon turn to boredom if it didn't proceed in tandem with the creative challenge of coming up with some kind of form or structure that seems especially appropriate to that subject.

**JL**  In the matter of coming up with a form or structure, I'm eager to talk with you about your new book on Tarkovsky's *Stalker*. I'm actually reading it in tandem with revisiting the film—the first time I've seen it in twenty years. I'm halfway through both book and film as I write this. The short book that covers another artifact—a book, a film, an album—in scrupulous close description (with plenty of digressions, of course)—is something I'm trying myself. Last year with a film, John Carpenter's *They Live*, and right at the moment I'm writing a short book on a Talking Heads album, *Fear of Music*. (I flatter myself I'm in "Dyerian Mode" when I do this.) If a novel is a mirror walking along a road (somebody said this; in a spirit of Dyerian laziness I'm refusing to Google it), a book like this is a mirror walking

113

hand-in-hand with somebody else's mirror. I'll admit I also became fascinated by a weird concurrence in our film-subjects: both *Stalker* and *They Live* are films that switch between color and black-and-white (and therefore both get compared to *The Wizard of Oz*), and both turn on a transformation of the everyday world at roughly the half-hour mark, where the ordinary is revealed as extraordinary. Of course, your film quite respectably avoids wrestlers and ghouls.

**GD** Here is an important difference between us. You could do these books as sidelines or diversion, almost, I imagine, writing fiction in the morning and then doing the film or Talking Heads stuff in the afternoon. I operate at a far lower level of energy and inspiration, but a higher pitch of desperation! Generally, I like the idea of short books on one particular cultural artifact as long as they don't conform to some kind of series idea or editorial template. The madder the better, in my view. I like the idea of an absurdly long book on one small thing. I think we'd agree that the choice of artifact is sort of irrelevant in terms of its cultural standing: all that matters is what it means to you, the author. I had so much fun doing the *Stalker* book I am tempted to do another, this time on *Where Eagles Dare*. In fact, I find myself thinking/whining, Why *shouldn't* I do that? Plenty of other writers keep banging out versions of the same thing, book after book, why should I always have to be doing something completely new each time?

**JL** Ha! I relish your image of my superheroic mornings and afternoons. I won't do much to puncture this, except say that Greil Marcus told me he allocates six weeks for these little books on *The Manchurian Candidate* or "Like a Rolling Stone." I took his encouragement and then took six months on *They Live*—I am now well into eight months on my hundred pages on Talking Heads (with three years of, er, contemplation behind that). But I'm glad you brought up the image of the long book on the brief artifact because what doing this kind of work has put me so much in mind of is the idea of "ratios of time"—i.e., writing about a film (or reading a book like yours on Tarkovsky, which extensively describes a film) you become so conscious of this allocation—the rate of attention-to-subject, or of prose-to-elapsed-time in the artwork. Of course, this matter is present for novelists, too, more subliminally, yet ubiquitous—the situation of the year that passes in a paragraph and the minute that takes thirty pages to describe. It becomes beautifully visible with something like *Stalker*—how do you write a 160-minute book? This leads me to the grave observation that for all your sense that your work is centrifugal and non-repeating, your true subject, no matter what you put in the foreground, is time. Jazz musicians—and Bob

Dylan—are known to have claimed that their effort is to "stop time," but it seems to me that's yours as well, or to capture exactly the sensation of its passage, which amounts to the same thing.

**GD** Funnily enough, at one point I thought of adding a paragraph in my *Stalker* book saying that it could be read in real time, i.e., in approximately the time it took the film to unfold. But then the book got longer, and I realized that to get through it in 160 minutes you'd have to read it very and—given the slow pace of the film—inappropriately fast. Generally I like the idea of shrinking the gap between that which is being written about and the way that it is written about. Having said that, the test of books like these is that they should be capable of being read and enjoyed by people who have no knowledge of the thing they're about. To that extent, the gap is increased so that one's book about this thing becomes an independent and free-floating—forgive the pomposity—work of art in its own right.

As for time, I'm glad to hear it! I'm doing a conversation at the ICA in London with Christian Marclay in a month. It will be nice to be able to say that our shared interest in time has been independently verified. Have you seen any of *The Clock* yet?

**JL** No, I haven't, only because I haven't been in any of the cities where it was on view, but by now I've read so many compelling descriptions of it—particularly Zadie Smith's—and responded so extensively to those, and gone on to see or re-see some of the films that are mentioned as being included, and noticed the moments of clocks in those films, that I feel I can quite competently weigh in on Marclay's piece and claim myself as having been influenced by it. I hope you'll be sympathetic to this stance as being some-what more than being totally full of shit, or somewhat less than totally, since from your Lawrence book and a few places in *Working the Room* I think of you as being receptive to the influence of books you haven't read completely, or have forgotten reading, or only heard paraphrased.

**GD** How interesting: to have seen bits of Christian Marclay's *The Clock* quoted, as it were, in the films he's lifted them from! I think of you as being one of two ideal viewers of *The Clock* (the other would be David Thomson), partly because of this issue of appropriation and creativity—"The Ecstasy of Influence"—and the obsessiveness you share with Marclay. But I also quite like the perversity of your continually missing it through the serial mishap of being in the wrong place at the wrong time! Anyway, I think you're not quite right about time being my big theme: I think the big recurring theme has been the desire to give up, to quit. I'm always on the brink of no longer being a writer. (That, needless to say, is exactly what's kept me going all these years!) *Stalker* lends itself very well to addressing this because the character called Writer is a washed-up writer going to the Zone for inspiration. His is the mirror I'm looking into on this journey. But yes, I think you're right in that I've always wanted to preserve certain moments. I'd trace this back to my teens, to reading Wordsworth and what he calls "spots of time," though for me they've tended to be scattered through my adult life rather than concentrated in childhood as he claims in *The Prelude*. It's part of a general romantic yearning, but I like the way that in Wordsworth it's so deeply earthed rather than being part of a more ethereal *ooh*ing and *aah*ing such as you get in Shelley. Following on from this, it's inevitable that those spots of time in Wordsworth are absolutely rooted in very specific places. Being in the right *place* at the right time! That's been a real constant for me: place. Especially places where time has stood its ground, where the temporal manifests itself in the spatial, where history becomes geography.

JL   That's especially true in your book on the Great War, *The Missing of the Somme*, isn't it? I'm in the middle of that one too—being half-done with two of your books, and having to race back and watch the rest of *Stalker* before I can allow myself to finish one of them. This seems like a particularly Dyerian—I'm sorry I keep using that annoying word—place to be. I'm glad the Great War isn't only half-finished, though! Reading the Somme book, I was struck by the way you capture an image of the whole of England acting as one great grieving and commemorative and self-flattering consciousness in the wake of the war—as if England became a kind of artist, grappling with a theme (or became a mirror walking down the road of history, for a while). This idea of capturing "spots of time" seems to fit here, too. The way the British public and its poets all began anticipating going on this journey of sorrowful remembrance before the occasion had actually taken place reminded me, strangely enough, of Geoff Dyer's, or "Jeff's," approach to going on vacation in books like *Yoga for People Who Can't Be Bothered to Do It*, or *Jeff in Venice, Death in Varanasi*, i.e., always speculatively laying the groundwork for retrospect.

GD   Yes, right. Lutyens's Memorial to the Missing of the Somme at Thiepval is where I became fully conscious of this time-in-space thing. The grieving collective consciousness is certainly there in the 1920s and '30s—though by the mid-'30s it takes on another, forward-looking quality as people realize that actually the peace had been a long time-out and soon we were going to have a go at the Germans—again. The self-flattering idea is very interesting too. In his history of the First World War (published in 1998, well after my book came out in the UK), John Keegan writes: "The Somme marked the end of an age of vital optimism in British life that has never been restored." Quite a claim! Now, apart from its accuracy, which is questionable—given the euphoria of various times—the swinging '60s in London, beating the Germans in the World Cup final in 1966, or the ecstasy years of the late '80s and '90s, for example—there's the tacit celebration of this loss of optimism (and maybe even an implied nostalgia if it ever returned!). But as with all myths, it contains a certain truth about British life, one that is so profoundly depressive as to be unimaginable in America.

As for speculatively, and similarly, laying the groundwork for retrospect in *Jeff in Venice* or *Yoga*—I don't see it at all: just a preservation of special moments, i.e., good ole-fashioned lyricism!

**JL**  I finished the Somme book last night. I had no choice but to stay inside the trance of it to the end, once I'd gotten any momentum at all. It's outstanding, one of your best things, I think. Amazing to me that it hadn't been published in the US before, and that I hadn't read it before, which shouldn't amount to the same thing but apparently did in this case. On page one hundred (of this edition, anyway), you make room for a pretty bad joke about a friend's bad driving and for a friend's good joke about dying in a car crash being good publicity for your unwritten book. It's an amazing act of confidence and generosity, I think, toward your friend and the reader both. It struck me that with your willingness to court inanity, even in the midst of your topic, you'd authorized yourself to be the writer of a book about such unspeakable sorrow—much more absolutely than you had, for instance, by telling us that your grandfather was in the war. Many thousands of people could say the latter and, there's no way to be polite about this, I mostly wouldn't want to read their books. They wouldn't have known to include the friend's joke, or even the friend in the first place.

A simple question: do you reread your old books? I don't, but I wonder about this situation of an older book becoming "new" in this edition, and whether that tempted you into looking into it.

**GD**  No, like you, I don't suffer from that masturbatory habit! But yes, the delay is quite interesting in that the combination of subject matter and photos inserted in the text—albeit with captions—gives it a rather post-Sebaldian quality. It was an important book for me in four ways, all of which are, of course, inextricably related: 1) in terms of my coming to feel at home in this neither-one-thing-nor-the-other hybrid territory; 2) in the development of a tone that could move between the kind of joking around you describe and rather solemn stuff, and a bit of history and literary criticism, etc., without any obvious changing of gears; 3) the evolution of a form that did without the structural prop of chapters in favor of something more organic and free-flowing; and 4) not even trying to be thorough, ignoring completely the stuff that didn't interest me.

**JL** And now, right on cue, I've finished your other new short book (this one authentically new, as opposed to just US new), *Zona*, and it appears to me, very happily, that you have just described the whole of Tarkovsky's brilliant movie in order to passingly (and for me, unmissably) explain why you're actually glad you don't own the film on DVD, as well as what you think of Lars von Trier, and why you and your wife don't have a dog yet. The freedom to digress is, of course, your great signature, and I was thrilled that you put it in footnotes, because every generous footnote now is a blow to reclaim footnotes from the judgment of an ill-informed audience that believes that David Foster Wallace invented them and therefore no one else gets to use them. This in a world where Nicholson Baker plainly invented the footnote! As a footnote to my own non-question here, I'll also mention that your two short books are officially the only two books I will have finished this summer, because what this spate of Dyerian study has interrupted for me is my summer of reading the new translation of Musil's *The Man Without Qualities*. You licensed this digression by mentioning Musil in the Somme book, toward the end, which reminds me that one of the best qualities a very short book can have is the appearance of somehow having mentioned everything that exists.

**GD** But I do have a DVD! How d'you like them bananas! I needed to have one to refer to the film from time to time, to make sure I wasn't getting things totally wrong, although my book is not necessarily a reliable record of what's going on in the film. Thank you for being so generous regarding the capaciousness of the little *Stalker* book. I know we share a fondness for Roberto Calasso, who was the biggest influence on this book. I love that line of Calvino's about Calasso's early book, *The Ruin of Kasch*: that it "takes up two subjects: the first is Talleyrand, and the second is everything else." As for digressions: I love what one might call the integral digression, or to put it another way, books where the very idea of the digression is rendered meaningless, as it is in Calasso, Nicholson Baker, and in quite a few of those American monologue-type novels. I'll return to this in a moment. But, for now, sticking to the film, I would just say that this idea of integral digression is integral to *Stalker* since the route they take through the Zone is, as Stalker points out to Writer and Professor, necessarily meandering and indirect. Now, a point of comparison: it seems to me in some ways that you and I are rather similar. We are both hobbyists, obsessives, inventoryists who have pursued these hobbies and interests outside of academia. That's the overlap of sensibility. But you have nailed your primary colors more loyally to the novelist's mast, to narrative fiction. Let me put this distinction another way: you are American; I am English. The American novel is able to accommodate a tendency to digress, whereas I feel the English novel is sort of to one side of where my main enthusiasms are, so I've found a way of digressing from the national norm. I throw this out as an off-the-cuff thought, so feel free to debunk. But I honestly, if mistakenly, believe I would have been more thoroughly a novelist if I'd either been born in America or had moved there—as I should have done—ten or fifteen years ago. (Oh, and in passing, I have never made much progress with the Musil.)

JL  I'm very interested in where you end up in this sequence of thoughts, since I've always noticed that when we talk about novels you do so very much with the conviction and investment of a fellow novelist. I remember you telling me once how much more important and transformative a figure Martin Amis was from the perspective of an English novelist (which I wanted to resist, but had to take your word for) and (more happily) that Alan Hollinghurst was the greatest living English novelist. I don't know whether these were studied positions or whimsical provocations you'll now claim to have no memory of making. The point is, it was *novelists'* talk. Whereas in your public statements, even when you're putting forward a novel, you're rueful and self-effacing about the role. I like the idea that you're sure you'd have been the novelist you aren't—even though you sometimes, actually, are—if you'd moved to the US. (Maybe you would have read Musil too. And you'd go to the gym more often.) How much have you followed the sometimes cartoonishly polarized debate about David Shields and the lyric essay versus the Moldering American Novel? You and your books are something of a symbolic token on the board, you know.

GD  Yes, I remember, and stand by, those two claims. Reading the new Hollinghurst—and, as it happens, the new Ondaatje—served as a rebuke to my occasional antinovel sentiments, because they reminded me of exactly the all-immersing pleasure I routinely used to get from many novels. So my objection, I suppose, to mediocre—but still so-called literary—novels, is that they offer "entertainment," when what I want is the "deep plumbing of consciousness." The quotes are from Shields, who I think articulates this kind of stuff very well. The problem, as Sam Lipsyte pointed out to me, is that the Shields anticanon ends up being rather skimpy and a lot of the stuff he most values is actually to be found in . . . fiction! It's like some command economy in which you end up having to import back the stuff that you have banished because you can't actually live without it. But, generally, I thought *Reality Hunger* was very exciting and original. Inevitably it spawned a lot of quite moronic debate over here too and people got very exercised about his alleged "plagiarism." What a yawn, especially for anyone—you and me, both—who had the privilege of being part of that amazingly stimulating conference on fair use (actually about the nature of creativity in the 21st century) organized by Lawrence Weschler a few years back.

JL  Well, it sounds like we arrived at exactly the same place with *Reality Hunger*, though perhaps from different sides (in a couple of senses: novelist's ego/essayist's ego, US/UK, and the fact that I was privy to Shields's writing it early on—after I'd published "The Ecstasy of Influence" essay, we were in a constant dialogue). Anyway, when it came out and the conversation was all about an ostensible "attack on the novel," I was disappointed. I mean, I guess that stuff was in the book, and consisted of a kind of provocation that couldn't be resisted, but it seemed obtuse to take it so literally. Some novelists I know were genuinely outraged. I had to consider that he'd really struck a nerve, but it's not a nerve I possess. I'm just congenitally complacent about the permanent vitality and relevance of the form I've chosen, I suppose. The fact of dull examples doesn't threaten that complacency any more than bad slices of pizza threaten the good ones.

Weschler's conference at NYU six years ago was a great moment, wasn't it? How much do you fiddle around with actual "appropriation" in your prose? Do you ever?

GD  Oh, yes. Those are the best bits! In *Paris Trance* I added a note at the end saying the text contained various "samples" from Hemingway's *The Sun Also Rises*. I thought I was so cool and hip, you know, saying "samples" rather than boring old "quotes"! And there are the lines from Thomas Mann's *Death in Venice* in *Jeff in Venice*. It adds layers and nuances, though it's often taken as just showing off. Maybe one of the reasons I'm drawn to this free-form, quasi-essayistic kind of book is that one has more license to quote, though as far as possible I like to find ways around saying "As X writes in his book *Y*, etc. . . ." I like unacknowledged quotations, unacknowledged till the end at least—something I got from Berger and Ondaatje.

I'd like to go back to where you say "I'm just congenitally complacent about the permanent vitality and relevance of the form I've chosen." I find this really appealing and persuasive coming from you, especially in connection with the subsequent pizza point. But then I think of examples, particularly in England, where there is a generic assumption of merit in a particular slice of pizza, irrespective of its individual quality, simply because it is derived from the recipe used by Dickens or whomever. There's a question of conformity versus originality or novelty.

JL  I'd forgotten about your outright "samples." You know, *Paris Trance* was the first of your books I read. It was new at the time, which tells you when I got aboard. I, of course, also take every opportunity to appear "cool and hip," but in that particular regard, I find it leads to a distortion. There have been so many stupefyingly silly attacks on appropriation in text, which associate it with some sort of provocative or ironic postmodern impulse in order to damn both. So I've usually wanted to emphasize how boring and predictable a move appropriation or reference really is, how much continuity it has with all kinds of fundamental traditions of reference and intertextuality, all taken for granted. It is only the big neon arrow pointing to the act that is anything new at all!

Which actually leads in very nicely to what you were saying about the assumption of the merits of the recipe from Dickens. This is going to be another English versus American thing for us—you, there, feeling so suffocated and hidebound by weary traditionalism; me, here, feeling so exasperated with the falsehood of a constantly moving frontier and the cultural amnesia that accompanies the myth of innovation: "Make it new!" and pretend you can't see how it's really quite old. For me, the useful insight about novels is how deeply even the apparently radical ones rely on the tradition, the old forms, the recipe from Dickens. I like that and find it nourishing. The "conformity," as you call it, doesn't irritate me. Bogus revolutions irritate me more. And if a novel isn't very surprising and memorable, in the end, and so many aren't, we turn out to have read them anyway, because we like novels, right? What's good in them is usually their conversation with the tradition, not whatever slightly preposterous and unworkable "new" thing they've done. As I've said elsewhere, I'd rather be trapped on a desert island with the collected works of Barbara Pym than those of Thomas Pynchon. (I don't know if I mean what I say here, or if I just want you to have to respond to it. But of course Alan Hollinghurst is hardly a radical innovator. As Phillip Lopate said to me once, in a fit of annoyance over someone criticizing something wonderful for not being "transgressive": "All excellence transgresses against mediocrity.")

GD  Yes, in England just now people are all falling over themselves about Hollinghurst's new book because they've realized what a great straight novelist the gay writer is! Of course he's always been a straight-down-the-line novelist, and, for at least three of the four previous books, a great one too. More broadly, these debates tend to get polarized between the traditional novel and experimental fiction—itself a largely historical relic. I like the idea of something that combines experiment and tradition: you know, *Pym*chon! In a version of that wonderful Lopate line, I've sometimes been tempted to say that all great art is experimental. But a moment's reflection makes one realize that it's not. As you say, a conversation with tradition is the important thing. That's what those hip samples are really about.

I fear I'm running out of steam here with regard to literature, but in jazz it's very boring when you get bands just repeating the kind of post-bop that was being played half a century ago—however well they do it and however exciting that original post-bop was and is. What I'm interested in, to the point of obsession, is an outfit like The Necks, who come along and completely blow away the idea of what a piano, bass, and drums trio can do, to the extent that it's maybe not even jazz. Translate that back into the realm of literature and I think that's also where a lot of my interest currently lies.

# Jennifer Egan
# and Heidi Julavits

JENNIFER EGAN  was born in Chicago, Illinois, in 1962. She is the author of *The Invisible Circus*, *Emerald City*, *Look at Me*, *The Keep*, and *A Visit from the Goon Squad*, which won the National Book Critics Circle Award and the Pulitzer Prize. A graduate of the University of Pennsylvania, Egan has also been awarded the Thouron Award, was a finalist for the PEN/Faulkner Award for Fiction, and is the recipient of a National Endowment for the Arts and a Guggenheim Fellowship. She lives in Brooklyn, New York.

HEIDI JULAVITS  was born in Portland, Maine, in 1968. She is the author of the novels *The Mineral Palace*, *The Effect of Living Backwards*, *The Uses of Enchantment*, and *The Vanishers*. A graduate of Dartmouth College and Columbia University, where she earned her MFA, Julavits is the coeditor of *The Believer*, from which she collected work for the book *Read Hard: Five Years of Great Writing from the Believer*. She lives in New York City

**HEIDI JULAVITS**  So, my spies informed me that you were a "real" punk in high school.

**JENNIFER EGAN**  I was not a punk in high school. (Ahem, who are these spies?) Except for blonder hair and no wrinkles, I have never looked much different than I do now. I did go to concerts at the Mabuhay Gardens, but always as a wannabe observer. The good news is I didn't end up shooting heroin with communal needles, as many punks did in the late '70s, just before AIDS was discovered.

**HJ**  Given how different your early work is from your more recent work, are there anxieties you had when you first started writing that no longer preoccupy you? Do you have new anxieties now?

**JE**  My biggest concern at the beginning was just being understood in a way that, looking back, seems very neurotic. I literally felt as if no one would understand what I was saying, even though I was writing a totally conventional novel. As usual, I had certain theoretical questions I wanted to explore in my first novel: I was interested in how the new mass media interacted with the '60s counterculture and heightened its intensity, and also in the "out of body" nature of media coverage and the way that might dovetail with a basic human longing for transcendence. I probably hammered those points a little too hard out of a fear of being misunderstood. I was kind of crazy about literary theory in college, I spent way too much time reading texts *about* texts. More and more I feel you'd better not try and say anything too clearly or too loudly in fiction, because you end up eliminating the mystery that's at the heart of any great literary experience. I'm also more aware of how I seem to work purely instinctively. For all of my theorizing about culture and the intellectual girding that I hope is in my books, I don't think a lot about the actual act of writing or the way I'm going to do it. So there's this possible overtheorizing in terms of intent but a total lack of theorizing about method.

**HJ**  But it also seems as if you're trying to expose or question method, especially in "Safari," a chapter from *A Visit from the Goon Squad* that I first read in *The New Yorker*. A term Zadie Smith used in her awesome essay "Two Paths for the Novel" is "not naïve." There's something extremely "not naïve" about "Safari." It features this really overbearing narrator, as if to say *without* saying, "Look, people, at how lopsided the power dynamic can be in these third-person omniscient so-called realist stories!" Tragically your characters are captives, not of past acts and experiences—from which they could still arguably recover—but of future ones. These flash-forwards are so much more chilling, almost like death sentences—in some cases, that's literally what they are.

**JE**  I feel like you understand the story better than I do.

**HJ**  (*laughter*)

**JE**  The principles guiding me in terms of method might seem kind of obvious. With *Look at Me*, which is more experimental than my first novel, I remember thinking, I'm really tired of the way pages of text look. I wanted mine to look different. I had this feeling of not liking to read a book where you turn these pages and they all look the same. The biggest thing that guides me is a basic attempt to move away from anything that feels familiar.

**HJ**  Meaning anything that's too close to your personal experience?

**JE**  If I've read it or done it before, then I'm not interested. My aesthetic, or my method, is basically guided by curiosity and desire. Again, there's nothing very sophisticated about that. There's no theory there. And I don't know what the novel should be, but I do know that—well, I was a National Book Award judge last year, and I read some great stuff. But I also found myself thinking that a lot of novels feel really constrained and unaware of the possibilities at hand. I find that curious, because the novel began as this explosion of craziness. I mean, look at Cervantes and Sterne. Two of the first novelists. There's nothing holding them back. They haven't learned to be afraid to do anything. You do need to be in control, and, in a way, the more chances you're taking the more you need to control them. But now I feel like the control is coming before the chances. For example, this idea that you can't change the point of view. *What?* Why? If you can make it work, you can do anything.

**HJ**  In the past you've written books that were clearly short story collections or clearly novels. How do you categorize *Goon Squad*, genre-wise, in terms of your own past work? Did you start writing it with a category in mind or did that kind of categorizing never influence your thinking?

**JE**  If I had been telling myself I was writing a novel I couldn't have done a damn thing. I would have had to just stop because I knew this did not meet even my own definitions of what a novel is, in terms of providing some kind of centrality. I wanted to avoid centrality. I wanted polyphony. I wanted a lateral feeling, not a forward feeling. My ground rules were: every piece has to be very different, from a different point of view. I actually tried to break that rule later; if you make a rule then you also should break it!

**HJ** How did you try to break it?

**JE** I tried to write a second piece from Sasha's point of view. But it was a nonstarter, even though I worked on it for months and months. I tried, but it was just so loathsomely familiar. So anyway, every piece would have a different point of view, but, in addition, every piece had to be a different world and have a different feel from all of the others. I imagined the book was sort of like those art projects you do as kids when the teacher makes you put a grid over a drawing and every person in the class is responsible for a little square, you match them all together and then, Oh my God! It's the same drawing. But in my mind, the way to do it was more of a Chuck Close painting, in that every small square was its own individual work, and yet they all added up to something bigger. I often actually have a visual idea of what I'm trying to do, which is odd because I'm not visual. I'm really a horrific draftswoman. But I conceived *Look at Me* as a figure eight. The vanishing point, the middle point that's both a presence and an absence, is this character Z, who has disappeared from one world of the novel and appeared in another, and whose past is a blank. He connects these two worlds. I wasn't wondering how that book fit into the tradition of the novel. It was more like, I'm just making my figure eight here.

**HJ** The Chuck Close analogy is very fitting.

**JE** Another one of my rules was that each piece had to stand on its own and be at the highest level, individually. Each one had to fulfill its own intentions completely, but also—ideally—in a surprising way. And then the idea was that the explosive combination of all these separate sounding units would be very powerful. But I was perfectly prepared for it to be mediocre.

**HJ** Did you write the pieces in the order in which they appear in the book?

**JE** No, not at all. In fact, four of them were written years and years ago. They were just written as stories, and published, all four. "You (Plural)," "Good-bye, My Love," "Forty-Minute Lunch" . . .

**HJ** I love "Forty-Minute Lunch." It's written as an article by one of your characters, but it's so raw, so revealing of its author. *And* so hilarious.

JE  And what's the fourth? Oh! "X's and O's." I had no sense that they linked up at all. And then I started working on "Found Objects," and it all kind of followed from there in a strange way because I wasn't even planning to work on this book. I was trying to work on my goddamn Brooklyn Navy Yard book, which I still haven't started.

HJ  You wrote a book to avoid writing a book.

JE  The Navy Yard idea happened during a fellowship I had at the New York Public Library. I've wanted for a long time to write about New York in the late '40s, that moment when we as a country felt the seismic shift in our global power and status. I got interested in the fact that thousands of women worked at the Navy Yard during World War II, often doing traditionally male jobs like welding and pipe fitting. Anyhow, the research itself took on a life of its own. I became immersed in the letters that a woman named Lucille Kolkin wrote to her husband while she worked at the Navy Yard during the war. Then I met and got to know Lucy's present-day family (she died in 1997), including her widower—the man she'd been writing to! Eventually the Navy Yard partnered with the Brooklyn Historical Society, and I've been working with an oral historian there, too, interviewing subjects. And then I got interested in the divers who repaired ships, and attended an Army divers' reunion in Virginia, where I actually got dressed in one of those two-hundred-pound suits they used to wear, with the lead boots—you get the idea.

HJ  So maybe *Goon Squad* could be seen as showcasing a similar chain reaction of curiosity—but you were "researching" fictional people.

JE  I initially got curious about Bennie Salazar, one of the other protagonists in *Goon Squad*, because he was briefly mentioned in the first story as Sasha's weird boss who sprinkles gold flakes in his coffee and sprays pesticide in his armpits. Having written that basically as a laugh line, I thought, Why would a person do those things? So then I wrote "The Gold Cure," basically exploring the answers to that question. The next piece I wrote was "A to B" because in "The Gold Cure," Bennie is recently divorced, and I got curious about his marriage, and why it ended, and who Stephanie, his wife, was. Before I started "A to B," for some reason I had decided that Stephanie's brother was my "Forty-Minute Lunch" narrator. Why did I decide that? I don't know.

HJ  It strikes me as a relevant form of interconnectivity, since it mimics how our curiosity fires these days. It's like Googling, where you're on one site and a marginal mention catches your interest, say a mention of Bennie Salazar, so you plug him in and boom, you fork off to this dedicated Bennie Salazar space.

JE  I was also thinking of *The Sopranos*, which I was crazy about. I loved the polyphonic quality of that show, and the way peripheral characters would become central characters. I was always curious about the decision-making around that, and the idea that, obviously, we're all peripheral to other people and central to ourselves. But my initial structuring idea, which didn't pan out at all, was that the book was going to go backward in time. I had an order in my mind, but when I read it through, it didn't work at all. Anyway, early on there was this linking up of "Forty-Minute Lunch" with "A to B." I loved importing that character, Jules Jones (an unstable, unhappy celebrity reporter who ends up attacking the starlet he's supposed to be profiling) and revisiting him after he's released from prison. And then I found myself having this weird sensation, as if the stories were putting out tendrils and attaching to each other. One of the great moments, for me, was realizing Sasha, from "Found Objects," was the same person as the protagonist of "Good-bye, My Love." I couldn't believe I had written two stories about women who steal wallets without realizing they were one person.

HJ  And that that person was you. (*laughter*)

JE  No, I'm the one that *gets* my wallet stolen. Finding the order was very tricky because I was looking for a system but no existing one could help me, which gets back to the question of why I don't read theory any more. I don't seem to do well with systems guiding me on those questions—my best guide is my own curiosity, and that's what I ended up using. I thought, Okay, having just read this story, what's the one that would be most satisfying to encounter next just based on these little tingling awarenesses of other people and other possible stories that might interest the reader?

HJ  Let's talk about how time functions in *Goon Squad*—I'm just going to call it a "book." That's a relatively uncontroversial genre classification, at least for the moment. Pretty soon I'll have to call it your "ebook."

JE  My "text."

HJ  Quantum physics comes up in a footnote in "Forty-Minute Lunch," which I found apt because while reading your "book" I thought a lot about the many-worlds theory. Every time I encountered your characters anew it wasn't as though I was moving back and forth on a horizontal timeline, but rather I felt like I'd been transported to a parallel universe that was occurring simultaneously.

**JE**  That's cool.

**HJ**  I felt like there was no time in your time. Time was eradicated.

**JE**  I don't experience time as linear. I experience it in layers that seem to coexist. I feel like twenty years ago was really recent even though I was much younger and had a different kind of life. Yet at the same time I feel like I'm still kind of there. One thing that facilitates that kind of time travel is music, which is why I think music ended up being such an important part of the book. Also, I was reading Proust. He tries, very successfully in some ways, to capture the sense of time passing, the quality of consciousness, and the ways to get around linearity, which is the weird scourge of writing prose. There is the sense that one thing has to come before and after another if you're writing a sentence.

**HJ**  Again, to cue that Zadie Smith essay, she writes that "realism's obsession is convincing us that time has passed. It fills space with time." What's interesting about your book is that it fills space with time, but it also fills time with space. My husband was just in Marfa, Texas, and he's been talking a lot about visiting the Chinati Foundation and the work of Donald Judd. He sent me photographs of this huge room with these big metal cubes in them. I experienced these temporal spaces in your book not as these gaps that were supposed to indicate that you didn't know what happened, or that we weren't supposed to know what happened; rather I felt as if I was wandering around in this minimalist space with just cubes in it or something. I had to go in there and just hang out for a second.

**JE**  It felt sort of like a chemistry experiment, as I said before. Here is a set of rules, that's what I'm going to do. And we'll put them all together and see what works. But my idea of going backward, as I mentioned, was a total bust.

**HJ**  I'm curious why.

**JE**  "Pure Language," according to the rules I had set, had to be the first story, because it takes place in the future. And I was so miserable because I just knew that the story would be meaningless if you didn't know who the people were. You can't begin with a convergence and expect it to mean anything, because there's nothing to converge, obviously. And then I had this lightning bolt moment when I realized: this is not the first story in the book. It's the *last* story in the book. Once I knew that, I adapted my rules to account for it: time goes farther and farther backward, and then it leaps into the future. So when I had all my pieces, except for the PowerPoint piece, I sat down and read it and realized it was very flat.

HJ  And you knew you needed a PowerPoint presentation!

JE  I had known that for a year and a half, that I wanted to write a PowerPoint story, I just couldn't do it. The impetus came from a sense that PowerPoint had become a true literary genre—I remember reading the summer before the last election that the Obama campaign's turnaround had happened in response to a seminal PowerPoint presentation, and thinking, it wasn't referred to as a "presentation" or a "memo," or a "paper," but a "PowerPoint presentation." And if PowerPoint has become that basic a form of communication, then I have to write some fiction in it.

HJ  I should probably admit that I was really dreading that story. I live in fear of the gimmicky story that fails to rise above its gimmick. And I didn't want you to fail as so many before you have failed, myself included. But within a few pages I totally forgot about the PowerPoint presentation format, that's how ungimmicky your gimmick was.

JE  The PowerPoint piece was the last big change I made to the book after it was sold. By then, it was pretty settled. I had very few choices in terms of content, which in a way was really interesting. There weren't that many avenues left to explore that wouldn't have required introducing new major characters—and it was too late for that. So I didn't have all that much room to move in.

HJ  It's liberating to be confined.

JE  There's this funny way, too, in which there's a larger plan that you're not consciously aware of. You've been participating in it, but you could say you created it without realizing it. And at some point you have to bow to that plan, which in this case meant finding the last little tunnel that I could explore without upsetting the balance of the book. The PowerPoint piece was a disappointment for a really long time; I'd never used PowerPoint, so I just pictured PowerPoint as slides with bullet points. My sister works at a global management consulting firm. She lives and breathes in PowerPoint. One of the templates in my PowerPoint story I stole from her, actually. But ultimately I realized that writing anything successful in PowerPoint requires that you break down a particular thought, or fictional moment, into its basic structure, and then illustrate that structure. I finally reached my true apotheosis as a PowerPointer when I began creating my own slide graphics out of shapes, rather than using templates. And I didn't understand until I was in the middle of that piece that PowerPoint does offer an achronological option, for multiple chronologies.

**HJ** And multiple POVs. You get the polyphonic quality.

**JE** In that way it does pull the book together, actually, because it epitomizes in this really extreme way all of the principles I'd been working on. The biggest drag about PowerPoint is just making the graphics work. Just making something like that (*points to a graphic*) actually line up right—it's a nightmare. That was my whole summer last summer: beautiful sunny days and me inside trying to make edges line up in PowerPoint. But the writing part, too, was really hard.

**HJ** The PowerPoint story is, nominally at least, about the most significant "pauses" in rock 'n' roll—meaning complete silences in the middle of songs. Are you one of those people with an encyclopedic knowledge of music?

**JE** Well, I acquired some knowledge of the industry to write this book. I'm no great aficionado, actually, of music.

**HJ** I guess writing with and about the knowledge of music isn't the hard thing to do. The challenge as a fiction writer is communicating the emotional experience of listening to music. Were there any successful antecedents that you sourced?

**JE** I read *High Fidelity* years ago. I really enjoyed it, but I found myself thinking, I don't really know this music. Nick Hornby and I don't share a musical palette, and therefore, in a way, the heart of it was lost on me. Music figures hugely in Proust, and I think that was probably more my model. I'd known for a while that I wanted to write about the music industry. I had tried as a nonfiction writer, but I could not for the life of me get an assignment that brought me into the music industry (though I did get assigned once to write about a pair of identical twin rappers called Dyme). But to write "The Gold Cure," I actually had to do a lot of research just to understand the technology. I found this producer/mixer who literally spent hours on the telephone with me, laying things out. I didn't even know the difference between analogue and digital recording.

HJ  So if you'd been paid to write about the music industry for a magazine, would that have staunched your interest?

JE  I probably would have still written this book because the time/music connection is so strong. And I'm always really interested in technology and how it changes culture. In a way there's no better lens to look at that change than through the music industry. It's not ever again going to be the way it was, or even close, and I felt very sad about that. Anyone who's grown up listening to albums and then to CDs can't help but feel sad about the atomization of music consumption. It would be like if we couldn't publish a book anymore, only chapters. So, in a way, writing about it became my act of wistful homage in a twilight moment. Have you read the book *You Are Not a Gadget*?

HJ  No.

JE  You must.

HJ  I did clock the guy's awesomely hirsute author photo.

JE  Yes, Jaron Lanier is very hirsute and he's very awesome. He was a true believer in the power of the Internet and the bounteous possibilities that it held. But now he's talking about how many of the people who were so ecstatic about the Internet are basically unemployed because of it. I think we're in that moment where old stuff is dying and it's not clear what's going to replace it. Bennie Salazar talks about an aesthetic holocaust. I don't think that. I'm hopeful about the iPad—both because it'll give Amazon a run for its money and because it may begin to offer a solution to the problem of newspapers and magazines not being able to profit from online advertising.

HJ  But not the Starfish, the "futuristic" handheld device designed for pre-verbal children you feature so prominently in "Pure Language." I bet you're not so hopeful about the Starfish.

JE  You know, it's not a bad idea.

HJ  Maybe you'll get a future cut of the profits. Speaking of preverbal children, I have a question to ask and I don't really know how to ask it without me sounding like a loser for asking it, and making you sound like a loser for answering it.

**JE** *(laughter)*

**HJ** Is there some cognitive shift that's come as a result of your having kids and subsequently having less time to write and think? Has caring for very needy beings had *any* positive effect on your brain? I thought of this question because I had this sensation when I read your book that the positive side of being sleep-deprived is you do feel like all your psychic boundaries have been eroded and you can coexist as all these different people you've been your whole life.

**JE** Initially I felt that there was a very negative impact. The book I was working on before I had my first kid was *Look at Me*, this huge undertaking. I had such a hard time holding it all in my mind. And then after I had kids, or even one kid, I thought, I'll never be able to do that again. I just don't have the room. And I don't think I've achieved quite that conscious breadth of thought since having children. So I'm really surprised, honestly, when people are excited by *A Visit from the Goon Squad*. As I worked on it, I thought, Well, this is kind of a lateral move, but I'm hoping I can get away with it and I'll come up with something really good for the next one. But I'm wondering now if, in some way, I kept my sights narrow so that I didn't feel overwhelmed by the task. I worked while also doing a lot of schlepping, and ordering from catalogues, and making of sandwiches. And talking about the work with my kids, because they're really interested in it, "What happens with the lady who steals the wallet?"

**HJ** Kids have such an excellent sense of "What comes next?"

**JE** They're very interested in results. Like, "So what happened?" Or in the case of my older son, "Who won?"

**HJ** Did you write any pieces for this book that didn't make the final cut? Any pieces where nothing happened and no one won?

**JE** In four cases I worked for months on things that were just dead on arrival. One was about Bosco, the overweight, terminally ill former rock star in "A to B," as a young guy. I really wanted to write about Bosco when he was still a rock star. Hopeless. Another was about Ted, Sasha's uncle in "Good-bye, My

Love," and his wife, Susan. I was so curious about her. But nope. Still, I like mentioning them to honor them a little bit. Another failed story was about Sasha in college, from her point of view. The fourth was Rolph, the little boy in "Safari" who we learn will later commit suicide as a grown-up.

HJ  I like that he existed as Future Rolph and then he existed as people remembering him after he was dead. There's a blank circle protecting whatever pain he went through. It's the fictional equivalent of a great rock 'n' roll pause.

JE  In "A to B," Stephanie says, "I feel like everything is ending." And her brother Jules says, "You're right, everything is ending but *not yet*." My friend David Rosenstock said about that piece, "I feel like this whole story is about that *not yet*." That really stuck in my mind. This whole book is about that *not yet*, what happens in that not yet. So that's a pause. And the great rock 'n' roll pauses idea, interestingly, comes from one of the failed stories, which was an earlier PowerPoint attempt, which I was trying to write without actually owning PowerPoint. I feel like what I don't do well is the top-down thinking that I used to embrace: this is what I'm trying to do, this is how I'm going to do it. Now I have a more inductive method, which seems to suit my slightly frazzled existence.

A big part of the struggle is having confidence and feeling a sense of momentum about one's own projects. I tend to think that if the kids need something I *have* to deal with that; I will drop what I'm doing to help them. When you're in that state of mind it's hard to believe that you could do anything much. I guess what I'm saying is I think that I've had more worries about what I could do than real hindrances on what I can do. The worry is that feeling so pressured in terms of time and choices makes it harder to have the sort of desultory meandering curiosity and flights of fancy that might lead to the riskier, difficult stuff. That would be the fear.

HJ  I would say that's a fear that hasn't really panned out, given the excellently risky nature of your post-kid work.

JE  But that was the worry.

HJ  Could we call it anxiety? To loop us back to the beginning? Begin with anxiety, end with anxiety.

JE  Maybe what's really changed with having kids is the way I *think* I think, rather than the way I actually think.

# Jeffrey Eugenides and Jonathan Safran Foer

JEFFREY EUGENIDES  was born in Detroit, Michigan, in 1960. He is the author of *Middlesex*, *The Marriage Plot*, and *The Virgin Suicides*, which was adapted into a movie. A graduate of Brown University and Stanford, where he earned his MA in Creative Writing, Eugenides is the recipient of many awards, including the Aga Khan Prize for Fiction, the Whiting Writers' Award, the Pulitzer Prize, and the Salon Book Award. He has been nominated for the Nation Book Critics Circle Award twice and is a Guggenheim Fellow. Eugenides teaches at Princeton University.

JONATHAN SAFRAN FOER  was born in Washington, DC, in 1977. He is the author of the books *Eating Animals*, *Everything is Illuminated*, *Extremely Loud and Incredibly Close*, and *Tree of Codes*. Foer, a graduate of Princeton University, is the recipient of many awards, including the *Zoetrope: All-Story* Fiction Prize, the New York Public Library's Young Lions Fiction Award, the National Jewish Book Award, and a *Guardian* First Book Award. He is Lillian Vernon Distinguished Writer-in-Residence at New York University.

**JONATHAN SAFRAN FOER**  It's been an awfully long time since we last spoke. Four years? And it's been a long time since the reading world last got new material from you. About seven years? What's been going on?

**JEFFREY EUGENIDES**  I've been writing a book.

**JSF**  Have you been happy?

**JE**  I've been absorbed.

**JSF**  One of my biggest problems as a writer is that I get tired of what I'm working on. Or rather, I feel that a project can't keep up with how I think about writing and how I think about the world. How were you able to commit yourself to one story for such a long period? And how did the passage of time influence what you were writing?

**JE**  Well, one of the hardest things about writing *Middlesex* was trying to stay true to the original impulse. I felt young when I began the book but something more like middle-aged by the time I finished it. All sorts of life-altering things happened to me while I was writing it, too. My father died in a plane crash. I became a father myself. William H. Gass says it's difficult writing a long book because as you go along, you get better, and then you have to go back and try to bring the rest of the book up to the same level. I did a lot of that. I obsessively went back and reworked the early parts of the book. Even so, I made sure the later chapters had the same voice and spirit as the early chapters.

**JSF**  And what about fatigue when writing? How'd you deal with that?

**JE**  My fatigue was alleviated by the structure. Nearly every chapter of *Middlesex* takes on new historical or emotional terrain. Once I was finished dealing with the Greco-Turkish War, I had to summon up Detroit during Prohibition, and then later I launched into genetic and sexological concerns. *Middlesex* has lots of different storylines in it, so when I had done all I could with one, I could refresh myself with another. The book allowed me to grow along with it. But there was pain, sure. There was lots of pain.

There must have been some kind of perverse comfort, too. I had this torture waiting for me every day, but at least it was my torture. The book was my jailer and we became friendly. I was like Patty Hearst with her Stockholm syndrome. Little by little the book expanded to fill every inch of my consciousness. It lasted as long as the Trojan War. But I didn't want to be Harold Brodkey. I knew before things got really ridiculous I had to set sail for home.

**JSF** Along these lines, *Middlesex* strikes me as a book that begins as a fairy tale (albeit a violent, racy, political fairy tale) and develops into a coming-of-age story. You have a daughter. Do you think the development of the style was influenced by her development?

**JE** My daughter was born midway through the composition of *Middlesex*. Her influence shows up in the plot, not the style. There's a preoccupation with birth and fetal development in the book. There's a lot about what women go through during pregnancy, and how beside the point men feel in the process. I see my daughter's fingerprints in those details, but the book took shape long before she arrived on the scene.

Nabokov said all great novels are fairy tales. The first two parts of *Middlesex* were conceived in the spirit of epic literature, which isn't so far from fairy tale. I wanted the book to exist on different levels. On one, it's an immigrant or family saga. On another, the book mirrors the progression of Western literature, something in the way the "Oxen of the Sun" chapter in *Ulysses* does. I've always loved that part of *Ulysses*, the way it begins with old English and goes on to Middle English, mimicking the styles of succeeding epochs and generations and even particular writers. I didn't do anything nearly as comprehensive, nor would I have wanted to, even if I could have pulled it off. But I did see the book as beginning with heroic epic narration and then, as it went along, becoming more realistic, more deeply psychological. The book, like its hermaphroditic narrator, was meant to be a hybrid. Part third-person epic, part first-person coming-of-age tale.

Since I was writing about a genetic condition, it also seemed incumbent on me to pass on classical literary forms to what is, after all, a 21st-century book. "Phylogeny recapitulates ontogeny." The traits of the ancestors show up in us today. I wanted *Middlesex* to be like that, a kind of novelistic genome. But I wanted to do all this without disrupting the story I was telling, without being too modernist or postmodernist. I didn't want these kinds of academic concerns to be the story; I only wanted them to *support* the story.

**JSF** It's a very fine line, isn't it? But do you consider yourself a postmodern writer? In the *New Republic*, Dale Peck recently said you were upholding the high literary postmodern tradition, a tradition Peck claimed was bankrupt.

**JE** On the issue of postmodernism, Dale Peck and I would agree more than he thinks. I don't see myself as a high postmodernist. I always say it like this: my generation of writers grew up backwards. We were weaned on modernism and only later read the great 19th-century masters of realism. When we began writing in high school and college, it was experimental fiction. I think now that a certain kind of academic experimental fiction has reached a dead end. *Middlesex* is a postmodern book in many ways, but it is also very old-fashioned. Reusing classical motifs is a fundamental of postmodern practice, of course, but telling a story isn't always. I *like* narrative. I read for it and write for it.

Recently I was reading an old panel discussion from 1975 called "The Symposium on the Future of Contemporary Fiction." Almost thirty years ago now, but they were basically debating the same thing. How do you make something new in literature? How do you move it forward? This discussion took place among Grace Paley, Donald Barthelme, William H. Gass, and Walker Percy. Barthelme and Gass, at the apex of their careers back then, kept going on about creating new voices by means of theoretical exertion. But it was Grace Paley who turned out to be right. It didn't appear that she was right, but now we can see she was. She said that new language rises again and again from human voices, not just new theories. If you look back now, you see that postmodernism hit a dead end, and what took over were the kinds of books—call them multicultural or whatever you want—that Paley was prophesying.

If there's anything new in *Middlesex*, it's not a matter of formal or theoretical development but closer to the new human experience Paley was talking about. The content in the book is new. The narrator, Cal Stephanides, is a real living hermaphrodite, not a mythical creature like Tiresias or a fanciful one like Orlando.

JSF  As long as we're talking about contemporary writing . . . Who's your favorite contemporary writer?

JE  Right now my favorite writer is A. A. Milne. Let me give you a sample of why:

*Rabbit leant over further than ever, looking for his [stick], and Roo wriggled up and down, calling out, "Come on, stick! Stick, stick, stick!" and Piglet got very excited because his was the only one which had been seen, and that meant that he was winning.*

*"It's coming!" said Pooh.*

*"Are you sure it's mine?" squeaked Piglet excitedly.*

*"Yes, because it's grey. A big grey one. Here it comes! A very . . . big . . . grey . . . Oh, no, it isn't. It's Eeyore."*

*And out Eeyore floated.*

*"Eeyore!" cried everybody.*

*Looking very calm, very dignified, with his legs in the air, came Eeyore from beneath the bridge.*

*"It's Eeyore!" cried Roo, terribly excited.*

*"Is that so?" said Eeyore, getting caught up by a little eddy, and turning slowly round three times. "I wondered."*

**JSF**  That brings me back to your daughter. Is it important to you to write something that your wife and daughter like? Would you be disappointed if they didn't like it? And if so, whom would you be disappointed in, them or you?

**JE**  As far as my daughter goes, I hoped *Middlesex* would appeal to all sorts of readers, but three-year-olds weren't on the list. I tend to be obsessively secretive about my work. A few of the early chapters of *Middlesex* appeared in magazines, but for the last four years or so no one saw it. If I can still make the book better on my own, I'm not eager to show it to anyone.

I don't think about my family while I'm writing. Or, I think about them constantly, but not as potential readers. I keep filial respect out of my mind until I'm done. And then compunction rushes in. During the editing of *Middlesex*, I took a few things out that might have stung my relatives. There may still be things in there that will sting. But to me, now, it's all made up. I blend fact and fiction until everything seems completely true and yet also impersonal.

**JSF**  Speaking of family, have you ever been ashamed of your writing? If yes, when and why?

**JE**  You mean ashamed as in embarrassed? Well, as you might expect, that was one of the hardest things about writing my hermaphrodite's tale. I have something of my mother's prudishness in me. It was hard for me to plunge straight into the anatomical features of my hero. It was hard for me to write about a life experience so different from my own. That's why it's a family novel, too. I couldn't inhabit Cal's consciousness without knowing his entire clan, without putting him into perspective as a child like any other, with parents and grandparents. There is full disclosure, eventually, but it's handled, as my mother would like, *tactfully*.

JSF  It surprised me, actually, how little of the book is "about" Cal. That is, while she/he narrates the novel, there's very little characterization, or plot involvement, until about three-quarters of the way in. I would never describe *Middlesex* as being about a hermaphrodite. I would describe it as a family epic, with a very unusual narrator.

JE  I suppose you could describe it that way, though Cal (as Calliope) is there from the beginning. She gets born in the first chapter. There are of course short sections throughout the novel concerning Cal's life as an adult in Berlin. Calliope's life story properly begins around page 250, exactly halfway through the book. It's a long book and her part on center stage takes up almost 250 pages itself, which is as long as many novels. And, as you say, Cal is telling the entire story, so he's there in every sentence.

JSF  What wouldn't you sacrifice for your writing?

JE  I used to be scared of that line from Yeats, "perfection of the life or of the work." I thought I'd never be able to make that choice, that I wasn't disciplined enough, or committed enough. It sounded so painfully ascetic. But now I find that my work pretty much is my life. I don't think I could operate without it. The lucky thing is that writing has only made me sacrifice things I can get along without: a frisky social life, a manly feeling of being "out in the world," office gossip, teammates. You can be married and write. You can have a family and write. So you do have a life, after all. It's waiting for you just outside your studio.

JSF  I'm sorry, frisky social life?

JE  Like the one you're leading now, young man.

JSF  Ahem. You allude, many times in *Middlesex*, to national epics, particularly Greek ones, of course. It seems to me that our modern epics— *Ulysses, One Hundred Years of Solitude, Midnight's Children*—have had their greatest influence outside the countries of their origin. Am I wrong in sensing some ambition on your part to write a Greek epic for an American audience?

**JE** I've always wanted to write a big comic epic. The books you mention are books I loved in my late teens and early twenties, and back in those days I dreamed of trying my hand at the same thing. I thought I'd better give it a go before I got too old, because I knew it would be physically and intellectually draining. And because the comic spirit might dissipate with age. I never set out to write a "Greek-American" epic. At first I just wanted to write a fictional memoir of a hermaphrodite. This summoned other literary hermaphrodites, like Tiresias. Hermaphroditism led to classicism. Classicism led to Hellenism. And Hellenism led to my family. I used my Greek ancestry because it worked in the story I wanted to tell, not the other way around. But with a name like Eugenides, what do you expect?

**JSF** Baklava?

**JE** I had that coming.

**JSF** Roth and Rushdie seem to be the two poles of your influence. Do you feel that way?

**JE** One review of *Middlesex* compared it to the early novels of Saul Bellow. Which was fine by me. (But can you imagine Saul Bellow writing about a hermaphrodite?) I bring this up because my supposed influences are always changing. When *The Virgin Suicides* came out, I was accused, in England, of being too influenced by Salinger, especially by *Franny and Zooey*. There was only one thing wrong with that—I hadn't read *Franny and Zooey* at the time.

Literary influence is like genetics, too. Rushdie got some of his fireworks from Günter Grass and Gabriel García Márquez. García Márquez got things from Kafka and Faulkner. So, with *Middlesex*, you could say I inherited traits from all these ancestors, not to mention good old Homer. But some of my stuff bears no relation to these writers. Different gene pool entirely.

Influence isn't just a matter of copying someone or learning his or her tricks. You get influenced by writers whose work gives you hints about your own abilities and inclinations. Being influenced is largely a process of self-discovery. What you have to do is put all your influences into the blender and arrive at your own style and vision. That's the way it happens in music—you put a sitar in a rock song and you get a new sound. It's hybridization again. Hybrid vigor. It operates in art, too. The idea that a writer is a born genius, endowed with blazing originality, is mostly a myth, I think. You have to work at your originality. You create it; it doesn't create you. If I look at the writers who have influenced me, I see that many things about their lives accord with my own. Take Roth, for instance. He grew up in Newark, a town not so different from Detroit. He was the son of middle-class American parents and the grandson of grandparents with funny accents. From this hardworking but hardly culturally elevated milieu he went on to study English and become a good college boy. Now take Rushdie. He came from exotic origins, Bombay, (exotic to the English, anyway) and went to Cambridge. With both these writers, there is belonging and not belonging. In my own case, I was sent to a private prep school in Grosse Pointe, a place that made me more aware of my supposed "ethnicity" than I had been in public school. This marked me. I think it's no surprise that I might be influenced by a writer like Roth who writes very much about being American but also about being Jewish. I also happen to admire his books.

But I don't want to take this similarity business too far. I love Henry James but I'm not much like him. Maybe that's the Grosse Pointe in me, though. After all, I went to black-tie affairs when I was sixteen. We smoked pot behind the bushes in our tuxedos. Very Jamesian.

**JSF** Your bringing up pot reminds me of something I think about every now and again. There's a timeless tradition of associating creativity with drug use. I've often wondered if writers and artists use drugs because they think they're supposed to. (Here I don't mean smoking the occasional joint, of course, but damaging stuff.) If you want to be as important as Jackson Pollock, you'd better be as degenerate. The same is true for depression. I know a lot of people who think that artistic creation is born in grief. I certainly don't believe that. It's just the opposite for me. I think that's why I asked if you were happy when you were writing *Middlesex*.

**JE** You're right that people can't become talented by adopting the weaknesses of great artists. Pollock was a great artist not because of his self-destructive habits but in spite of them. Lots of people drink too much. Only a few of these people paint well. Same goes for depression. The depressives who write well do so by battling their depression, though it may color their work in significant ways. I tend to think I write best when I'm feeling happy, too, but writing a novel takes years, and you can't be in a good mood every day. So you have to learn to write in whatever mood you happen to be in. Extrapolating this over an entire lifetime, you have to learn to write with whatever disposition you've been born with.

**JSF** In *The Virgin Suicides*, the narrative voice was a first-person-plural "we." *Middlesex* is told by a hermaphrodite who was raised as a girl and later started living as a male. Obviously you like to complicate the narrative voices in your fiction.

**JE** I like impossible voices. Voices you don't hear every day. The "we" voice in *The Virgin Suicides* came easily, however. It was the first thing I had, really. The first paragraph was told by this collective narrator and the book grew from that. With *Middlesex*, it was different. I had a story in mind but I didn't have the right voice to tell it with. The voice had to be elastic enough to narrate the epic stuff, the third-person material, and it had to be a highly individualized first-person voice, too.

For a long time I didn't believe what I was writing, but then I gave Cal permission to zigzag between first and third person, and then I did believe it. A lot of time passed while I was screwing around with all this, but then I finally had my starting point. All I had to do was write another 530 pages.

**JSF** There is a chapter in *Middlesex* that deals with the rise of the Nation of Islam in Detroit in 1932. It's one of the many disparate elements that somehow get woven into the story of the Stephanides family. Did you have that in mind from the start? And how did you balance telling the family's story, and the country's story, which you were also obviously tracing?

**JE** Pretty early on, but not immediately. When you're writing a book, everything you come across seems to fit into it. When I was working on the early chapters of *Middlesex*, I read an article about W. D. Fard, the founder of the Nation of Islam. My grandparents were silk farmers in Asia Minor. I was already dealing with the silk farming in the book when I came across this mysterious historical personage. Fard described himself as a mulatto. No one knew where he came from, but he was reputed to have been a silk merchant. Fard seemed ordained to become part of *Middlesex*, and the more I learned about him, the more his story amplified the book's themes of genetic mutation, metamorphosis, and racial conflict.

I didn't see myself as tracing the country's story so much as the history of Detroit. And it wasn't a question of balancing the Detroit history against the family history. I needed the history in order to tell the family story, in order to put my characters in a real place and understand what their lives were like. I have a perverse love for my place of birth. I think most of the major elements of American history are exemplified in Detroit, from the triumph of the automobile and the assembly line to the blight of racism, not to mention the music, Motown, the MC5, house, techno. All made in Detroit. So I guess you're right. In telling a little bit of Detroit history I was telling the story of the nation as a whole.

**JSF**  Do you consider *Middlesex* a historical novel?

**JE**  No. Historical novels take place purely in the past. *Middlesex* runs up to the present and the history in it is an itinerary of the journey taken. I'm chronicling the transmission of a genetic condition as it passes down through a Greek-American family. There's a generational aspect to the book, and so there's history. But the book constantly cuts between the present and the past, and the past exists in Cal's memory or reconstruction of it, not as a period piece. There is a lightness of touch and a sense of comic self-dramatizing that, I hope, mitigate the stuffiness of historical novels. Still, I tried to be accurate about the historical events in the book, from the burning of Smyrna in 1922 to the Detroit Riots in 1967. I spent a lot of time in libraries reading microfiche. I visited historical museums to see what kind of radios people listened to in 1932. So I wasn't cavalier about the history. One of the joys of writing the book was coming to know my grandparents through the act of imagining their contemporaries. My grandparents died when I was relatively young, so this was a way of meeting them again, as an adult.

**JSF**  Once Callie's condition is discovered, she ends up at a gender identity clinic. The sexologist there, a Dr. Luce, puts her through a barrage of tests to determine her "true" gender identity. Much of this part of the novel concerns the nature/nurture debate in regard to gender identity. How did you see this playing out in the novel?

**JE**  I grew up in the unisex '70s. The heyday of nurture. Everyone was convinced that personality, and especially gender-specific behavior, was determined by rearing. Sexologists and feminists insisted that each child was a blank slate and that rearing determined gender roles. Now everything is reversed. Biology and genetics are considered the real determinants of behavior. Having lived through the demise of the first oversimplification, I suspect the imminent demise of the current one. Right now we exaggerate the role of genes in controlling our destiny. As Cal says, the ancient Greek notion of fate has today been carried into our very genes. But that's not the way it works. Genes and environment interact during a specific, crucial developmental period. They coauthor the human being. Biologists understand this, but the culture at large still doesn't, quite. So we have these pat theories about evolutionary causes for our present behaviors. Men can't communicate because twenty thousand years ago they had to be silent on the hunt. Women are verbal because they had to call out to each other while gathering nuts and berries. This is just as silly as the previous nurture explanations.

The life of my hero plays out this debate. Callie is reared as a girl but, due to her virilization at puberty, adopts a male gender identity. Cal "operates in society" as a man. But that doesn't mean that he's really a man. Nor is any man exactly like any other man. Between the alternatives of nurture and nature, I argue for a middle place. That's one of the meanings of the title, obviously. But the *Middlesex* I'm talking about is not only a third gender category. It also represents a certain flexibility in the notion of gender itself. It's a very American concept really. It's a belief in individuality, in freedom. I think we are freer than we realize. Less genetically encumbered. Researchers expected to find two hundred thousand genes in the human genome. Instead they found about thirty thousand. Not much more than a mouse has. There literally are not enough genes to account for our human capacities. How did we become the way we are? The mystery is still unsolved. *Middlesex* is Cal's account of his own formation, his journey of self-discovery.

**JSF** Another issue that's sure to be discussed in relation to your book is whether or not "voice" is gendered. I didn't notice a dramatic shift in voice when Cal moves into manhood. Should I take that to be your answer to the question you beg?

**JE** I tend to believe there's not an innate difference between the way women and men write. Or at least I believe that differences between individuals are more significant than differences between genders. You're right about Cal's voice. It doesn't change, and it shouldn't. He's all grown up when he writes his story. If innate language abilities exist between males and females, this would result from brain chemistry and the formation of the brain in utero, in response to different levels of hormones. Calliope's brain would be that of a male and, as it happens, a heterosexual male, since she is attracted to girls. Well, I know something about that. Cal looks like a man and talks like one, with a deep voice, and he writes as a man might, too. So I didn't have to settle that thorny question. Cal's voice is his own, as I think everyone's is. Still, he was a girl at one point and has to render female experience credibly. When I finished the book, I gave it to Karen, my wife, to read, and to a few other women. I asked them to tell me what I'd done wrong. Future women readers can make up their minds, but my consulting group said that I had the emotional stuff right. What I didn't know much about was toenail polish. I had to ask a lot of questions about details like that. But Callie's life, her attraction to her redheaded, preppy best friend, her pubertal anxieties, her longing—all that I felt I knew about. Calliope Stephanides, the fourteen-year-old male pseudohermaphrodite and girls' school student—*c'est moi*.

**JSF**  Do you ever feel feminine? Have you ever felt feminine? (This is a serious question.)

**JE**  It's a very serious question. And the male author of a novel about a hermaphrodite couldn't fail to answer it in the affirmative. (Was that diplomatic enough?) My parents had two boys before me. They wanted me to be a girl. They even had a girl's name picked out for me: Michelle. I remember being little and hearing that Beatles song "Michelle" and thinking about the fact that I was supposed to be a girl but wasn't. This was a minor thing; please don't draw too many psychiatric conclusions. Did you know that Hemingway was made to dress like a girl until he was eleven or so? You could say he overcompensated in later life. When I was thirteen or fourteen I was very pretty. It seems amazing now, Jonathan, but that was the case. I'd be hanging out with a bunch of girls and one of their mothers would come out and say, "Would you girls like something to drink?" Bellow says in *Humboldt's Gift* that being a poet is "a school thing, a skirt thing, a church thing." So I'd say that to be a writer you have to have something feminine about you. As these tiresome categories go, anyway. Gender is a continuum and everyone falls in a different spot. There's no other way to think about it, really.

**JSF**  I've felt that the visual arts influence my writing more than literature does. What art do you like to look at? What has been the role of art in influencing your writing?

**JE**  The visual arts haven't influenced my writing more than literature has. With *Middlesex*, though, I had two visual models in mind. One was the interior of a Greek Orthodox church. Those gilded interiors covered with icons, faces everywhere you look. And dark grottoes where candles are smoking. And lots of noise from people talking during the service. And the big face of the Christ Pantocrator on the dome, looking down. That was like my narrator, Cal, both omniscient and not, both transcendent and immanent in creation, born of woman. The other image in my mind was the Diego Rivera mural at the Detroit Institute of Arts, depicting the automotive industry (*Detroit Industry*, 1932). I urge anyone who ever ends up in Detroit to go see it. I grew up looking at it and it still has a totemic power over me. Interestingly, long after I started *Middlesex*, I went to see it again and noticed the four races of humankind up near the ceiling. My attention had always been on the assembly line and smokestacks on the lower panels. But now I saw the four races. And Rivera had rendered them as hermaphrodites. This was back in 1932. I never knew about any of that as a kid. I just loved the activity of the mural, all the colors, and the feverishness of the workers, and the social implications, and the fact that so much was going on. Just like on the walls at church. I wanted *Middlesex* to be like that, both teeming and serene.

JSF  Teeming and serene. I really like that.

JE  Well, I didn't feel serene. Not while writing the book. But that was the idea.

JSF  You working on anything now? Someone once said that every book is a response to the previous book. What kind of response will *Middlesex* call for?

JE  It calls for something short, tangible, and easily verified. I'm working on a short nonfiction book about Berlin, part of the Writer and the City series for Bloomsbury.

# Brian Evenson
# and Blake Butler

BRIAN EVENSON was born in Ames, Iowa, in 1966. He is the author of a dozen books of fiction, including the story collection *Windeye* and the novel *Immobility*, both of which were finalists for a Shirley Jackson Award. His novel *Last Days* won the American Library Association's award for Best Horror Novel of 2009. He is the recipient of three O. Henry Prizes as well as a National Endowment for the Arts Fellowship. His work has been translated into five languages. He lives and works in Providence, Rhode Island, where he is Royce Professor of Teaching Excellence in Brown University's Literary Arts Department.

BLAKE BUTLER was born in Marietta, Georgia, in 1979. He is the author of several works of fiction, including *There is No Year*, *Sky Saw*, and *300,000,000*, as well as a nonfiction book on insomnia, *Nothing*. A graduate of Georgia Tech and Bennington College, where he earned his MFA, Butler edits the literature blog HTMLGIANT and the journals *Lamination Colony* and *No Colony*.

**BLAKE BUTLER** *Windeye* seems to have a different texture than any of your previous books. A familiar reader probably won't be surprised by the content, but there's a different tone and quality to the way you're delivering the story this time. Your characters seem particularly disoriented, maybe even muffled by what they're up against.

**BRIAN EVENSON** More than any of my other books, this book is about loss. It's also about characters who are having a hard time navigating their world. In many of these stories, the reality of the world is either collapsing or threatening to collapse—there's a sense of something having disappeared. I too feel the book is different, but since these are themes I've touched on elsewhere, I'm trying to figure out exactly *what* is different. Contentwise there are stories that could potentially be in my other books. Perhaps the book is more sober? The humorous element is not as prominent, and there are stories here that are much creepier. They're *always* creepy, that's the thing. (*laughter*)

**BB** The tone is sober. The narrators seem like they've been under pressure from what they've been through. And now they're like, Okay, I'm going to really figure out what's happening. But the more they try to focus, the more the story pushes their world away.

**BE** That's a big part of it. In the title story, the narrator is trying to figure out, to no avail, how he's lost part of his reality. Finally he just decides that he has no choice but to go on with life as it is, even if he's certain that something that should be there is missing. That's a sobering surrender.

**BB** There's so much obsession with appendages and grafting. A character loses an ear and then an ear is grafted but it's not his ear. Another has the same thing happen to his arm.

**BE** You start to see this in my novel *Last Days*, where there was a sense that you lose an arm but you still feel like the arm is there somehow. Here it's the reverse. You have something grafted back on and you're convinced it's not yours. This thing both *is* you and is *not* you at the same time. It's unsettling. Weirdly enough, there are aspects of this book that are more autobiographical than my other books. The kids locking each other in the toy box in the title story at the opening of the book—that was something my sister and I used to do to each other. We had this normal-sized toy box, but it had this little cubbyhole in the bottom that was just big enough to crawl into. When I was about four or five, one of us would crawl in and the other person would close you in and pretend like they were going to leave. In that sense, it's this return to certain things that feel familiar to me. But it's also a search for these moments that unsettle your sense of reality and then how you, regardless, build a life on top of them. You know, I had a tumor in my neck about a year and a half ago. To get it out, they had to take my left ear and peel it back and then put it back in place. No one told me before the operation that they'd have to cut the nerve so I wouldn't feel my ear. So, afterward, there was this really strange period where the nerve was there and not there, flailing, trying to reconnect. My brain was figuring out ways to pretend there was something there. There was a period that I described in "The Other Ear" where it felt like my ear was tightening like a fist and then opening wide like a fan. It was like an alien presence on the side of my head, out of my vision. That was the start of that obsession with both feeling connected and distant from myself at the same time. This opened up to larger epistemological issues, starting with the question of how you can know if what you're experiencing is real. So many of these stories are struggling to find an answer to that question. Their characters are trying to figure out ways to continue on, try to calm the world down so they can feel like they can stand on something, even though it's no longer solid.

**BB** Do you put yourself in your characters' feelings, are they tools, or both? Some of the stories specifically explore the role of the detective as being mostly useless beyond his ability to ask critical questions, while other less objectively described characters' emotions are formed in the very act of trying to find an answer. The area between those two extremes here is so rich.

**BE** Yeah, there is an investigation of the nature of character that goes on in the book too. On the one hand, you think of characters as a kind of noise or words on a page. You know, a collection of bits of language that cause a particular effect. On the other hand, we tend to respond to characters as if they're living, breathing things. Certainly I do; I feel very attached to some of my and others' characters, like I could have a coffee with them. So there are moments where characters are fairly empty vessels; they're serving a function within the story. And there are other moments in which they refuse to play that role, they insist on acting human, and they become uncomfortably close. The book as a whole is playing around with the degree to which fiction is something that's mimetic and producing a reality and the degree to which fiction is something intensive that's having an effect and making the reader experience something.

**BB** The book opens with "Windeye," which sets an oddly emotional tone, developed through the boy's confusion over whether his sister actually existed. Then "The Second Boy" changes the position slightly, beginning with these boys who also have trouble being sure of what is real. This story falls into a looping mechanism where you tell the same story again and again, and the moments that seem most vivid are the tiny glitches in what carries over. I kept thinking about Deleuze's *Difference and Repetition*.

BE It was deliberate to have those two stories at the beginning, because they do mark a continuum for what the other stories in the book do. "The Second Boy" is a kind of ghost story. And also a story about storytelling, about the way in which language works. The funny thing in that story is that a lot of the joy, for me, was in the minute description of the winter landscape—in talking about how the frozen leaves look, about what happens to the bark as it catches fire. There's an attempt to create a tangible world that doesn't seem to be located anywhere except in the story. Then, as evening comes, Leppin keeps on having this experience of the reappearance of Dierk. I'm not sure if that's real or not, and neither is Leppin. By the end of the story, you have the sense that he's in a trap that could potentially go on forever—the repetition becoming very intense. So, yes, I do think both those opening stories have this poignant quality that you don't find as much in my earlier work.

BB Have you ever scared yourself?

BE When I was writing "Munich Window" (in *Altmann's Tongue*), I fell so deeply into that logical, precise, and yet self-justifying voice that it got to be terrifying. I felt very intimately the evil of it. As time's gone on, I've developed ways of focusing on language more and protecting myself from that. A lot of my stories deal with pretty grim, weird stuff. I try to deal with that material in ways that are not necessarily grim and weird. There are aspects of "Grottor" that scare me a little bit—I don't particularly like the dark and once I did almost get stuck in a narrow tunnel in a cave. Also, Grottor himself is quite troubling, particularly when he's dressed as someone else. There are moments when I realize that the stories are inexorably headed to a dark place. That's when it gets frightening.

BB You said in another interview, "People have a lot less of an internal life and a lot less of what has been called consciousness—at least coherent consciousness—than has been believed." This book in particular seems embroiled in trying to grapple with the gray area between knowing and not knowing.

**BE** I've been pretty skeptical of the standard ways of describing consciousness. We have these models for understanding how consciousness works—the Freudian model, for instance—but I don't think they accurately get at what's going on. So much of what we think is internal stuff is programmed for us by language or by culture. I think that "consciousness" is thinner than we like to believe. I'm interested in Thomas Metzinger's work—he suggests that consciousness has put us in this kind of tunnel where we are perceiving a *representation* of the world rather than the world itself. That representation is much less articulated than reality. We recreate this representation of the world in our heads and get rid of all the surrounding noise. Anything that doesn't seem significant we erase or ignore and then we go ahead and live our lives according to what's left. This gives us a sense of subjectivity. I buy that. I don't think we apprehend the world as directly as we like to think. This question of what's real is very vexed.

**BB** The story that turned *Windeye* on its head for me, in particular, was "Legion." It starts to tell a story and then it says, "Wait! I need to tell you something else before I tell you this." And then it tells you that the only reason it's telling you any of these stories is to set up the next, as if we're both being deceived and, at the same time, prepared for something to be done to us—it's a keyhole of sorts. There are a bunch of moments like that, where you're pulling back the curtain.

**BE** And there are detective stories in the book as well as a story that's talking about detective stories. There are lots of moments where storytelling becomes the topic of the book—the inability to tell stories or the inability to get to the story you need to tell. You could probably make an argument that fiction for me is this attempt to work through and explain something that just can't be explained. You tell a story, but it only puts you on the threshold of the next story that needs to be told, the real story that you meant to tell. That ends up opening a kind of void.

**BB** It seems like it's not that we're asking an unanswerable question, but that we're not built to answer it in such a direct way. There *are* answers. The book opens and ends with houses. I don't know if the houses in "Windeye" and "Anskan House" are the same, but I feel like they both know more than anyone else.

**BE** That's a really interesting way to look at it. There is this strangeness of having these two almost magical houses at the beginning and the end of the book—there's a recursiveness to the structure. Both dwelling spaces harbor things that we don't normally expect dwelling spaces to have—one has a window on the outside that doesn't exist on the inside and the other has a kind of strange semihuman presence. Repetition is prominent throughout the book as a whole. I don't know why it's so panicking to hear the same story twice but in a slightly different way, but it's something I really love.

BB  When I was in Providence to visit your classes and you took me to my hotel, it had this very particular look to it. The first thing I thought was, Is Brian taking me to Anskan House? I never saw anyone else in the hotel, and I felt I was trapped in one of your stories.

BE  We always try to do that, rent the whole hotel and just put one person in it to freak them out. (*laughter*) Houses are critical through the collection as a whole. In "The Moldau Case" someone is upstairs writing about something that he thinks is happening on the first floor. And what actually is going on is happening in the basement. So the house is split into these different areas of knowledge and perception. That's a response to Gaston Bachelard's *The Poetics of Space*, which speaks very specifically about the metaphorical resonance of different parts of the house in literature. In "Tapadera," the dead boy keeps on trying to get back in the house. With "The Oxygen Protocol," it's not a house so much but an enclosed space within a domed city that is running out of air. Then you have an enclosed ship in "The Sladen Suit." The suit itself becomes a kind of small house. Not all the stories are set in houses, but a lot of them have people who are trapped in some way or another.

BB  That leads me into wanting to talk about your settings; they seem so vivid, and yet they're not made in any of the ways that we would normally be told to set locations for a story.

BE  I do tend to key in on small details that have a phenomenological feel to them, and also on the way in which individual bodies interact with those details. In "Windeye," what makes the house real for me is the way that the shingles on the side are buckling and coming out so that you can stick your hand up under them. That kind of palpable detail is enough to allow the reader to generate the rest of the house around it. There are some specifics in the way the house is described in "The Dismal Mirror," for instance, the curtain in the middle of the bedroom the brother and sister share, and in the way that the grounds and the land are described. But still, I don't give all that many details or give you enough to pinpoint it on a map. I'm more interested in thinking of the reader as someone who is there to help generate the story. My work is not mimetic or imitative of life; it's more of a catalyst that works with the reader to create an experience. The reader has to invest in it—hopefully what I'm doing with the words is putting the reader in the position where they can do that in a productive way.

BB "Anskan House" has a line that underlines that exactly: "A house stands empty long enough, unlet and uninhabited, and then something comes to be part of it. It's not a person nor exactly a house, but something in between."

BE We invest objects and houses with personality. Those things that are closest to us and that we surround ourselves with have gone from being *just* things to becoming something else—they've taken on consciousness. I like that. I hardly use any metaphors in my work. The metaphor is second-order perception, it moves us away from the connection that we have to things and objects, and doesn't allow us to experience them in the same way. With metaphors, we're able to make this leap in terms of thinking about things, but that leap strikes me as more of an intellectual leap than a bodily leap. I am interested in bodily perception.

BB Would you say you learned that from Beckett? I know you really admire *Molloy*.

BE One thing I've learned from Beckett is that he lets things happen and doesn't necessarily explain them. He just figures that you'll be able to go along with him and catch up. He has these almost synesthetic moments that are very subtly done. Also, I think he has a pretty big skepticism of metaphor and the sense of doing *without* things. Seeing what you can do with a stripped-down style is something that I'm interested in. I got that from Beckett, very much so.

BB What about Gordon Lish? How was your experience with him?

BE I wasn't ever in his New York class, but he did publish my first book at Knopf and several of my stories were in the *Quarterly*. He was really good at making me pay attention to the way in which language was working and to the dynamics and the structure of a sentence. I've always been a little bit off in my own space, and it was great that Lish was willing to let me be there, and understood it. I've always been more interested in plot than a lot of other writers who worked with him. If you become really focused on the sentence, the danger is that you stay so focused on the sentence that you have a harder time moving to larger structures. So the trick is figuring out how to become focused on the sentence and build that into something that still has drive and momentum to it over the long haul.

BB So how do you balance those two things, plot and sentence, while creating?

BE It's about keeping a velocity and sense of direction in mind and, at the same time, paying very close attention to each footstep you're taking along the way. I don't plot things out in advance usually. For short stories especially, I only have a vague notion of one or two things that might happen, and then things develop from there. In a story like "The Adjudicator," there's this moment early on where the character unearths an arm. Until he did that, I didn't know it was going to happen. That suddenly started to make me interested in his relationship to the arm and ended up directing the story. I find it necessary to be open and allow these moments to happen. Or, for instance, "Anskan House" is a response to the Rudyard Kipling story called "Wish House," but it's quite different from it: the Kipling story is a conversation between two older women. Riffing off of that story gave my story a structure I could play around with, something both to follow and diverge from. With "The Second Boy," I didn't know the story was going to restart until he'd been wandering in the woods a while and found his camp again. Then it made perfect sense to let it restart.

BB You have a lot of section breaks in most of your stories, little pauses. I like having those gaps; it's almost like the story gets to think for itself.

BE That breath or pause often allows me to move in a direction that's more startling than if I were just writing a continuous prose line. That openness keeps me interested. I've sat down and written a sixty-page outline of something—when I did that, I knew how everything was going to go. But I wasn't actually interested in writing it any more. (*laughter*) There is a vertiginous freedom to being able to perceive possibility in the virtuality of the space that's opening for you. Writers—their conscious minds can often take over things and shut them down. So it's a question of trying to turn off your conscious mind enough that things can happen, things that will take the story in ways that you don't expect and that are going to be productive for readers. There are moments when you just shouldn't have your ass on the chair. You're better off going on a walk or having a drink, doing something that distracts you and lets your mind do its work without you there. You can't push it. I mean, with *The Open Curtain*, I tried to work through the problem by writing page after page after page. I threw all those pages away. The book wrote itself when it was ready to write itself.

BB  Do you do a lot of revising?

BE  I do. When I revise, I bring out patterns and repetitions a little more. I mean, it's a combination of both bringing out patterns and hiding patterns at the same time. Feeling something below your skin will have more of an effect than if it is out there really obviously. "Windeye" is pretty close to how it was written; there were one or two minor changes. But many of the other stories in the book were revised a lot. It's a question of getting to the point where things feel right.

BB  I like the subdermal idea. Especially when you are writing a draft in a fast-paced way, when you go back and look at it again you find there's a whole other thread buried in the story. Finding the right ones to be expanded or trimmed or cut—that's where the story can take on this other life that we're talking about.

BE  Writing is almost a hydraulic system. You have all these things that you're regulating. You want to get the levels right. If you're not careful, something will overflow or go dry. And so a lot of the revision, for me, is about small details, sound, and the repetition of certain kinds of rhythms within the piece. There's a kind of decisive rhythm that I often use deliberately in my work—it's focused around significant events. A lot of the effect of fiction is not what you can see on the page, it's what you feel. I love stories that do something to me in a way that I can't quite understand. And I love writing stories in which I can't manage to figure out how I produced an effect, but I know it's there.

BB  I remember reading that when you wrote *The Open Curtain* you wrote up almost five hundred pages trying to get the ending right. After I learned that, I had to go back and read the book again, and it felt like the mental presence of those other endings opened the book in a certain way, as if the ending were surrounded.

BE  I've reread the discarded parts of *The Open Curtain*. There are all these ghosts of things that just didn't work. I had to give them up. So, mentally, for me, there's this strange layering of different stories, of abandoned alternatives. But, you know, on the finished page, those abandoned possibilities are probably not visible. One of the stories in *Windeye*, "Grottor," started with material from the pages of *The Open Curtain* that I ended up throwing away. So for me "Grottor" feels like the ghost of *The Open Curtain*.

**BB**  Do you feel haunted by the things you delete?

**BE**  It's starting to sound like that. I mean, all these possibilities of fiction accumulate. One way that a lot of my stories start is from reading something and seeing it go in one direction and thinking, Hey, I could take this in another direction. In fact, "The Second Boy" originated with a passage from Roberto Bolaño's *The Savage Detectives* in which a boy falls down "a shaft or pit or chasm up the mountain." The ambiguity of that phrasing opened something up for me. A lot of my stories come from the path that another story could have taken but didn't take. They attempt to animate these moments that could have existed but didn't.

**BB**  So what leads you to your choices? Is it logic or a guttural thing?

**BE**  It's instinctual, sometimes slightly random. You come to a point in the piece that you're working on that could go in several distinct ways. I often tend to want to make a less obvious choice. Doing that often gives rise to both anxiety and elation. I've always done that, but I started consciously doing it when I was working on the stories that make up *Contagion*. There was a moment in writing the story "Two Brothers" when I realized that it was possible for the brothers to almost swap identities. That ended up changing the whole landscape of the story and making the house within, which before had been fairly solid, into something that seemed to be expanding and changing. Trying to write yourself out of the narrative corner you've put yourself in can be really worthwhile.

**BB**  I wonder if that relates to music. I know you're really into music that has this kind of ambient effect or mood, but you don't ever really talk much about sound in your work.

**BE**  I write to music and listen to a lot of experimental stuff, noise stuff, and things like that—Sunn O))), for instance, or Earth or Hecker or Lightning Bolt or Merzbow—but, actually, just a wide variety of very different kinds of things. I can become very obsessed with little details, like the way in which a certain bass line is working, or how things are coming together, and the collision of different things. If I begin listening to a piece of music when I start a story, I'll listen to it dozens of times while I'm writing it. I don't talk about music in my fiction very much, but something curious happens when I'm listening. With a lot of the music that I like, I have the impression that if I turn it up a little bit louder, I'm going to hear something in it that I can't quite hear otherwise—something that's being kept from me, though

161

I'm feeling it's there. It gives me the sensation of being on the verge of something.

BB  I'm always interested in the way you end things. They are often recursive. Ostensibly your stories could go on forever until the character is dead, but even sometimes when they could be dead it still continues. How do you know when you've reached the end?

BE  It varies from story to story. There's this strange dichotomy in several stories where there's this projection far into the future but also a looking back on something. Also there is often this moment of acceleration or a shift that occurs where the stakes get changed or raised—that's a way of exiting the story. Or things start to happen in a different way and that allows for a way of stepping out or aside from what's going on. In this collection the stories have a new kind of urgency. It might have to do with where I am in life. That urgency probably also has an effect on the way in which the endings are working in the collection. Often there is this act of surrender on the part of the characters—they're on the verge of either giving something up or starting something new. With "Legion" there's this moment where something is going to begin—it's horrible, but it's also this genuine attempt to come into a new sense of consciousness.

BB  I think that encapsulates what I was talking about earlier, each text preparing the reader to be more fully opened by the next.

BE  It's ending with this sense of beginning as well. There is the sense of taking an ending and turning it inside out so we move into a more drastic space. We know that something awful is going to happen, and then we go on to the next story.

BB  The multiplying tensions elevate the urgency beyond urgency. Instead of trying to describe the indescribable, you make us enter it.

# Nuruddin Farah and Kwame Anthony Appiah

NURUDDIN FARAH  was born in Baidoa, Somalia, in 1945. He studied in India and England, and is the author of numerous books, including *Maps*, *Links*, and *From a Crooked Rib*. Farah has won many international prizes, among them the Premio Cavour in Italy, the Kurt Tucholsky Prize in Sweden, the Lettre Ulysses Award in Berlin and the Neustadt International Prize for Literature. His work has been translated into over 20 languages. He lives in Minneapolis, Minnesota, and Cape Town, South Africa.


KWAME ANTHONY APPIAH  was born in London, England, in 1954. He is the author of numerous books, including *Cosmopolitanism: Ethics in a World of Strangers; The Honor Code: How Moral Revolutions Happen;* and *The Ethics of Identity*. Appiah, who earned his PhD at Cambridge University, has taught at the University of Ghana, Cornell, Yale, Harvard, and Princeton University. He is a professor at New York University and lives in New York City and New Jersey.

**KWAME ANTHONY APPIAH** Let's start by talking about what you're doing now.

**NURUDDIN FARAH** I'm at a residency program in upstate New York, Art Omi, enjoying the quiet and rewriting a novel. I work in a very concentrated manner on a rewrite, working eighteen hours a day, sleeping very little. This way I see where the weaknesses of the story are. I rewrite the novel as many as four or five times. I always start from the beginning and go through it without stopping, then put that draft away and three or four or six months later go back and rewrite it again more or less from memory.

**KAA** And you keep all these drafts?

**NF** I keep the drafts, some very bad, some not so bad, until I'm done with them all.

**KAA** There will be lots of literary archaeologists who would love to get their hands on the whole process.

**NF** I don't think the drafts would be of much use to anyone. If you saw some of the earlier drafts, you would think I didn't know how to write—and maybe I don't. I write fast and then rewrite just as fast. For the first time, though, I've done a novel of about 570 pages and am cutting it down to three hundred-plus pages. Normally I work the other way around: I write a book of one hundred pages and then make it much longer. What I hate most is to publish a novel very similar to my earlier ones. To make sure that that doesn't happen, I convince myself that I'm new to writing, that I am doing it for the first time, in the hopes of producing something completely, absolutely different. To me anyway. I do that each time I write an article or a novel or a play.

**KAA** So the writing process doesn't change depending on what the novel is about?

**NF** It is the method that is important. I approach writing as though it were a game that I play alone, in a room by myself. It's not the most pleasant profession—how can it be? You lock yourself away in a room and face an empty page, daily. Writing, as a profession, is tedious, not very enjoyable. Nor is it highly appreciated, nor understood.

**KAA** So how did you come to be in this unpleasant business of writing?

NF (*laughter*) My interest in writing started long before I knew how one went about it. You could say it started as soon as I learned the first few letters of the Arabic alphabet, which I found most fascinating, as Arabic calligraphy decorated the walls of our houses. I was so enthralled that I kept copying them. And because many of our townspeople were illiterate, a large number of them believed that I was engaged in an activity that was rewarding. Even my parents linked my busyness to the sacredness of Arabic as a language, the tongue of the Koran—unaware that I was only taken with the script's decorative quality, not its holiness. Somalis tend to be very religious but have no deep knowledge about the Koran or about Islam. Reading and copying became my means of escape.

Then I came into contact with secular writing in Arabic and was equally fascinated, in fact more so when I discovered that my name, Nuruddin, happened to be that of a prince's in *A Thousand and One Nights.* Mischievous, I would cut *Nuruddin* out of every *Thousand and One Nights* copy that I got hold of (*laughter*) and tape them in my exercise books. Then I would boast to my playmates, "Look, I am a writer." Later I showed similar interest in the English-language textbooks at the school I went to, which was set up by an American evangelical mission dedicated to converting us to Christianity. I would say that my first attempt at writing occurred when I was fifteen and tried to recast a folktale in which rats plot against the cat that has been attacking them one at a time. In my desire to make the story mine, I replaced the names of the rat and cat characters of the folktale with the names of my classmates.

KAA (*laughter*)

NF  I gave the good lines to the ones I liked and the bad lines to the ones I didn't like.

KAA So you were retelling a folktale?

NF  Reshaping it *and* imposing my own likes and dislikes upon it. By then, at any rate, my brother had given me books to read, Dostoyevsky and Victor Hugo in Arabic. He also gave me books in English that I was unable to read, let alone understand, because I had to underline every word, go to the dictionary and look it up. My brother then suggested that perhaps I should read the dictionary from cover to cover once a year, which I did for several years.

KAA So you had two languages as a child, Somali and Arabic, and then your brother got you into English. But you were quite serious about the Koran, weren't you? And you know it very well.

**NF** My father was very serious about my learning the Koran. I was the fourth son. A tradition followed by families with many male children is to devote one of them to the study of the Koran and religion. I was the one chosen, assigned to the spiritual side of things. I had an excellent memory and could recite the Koran from beginning to end at an early age, so my father assumed that I would be good material. Unfortunately, though, my memory became unreliable the older I grew, especially when I started fooling around with some of the texts. You see, I was born toward the end of 1945, when a lot of the old traditions were being rejected or challenged, as was the case everywhere in the world. The world was changing from what it used to be to something that had never been known. All this was affecting our lives and our way of looking at the world.

**KAA** You were born when the Ogaden was under British control.

**NF** Yes, and my father was in the British civil service as an interpreter for the British governor. He was transferred from the town in which I was born, Baidoa, which had been Italian and then taken over by the British when the Italians lost the war, to the Ogaden. Then the British handed over the Ogaden to Ethiopia as compensation to Haile Selassie. By 1948, my father had saved enough from his interpreting job to start farming. He grew sesame, maize, lettuce, lemon, papaya.

**KAA** So your first memories were of the farm?

**NF** The farm was ten miles away from where we lived in town. I remember being taken there as a small child—carried on somebody's back or shoulders. When I got bigger I walked, and helped on the farm.

**KAA** Since then you have lived in many places: India, Gambia, Nigeria, South Africa, Uganda, Germany, the United States.

**NF** Yes, but I have remained loyal to the idea of Somalia. I say that all the things I know about all the other places I've lived can be put into an article of about a thousand words, no more than that. Of course, I can set novels in these countries, but when you think about them seriously, such books will be of small literary value.

**KAA** It's because of Somalia's political history that you had to leave Somalia. You didn't choose to be in all these other places, you were an exile. Isn't that true?

NF  Yes, I didn't choose to leave Somalia.

KAA You had left, but then you couldn't go back. What happened?

NF  In the early '70s I started writing my second novel in Somalia. I had published my first novel, *From a Crooked Rib*, in 1970, and it became very popular, very well liked, a cult book, especially among women—incidentally, it's just been reissued by Penguin Classics in the U.K. I wrote *Crooked* as a student in India. I began work on my second novel—

KAA You wrote your first novel in English?

NF  Yes.

KAA I'm sure that people have asked you this often, but it is an interesting question for someone who could have written in Arabic or Somali or English: How did you make that decision, or did you just find yourself writing?

NF  I chose to write in English because Somali, my mother tongue, had no orthography in those days. Now why did I not write in Arabic, Amharic, or Italian? The way it happened, a good, solid American typewriter decided that I would write in English. It was a Royal, and I adored it. I liked hearing the sound of it when I typed. And I couldn't find a good enough typewriter in any of the other languages that I might have written in. There is another important factor: I've received much of my intellectual makeup in English. Also, being a very practical person, I was aware that Amharic has far too many letters for a typewriter—it's too complicated. Arabic was out of the question because Arabic typewriters weren't common in our peninsula— and anyhow, Arabic was foreign to me too. Somali had no script until the fall of 1972. And soon enough, I started to write a novel in Somali, which was published serially, a chapter a week, in the only Mogadishu daily. The publication was discontinued because the censorship board people didn't like a couple of chapters, and, silly as I am, I insisted, when asked to explain, that I would not allow the text to be cut. Fancy that! "This is *art*," I argued. "You don't explain art; you take it or leave it." So not only was the publication of my novel in Somali discontinued, but the censorship board also banned *From a Crooked Rib*, at that time my only published novel. I was reduced to a nonperson. I was teaching literature at the university in Somalia, but in order to avoid further complications with the regime, I left, in 1974, on a British Council scholarship for England, to do a master's in theater at the University of Essex. Two years later I published *A Naked Needle*, a month prior to my expected return to Somalia. Several favorable reviews in the British press described the novel as satirical—in a way hostile to the regime of Siad Barre. So when I rang one of my brothers to pick me up at the Mogadishu airport, he said, "Apparently you haven't heard—you are enemy #1 now. We suggest you find something else to do, and that you forget about Somalia." And I became an exile.

KAA You have this place that you say is the only place you want to write about. And not only are you cut off from it in the most direct way, but you don't know how long your exile is going to last. Siad Barre's legacy might be there for the rest of your life. So you have to travel the world. You can go everywhere except Somalia—and yet you go on writing only about Somalia.

NF Siad Barre is now dead and buried, but what he left behind continues to haunt us—because dictatorships always leave behind deranged minds, lots and lots of unaccounted-for evil. The Somali civil wars result from his dictatorship. I can go back whenever I please—I've been there three times this year alone. But there is an additional complication: I have a young family, and they are happy in Cape Town, where we've bought a house. My wife has a wonderful job, and the children are contentedly settled. And even though I wish I could relocate and live permanently in Somalia, I'm not likely to insist on this, as it will mean uprooting them. Moreover, as things stand, Somalia is not a workable proposition: no functioning schools, no job for my wife, and so on. Who knows, South Africa may turn out to be an unworkable proposition, and then we'll rethink. In the meantime, I continue having faith in the world I know as an exile, and I will continue writing about a country in which I cannot live, in a language that's not my first tongue—

KAA Or your second.

NF —or my second, or my third. (*laughter*) These contradictions help me reassess my position. And in a way, these discomforts help me visit in my imagination the very neurosis that is part of me, the neurosis that sharpens my focus on my subject matter, the land that I'm cut off from.

KAA In your first novels you wrote about Somalia as a place shaped by tension, but nevertheless a place where people have loves and lives and relations with their families. There were questions about how women would find their place in gender relations as the world changes. You actually didn't go straight at Siad Barre all the time.

NF That's what I would challenge my fellow Somalis to do: to talk not about Siad Barre but about the regime. It is not the man, it is the system that creates the man—the two are symbiotic. "Study the structure of the Somali family," I would challenge, "and you will find mini-dictators imposing their will without regard to the sensitivities and sensibilities of the weaker members of the family unit." The tyranny of tradition rules in Somalia; Islam is the only faith. I would then paraphrase Wilhelm Reich: Every half-schooled father is the principal representative within the family of the authoritarian structure of society. This is something I come back to often in my analysis of Somali society. We become replicas of the tyrant whom we hate. We hate these warlords, these dictators, and fight against them to the point that we become dictatorial. This is what has destroyed many of the great nationalists in Africa: they became authoritarian, just like the colonialists against whom they fought. A question: What happens when you rid yourself of the monster? You become a monster.

KAA What's interesting, though, is that the women in your novels, both older and younger, are very strong people.

NF You wouldn't survive in a place like Somalia—and I love Somalia, but I'm the first to admit what a terrible place it can prove to be—you couldn't really and truly live there unless you were strong. I doubt there can be an interesting female character in a novel set in Somalia unless she is strong-headed. Let me generalize. A woman who is trampled on, who is unable to speak her mind is not worthy of becoming a character in a novel written by an ambitious writer who thinks he or she knows what he or she is doing. All societies are horrid to women, just awful. I've modeled my characters after women like my mother, who was strong. I am happily married to a strong woman. I love it when my wife holds her ground and says, "You are out of line." One must be able to say that to one's parents, one's spouse, the president of one's country. For me that is democracy.

KAA What you're talking about is a kind of democratization of the whole of social life. Where does your strong commitment to that come from? Looking at Somalia, and for that matter at almost any country, you can see that the world is full of people who want to be heard themselves but are not necessarily interested in hearing other people. I'm curious whether you think it's something in the Somali tradition, or in your family, or in your experience as a traveler, as a migrant—

NF That commitment comes from my mother, who was wiser and more articulate than my father. Unlike him—he couldn't abide anyone who disagreed with him—my mother had the ability to listen. Listening is a faculty lacking in many people, more specifically among men and among dictators. When you listen, you arm yourself against your enemy. You must listen until the other party has finished speaking, then it is much easier to prick holes in their arguments. That's how my mother used to do it. People don't listen or have the patience or make the time. It is small-minded to be too arrogant or to think you know enough. I speak slowly, and usually before I finish what I'm going to say, a lot of my interlocutors lose interest in what I am saying, and then—

**KAA** This comes out in your writing, this sense of what can happen if people treat one another properly. Of course, one way to discover that is by seeing what happens when people *don't* treat one another properly. You are able to go back to Somalia now that Siad Barre has been chased out; it's not a safe place, but at least you haven't been sentenced to death by the president of the current administration.

**NF** (*laughter*) Not yet.

**KAA** Have you had a chance to talk about some of these ideas with people in Somalia?

**NF** One of the things I've said to many of the politicians and the warlords is to listen to what the other guys are saying. If you listen, you won't need to pull out a gun. In short, let us take the gun out of Somali politics, even if someone says things that you don't like. Just look at them after they've finished; don't say anything. Listen some more, and they will have changed their mind. Last year I spent close to two months talking to as many of the warlords as I could with a view to making them "think peace and talk peace." And I am planning to return and listen to the various interest groups, some of them armed and some not. When in Somalia, I gave public lectures at the universities and at other venues. I am hoping that peace will become more fashionable in my country, that the warlords who have looted, plundered and taken possession of other people's properties will return some of these, having enjoyed the fruits of their plunder for some time now.

**KAA** So they now have an interest in the kind of ordinary, everyday stability of life that they destroyed. Is your next novel also set in Somalia?

**NF** Yes, I'm still writing about Somalia.

**KAA** What can one write about Somalia now?

**NF** The civil war, and how people live through a civil war; how they express themselves, gather their broken selves with a view to mending their damaged memories and cure their illnesses. More and more Somalis, especially from North America, are going back to Mogadishu to help in the reconstruction. And some of them are beginning to listen. You see, the problem with the American intervention was this: the Americans didn't listen to the Somalis. They barricaded themselves in their fortresses in Mogadishu, raided this or that warlord's redoubt and then quit the country. My new novel, *Links*, is about the Somali civil war between 1992 and 1996, including the period when Admiral Howe was fighting it out with General Aidid. In the novel, I try to view the city as the principal character, and the people living in it or visiting it become secondary characters.

**KAA** It's the life of a city.

**NF** It is about a dog running into the dusty street with its tail between its legs; about a mini-tyrant turned beggar who was in the service of Siad Barre; about how the city is divided, and what role corruption plays. People living in the city become witnesses to the terror, or a casualty, or a cause.

**KAA** Does the fact that you have been able to go back to Somalia in the past few years make a big difference to the writing? Or had you been in touch through your contacts there?

**NF** There's a cliché, isn't there, that one never goes back to what one has left, as things will have changed. My writing has benefited in the six or seven years since I've been able to go back, becoming sharper where before it may have been dull around the edges. But I have lost the power to philosophize and mythologize. Previously, I was able to obfuscate matters, and thus sound more poetic. Years ago, if I wasn't sure of the street names, I concentrated on an area of the city rather than a particular street. Now, because I know the names of the streets, there are other interferences, and so there are fewer abstractions in my writing. I don't know if this is good.

**KAA** In a way, not being there all that time freed your imagination.

**NF** Yes. I made more art out of it. I ask myself if I am losing the art, if you see what I mean. Or perhaps my writing will have become dated in a few years.

**KAA** So specificity hinders your travel in the direction of abstraction.

**NF** Yes.

**KAA** This novel is being written in English. Are you tempted to write in Somali?

**NF** Well, I borrow from the day before yesterday, because I am working on lots of things at the same time—one of them is a novel in Somali in the shape of a film script. That I am in exile and that there is no fully functioning Somali state are disadvantages. I am like a one-man company, and nobody invests in the ideas of a one-man company—not lucratively. If there were a functioning state in Somalia, film and television companies in Italy or Germany might have expressed their interest in collaborating with me—country to country; you call this bilateral—but there you are.

**KAA** You mentioned that at the start of your career you published in Mogadishu. What is happening there for new writers?

**NF** There is little publishing happening in Mogadishu, though you can publish short stories in the newspapers. Incidentally, there are more newspapers now than there have ever been in the history of Somalia. In the days of Siad Barre there was only one government-run daily. Nowadays you have about thirteen newspapers. The print quality is atrocious and the text is presented in four-page cyclostyled broadsides centered on the day's happenings or the week's—but they are very interesting.

**KAA** But Somalis are welcome to read fiction and poetry, assuming they want to.

**NF** Yes.

**KAA** What about the radio?

**NF** I do radio things quite a lot, programs for the BBC Somali Service and also for local radio stations. Somalis being oral, they take you seriously when you speak on the radio. Recently, in Mogadishu, I did an hour and a half of live radio and television call-in programs. Many listeners called in to tell me what they thought about my political interventions: promoting peace and dialogue and trying to silence the guns. This would not have been possible in the days of Siad Barre.

173

**KAA** You're very well known, of course, among Somalis in the diaspora. Because of the war and the dictatorship, there are Somali communities in many American and European cities. Do you travel among them to speak?

**NF** In my travels, I share with the Somalis in the diaspora my views about my visits to Somalia. Hundreds of thousands of Somalis are scattered throughout Europe and North America. And even though they have no intention of returning, they've brought the trauma of displacement, with which they are burdened. They're not educated enough in their new language and they can't pick up a job quite so easily. It's as if they left their minds back in Somalia and brought only their bodies with them—it is because they're still connected to Somalia. I tell them that if they do well where they are they'll do well for Somalia; that if they don't do well there, then Somalia will also suffer. I advise them to decide once and for all: either here or there. If they are going to live in America as Americans, then they should let their children go to school and participate in everything—fully. In other words, they can be Americans and yet keep their Somaliness, which is important to their psyche. I remind them that nobody is going to take their Somaliness away from them. But if they continue looking back, then they won't look forward and they're not going to go anywhere, they will not succeed here.

**KAA** Are there writers in the Somali diaspora?

**NF** Diasporic Somalis are writing in Dutch, Norwegian, Swedish, French, but some have decided to continue writing in Somali even though they live in Europe or North America. They write more comfortably than those still living in Somalia, because they have the peace to write.

**KAA** The other reason you can go on writing is that you have a huge, worldwide audience. You've made Somalia a real place for people who otherwise would never have thought about Somalia except for what they hear on the news from time to time.

**NF** In my cynical way, I say that the world needs a Somali, a Ghanaian, a Frenchman, a Mexican, a Chinese and an Indian—to mention a few writers from these nationalities. There is a party to which the world invites one or two people from each place. I am the Somali invited to this party, and you are perhaps the Ghanaian. That's why you and I are who we are—world writers.

KAA The difference between those countries and a country like, say, Germany is not so much the difference between a rich country and a poor one. In Germany perhaps they are too preoccupied with writing from other places. They're not paying attention to their own.

NF Maybe the Germans and the French are genuinely interested in other people's cultures. Maybe this is why almost all my novels have been translated into German and French. That the world is a marketplace is not a bad thing. We, in Africa, buy manufactured goods from America, Germany, England, and France. And they buy and publish our writings. Even so, the fact that Somalis know more about America, Britain, or Germany than they know about Ghana is disturbing. Because the media and present-day technology is tilted that way. In another context, I'm reminded of a Somali poet who prayed, "Lord, either do not show me the things that I see or please make everyone else see them too."

KAA I wonder if part of the reason you do have a wider audience with different types of people is that you're discussing the question of how society is corrupted by dictatorship, and that's not a specifically Somali question; and you're discussing relationships between women and men across the generations. These are obviously questions that interest and engage people elsewhere.

NF I'm reminded of a meeting I once had with Friedrich Dürrenmatt—

KAA Really?

NF We were taking a flight together from someplace or other and he asked me if I had read some of his books. I said, "Yes, I have." And he said, "I won't ask you what you thought of them. But I haven't read your books. So tell me, Mr. Farah, why should I read your books?"

KAA (*laughter*) Well, what's the answer?

NF I said that if he read my books he would find a worldview that he couldn't find in a book by a German, a Swiss, a Nigerian, an Arab and so on and so forth. He said, "What if I am not interested in discovering another worldview, because I am content with mine?" I responded that no matter how happy one is with one's worldview, the truth is that our world—as Swiss, as American, as Somali—is incomplete without the additional worlds that will be brought to bear on that world, to make it richer and more fulfilling.

# Paula Fox
# and Lynne Tillman

**PAULA FOX**  was born in New York City in 1923. She is the author of many books for children and adults, including *A Place Apart*, which won the National Book Award; *The Slave Dancer*, winner of the Newberry Medal; *One-Eyed Cat*; *Desperate Characters*; *The Widow's Children*; and *News from the World*. She is the recipient of a Hans Christian Andersen Award for her contributions as a children's writer. A teacher and literary critic by profession, she has taught at The New School and Long Island University, and is the former editor of *Commentary*.

**LYNNE TILLMAN**  was born in Brooklyn, New York, in 1947. She is the author of several novels, collections of short stories and nonfiction books, including *No Lease on Life*, a National Book Critics Award finalist and a *New York Times* Notable Book; *American Genius, A Comedy*; *What Would Lynne Tillman Do?*; and *Haunted Houses*. She is the recipient of a Guggenheim Fellowship, and is a Writer-in-Residence in the English Department at the University of Albany. She lives in New York City.

**LYNNE TILLMAN**  You're a profoundly psychological writer, and also socially and politically engaged. In your first novel, *Poor George*, George Mecklin thinks, "We live on the edge of disaster and imagine we are in a kitchen." Absolute Fox! How did George come to you? How did you decide to write a male protagonist?

**PAULA FOX**  To answer the last part first: I didn't even think about it. It would be false naïveté to say that I didn't realize what I was doing. I did remember hearing, on NPR, in a time of extreme feminism in the late 1960s, a woman being interviewed who said, "Imagine! A man writing about a woman!" I thought of Thomas Hardy, Marcel Proust. I thought, Of course, this kind of extremism accompanies everything that has to do with human affairs, as we see in contemporary life. What engaged me most in writing *Poor George* was a story I was told in about three sentences by someone I knew casually. He said, "I heard this story about a man who took a boy into his house . . ." I thought of things that might happen. I didn't actually think because a story grows, with me, in a series of images. I have acute memories of the past. I can remember the wrinkles in my father's jacket, when he was lighting a cigarette, sixty-five years ago. I can see the wrinkles, the cigarette. I have a very visual memory. I started visualizing a place where George lived, and from there, I invented a whole life for him. But one always writes about one's self in a certain way. There's no way you can write about anything that you know as well as yourself. In a certain sense, whatever is imagined is always based on an inner sense of self. Now, I don't know what that means, particularly after reading in the *Times* today about all the discoveries about the brain. I don't know where the invention of stories comes from. With the violin, you have to begin with some kind of musical ability; you can't sing without an ability to sing. Then you need training. I think you need training for everything.

**LT**  Before you wrote *Poor George*, had you been writing short stories?

**PF**  Yes. I've been writing since I was seven. I wrote my first story ever, when I was seven, about a robber who comes into a house and kills everybody, but miraculously they all come alive. Actually, I sent out a lot of stories in between working for a living. I kept getting them back, except for two, which the *Negro Digest*—which is what it was called then—published. I was in my twenties, and they tried to find out if I were black.

**LT**  Was it because you write black characters?

**PF**  Yes, that's what I was writing about: black. I didn't feel any constraint about writing about anything, except kind of ordinary constraints of life. It seemed to me that the tracks hadn't been made yet, in certain areas—by me. So, I made my own tracks, not that there weren't lots of tracks around.

**LT**  There's a fearlessness in your work. As you just said, you didn't feel those constraints. Most white writers do.

**PF**  I think it's not fearlessness as much as a kind of innocence. I think it was fixed in my mind when I was very little. There's a scene in *Borrowed Finery* that occurred in my brief time with my parents in Hollywood. I had locked myself out one night, my parents were at a party, and I stayed with neighbors. When I came back the next morning, my father had brought home a different woman from my mother. I said, "Daddy, daddy," coming up the stairs to his room. He rose up in the blankets—you know what a man looks like with blankets falling off of him—and in a rage. He grabbed me up and rushed downstairs with me, into the kitchen. There was a black maid ironing. He raised his hand to spank me, and she said, "Mr. Fox, that isn't fair." She rescued me. It must have taken so much courage for her to do that in 1929. I was very struck by that. I think what it did was, it instantly opened a kind of corridor, so that I went down it. Not because I was fearless, but because it was there. It just presented itself.

**LT**  All of your novels are about justice and injustice.

**PF**  I feel very strongly about that.

**LT**  In *The Western Coast*, your third novel, Annie's friend Cletus, who's black, is beaten up. It's a horrible scene. Annie's relationship with him changes because he can't continue to have the same feelings he had about white people after that.

**PF**  Cletus is based on a dear friend of mine who is dead now. He had a white mother and a black father. He didn't get beaten up. The ease between Annie and Cletus is based on my relationship with him. You take certain things from life, then you enlarge or diminish them. You ornament them or leave them plain. You strain out the truth. Years ago, when I was looking at a manuscript of mine that was on the floor, turning the pages, suddenly this brain bulb went off. I thought, I have to try to tell the truth, even when it's *and* and *the*. This was around the time that Mary McCarthy had claimed even Lillian Hellman's *ands* and *thes* were lies. My own thought is that we can't know the truth, but we can struggle for it, swim toward it, fight for it.

LT  Toward the end of *The Western Coast*, which takes place in LA during World War II, Annie drives cross-country with Mason White, a black soldier. She gives him a lift to Texas and sees the racism in America—they can't go into many places.

PF  That happened to me. I picked up a black soldier, and we were thrown out of a dozen places in Texas, so many bar-cafés in these little one-store towns. These old men—everybody else had been drafted—they'd be rattling their bones at us. I said, "But he's a soldier, how can you?" They said, "Well, we got our ways down here." I remember the idiocy and limitation of what they said. I didn't feel it at the time to be an idiotic limitation. I do now. I felt it then as a wall that wouldn't give way. I just knew it would never give way with those people.

LT  You have a visual memory and write powerful visual images. In *Poor George*, you write of George's distress and his troubled relationship with his wife, Emma: "There was a boiling sea of acid in his stomach—he longed for a pill. She dropped a cup and the handle broke." You can see him agitated, their tension.

PF  I think that also there's a certain thing that happens—that there is silence between actions. There's so much silence in our lives, despite all of the terrible noise every day. There's an awful silence in between things.

LT  You leave a lot of space between characters, and inside characters' minds. It makes for a lot of anxiety.

PF  I know, in writing it too.

LT  In *Desperate Characters*, your second novel, and *Poor George*, the middle class isn't allowed to enjoy its comforts.

PF  No! That's why I'm not read!

LT  In *Desperate Characters*, Sophie Bentwood can't enjoy eating in the garden of her Brooklyn house because of a wild cat. George Mecklin's house is invaded by the delinquent teenager he sort of adopts. The Bentwoods's summer house is vandalized, which goes back to your first ever story about robbers.

PF But the Bentwoods don't miraculously come alive; they're not killed. I took a rather uneasy pleasure in writing about a family who were getting eaten, getting eaten to death, for being so opulent and luxurious. Summer people.

LT The neighbors are enraged at them. George Mecklin's also enraged. You write, "George felt as if his own personal army had just fixed bayonets." He's a teacher, supposedly civilized, a middle-class man. Much of your imagery about him, your metaphors, uses militaristic language and is violent.

PF I think it's what certain people in this country would use; I wouldn't say, "with his cutlass drawn." The militaristic imagery seems apropos to me. I have a certain sense of what suits and doesn't suit in my range, inside of my range.

LT Like Edith Wharton, you're able to make inner worlds visible through external objects. The cup's handle breaking, the image of a personal army in him. You internalize through what's external, to create a psychological space. Did you read her?

PF She and Henry James, whom I admire a great deal, didn't have as much effect on me as Willa Cather and Thomas Hardy. I love two of Cather's books so much, *Death Comes for the Archbishop* and *The Shadows on the Rock*. Of course, there's George Eliot, whom I love. D. H. Lawrence was a great favorite of mine, I have read him over and over. His blood and sex ideology gets in the way of his finer observations and philosophical musings. I think ideologies are terrible for people—any kind. We have to be very careful to avoid them, and sometimes we can't.

LT Your characters give way to their ideology, to what they're in, or fight it—feel oppressed by the middle class or against it, like Otto Bentwood's partner, Charlie, in *Desperate Characters*. Otto tells him there's no alternative. In your novels, there's a sense that they're living inside something. Some fight it, some don't.

PF That's a very accurate description. I never thought of it exactly that way. But I don't think about my books in a way that a very good reader would think about them.

LT How do you think about them?

**PF**  I see things I like in some of my children's books. I like the section about Paul Robeson in *The Coldest Winter*. It's very hard for me to say. There's something I think about age that makes you feel, there's a certain sense, that you've done what you could do to ameliorate the condition of life, and it's very limited. Unless you're Madame Curie.

**LT**  In *The Western Coast*, you approach World War II and the Communist Party in America through Annie's experience of them. She's a drifter. One of her lovers, Myron Eagle, says to her, "You must make judgments. How can a person live without them?" That's a central question in your work.

**PF**  I feel it in my own life. You can't go around with your mouth open, because some buzzard will fly into it. Or some cobra will strike. I think you have to be able to give up judgments, when it's time. But you have to make them too. Otherwise, everything is disorder and chaos.

**LT**  Max, for instance, in *The Western Coast*, is in the Party, but he steps back from its ideology and observes it. He's an incredibly interesting character because of that.

**PF**  I think that you have to be attached and detached at the same time—who knows to what extent we can be detached?—but enough so that you can see what it is that you're up to. I had an image once: a lynch mob, a victim, and a mediator. And I was all three. I didn't exclude myself from any group. In some way, that sense of being absolutely susceptible to all of it, to human flaws, to virtues, to circumstances, to experiences—has helped me a lot. Because I tend—as we all do—to close in on myself; I have to keep it, especially when I write.

**LT**  You never let any of your characters off the hook. You don't write stories of redemption, which, from my point of view, is an American disease.

**PF**  No, I know, it's "Have a good day!" I wrote recently to the Royal Folio Society in England. I owed them seventy-five words about Proust. I said that I'd gone one day to Père-Lachaise cemetery and had seen the tomb of Gurdjieff, a spiritual healer. It was covered with flowers and candles, some lit the morning or afternoon I was there. I found Proust's—black marble. And on it a little metal juice can that had contained frozen orange juice, and in it one small bramble rose. I wrote, Gurdjieff said we could reach a higher consciousness and be in control of our lives. Proust taught nothing, but he wrote the most extraordinary book of the 20th century, *In Search of Lost Time*. And he didn't believe in ordinariness. But the childish ideas, that smiley face! It's like naming the atom bomb the "peace bomb." It's a kind of perversity.

**LT**   In *Desperate Characters*, when Sophie and Otto go for a drive, she sees a poster of an Alabamian presidential candidate. You wrote: "His country, warned the poster—vote for him—pathology calling tenderly to pathology."

**PF**   That was based on George Wallace. (*laughter*)

**LT**   Your fourth novel, *The Widow's Children*, like *Desperate Characters*, takes place in a weekend. It's a very disturbed family romance. Laura, the mother, Clara, her daughter, her brothers, all have terrible relationships. The family is supposed to be celebrating. Laura keeps it a secret that her mother has just died. It's an intriguing withholding on her part, and strategy on your part as author.

**PF**   A lot of things went into that. I don't think in advance about psychology because then I'd be a psychologist. I think there is an impulse in Laura to keep it private. She was possessive about her mother's death and her mother, in a very primitive way. There are lots of reasons. She wanted to punish her daughter and her brothers. But that was also very primitive—to punish them for everything, for being themselves, for not paying attention to their mother, for neglecting her, for their laughter, for their lives. And then there was a child's secrecy. That is very significant for me: a child's secrecy and horror, because Laura was frightened by the death of her mother. If she didn't say it, then it didn't happen.

**LT**   Like magical—

**PF**   Magical thinking, exactly. Her main reason can fit under the subtitle "mischief," of a certain psychological bullying, viciousness, revenge. There are other reasons, but they're less significant.

**LT**   *The Widow's Children* is structured in sections: Corridor, Drinks, Restaurant, specific places or times in which we expect things to happen or not to happen.

**PF**   The corridors of our lives are very different. We pass through them on our way to different places, but they also exist in themselves as places where things happen. In the restaurant, Laura looks around; Clara, all of them, are at the table, and they're moored in middle-class-life comfort. It's the hour of drink, persuasion, assuagement, and satisfaction, but not at Laura's table.

LT   The discomfort . . .

PF   It's very extreme, and Carlos, Laura's brother, can't wait to get away, to escape. They all want to escape, except for Laura's longtime friend Peter, who begins to sense, who sees how bad his choices were, but how inevitable.

LT   In the last paragraph of the novel, after Laura's mother's funeral, Peter remembers his childhood.

PF   I remember the last line. He had "known the cat and dog had been let out because he saw their paw marks braiding the snow, and felt that that day, he only wanted to be good." That's a kind of hope. We all wish we were good.

LT   Your characters all want to be good.

PF   Yes, I think that's true. Except for Laura.

LT   Each of your books is quite different from the others, though there are recurrent themes, like justice, injustice, people trying to see their own flaws, wanting to be good, honest. *The Widow's Children* stands out as something unto itself.

PF   It's so dense and compact a book. But I think in the last novel I wrote, *The God of Nightmares* [set in New Orleans], I kind of eased up on pounding away at my themes. That's really my most hopeful novel.

LT   Do you know why?

PF   No, except that it has a kind of easing.

LT   I think it's that, in the text itself, there's forgiveness.

PF   I think that's true. Oh, yes.

LT   There's the protagonist Helen's mother's letter to her. Her mother's dying, and she asks Helen to forgive her. She also forgives Helen.

PF She says you have to forgive me for myself. Because we're all helpless, the way we are, until we can strike a judgment, a point—that's why judgment comes in . . . I was just having a very complex thought. I don't know how to speak about it.

LT At the end, Helen discovers that Len, her husband, was in love with her best friend, Nina, years ago. She feels terribly betrayed.

PF But after their fight, she passes her hands over his body while he's asleep. Yes, it is forgiveness.

LT Was your complex thought about forgiveness?

PF We can't forgive easily. We have to take into account what was done. Various people get treated so badly. People get mistreated all the time. Black people were treated as an entity in a terrible way. We're such primitive creatures that we go by what we see, which is a different skin tone. Part of us is primitive.

LT Helen leaves New Orleans, marries Len, and the novel jumps into the future, when she thinks, "We were no more than motes of dust, drifting so briefly through a narrow ray of light that we could have no history." All of your characters experience that.

PF Yes, it's a kind of profound life melancholy. But it's offset by feelings of affection for other people and, in this case, particularly for people in the French Quarter, who took Helen in, so to speak. She had such a good time when they told their stories.

LT The secondary characters are wild, vivid figures. It's a war novel, like *The Western Coast*, but even more so. People go to war, come back, and don't, which is felt in the entire city.

PF Everything was made very precious by that sense of leave-taking. I just suddenly remembered the black man looking at the ship, and Helen and Nina saying, "What do you think he was thinking about?" Nina says, "Getting away." I did see a black man looking at a ship while living on the Mississippi. But I don't know if he was longing to get away.

LT Your fifth novel, *A Servant's Tale*, begins with two words, "Ruina! Ruina!" It covers a lot of time and history. Luisa Sanchez is a character of great abjection. As a child, she comes to New York, America—El

Norte—from San Pedro, where her mother was a maid, her father, the son of a plantation owner. When she grows up, Luisa decides to be a maid.

PF  You know what one of the reviewers said about that? A black woman in *The New York Times* wrote, "Why didn't she pull herself together, go to college, and get a degree?" It's like a corporate person rearranging a book of taxes, when they say it should go here in this column rather than here.

LT  Women writers are meant to write women characters who uplift the sex, like black writers—women and men—are urged to uplift the race. By your having Luisa make that decision, it flies in the face of—

PF  The American Dream.

LT  Horatio Alger, middle-class values. The novel confronts claims and feelings—ideologies—that Americans hold dear. Luisa wants to be a servant.

PF  Americans hold family values dear, even as they're killing their own children. I think that people in terrible situations lie to themselves about the situations they're in. I feel that lying is the great human activity; being right is the great human passion. Because if you're not right, you're nothing.

LT  Luisa marries Tom, a public-relations manager; they met at a political meeting in Columbia University. You feel part of his interest in her is her ethnicity, her so-called authenticity, and his wanting to overcome his middle-class ways. Then he tries to change her. But Luisa will not be changed by anyone or anything.

PF  Yes. This is what has happened to her: she wants her childhood back. She doesn't give it up until the end of the book, when she's able to think about something else. She wonders about Maura, one of the boarders in her parents' apartment. Luisa is the victim of herself. She's given everything over to reconstituting, discovering, her own terrible, lovely childhood and her grandmother. That's what she wants. She goes back to San Pedro and discovers that it's all changed, but the old witch is there. Gradually, in that last section, she recognizes it, without being able to name it, but the only way a reader knows that she's recognized it is that she can think of something else, in a way that's absolutely free of everything.

LT  Thinking about a person other than herself gives her the possibility of another future.

PF  I knew that she wasn't going to act the same way afterward. Even though so many years had passed, and she hadn't seen Ellen Dove, her black friend, I thought Luisa would contact her again and see about getting a law degree or something. (*laughter*) Then there was the last story in *The Coldest Winter*, "Frank."

LT  One of the boys you were teaching.

PF  Yes. Narcissism is not a good thing to have in the sense that you fill in everything with yourself, and people suffer so. You don't just have to be an indulged, rich child to be narcissistic. In fact, it's the opposite. The poor children. The world's filled up with questions of the self and the sense of the self. It's a dreadful, agonizing torture. And that's what happens to people, it seems to me, who have deprived, difficult, complex lives—when it's very extreme, out of some kind of alarm, everything in one's self—whatever it is—rushes to fill in all the spaces. So I used not the usual, sentimental relativism, that is, something larger than the self, but something other than the self.

LT  That's a very important distinction. You wanted Frank to go to an observatory and look through the big telescope, to see the stars.

PF  I had taken a course with Professor Motz, Lloyd Motz, professor of astronomy at Columbia. This was in the 1950s. I had a year with him, and I couldn't go ahead because I hadn't been to high school. I had only been there for three months. I didn't have the trigonometry I would have needed. I also couldn't go on with geology, which I loved.

LT  You had only three months of high school?

PF  Yes, pretty much. But I went to Columbia for four years, and managed other courses outside of the science courses. I'll tell you, my father was a terribly irresponsible man. He had a lot of charm, but he was an alcoholic.

LT  In your memoir *Borrowed Finery*, when you were going to meet the daughter that you had given up for adoption, you wrote, "In the face of great change, one has no conscience." You were hoping the plane would crash.

PF  That's right.

LT  When your characters have to face change, they'll do or think anything.

Again, you're fearless; your characters don't couch their thoughts. Most writers would avoid their characters thinking what yours do.

PF   My husband, Martin, thinks it's because I didn't go to college. (*laughter*)

LT   Your characters have prejudices. Again, white novelists mostly shy away from writing about race, which is obviously a major subject.

PF   Yes, it is. It seems so important to me. My friend Mason Roberson, who was a writer and part of the Harlem Renaissance, lived in Carmel for a while. We used to have very funny phone calls. He wrote continuity for *Sam Spade*, and one day he called me up when I was living in San Francisco. He said, "I have a question to ask you." I said, "Shoot." He said, "What's 'shortnin' bread'?" (*laughter*)

LT   You also write about your mother in *Borrowed Finery*. You go to see her after thirty-odd years, when she's dying. She offers you a family photograph, but then she hides it under her bed covers.

PF   She was such a savage that she didn't try to conceal anything about herself, though she concealed the picture very effectively. There was something remarkable about her that way; she would never pretend to be anything. I spent very little time with her, but once when she was in New York, with my father when they first came back from Europe, she was in a little brownstone on the East Side. I remember looking down a flight of stairs, and there was a brown, straw baby carriage with a hood. She looked down at it and said, "You know, the woman whose carriage that is killed her baby last week. Isn't it interesting to look down and see that carriage?" She was a terror for me. Any creature can give birth and walk away, and I thought that's what she'd done.

LT   Maybe the one thing you got from her of value was her honesty.

PF   Exactly, that's what was remarkable about her. She never tried to be any different than she was.

LT   I want to ask you about friends, groups, if you saw or see yourself as part of a literary movement. So many literary histories make assumptions about writers in that way.

PF   No, I don't feel that I'm in any particular group or movement. It's hard for me to feel that I belong to any group. That's a limitation for me, in myself. It's partly because I was always on the outskirts as a child—of my own life, in my family. As a writer, I feel like one voice among many. I hope that I don't dishonor the art of writing as I am passing through. It's my hope that I don't damage it in any way.

LT   Was it a struggle for you, the response to your books when they came out, and your novels going out of print?

PF   It was, but I've gone on. When *The Widow's Children* was turned down by Harcourt Brace, by Bill Goodman, who had taken *Poor George* on, he said it was the best novel I had written so far, but that my track record was very poor. That was a terrible thing—the track record idea. Of course, what else is new? This is a country so nakedly based on money. Other places try to conceal it.

LT   You said you didn't want to dishonor writing. That would be impossible. Your writing is truly wonderful. You are a great writer.

PF   Thank you. That's lovely to hear. I don't know what to say.

LT   Are you going to write another novel?

PF   I'm working on a short novel. It's called *A Light in a Farmhouse Window*. It takes place in contemporary France. There's a little part of it that goes back to 1321, when heretics occupied some small villages in the Pyrenees. They were the Cathars, and they were, like the Albigensians, completely wiped out by the Dominican priests. I'll tell you one story that I use: A Dominican priest was describing a village late at night to some horsemen, a gang, and one of the Crusaders tells him there were only twenty heretics in the village. The total population was two hundred. The Dominican priest said, "Kill them all. God will know his own."

# Jonathan Franzen and Donald Antrim

JONATHAN FRANZEN was born in Illinois in 1959. He is the author of the novels *Freedom*, *The Corrections*, *Strong Motion*, and *The Twenty-Seventh City*; the essay collections *Farther Away* and *How to Be Alone*; a personal history, *The Discomfort Zone*; and a translation of Frank Wedekind's *Spring Awakening*. He lives in New York City and Santa Cruz, California.

DONALD ANTRIM was born in New York in 1958. He is the author of the novels *Elect Mr. Robinson for a Better World*, *The Verificationist*, and *The Hundred Brothers*, and a memoir, *The Afterlife*. In 1999, *The New Yorker* named him one of the "Best Writers Under 40." In 2013, he was named a MacArthur Fellow. He teaches at the MFA program at Columbia University and lives in Brooklyn.

**DONALD ANTRIM** It's been nearly ten years since the publication of your second novel, *Strong Motion*, and a few more years since *The Twenty-Seventh City* came out. I'd like to hear you talk about what went on during the years after *Strong Motion*—how your new novel came to be and what was happening in your personal life and in your family. I also want to hear some of your ideas about writing in general. Before we begin, I want to say that *The Corrections* seems, to me, profoundly and substantively a departure from your earlier books. In each of your novels, you devise intricate, sophisticated plots. You bring the reader along on a ride. *Strong Motion* and *The Twenty-Seventh City* both grow out of daring, somewhat implausible-seeming gambits: massive earthquakes in the suburbs outside Boston, the appointment of a corrupt Asian Indian woman as chief of the St. Louis police. As you think about them now, with *The Corrections* nearing publication, would you say that your first two novels belong together?

**JONATHAN FRANZEN** Yes, in that I continue to be interested in the dramatic intersection of personal, domestic stories with larger social stories. In the first two books, there were these large, externalized, heavily plotted dramas, at the focus of which were individual families. The new book goes about managing the drama very differently.

**DA** You were younger when you wrote those books—considerably younger when you wrote the first.

**JF** I was about thirteen, in some ways, when I wrote the first book. Approximately eighteen when I wrote the second.

**DA** Well, if I understand what you're saying, then—

**JF** I was a kid. And let me step back here and say that I was a very late kid—growing up, I had parents who were much older than I. To a substantial degree, my social life consisted of interactions with serious grown-ups. And in a funny way that's what the first book, *Twenty-Seventh City*, was: a conversation with the literary figures of my parents' generation. The great '60s and '70s postmoderns. I wanted to feel like I belonged with them, much as I'd spent my childhood trying to be friends with my parents and their friends. A darker way of looking at it is that I was trying to impress them. The result, in any case, was that I adopted a lot of that generation of writers' concerns—the great postwar freak-out, the Strangeloveian inconceivabilities, the sick society in need of radical critique. I was attracted to crazy scenarios.

**DA** Is this urge to become a younger peer of those writers who were prominent when you and I were growing up—

**JF** And we're talking about Pynchon, DeLillo, Gaddis, Heller, Barth—

**DA** Certainly. But it sounds to me as if, with *The Corrections*, you wanted to make those conspiracy plots fall away, and that you wound up with a different kind of emotional landscape. For instance, Chip Lambert, the middle child in your fictional family, gets involved in a variety of dubious and self-destructive scenarios. There's a love affair with his student, and, toward the end of the novel, a trip to post-Soviet Lithuania, which is fairly disastrous. Chip's behavior seems like a result of his financial incompetency and his questionable sense of himself as a man in the world, more than a reaction to enormous forces beyond his control.

**JF** Actually the forces are substantially the same, but in the new book they take the form of interior urges and anxieties, rather than outward plot elements. We may freak out globally, but we suffer locally. Not that I take any particular credit for this shift of emphasis. Jane Smiley has this theory of an alternation of literary generations. Smiley thinks there are two fundamental possible preoccupations for the novelist. One is a kind of venturing forth to discover the wonders of the world, à la *Robinson Crusoe* or *Don Quixote*. That school of outward-looking fiction reaches its culmination in *Candide*, in which the world turns out to be full of horrors. Voltaire's lesson is: go home, cultivate your garden. And so the adventurous world-seeking novel is succeeded by the great 19th-century domestic novel. Which itself then culminates in Kafka: you can stay home, but home is a horror, too. Within American literature you find the venturing-forthness in Twain and Hemingway, the at-homeness in Wharton and O'Connor. The dichotomy is gender-specified to some extent. But I feel like I'm essentially participating in one of those swings, a swing away from the boys-will-be-boys *Huck Finn* thing, which is how you can view Pynchon, as adventures for boys out in the world. At a certain point, you get tired of all that. You come home.

**DA** Speaking of boys, or men, in the world, you've written for *Harper*'s about the novelist as an increasingly marginalized figure in American society. Do you have feelings or anxieties that you've been aware of in recent years, not so much about writing a particular book, but about living as a writer of fiction?

**JF** I look at my father, who was in many ways an unhappy person, but who, not long before he got sick, said that the greatest source of satisfaction in his life had been going to work in the company of other workers. He got up every weekday morning for forty-plus years, put on a nice suit and a hat, went to this wonderfully structured environment, and did work that he perceived to be important and constructive. I think any artistic child of a businessman is prone to a sense of the *slightness* of what he or she is doing. Of the uselessness of art. This uselessness is intrinsic, of course, and that's part of art's charm. But it's useless nonetheless. And when you compound this with the general dimunition in the stature of the novelist since the days of Hemingway and Fitzgerald, who were celebrities to a degree that novelists of like caliber nowadays simply can't be, when you compound this with the sense of being in one's father's shadow, well, you risk feeling like a little kid. My first response to this feeling of smallness was to try to know everything, to exude confidence and total command. But when the world refuses to be changed by what you're writing—when the world takes, essentially, no note of it—it gets harder and harder to persuade yourself that your desire for total control, and your head-on engagement with Big Issues, is meaningful. So I've spent a lot of the last decade retooling. There were also changes in my private life that made it clear that the premises I'd begun with were no longer sufficient.

DA  Let's talk about your private life. I suspect that your experiences with family, and what I know about what you've gone through during this chunk of time, have a huge bearing on the ways in which family becomes, in this new novel, more central and preoccupying than in earlier work.

JF  Well, my father died in 1995. Up until then I'd been trying, sporadically and unsuccessfully, to write a book that was similar to the first two, with an elaborate, externalized, and exceedingly complicated plot. Within a few months of his death, I began writing stuff that came from a very different place.

DA  During those years, you actually worked over and discarded a huge amount of material. I have the impression of you tossing out about three or four possible manuscripts.

JF  Yes and no. Even before *Strong Motion* was published, I had an idea for a third book. I tried to write it, I found it wasn't working, and so I changed it. And I kept changing it, and changing it, and eventually nothing was left of the original, although it was still connected to the original in the way that my body now is connected with my body at the age of twelve—all the cells replaced, but very gradually. Finally, about six years in, I said, To hell with all that. Material that was more urgent had announced itself.

DA Other things were happening in life as well. Several years ago, your mother passed away.

JF Yeah, my mother more recently. Frankly, though, the thing that enabled me to get those first two books written was that I had a very stable home life. I'd gotten married pretty much right out of college, to someone I'd gone to school with, also a writer, and we had a very quiet, very steady domestic life that we dedicated to reading and writing. That's really all there was, except for tiny little doses of family and an honorary friend or two. Ours was essentially a universe of two, set up as a kind of antidote to the overwhelming family universes that each of us had come from. As long as that marriage lasted, I could just shut down questions on certain important personal topics. Is this relevant?

DA You're doing fine. Keep talking.

JF Well, at a certain point our universe of two started breaking down. My first book was a big success. Her first book she couldn't sell. By the time I was writing the second novel, there were tensions. And, in ways that are terrible to recall, those tensions just got worse. The early '90s were taken up with ever-more-desperate attempts to preserve a marriage, and then, finally, after that bargaining stage was over, accepting and mourning the death of this immensely important marriage. And meanwhile my father's mind was dissolving with Alzheimer's, and my mother was getting sick. Maybe it's no surprise that the book I was trying to write in those years would change. What seemed to me important was changing weekly, daily, almost hourly. I think the last time my wife and I were together in public was at my father's memorial service. Not long after that, something loosened up. There was a space in which I could actually start to write again, a little bit, something that was mine and not ours.

DA Let me ask you something. You're talking about a growing discontent with work that had been supported by the conditions of your life, followed by a period during which your family, not only your marriage, but your own family—

JF All the people who were most important in my life—

DA Are no longer there. Given that you were having these experiences that you couldn't control, to what extent were you conscious of exploring what was happening as it happened?

JF I'm uncomfortable with the idea that suffering creates material for art, or that conflict and trouble are what the novelist thrives on. I think it's more accurate to say that the attempt to be a living, productive artist is often what creates the trouble and the conflict. I had an immense conflict of loyalties, for example, regarding my marriage. I felt explicitly that if I would just stop being a writer, I could make the marriage work. And it wasn't just my marriage. My mother had my father on her hands. Ever more trouble out there. And I would go back home to the Midwest for four days, and then I wouldn't go again for six, eight months. I had to preserve my emotional equilibrium in order to do my work. I felt terribly guilty about that, because in a sense, why not take three months and go and really help out? But I couldn't, I would have gone crazy. We would've been irritating each other the whole time. But—and this is my point—the fact of who I am is what would have created the irritation. And who I am is a man who writes novels.

DA You're describing something pretty difficult, the guilt over not being able to go home, and in the meantime exploiting, if not the more concrete and remembered experiences and events of family life, then something immediate in your relationships to your mother and to your father, just as you are losing them. So, I'm imagining that this could be a fairly frightening time.

JF Oh. Of course.

DA Do you also feel guilty for having written the book?

JF No. I don't. Not at all. It's akin to the flip side, as I keep trying to stress. There's a flip side. That I was writing the book was what was creating much of my trouble.

DA Yes.

JF And the book in turn stands as a record of who I am. I wouldn't wish it away any more than I would wish my personality away, or my privacy and individuality. It was a taboo-a-week in terms of its creation. I was constantly thinking, You can't write about *that*. Each taboo was accompanied by a set of technical problems—how to make the material interesting enough to justify violating the taboo. But no, I don't feel guilty. The most important experience of my life, really, to date, is the experience of growing up in the Midwest with the particular parents I had. I feel as if they couldn't fully speak for themselves, and I feel as if their experience—by which I mean their values, their experience of being alive, of being born at the beginning of the century and dying towards the end of it, that whole American experience they had—I feel as if I'm part of that, and it's part of me. One of my enterprises in the book is to memorialize that experience, to give it real life and form. Even if both of my parents would have personally hated the book, which they may very well have, I still don't feel guilty about it.

DA Writing this novel was a kind of constant correction against some other novel you could have written but didn't want or need to, and it's a correction against something that might've been easier, in favor of something that feels dangerous.

JF Right.

DA Prohibited.

JF I did a nonfiction piece five years ago for *The New Yorker* about the tobacco industry and my own cigarette smoking. At the time, I was still concealing from my mother, whose father had died of lung cancer, that I was myself a cigarette smoker. I was talking one day with my editor at *The New Yorker*, Henry Finder, and he said: "How about the tobacco industry, do you have any interest in that?" I said: "That is the one thing I absolutely can't write about." And he said: "Therefore you must write about it." And that became a kind of rallying cry for the book. The more I felt, Don't write that, the more I knew I was on the right track.

DA Of course, writing the thing you can't write is an opportunity for a certain amount of destabilization and confusion.

JF It's bound up with shame. The resistance manifested itself as shame. "No, I can't be that straightforward and, no, I can't drop that mantel of utter mastery of fact and total control of data, because then I'll appear as this weak, puny boy, and not as the sort of striding, dadlike man that I wanted to be." Simply to write a book that wasn't dressed up in a swashbuckling, Pynchon-sized megaplot was enormously difficult. I spent years trying to somehow make it nonetheless work before I realized this thing's dead, and no matter how terrifying it is to let go of that kind of plotting, I have to let go.

DA Were the Lamberts in those earlier versions?

JF The Lamberts crept in little by little. I was developing the character of Chip, and, as a matter of process, I was trying to learn to write scenes in which I would conceive of a character and then make the character extremely uncomfortable. With Chip, I had the idea of a would-be East Village hipster—and then here come his grotesquely square Midwestern parents on precisely the day when his life is falling apart. Hence Enid and Alfred Lambert. Eventually I threw away almost everything that was not Lambert-related.

DA *The Corrections*, like the earlier two novels, is, however different, none-theless a big, complex book. It carries us along, and to me at least it's much more involving than the earlier books. I think this has something to do with the plot unfolding to reveal its own origins in choices made by the characters. The Lamberts' lives are complicated again and again by their own actions, their lives are complicated by their own lives. In *The Corrections*, the conspiracies become personal. I'm thinking of Alfred's Parkinsonism, his slow decline, as a kind of conspiracy of the body against itself. Alfred in dementia envisions a conspiracy of sentient turds. At the end of his life he imagines his nurses in a conspiracy against him. His paranoia is an illness of the mind created as a symptom of an illness of the body.

JF These are life-sized conspiracies. Gary, the older son, believes that his wife and children are conspiring to cast him as clinically depressed so as to win certain domestic battles, particularly the battle over whether his family is going to go back to the Midwest for Christmas. Gary becomes deeply paranoid himself, wondering not only whether he may indeed be mentally ill, but also whether his wife and kids are conspiring to *make him feel* mentally ill. There's all the stuff that you might get in a typical conspiracy novel, except that here the conspiracy is a family matter. Likewise Gary's contorted attempts to avoid turning into his father, and his paranoid suspicion that he's failing. His attempts to improve on his father's life make him all the more like his father.

DA Were you very aware, while writing *The Corrections*, of the Lambert children embodying or rejecting distinct aspects of their parents' strong, domineering personalities?

JF To say that the book is thematically self-conscious is to put it mildly. I come from a kind of old-fashioned Midwest, and I live in a technocorporate, postironic, cool, late-late-late Eastern world. The two worlds hardly ever talk to each other, but they're completely, constantly talking to one another inside me. And certainly my enterprise in the book, and probably the enterprise of most novelists at some level, is to take different strains in their own character, different modules in their own personality, and create whole characters on the page. I have my parents talking to me in my head and then other parts of myself talking back. I think this is potentially an interesting conversation. Something almost everyone does is vow not to be like his or her parents. At the same time, we mourn certain ways in which we're not like them. Talking with one's parents becomes a way of talking about the changes that have been wrought in the last fifty years by the various technological and political developments that we've seen in our lifetimes. Again, these are issues that the postmoderns were also writing about, but presented in a way that makes them more personal, relates them more to the family romance and the emotional life of the author.

DA  Sometimes we create ourselves as our parents to the extent that we rebel against them.

JF  Right, so there's this drama of trying to correct, of trying to be different. This is what much of life is about.

DA Did you find in writing this novel that the converse could also be true, that the extent to which you accepted your parents in you gave you some freedom to be not them, someone of your own creation?

JF  Yes. Here's an example. There were about twenty years during which I basically couldn't talk to my mom, and I concealed everything about myself from her. Sometimes I could hardly stand to be in the same room with her. This sense of mortification started at about age twelve and continued into my mid-thirties. Some of it had to do with her refusal to see what kind of person I was, and her specific disapproval of writing as a career. A different person, a different son, might have shrugged it off. And to some extent I did shrug it off. Or, actually, what I did was get married. I found a woman who liked what I liked. But then around the time my father got sick and my marriage was falling apart, something changed with my mom. She became more forgiving of all of her children, certainly of me. In the five years before she died, she underwent a transformation of her own. She discovered that she actually was happier being a less critical and more generous person. And as that happened, suddenly this window opened in me, and I realized, Well, you know, I'm actually a lot like her. I no longer had to deny that there was any connection between us, you know, I don't know how I ended up with this mom.

DA This oscillation between acceptance and rejection is something the Lambert children struggle with all the time. They struggle heroically to avoid coming home. But of course they do come back again, near the end of the book, for Christmas. Christmas is an obsession with Enid, reenacting the rituals that seem obsolete and sad, like the Advent calendar on the door.

JF It occurs to me, as we speak, that Christmas is Enid's novel. Christmas is the thing to be achieved. She wants it to have formal perfection. It's something she works on, she's obsessed with it, year round. Enid is an artist of Christmas, and she's tired of her daughter-in-law's inferior artwork. She'd like one last chance to produce a really good Christmas of her own. By which she means something old-fashioned — much as *The Corrections* itself is old-fashioned. And yet, because of the changes that have occurred in the family, and also because we live in a changed world, a fully old-fashioned kind of Christmas is no longer feasible. The holiday becomes, instead, a comic and tragic disaster. Well, probably more tragic than comic. I think of art in general, and certainly of a novel, which is an extremely conservative medium among the arts, as being about various familiar forms and rituals. There's nothing really new to say about the human condition, and so every novel is kind of a ritual reenactment, or retelling, of familiar stories, which proceed along expected but somehow satisfying lines. This ritual aspect is one reason why, for me, in a larger way, art in general and literature in particular have basically replaced the Christianity of my parents' generation.

DA Another way that the Lambert children all act out this business of escaping from home, or thinking that they're escaping from home, is through sex.

JF An escape from Alfred's puritanism.

DA Maybe I could just run through some of the sexual scenarios in the book. There are great, long passages of sex.

JF God, I was unaware of this, but go on.

DA Well, let's see, there's Chip's academic career-ending affair with his student Melissa. There's Denise's affair with the man in her father's office, another defining and destructive act. Later in life, Denise begins an obsessive, obliterative affair with the wife of the man backing her successful restaurant in Philadelphia. That's not a great idea on the face of it. Denise is pretty much undone by sex, and so is Gary, who I think of as the orderly, sentimental son. He seems bewildered and frustrated over sex, and the lack of sex, and its replacement by angry domestic fighting in his marriage. There is also, at one point, Enid's attempt to give Alfred a blow job. She's trying to seduce him into using inside information to make financial investments that could change their lives. Alfred won't tolerate the suggestion of a shady financial move any more than he'll tolerate Enid's blow job, and you could say that Alfred's fear of a blow job causes Enid to feel, and possibly to be, poor.

JF  (*chuckling*)

DA  The evidence, to me, is of sex as a kind of report on the state of affairs between people who wind up alone.

JF  Oh, that's harsh.

DA  Is that too harsh?

JF  I think that's harsh. I think the sex is there partly because I feel like it's something I can write well about and I seldom see written about well, and so I naturally gravitate to it. But my breakthrough, the thing I learned in writing this book if I learned nothing else, was that a good way to write a scene, a good way to write a book, is to define a character by what he or she *wants*. Sex is useful to the storyteller because the wanting can be so extreme. The wanting is so blunt and ferocious. It's a great plot device; once you take away conspiring Indians, or serendipitous earthquakes, you need something else to drive the plot.

DA  Yes.

JF  These are hungry people. There may be a lot of sex in the book, but there's even more food. I feel as if I gravitated toward food and sex because I myself was hungry in a million ways—sexually hungry, literally hungry, hungry to have a new book done, hungry for attention as any novelist is. But I was also looking for a counterpoint to the relative abstraction of the cultural or political or linguistic preoccupations that drove the previous generation of big novels. Saying "I'm hungry and I want something" is a form of correction, a correction towards more traditional and humane motives for a novel.

**DA** There are many, many corrections in *The Corrections*.

**JF** Market corrections, and prisons. And Chip is obsessed with making corrections to his screenplay that he's trying and failing to sell.

**DA** Enid's attempt to correct her mood with what turns out to be a club drug that she gets from a bogus doctor on a cruise ship. And Alfred thinking about his young daughter Denise and about how he planned to give her some of the gentleness and indulgence that he withheld from Gary and Chip. But then you say, and I'm quoting, "What made correction possible also doomed it."

**JF** Yes, a bunch of things going on there. For one thing, I've found that it's possible to go for years or even decades without telling yourself the truth about your life. The most important corrections of the book are the sudden impingements of truth or reality on characters who are expending ever larger sums of energy on self-deception or denial; and what's being denied, of course, is usually awful news. Death, for example. I also increasingly consciously saw the book as part of a conversation about American progress, the idea of self-invention. We live in an age of self-improvement, in a self-improving country with a long history of self-improvement; and I am reasonably obsessed with *Gatsby*. As for the particular line, "What made correction possible also doomed it," in a sense that's simply the tragic spirit. Every gain is offset by a loss, and most losses bring some sort of a gain. That's the spirit of the book as a whole. Beyond that, I'd rather not interpret the line. I think it's interpretable, but I don't want to be the one to do it.

**DA** That's fine, that's fine.

**JF** But where does that leave us?

**DA** Well, that leaves me with another question. You mentioned that you have a self-conscious awareness of your own thematic material.

**JF** Oh God, yes.

**DA** Describe what you think the thematic concerns of this novel are, aside from what we've already talked about. More to the point, what do you think your large preoccupations look like, now that you've written three novels?

**JF** I'm not sure what my big preoccupations will turn out to be. We were talking earlier about the sense of being a threatened writer with a threatened sense of importance, and therefore a threatened sense of personhood. From my perspective, I feel like I'm part of an embattled, retreating cultural minority that cares about books and about the values that have traditionally been associated with literature—tragic and comic values. But these values are threatened by materialism, materialism in two senses. First the sense of preoccupation with things and with money. Potential readers are busy experiencing other entertainment and earning the money to buy the fancy technological equipment necessary to enjoy it, and so forth. And then, even more to the point, there's a vulgar intellectual materialism that is encapsulated, for instance, in the currency of the term "clinical depression." If I say, "At that time in my life I was clinically depressed," in a way this ends the conversation. It replaces a potentially interesting story with a very simple, material story. "I was clinically depressed. The chemicals in my brain were bad. And I took this material thing into my body, and then the chemicals in my brain were better, and I was better." Obviously I'm not trying to minimize the seriousness of actual profound depression. But what we gain as science learns how to correlate the organic with the psychological, we lose in terms of the larger conversation. The poetic, the subjective, and particularly the *narrative* account of what a person is and what a life means—I feel like the novelist's vision is engaged in a turf war with the scientific, biological, medical account.

DA The conversation around something like clinical depression forecloses a larger conversation about grief or loss.

JF  Exactly.

DA  Or about changes in life that are frightening or even terrifying.

JF  Or about harmful changes in society that we might want to resist.

DA  I think the novel, and the business of being a novelist, and thinking not only about one's own position as a novelist in the world, but also about the lives of characters who populate a novel—this is a way to keep the larger conversation from being foreclosed.

JF  I hope so. I certainly see that in your own novels.

DA  We'll talk about that another time. I have one more thing to ask you. Is *The Corrections* the book you want it to be? Are you proud of it?

JF   I wrote much of it very quickly. I wrote 80 percent of it in the last year. I was on a federal jury when I was finishing it. I came to the point when I had two days left to write the last section of the last chapter and then the epilogue. I wrote each of them in a day, and I finished each day crying and not sure why, whether because the content was reminding me of sad content in my own life or because I was letting go of something that had given my life structure and meaning for nearly a decade. There was, as I was getting the last pages down, just this sense of grief. It nonetheless felt very sweet. When I handed the book in, I had a feeling I'd never had before and fear I will never have again—the feeling that I'd actually done what I set out to do. I'd spent a couple of years thinking, My God, if I can pull this off, it'll be good. But then I would get so terrified and excited by that prospect that I wouldn't sleep and wouldn't work until I fell back into my proper working mode, which is moderately depressed. Once I was moderately depressed again, I could continue to work. But at the very end, when I was done, I did have one moment of pure elation. Of Yeah! Okay!

# Mary Gaitskill
# and Matthew Sharpe

MARY GAITSKILL was born in Lexington, Kentucky, in 1954. Her books include the story collections *Bad Behavior* and *Don't Cry*, and the novel *Veronica*, which was nominated for the National Book Award and the National Book Critics Circle Award. Her work has appeared in *The New Yorker*, *Harper's Magazine*, *Esquire*, *The Best American Short Stories*, and *The O. Henry Prize Stories*. A graduate of the University of Michigan, where she earned her BA and won a Hopwood Award, Gaitskill is the recipient of a Guggenheim Fellowship.

MATTHEW SHARPE was born in New York City in 1962. He is the author of several works of fiction, including *Nothing Is Terrible*, *The Sleeping Father*, and *You Were Wrong*. A graduate of Oberlin College and Columbia University, where he earned his MFA, Sharpe has taught creative writing at Columbia, Bard College, New College of Florida, and Wesleyan University. His writing has also been featured in *BOMB*, *McSweeney's*, and *Zoetrope*, and has been translated into nine languages.

**MATTHEW SHARPE**  When did you think writing might be something that you would do as a vocation?

**MARY GAITSKILL**  When I was eighteen or so. I was indignant about things—it was the typical teenager sense of "things are wrong in the world and I must say something."

**MS**  Do you remember what you thought was wrong in the world?

**MG**  This will sound silly: it wasn't social injustice, some people being poor and others being rich, or anything like that. I was living in Toronto at the time. Every summer we'd turn the main street into a mall; we'd close out the traffic and there'd be street performers and people selling things. I used to sell flowers and trinkets, and the boyfriend I had was a frisbee player. He and his partner made money doing that. They were really good-looking guys and they'd take off their shirts and people went nuts over them in an extreme way; beyond reacting to what they were *actually* doing. They represented something to people—nonconformism, I guess, freedom. I thought it was fucked up. It was my first close-up reaction to watching people turn somebody else into something like a superstar. I thought it was gross—people taking their own creativity or spark and projecting it onto somebody else. Now I don't think that kind of projected idealism is all bad. I mean, I was a teenager then, so I was being very puritanical. I wonder if I wasn't also jealous of the objects of this adoration.

**MS**  When did you start writing the stories in *Bad Behavior*?

**MG**  When I was twenty-five or twenty-six.

**MS**  How many years did it take you to write that book?

**MG**  Six.

**MS**  Do you remember which story you started working on first?

**MG**  "Something Nice."

**MS**  That's the one about the woman who's temporarily being a prostitute.

**MG**  It's told from the man's point of view, a character people have wrongly described as stupid. Fred is a romantic person. I don't think it's stupid of him to entertain fantasies of love. A phrase I remember was, "Dumbbell Johns who fall in love with hookers," and I'm like, That's not stupid, that means he has *feelings*. You could say it's a little *foolish*, but that's different from *stupid*.

**MS**  *Bad Behavior* had a pretty big impact, right?

**MG**  For a book of short stories by an unknown, yes.

**MS**  And how did that affect you?

**MG**  It was life changing.

**MS**  Do tell.

**MG**  I was stunned—I mean, my agent couldn't sell any of the stories to magazines. I wasn't expecting it to get reviewed in *The New York Times* particularly; I thought it would maybe get one of those "Books in Brief" articles that now are the reviews.

**MS**  And how did it change your life?

**MG**  I was able to pay my student loans and eventually quit my job. I could buy nice clothes—

**MS**  What was your job at that time?

**MG**  I was a proofreader. All of this changed my psychological attitude as much as anything, though that took a while. It changed my whole idea of who I was, but it was uncomfortable because I felt like my public identity was far outsized compared to my private one. At the same time it was also constricted.

**MS**  Yeah, actually here are a few lines from "Today I'm Yours," a story in *Don't Cry*: "I did not realize I had made monsters, nor how strong they were, until the book was published and they lifted the roof off my apartment, scaled the wall, and roamed the streets in clothes that I never would've worn myself. Everywhere I went, it seemed, my monsters had preceded me, and by the time I appeared, people saw me through their aura." Was that your experience?

**MG**  Yeah. I was actually not a sophisticated person; I was lonely, socially ignorant, very shy. When I say that, people don't believe me because the stories were perceived as bold. I also could blurt things out that were quite forward, but that didn't mean I wasn't shy; I simply didn't know how to communicate very well. I've changed quite a bit, but I'm talking a long time ago. Suddenly I would be at these parties, or at dinners with, like, Sonny Mehta and some big agent. I had no idea what to say, and I felt that people expected me to be really sharp. They'd say things to me as if they were expecting me to hit the ball back really hard, and I would just freeze.

**MS** I see that in your characters a lot. There are these people who are unusually perceptive but are often trying to crack the code of some social situation: there is this constant effort to figure out who's doing what and who's where in the pecking order. There's often this sense of people standing at the edge of a party and wondering, Are all these people having a good time or are they as baffled as I am?

American culture and recent history are constantly woven into your books. In *Don't Cry* the Iraq war comes up explicitly in "The Arms and Legs of the Lake." "College Town, 1980" has the vibe of the recession that we had leading into the Reagan era. You're also constantly referencing pop music.

**MG** I don't think of it in terms of referencing it; it's just very poignant to me sometimes, the way music will hit a person at a certain moment or will be playing in a person's head. It's just a naturally expressive thing for me.

**MS** Yeah, there seem to be a number of dads in your stories who intentionally put on certain songs to try to recapture a feeling or to make up for certain lacks that they feel. There's Alison, the narrator of *Veronica*: "My father used to make lists of his favorite popular songs, ranked in order of preference. These lists were very nuanced, and they changed every few years. He'd walk around with the list in his hand, explaining why Jo 'G.I. Jo' Stafford was ranked just above Doris Day, why Charles Trenet topped Nat King Cole—but by a hair only. It was his way of showing people things about him that were too private to say directly." And then later in the book these singers go out of vogue and the father can't use them as shorthand for conveying his feelings.

You said in one interview about *Veronica* that you wished some of the critics had touched on the question of form and formlessness. Can you say more about what you meant by that?

**MG** Music is part of it. Music is a form that tends to give shape to rules, social mores, social attitudes, feelings—it does this in a very *beautiful*, fluid way. To me the issue of form and formlessness is most strong in the theme of mortality versus a human wish for immortality of a sort. Take, for example, the definition of beauty in fashion. Remember what Alison says at the beginning? She says when she was young she didn't know what *beautiful* was. She looked at this woman who everyone was saying was beautiful and she didn't even know what they were talking about. I experienced that when I was a child. If I loved someone I thought they were really beautiful. And then eventually, I began to get it, the social *concept* of beauty. Not that I think *beautiful* is completely imaginary, but beauty is so wide ranging and fluid. Yet there's a need to say: "This is what it is, and it's not changing; we're taking a picture of it to hold it still." It's like an impulse to put up a building meant to last forever. An urge to grab and hold something in place when nothing human can be grabbed and held in place. We come into these physical bodies . . . whatever we are takes this shape that is so particular and distinct—eyes, nose, mouth—and then it gradually begins to disintegrate. Eventually it's going to dissolve completely. It's a *huge* problem for people; we can understand it, but it breaks our hearts. And so we're constantly trying to pin something down or leave a trace that will last forever. "And this is the only immortality you and I may share, my Lolita . . ." What other immortality will anyone share?

**MS** There's a moment at the end when Veronica assumes a beautiful form in the dream of David, a minor character who takes in Veronica's cat after she dies of AIDS. He tells the dream to Alison, who's been narrating her friendship with Veronica throughout the novel. In the dream he's at a party at a beautiful mansion and describes the beautiful guests:

*There was one woman he noticed in particular; even though he saw her from behind, there was something familiar about her. She wore a beautiful man's suit tailored to fit her. On her head of gold-blond hair sat a fedora, angled rakishly. She was talking to two men, and even from behind, her poise and intellectual grace were visible. As if she could feel David's eyes on her, she turned to look at him. It was Veronica!*

Alison relates the dream to her sister and she says, "And that's what Veronica was really like, under all the ugliness and bad taste." I see that as one of the times when a character in your story uses form in a happy or useful way.

**MG** You could say that dream appeared in David's head as something from the other world conveyed to him in a form that he can understand and translate. It's also for his own benefit. He'd probably prefer to think that when people die, especially people who've had terrible lives, there's a possibility that they're going on to something ideal and beautiful. It's a compassionate gesture towards this woman, Veronica, but it's also comforting for him. Or you could say that it really is a communication from Veronica herself, letting him know, as the person who's taking care of her cat, that things are going well for her. She's putting it in a form that can be translated to human beings as good: a beautiful party, a beautiful home, a beautiful haircut.

MS  At the end of *Veronica* a fairy tale is reiterated. The novel begins with Alison describing how when she was a child her mother would read her the story of a wicked little girl who is sent to work for a rich family. At one point the family gives the girl a loaf of bread to take back to her mother. When she has to cross a swamp, rather than get her fancy shoes dirty, she puts the loaf of bread down using it as a bridge and sacrifices her mother's meal. Then she and the loaf of bread descend into this world of demons. One of the most amazing moments in this novel is when Alison describes not only hearing the story, but, since she is leaning against her mother, feeling the story. "I felt it in her body, I felt a girl who wanted to be too beautiful. I felt a mother who wanted to love her. I felt a demon who wanted to torture her. I felt them mixed together so you couldn't tell them apart." And then, at the end of the story, Alison projects herself and Veronica into this fairy tale by seeing the two of them as demons who become human by looking upon each other with pity. So this again seems to be an example where people project themselves into fantasies as a way to constitute themselves more salubriously.

MG  Fantasies can be very good for people. I had a conversation with someone recently who thought that sexual fantasy was always a by-product of damage to a person. I thought about that quite a bit . . . . I'm not entirely sure what she meant by it but it was an interesting idea to chew over, certainly. I tend to think a fantasy, if it's an obsessive fantasy, can be a way of retreading over and over again something that was painful for you in an attempt to heal it, so I suppose that it could be described as a product of damage. But I also think of it as a creative thing, a way to give form to something inchoate inside yourself. That's why Hans Christian Andersen's stories are powerful—they come from a deep place, like that story of the girl who trod on a loaf of bread. There's so much violence and cruelty in this story and yet also a sense of purity and redemption, since someone is able to escape a violent, painful knot they've gotten themselves into. So yeah, Alison could use that in her own mind to make sense of who she is in the world and what's happened. She has been bound in a dark place and although she's gotten free,

213

she's a marginal person outside the big story, you know, but her story also has its own power and beauty.

**MS** Did I understand you correctly that your friend said that sexual fantasies are the result of damage? That implies that people who aren't damaged, if there are such people, don't have sexual fantasies. I thought everybody had them.

**MG** Yes, most people do; I would find a person who didn't have them strange. I think she meant particularly elaborate, grotesque kinds of fantasies about things that she didn't really want to have happen to herself.

**MS** I have a relative who repeats the assertion that this whole business of everyone having a dark side is not true, that some people have "dark sides"—this is her term for it—and others don't, and she resents Freud for suggesting that everybody has this nasty person or animal within them who wants to kill and devour. My assertion is always that the scariest ones of all are the ones that don't believe they have a dark side.

**MG** Yeah, it's even beyond us, what we like to call "dark," and I don't even like the word very much in this context—

**MS** Well, I mean, aggression, violence, willing pain on oneself or another person, is that the kind of thing you're talking about?

**MG** Yes, but it's not only a question of individual people's feelings or psychologies. Again, this has to do with form versus the formless. A lot of what makes crazy people not be able to participate in society, in a way, is that their personality doesn't take a recognizable form that functions well in the overarching social forum. The things that we experience as violent or destructive are huge formless forces that sometimes take form in us. Fantasy seems like a pretty harmless and creative way to express them.

**MS** Another example of somebody using a fantasy or a fiction in a helpful way is Dorothy in *Two Girls, Fat and Thin*, whose father has sexually abused her. She's having a crisis—almost a dissolution of self, it seems—at this community college, and then turns to the novels of Anna Granite. They save her.

**MG** In a way, yes. You could also say that she's been very limited and deluded by trying to live her life according to this other person's ideas as expressed through fictional characters.

**MS**  So this is an ambivalent use of fantasy?

**MG**  At a certain point it's useful to her but there's a lack of fluidity. She makes it to be like "This is it, this is the literal truth," whereas if it were something that's held a little more lightly, it might not have that limiting effect.

**MS**  This reminds me of parts in *Veronica* where Alison uses the metaphor of a series of ten photographs to describe the different ways that a given moment could be seen or interpreted. The first moment is when Alison describes how she got into modeling: "One night at work, Veronica asked me how I got into modeling, and I said, 'By fucking a nobody catalog agent who grabbed my crotch.' I said it with disdain—like I didn't have to be embarrassed or make up something nice, because Veronica was nobody— like why should I care if an ant could see up my dress?" Then at the end of that scene, she reflects, "Imagine ten pictures of this conversation. In nine of them, she's the fool and I'm the person who has something. But in the tenth, I'm the fool and it's her show now. For just a second, that's the picture I saw." That seems to be an acknowledgement of the attempt to freeze moments into retainable images as well as of the fluidity that lies beneath the frozen ways in which we construe experience.

**MG**  At this moment I feel obliged to acknowledge a part of life that's not subject to fantasies or projections and doesn't care about how anyone sees it. I'm reading from a book of Simone Weil's letters, *Waiting for God*. It was introduced by Leslie Fiedler, and he says something that I like very much:

*This world is the only reality available to us, and if we do not love it in all its terror, we are sure to end up loving the "imaginary," our own dreams and self-deceits, the Utopias of the politicians, or the futile promises of future reward and consolation which the misled blasphemously call "religion." The soul has a million dodges for protecting itself against the acceptance and love of the emptiness, that "maximum distance between God and God," which is the universe; for the price of such acceptance and love is abysmal misery. And yet it is the only way.*

**MS**  Wow . . . Well, since we are talking about God, let's talk about the Chekhov story "In the Ravine." It comes up twice in *Don't Cry*. The writing teacher, Janice, who appears in "Description" and in the title story, talks about the importance of its descriptive passages, the soft open quality of description right after this woman's baby has been murdered. I was also struck by how, at least until the end, Chekhov's story doesn't have a protagonist.

**MG** It's fitting that a protagonist isn't that important in "In the Ravine" because it's about a very big picture of life. If you were going to tell this story from Lipa's point of view, the tragedy of losing her child would not be anything that she could quickly step back from. She would be completely in her feelings. But a bigger eye looks at her as this little person wandering through a forest and still notices the soft darkness and the sounds coming through the night. Chekhov doesn't describe the scene as "beautiful," but you feel the mystery and beauty of these things: the sound of birds, the sound of men's voices, the sight of someone's face half lit by the fire. You wouldn't get anything but despair if you were in Lipa's point of view—the foundation of her life has just been shattered. I would be hard-pressed to analyze why I consider "In the Ravine" such a beautiful story, though part of it is in those qualities of description where we are made acutely aware of the smallness and fragility of human beings, the strangeness of the world. Also how it expresses people's will to live and their brutality and tenderness and vulnerability, beyond what the human heart can bear, coming up against this hard, beautiful world.

**MS** But also cruel and ugly. The nastiest character in the story is this very seductive woman, Aksinya, who triumphs over the kinder characters. She has a willfulness and strength that others can't contend with.

**MG** Yeah, she has a female sexual vitality that is part of what makes her wicked. Lipa's vulnerability and passivity are part of what makes her good. I don't entirely *like* the idea of a feminine ideal as something that passive. I mean, Aksinya has just murdered her child and Lipa doesn't even say anything! The family thinks that Lipa is to blame for not caring for her child and she doesn't even dare to tell them it wasn't an accident. It disturbs me a little to see this passivity equated with purity and moral goodness. At the same time, it's rather appalling that we've come to idealize vitality and strength to such a degree that somebody like Aksinya would probably be the heroine in a modern story. She has gumption, and how! In an American story she wouldn't be a murderer. She would be the strong one who carries the day and has a successful business. And Lipa would just be drooping around chewing gum and scratching herself, and on welfare, probably, and considered bad because of that.

**MS** Yeah, this business of the meek shall inherit the earth doesn't dovetail very well with the American ethos, does it?

**MG** Well, the meek are despised now unless they're very, very cute. But often in our culture people who are actually the meekest come across very aggressively—their aggression is masking a deeper passivity, so they're doubly looked down on.

MS  There's that final image where Aksinya's father-in-law—who after all was himself a villain, if only of a monetary kind—is deranged and no longer eats in his own house, where Aksinya has made him irrelevant. He's wandering down the road half out of his mind, and Lipa and her mother treat him very kindly and offer him food.

MG  Yes, to me Lipa is the one who does have the deeper triumph in the story, even though she's lost everything and is essentially doing slave labor for Aksinya. But she nonetheless is walking down the road singing in this big beautiful voice, and she is able to extend generosity and help this poor man who's been destroyed by his own wickedness. And that is a bigger kind of triumph, absolutely. I think sometimes the powerful of society can allow the weak to have that kind of triumph while they sit on their bags of money and have a sentimental enjoyment of a story where the trampled-on person, safely out of the way, is having her spiritual triumph. I just can't help but look at it from a couple of different points of view.

MS  A lot of the women in your stories are people who, by contemporary society's standards, are failures. The protagonist of "The Agonized Face"—

MG  Well, actually Alison in *Veronica* would be a better example of that. The person in "The Agonized Face" has been married, she has a child, she's working a job that many would find glamorous. She may not have an ideal life, but certainly, by social standards, she is not a loser. Before *Veronica* was published, I was talking about the manuscript with a publicist who I don't think liked it much. She said at one point, "Well, Alison has *nothing*." I was shocked at that, but it's true—she's living much worse off than the woman in "The Agonized Face." She's on welfare, she's ill, she doesn't appear to have many friends, she's never been married, she doesn't have children— these are the building blocks in the most conventional sense of how women are defined as being successful or not. By those standards, she really doesn't have anything. Yet, she's learned so much from her life experience and is someone who can have a deep experience just walking through the woods— not everybody can do that.

MS  In an essay about Nabokov you said, "Sometimes I write from the point of view of characters whom I would dislike as people, not as a perverse exercise but because this cracks the story open and makes me see it in a way that I would not see it naturally." Is that the case with the narrator of "The Agonized Face"?

MG  Yes, although I wouldn't say I dislike her; I wouldn't go that far.

MS  She goes to hear somebody she refers to as a "feminist author" at a book festival. And the feminist author reads a story that bears a striking resemblance to your story "Turgor" in *Because They Wanted To*. And this woman, the narrator, is offended by the "Turgor"-like story; she considers it a cheap, pornographic description of sexuality even though the "feminist author" has just given a speech in which she's said that she doesn't want to be defined in those terms. Did writing from her point of view, as you say, crack the story open for you, or did it help you figure out something that you didn't know?

MG  Yeah. Sometimes when you go to what seems to be the opposite of your point of view, a whole gets created.

MS  Something which I see in your work as well—we've touched on this already—is the way that stories can heal. I wonder if there have been times in your life where you have felt healed by a story.

MG  Healed is perhaps a little too strong a word.

MS  Helped?

MG  Nourished. Stories or books which I find most satisfying in that way are those that fully express something. Sometimes human life seems so partial or incapable of full expression, of whatever is at the core essence of a person or situation. I feel a level of frustration with that, so when I see someone who is able to give full expression to whatever it is—I mean expression to the point of being able to glimpse those things that are always going to be outside our range of vision . . . There's nothing more profoundly satisfying to me.

# Kimiko Hahn
# and Laurie Sheck

KIMIKO HAHN  was born in Mount Kisco, New York, in 1955. She is the author of numerous collections of poetry, including *The Narrow Road to the Interior*, *The Artist's Daughter*, and *Toxic Flora*. A graduate of the University of Iowa and Columbia University, where she received her MA in Japanese Literature, Hahn has been awarded the PEN/Voelcker Award for Poetry, an American Book Award, and the Theodore Roethke Memorial Poetry Prize. A Guggenheim Fellow, Hahn has taught at New York University, Sarah Lawrence College, and the University of Houston. She is currently a Distinguished Professor in the MFA Program at Queens College, CUNY.

LAURIE SHECK  was born in the Bronx, New York, in 1953. She is the author of several collections of poetry, including *Captivity*, *Black Series*, *Amaranth*, and *The Willow Grove*, which was a finalist for the Pulitzer Prize. She is also the author of the hybrid work *A Monster's Notes*. Her honors include fellowships from the Guggenheim Foundation, the Ingram Merrill Foundation, the National Endowment for the Arts, and the New Jersey State Council on the Arts. Sheck has taught creative writing faculty at Princeton University and currently teaches in the MFA program at The New School.

**LAURIE SHECK**  When I first picked up the manuscript of *The Narrow Road to the Interior*, I was struck by the spacious feel of the work on the page. It felt like the record and embodiment of a mind exploring, moving around. Lots of white space in places. Text that looked like short blocks of prose, other pages with long indented lines, others with short lines. It had a wonderful feeling of both pattern and variation, randomness and order. The Japanese form *zuihitsu* that you use a lot in this book means "running brush," and the book feels very much like that. It incorporates a sense of process, movement, juxtaposition, collage. Would you talk about the zuihitsu—what it is, what attracts you to it, and how you came to it?

**KIMIKO HAHN**  This might be a strange analogy, but I like to think of the zuihitsu as a fungus—not plant or animal, but a species unto itself. The Japanese view it as a distinct genre, although its elements are difficult to pin down. There's no Western equivalent, though some people might wish to categorize it as a prose poem or an essay. You mentioned some of its characteristics: a kind of randomness that is not really random, but a *feeling* of randomness; a pointed subjectivity that we don't normally associate with the essay. The zuihitsu can also resemble other Western forms: lists, journals. I've added emails to the mix. Fake emails.

**LS**  I love the emails, the combinatory texture that arises from using a very old Japanese form while imbuing it with details and images from the twenty-first century. I think it's also interesting at this juncture for an American writer to explore ways in which strict boundaries of genres can be broken down.

**KH**  Maybe here is one place to pick up where the modernists left off? The technique of collage is really compelling to me. Letter writing, diary form—real and invented—I like to use within the zuihitsu itself. Of course the Japanese also used artfully composed diaries—*nikki*—that included poetry. My pieces that resemble a diary are far from a record of whatever I was doing that day—probably. So that's what I'm trying to do: mix up genres within the zuihitsu and sometimes include fabricated material. As for my own history with this form, because I studied it mainly in translation at Columbia, I have to say it was more an academic appreciation. Then about ten years ago, Ed Friedman, who was the director of the Poetry Project at St. Mark's, held a millennium celebration of Sei Shōnagon, author of *The Pillow Book*, which was written around 1002 A.D. He asked me if I wanted to participate, and of course I jumped at the opportunity. It was only then that I sat down and actually wrote a zuihitsu—"The Downpour."

**LS** When I first picked up *The Pillow Book* many years ago, it looked like prose to me. It's interesting you saw its potential as a form for a poet to use.

**KH** I probably saw it as prose too, to tell the truth—although, you know, as an undergraduate, I read *Paterson*, which even then began to subvert my notion of what a poem should *look like*. It gave so much permission! But I don't think I appreciated the potential of the zuihitsu until after I wrote "The Downpour." A few years later, when my mother died, I immediately wrote a number of poems and they were sentimental in the worst possible way. I reformed them into paragraphs, and the paragraphs seemed to absorb the sentimentality in a way that a lineated poem could not. That was interesting to me, how grief could be expressed differently in paragraphs: how form changes content. Different from discursive or meditative poems, I think.

**LS** I can see that. The zuihitsu gives you enormous freedom to get on the page a mind that is associative, alive, intuitive. Calvino wrote in *Six Memos for the Next Millennium*, "Who are we, if not a combinatorial of experiences, information, books we have read, things imagined. Each life is an encyclopedia, a library, an inventory of objects, a series of styles, and everything can be constantly reshuffled and reordered in every conceivable way." I thought of that passage when I read your new book because you seem to treasure the fact that a self is in a way encyclopedic, ambiguous, full of reachings in various directions.

**KH** I like his word *inventory*. I would say that each piece is an inventory, and that the whole book is an inventory.

**LS** Something else struck me about your use of the zuihitsu. There's not one central point, not a dominant center, but interacting parts. John Berger said that with Cubist painting the spectator feels the discontinuity of space and is reminded that his view is bound to be only partial. It seems to me that's something you're willing to live with, the anxiety and the ambiguity of things being partial. In fact you celebrate the fragment in many ways.

**KH** Ambiguity is the opposite of clarity—so, in my mind, it shares a necessary relationship to clarity, if that makes sense. We know it as an important tool in poetry—like double meanings, which are highly valued in Japanese poetics. Also, leaving things partial can either be or be akin to synecdoche. I've read that Japanese refer to such suggestion as fragrance, *kaoru*. You don't need to say everything, because the fragrance will continue, and you can keep experiencing what the fragment suggests even after the piece formally closes. Just because something is partial doesn't mean that the whole is not, somehow, present. It just means that something is not going to be fully extended or even fully realized as an image. In putting together *Mosquito and Ant*, I wondered how much could be left out before losing, completely, the sense of a piece.

LS  Doesn't that seem faithful to what "thinking" is?

KH  Yes, thinking and feeling, combined—and in terms of poetics, what we think of as mystery, or resonance, closure and anti-closure.

LS  You have ways of bringing in fragments and leaps of thought that end up giving the work a great deal of associative richness.

KH  I've always been interested in a sort of dialectic: where there's blurring and ambiguity, there's, finally, clarity. Where there's contradiction, there's clarity. Where there's intuition, there's reason. Fragmentation, wholeness. All these things can coexist.

LS  The Japanese notion of *sabi*, of the beauty of irregularity, of the unfinished, the idea that the flawed bowl is the beautiful bowl, seems relevant here as well.

KH  Yes, and in addition to the Japanese, a sensibility that is hopefully reminiscent of what Louise Glück has called disruption and ruin. For my own purposes, if a piece feels too smooth I seek to rough it up, put in flaws, put in contradiction, because for me that makes things more compelling. And rather than subject or theme, I look for an organizing principle—which strikes me as more spatial and coincides with your point about thought process. An organizing principle isn't necessarily concerned with content.

LS  The tension in your work between an organizing principle and randomness makes the work feel beautifully wrought.

KH  Funny—I started to mis-hear you when you said beautifully wrought. I thought you said beautifully *raw*, which I hope it is as well. That's the dynamic, that even though it is wrought, there's that randomness. After I write a zuihitsu I'll go through and I'll make sure it looks not only random but unfinished. I might take certain things out, scramble other things up and place certain things in, all very, very consciously. I'll lay the pages out on the floor and use highlighters to see where I have certain elements—images, motifs, words—come up and I'll move things around, and shape it so there's a certain pacing. The asterisks help also. The text in between the asterisks, I hope, are little pieces in and of themselves—they could be read out of context. And I find that all very pleasurable. And of course *wrought* can indicate perturbed, worked up. I love the notion of crafted disturbance!

LS  Throughout *The Narrow Road to the Interior* you use another Japanese form as well, the tanka, and you make reference to and draw on several writers from the Heian period. What draws you so strongly to this particular period?

KH  I first fell in love with that period when I found that women dominated the literature—for me that was extraordinary. As an undergraduate I was studying Japanese literature in translation when I learned that the men during that period were writing in Chinese, the way Western men would write in Latin. In other words, the educated people would write in a language that was not their spoken language. Women, who were not formally educated, would write in Japanese. And so while the men's writing became increasingly stultified, the women produced incredibly vivid writing, to the point where some men actually wrote in a female persona, in Japanese. Soon this became literary diction. So it was women who dominated what is considered the golden age of literature in Japan. That was my initial attraction to that era and especially to *The Tale of Genji*—which is such an incredible soap opera, and considered the world's first psychological novel. It has such a wealth of themes: longing, incest, karma and the female figure being both powerful and utterly without power. All that fascinates me. And it's such an alien world because the women—aristocratic women—quite literally lived in the dark, in a sort of twilight because while the architecture opened the rooms up to the outside, it also utilized screens to create walls. Between the screens and the candlelight—the lighting was quite dim, shadowy. This created a perfect atmosphere for liaisons—as well as for mistaken identities. The men, of course, lived in the real sunlit world.

LS  A twilight, yes. You write in the book, "Those women waited in boxes of semi-darkness, complexions pale as daikon, for the men." In the last piece, "Conspiring with Shikishi," you quote not only her poems but those of the predecessors who influenced her, and then you respond in turn. So it sets up this wonderful chain of responsiveness, which raises the whole idea that writing is itself a form of reading, a form of responsiveness.

KH  That section also includes Hiroaki Sato's translations of Ōe no Chisato and Taira no Kanemori, and several anonymous poets—so I'm responding to all of those poems, to his version of them. So there's that complexity. It's a tradition in Japanese literature and in my presumptuous way, I thought, I'm just going to stick myself into that current of Imperial anthologies and have fun, and so I did.

LS  Yes, well, writing's partly a conversation with the writing that's come before it. Your series of tanka, distributed at key intervals throughout the book, chart the minute, often seemingly unremarkable moments of daily life through the various seasons. As far as I can tell, they move from the summer of 2000 to the summer of 2002.

KH  Yes, they are a different chronological thread and as you point out, have a different relation to time. In the tanka form I found a way to pause and to just pay attention. At one point my life became very complicated, disorganized, and I lost my writing routine. So I thought, now is the time I should—at the very least in order to get back to a routine—I should try my hand at these. Around that time I was on vacation and by chance, at a secondhand bookstore, I found the book *String of Beads: Complete Poems of Princess Shikishi*—which I already owned, but I purchased again—and I read them and actually took notes on the progression. I found different ways that she progressed in this very short form, and I imitated her minute strategies. I'd resisted the tanka form for a long time because it so often seemed to use the same almost programmatic movement: mainly observation/enlightenment, and that felt too predictable. But she taught me otherwise. I wrote maybe several hundred over a two- or three-year period.

*From grasses fretting with oysters and crabs, the mud stutters and I can tell you wait for another dusk to ask me. And I am not impatient.*

LS  One obvious question is how your interest in Japanese literature might tie in with your own background. You're the child of a Japanese American mother and a German American father. When you were a child was *The Tale of Genji* something that your mother would read to you, or was Japanese literature something that you came to later on?

KH  I came to it in college. I did have Japanese folktales growing up. When I was a very little girl my mother would occasionally read stories to me in Japanese even though I had no idea what she was saying. So there was always the idea that there are languages that you don't speak but you can feel and love. You don't have to understand something for it to be a pleasure. Looking back all these years later, my memories of my mother reading to me—for me those are the most precious memories of our relationship.

**LS** Was Japanese spoken in your home when you were growing up?

**KH** No, we spoke English. But because my grandparents on my mother's side didn't speak English, language had that ambiguous aspect—for my whole family, I think. My parents spoke to one another in Italian when they didn't want my sister and me to understand them—Italian they'd picked up when my father had his Prix de Rome for painting. So there was this on top of the Japanese.

**LS** But then how did you communicate with your Japanese-speaking grandparents?

**KH** We all spoke in baby words, so they would say *good girl* or *nice food*. Or they mixed up language—which is what pidgin is, in part. "You good girl, *ne*, Kimi-chan." Partial communication. Also, I didn't see them very often.

**LS** They lived pretty far away, in Hawaii?

**KH** Yes, my mother grew up on a plantation in Maui and then moved to Chicago right after the war. She went to secretarial school and art school. My father was at the Art Institute. They met at the Y, married and came east a few years later. I grew up in Pleasantville, New York.

**LS** When you were growing up, did you feel like an Asian American; were you labeled that way? Did you feel mixed?

**KH** Well, I did feel mixed: I was considered Japanese by most Americans, especially Caucasian Americans. You know, "the Other." There's an Asian American anthology from decades ago called *American Born and Foreign*. So that's sort of what I felt like growing up, in the suburbs. When we lived in Japan for a year I was considered American. "Impure," someone later informed me. So I was never really considered one thing or the other.

**LS** How old were you when you lived in Japan?

**KH** I was nine.

LS  Did that confuse you—that in the United States you were considered Japanese, and in Japan you were considered American?

KH  Yeah, it wasn't very *pleasant* to never feel I belonged in either place. Not in Pleasantville, or Tokyo. Ironically, though, my mother, because of the war and being second-generation Japanese, rejected her Japanese background, which was pretty typical of that generation, while my father, on the other hand, was deeply curious and was studying Asian culture even before he met my mother. So it's through my father's interest that we came back around to my mother's culture. We actually had a lot of Asian art objects around our house growing up, especially after living in Japan for a year. So I studied Japanese dance and flower arrangement and a little bit of tea ceremony and calligraphy. There is further irony, since a great many third-generation Japanese American activists did not know as much about the roots of East Asian culture as I did—the Eurasian.

LS  Your year in Japan must have been quite extraordinary.

KH  It was. My father took a sabbatical year to study art. We lived in Tokyo, which was gearing up for a wave of *gaijin* [foreigners] to attend the Olympics. Our apartment was a traditional two-room setup where the living areas were transformed into bedrooms at night by way of rolling out futons on the tatami floors. It was a lovely way to live, actually. I attended Japanese school and walked the, I don't know, mile to school by myself. I think of a nine-year-old doing that now—living in a foreign country and being on her own—and it feels a bit frightening. But it wasn't then. We traveled within Japan—seeing a lot of shrines and temples—then returned to the U.S. by continuing east and so visited Taiwan, Hong Kong, Thailand, Cambodia, India, Egypt, Italy and Portugal. Cambodia was my absolute favorite—that was in 1965 and a bit of a risk, really. I didn't know that, of course. We went by pedicab to see Angkor Wat, and my little sister and I rode on an elephant through the ancient moats, monkeys chattering overhead. I remember seeing enormous half-buried temples with trees growing out of the heads of stone deities. At the inn we slept in a huge bed covered with mosquito netting. It was magical.

LS  You've mentioned that your mother turned away from her inherited culture in many ways, and yet in *The Unbearable Heart* you write of the Buddhist rites associated with her death. Was there any Buddhist practice on your mother's part? And what about in your life?

KH Only marginally. An underground stream. We attended a Protestant church, but I knew my Japanese grandparents were Buddhist, and we had a Buddhist service for my mother when she died. I guess the main exposure—every Saturday morning—came from Japanese language and dance classes at the temple on Riverside Drive. There's a dance festival in July that commemorates one's ancestors—and my sister and I always danced. Not my mother—I'm not sure why. So the sense of a Japanese heritage was both present and submerged. I only saw my mother in a kimono once; when I was in kindergarten she came to school for a kind of United Nations celebration. Her style of dressing, though, was influenced by Asian fabrics and muted colors. When she died, I considered becoming Buddhist, as a way of staying connected to her, I guess—but you know, I just can't pray to a male deity. It's just not in me.

LS Your mother died suddenly—

KH Yes, and I'd never felt as deeply—not any feeling—as I felt, and still feel, grief for my mother. A neighbor's phone call woke us up before dawn— this was thirteen years ago—and she told us that my parents had been in a car accident and that my father was in intensive care with broken ribs; that my mother, however, had died instantly, which he didn't know. So my then-husband and I, along with my sister and her husband, drove up to Yonkers to tell him, to begin the process of taking care of him and all the things one has to do when someone dies. We also had to tell my girls, who were three and six. At the time I was working on a long piece inspired by Said's *Orientalism*, and I had to put it aside. Nothing made any sense. I did immediately begin to scribble though—and out of those scraps came *The Unbearable Heart*. A poet friend told me how strange it was that the figure of the mother was actually dead, because in previous books there was so much longing to find her, to be with her; she felt fairly absent in my childhood and now she really was absent. He was right. Some of my grief is that I'm still looking for her, although I do get a tremendous amount of affection from my daughters. My husband's two daughters are very affectionate as well. I'm very, very fortunate.

LS In *The Unbearable Heart*, you wrote, "I have decided to write a language of disruption." And that book is full of shatterings, disjunctions. This new book, *The Narrow Road to the Interior*, on the other hand, evokes a very different kind of feeling, the feeling of a journey, for one thing. The title comes from Matsuo Bashō—so here's another influence, a seventeenth-century Japanese writer. And it comes from his travel journal. Did the governing idea and title of the book come to you early on in the writing process? Basho's journal is referred to specifically in one of the poems, "Sparrow."

KH The title probably came from working on that particular piece. The title to his book has also been translated as *The Narrow Road to the Provinces* and *The Narrow Road to the North*. There are about five different translations into English, but I love "interior" for its obvious double meaning, geographical and psychological. Also I just love the sound of the word interior.

LS In that journal, Basho writes at one point, "The journey itself is a home." Your book strikes me as being very much in that spirit. It seems to me that one of the things your book is doing is investigating the idea of home, interrogating this from many different angles—asking, What is a home?

KH Your words make me shiver—that has long been an issue for me. The issue of belonging I described earlier. Where do I feel at home? Whether it's feeling at home in a location or in my own skin, I've rarely felt at home. I can feel more comfortable in a hotel, oddly enough. What I'm hoping is that the journey in this collection is about flight but also about learning to stay. Not so much with a man, because the speaker, the character, leaves her husband and moves on to another relationship, but that she's learning how to be a mother, to stay when it's emotionally difficult to do so for a variety of reasons.

LS There are various kinds of home in the book: one finds a home in predecessors, in being with one's daughters, in one's own writing . . .

KH And not even in one particular location, because it keeps moving. Literally, a sublet.

LS There's a sublet in your book, an apartment with a yellow kitchen table, and the speaker seems very happy there.

KH She was very happy there. For the first time in a long time, she was without a man in the house and just with her two daughters, and suddenly she was happy in a way that she had never felt before. I am saying "she"—as if it were not me!

LS In your work there's a recurring theme of a very female world. I don't know what would have happened if you had had sons.

KH (*laughter*) I don't know either! I think of *Grimm's Fairy Tales*: all the little girls who go out and are very important after all, whether it's *Little Red Riding Hood* or *Sleeping Beauty*—those stories were mother's milk to me. That's what I grew up with. So the world, in that sense, is very female to me. Though, admittedly, the mother is often dead in those stories and the father quite present!

LS I wonder, speaking of home, when your children were growing up, where did you do most of your writing?

KH All my writing was done in coffee shops. I couldn't focus at home. Not to generate raw material. I would take them to a babysitter, or later, to school, and I would keep on walking to the nearest café. When I'm at home I try to do laundry at the same time, and then there's the telephone, and I'll get up to get a cup of coffee, then I'll notice there are things that need to be done. Emailing is a terrible distraction among many. Now I have a little study, which I've never had before, and I find there are distractions even there. In a coffee shop or library there are other kinds of distractions, but not personal ones. Even before I had children, I'd work outside my apartment.

LS Do you take your computer with you?

KH No, I write longhand on college-ruled yellow pads, then later type a kind of second draft on the computer—that begins the process of revision. I might bring along a book or newspaper with me, to "talk back" to sometimes.

LS In Harold Pinter's recent Nobel remarks, he talked about the difference between political language and literary language. He said, "Literary language, language in art, remains a highly ambiguous transaction, a quicksand, a trampoline, a frozen pool which might give way underneath the author at any time." You seem very comfortable, even curious, about ambiguity, even contradiction, in language. You're also very attuned to the sounds and physical properties of words. You seem to just love them. I'm thinking about the ending of "Sparrow": "I could not return to the body that contained only the literal world. Where sparrow does not suggest sorrow, where sorrow does not suggest sorry." We hear language in the process of echoing and revising itself.

KH I feel if a writer doesn't love words then they shouldn't bother. It's like a potter who doesn't love the slickness of clay. Never mind what they make with that clay, but don't you just have to love clay? To me, whether I write a successful poem or not, I just want to play with words. It's what I love to do.

LS  Yes, that comes through.

KH  If it doesn't, then I'm not doing what I want to do—sharing that passion, because it is not just about talking or expressing myself, or beating my breast, or telling a story, or any of those things. It has to do with just loving words. The way a child loves to learn words and to use words. I am really trying to get back to those early moments—what a sound is, what that sound eventually becomes, the idea that a sound has meaning. And if a word suggests many meanings, so much the better. It will reverberate. I think of Gertrude Stein; I think of the Japanese use of double meanings. We think of puns as being ridiculous, but in fact double meanings are an absolutely essential way to make the most out of economy.

LS  We've talked about the influence of Japanese literature on your work, but what about English and American influences?

KH  I'm very interested in Emily Dickinson and John Donne—at the moment specifically for their use of scientific and/or religious diction. It absolutely stuns me. To use the word *quartz* to talk about a numbing moment, or to write, as Donne does in "A Valediction: Forbidding Mourning," "like gold to airy thinness beat"—that use of alchemy—it's just amazing. And then some of my Asian influences have come second- or third-hand through Williams and the Imagists. Eliot's *The Waste Land* gave me permission very early on to bring things together from different cultures in one piece. And Eliot and Dickinson for the erratic way they sometimes present formal elements: whether his rhyme in "Preludes" or her dashes or slant rhyme. Then of course there's influence from rock 'n' roll and popular culture in general.

LS  In your book you ask if women writers have a place in Western literature and your answer is yes and no. How do you locate your own work within this?

KH  I'm interested in bringing the female voice to the fore—also to see if that voice is qualitatively different. One dated literary myth is that women create babies and men create stuff—such as artistic masterpieces. But of course such myths are merely part of the larger picture of excluding women from having their say. That's changed to a great degree. Dickinson's, Plath's and Glück's use of metaphor is, for me, very female. Each is like a shamaness.

Magical. Disturbing. Powerful—but in a way that allows for vulnerability. There is also a shared tone and stylistic compression. Adrienne Rich's "Calle Visión" also. Of course, any good art is going to be connected to the body through cadence, at the very least. Whitman's loping lines or O'Hara's prosaic meanderings. Still, I wonder as women's poems are further included in the canon over the next fifty years, if there'll be qualitative differences. I hope so, actually. For myself—I do wish to write from the body, from this female body. From the sacred and the scandalous, the luscious and the aging.

**LS** In writing, there's a sense in which body and mind are inseparable, and maybe even genderless on some essential level. Dickinson's dashes, Whitman's ellipses carry processes of thought that activate the page in ways that feel totally alive, precise, electric. Your use of "luscious and aging" reminds me of Whitman. I wonder what you're working on now?

**KH** Over a year ago I was commissioned to write a film text for photographer Peter Lindbergh and filmmaker Holly Fisher, and it's just being completed now. Over the past year or so I've been working on a new series of regularly lineated poems. They're based on outside source material, mostly from the *New York Times* science section. In general, whatever I find curious becomes my material. I think human beings are often drawn to the exotic, where a measure of license or a view of the Other is a kind of reverse mirror. For some, like Flaubert, this meant sex tours in foreign countries. For some it might mean cross-dressing. Lately for me I'm drawn to language that feels exotic, and this is the language of science. It is my exotic. The working title is *Toxic Flora*.

**LS** It's interesting to hear about this movement into such different subject matter. But then again, *The Narrow Road to the Interior* is in many ways engaged with the whole idea of movement, of change. As we talked about earlier, in your writing the Japanese women are often waiting. But early on in your book there's the image of a train and a journey. In many ways your book enacts the antithesis of waiting.

**KH** That's good. That was my unconscious hard at work or my life hard at work.

**LS** Well, it struck me, and the book ends with a dash. The dash can be such a charged, dynamic gesture. You could say it's almost the opposite of waiting in a box of semi-darkness. I wonder how you see that dash?

KH  Well, that was also unconscious, and that's probably a good thing. It's funny, how the word *dash* goes back to ambiguity and wordplay, how the word dash is obviously a punctuation mark, but it also means not to wait, to leave.

# Wilson Harris
# and Fred D'Aguiar

WILSON HARRIS was born in New Amsterdam, Guyana (then British Guiana), in 1921. He is the author of many novels, including *Palace of the Peacock*, *The Guyana Quartet*, and *The Ghost of Memory*. For his work, Harris has been awarded the Guyana Prize for Literature twice and the Premio Mondello dei Cinque Continenti. He has been awarded honorary doctorates from the University of the West Indies and the University of Liège. In 2010 he was knighted by Queen Elizabeth II.

FRED D'AGUIAR was born in London, England, in 1960. He is the author of numerous books of prose and poetry, including *Mama Dot*, *Feeding the Ghosts*, *Children of Paradise*, and *The Longest Memory*, for which he was awarded the Whitbread First Novel Award and the David Higham Prize for Fiction. A graduate of the University of Kent, D'Aguiar has also been awarded The Malcolm X Prize for Poetry, the Guyana Poetry Prize, and the Guyana Prize for Literature. He has taught at Amherst College, Bates College, the University of Miami, and is currently a Gloria D. Smith Professor of Africana Studies at Virginia Tech.

**FRED D'AGUIAR** You began as a poet in British Guyana. Your early poems, published in Guyana in 1954 and reissued as *Eternity to Season* (1978), revere a European classical tradition characterized by Greco-Roman and Judeo-Christian iconography. There is an implied mission in this early poetry to revise the given frame of a classic poetic tradition derived from England and for it to accommodate the tropics of the New World. Could you say a little about the Guyana of the late '30s and '40s that led to the formation of this revisionary sensibility?

**WILSON HARRIS** The word "Guyana" is based on an Amerindian word that means "land of waters." There is magic in this contrast in which the specter of land moves, the ghost of rock resembles a tide, in rivers that run. Such magic is the dance of place.

The '30s and '40s were a time of severe depression in coastal and urban regions of Guyana. Property values were at rock bottom.

In 1942 I had taken and passed the surveying examination—land and hydrographic surveying, mathematics, astronomy—and was on a major surveying expedition in the deep interior, the Cuyuni River interior, a river that has its headwaters in Venezuela. I was a junior officer of the government survey party.

This expedition was a revelation for me: multitudinous forests I had never seen before, the whisper or sigh of a tree with a tone or rhythm I had never known, real (it seemed) and unreal footsteps in the shoe of a cracking branch, mysterious play in the rivers at nights, distant rain bringing the sound of approaching fire in the whispering leaves, horses' hooves on water on rock, the bark of dogs, of technology in the bruised tumult of a waterfall . . . Much more that witnessed to the living water and land one had assumed to be *insentient* in the coastal and urban regions. This was another planet, a *living*, unpredictable planet.

I found it impossible to write what I felt, but persisted. There were clues in ancient Homer speaking of the gods as animals and birds arising and descending from spaces in and above the earth. This reminded me of the pre-Columbian god Quetzalcoatl, *quetzal* (the bird), *coatl* (the snake). There were clues in the one-eyed Cyclops that I now saw standing like a lightning-struck tree in the forest. But such clues came home to me as "museum pieces" divorced from their genuine and original sources. I had never felt such a divorce so acutely, so sharply before. I had accepted it all along as natural. My busy activities were all that action was. Now, however, in the depths of the multiform pressures of what seemed other than the nature I had known, in the sudden station of a tree, in the sudden station of a rock, like watchers that were potently alive, potently still, there was *something else*, something akin to a bloodstream of spirit that ran everywhere with an astonishing momentum that made my former activities pale into a fixity or immobility. Was it *natural* that an immobility at the heart of a busy world dominated the cultures that I knew? Was it *unnatural* that each prosperous group, or tight-knit state, accepted itself as inherently superior, others that strayed from a given path as deserving of rebuke or of violence to be meted out to the inferior?

I had had a glimpse of something immensely precious, but the question remained: How does one combine with, and transfigure, a cultural fixity that passes for action ingrained into one's education? How does one bring into play—through various aspects and layers—a sense of profoundest cross-culturality beyond the immobility of habit or of virtue that exterminates all unlike itself?

This was the beginning of a task I could not evade—if I may put it that way—that lay in the incorporation of shells, of the branches of trees, of wood in oneself like a skeleton—interiorly and imaginatively in oneself—as much as exteriorly in diverse and complex nature. This gave me a sensation that conflicts in the past were unfinished and could be seen afresh beyond the frames or limitations we had imposed on them and on ourselves. I found myself intuitively moving into a poem I called "Troy," which was written in 1950. I shall quote but two lines from that poem:

*the strange opposition of a flower on a branch to its dark*
*wooden companion*

In that poem I knew an intuitive tremor of "flower and wooden branch" erupting in myself and transforming the flesh of fixity.

The dance of place had begun.

FD'A  Your novel *Palace of the Peacock* (1960), the first of twenty-three published works of fiction, startled readers with its story as much as by the way you tell it. I remember when I first came across the book in 1978 how surprising the diction seemed to me. To begin with, no single narrative detail stood for one thing so much as at least two equally plausible things. For example, in the opening scene when a horseman is shot, he appears simultaneously to hang in the air as well. The diction and syntax say one thing and imply another shadow reality. Adverbs and conditional clauses splinter verbs and main clauses into multiple options working against their first sense and promoting alternative meanings of those first implied readings. These local effects in the prose are thrilling to read but they ask a larger question of the reader who is forced to revise his or her expectations of linearity and of the narrative.

**WH** *Palace of the Peacock* actually had its beginning in the Cuyuni River expedition, a beginning that was "mute" or "without a tongue." It was a challenge for which I found myself without expression. This puts it as simply as I can. The shock of contrasts in river, forest, waterfall had registered very deeply in my psyche. So deeply that to find oneself "without a tongue" was to learn of a "music" that was "wordless," to descend into varying structures upon parallel branches of reality, branches that were rooted in a stem of meaning for which no absolute existed. It took me seventeen years—through "Troy" and *Eternity to Season* and above all through three experiments with novels, all of which I discarded—to strike the right rhythm and note with which I wrote *Palace of the Peacock* in 1959, the year I left Guyana. I had sensed a crucial change occurring in the narrative at the end of the third novel I had discarded before I left. I had achieved, it seemed to me, a blend of lands and precipitous places, Cuyuni and Potaro, the River of Kaieteur.

*Palace* opened, it seemed to me, a new world of fiction that made a succession of novels possible—with varying dimensions—the latest of which, the twenty-fourth, titled *The Mask of the Beggar*, is to be published in 2003.

I led members of the crew in the Cuyuni whose names appear in *Palace*. There are Carroll, the singer, "a boy gifted with his paddle as if it were a violin and a sword together in paradise"; Vigilance, "sparkling and shrewd of eye, reading the river's mysterious book"; old Schomburgh, "agile and swift as a monkey for all his seasoned years"; the daSilva twins, "thin, long-legged, upright spiders, of Portuguese extraction"; Cameron, "brick-red face, faster than a snake in the forest with his hands"; and Jennings, "the mechanic, carved out of still wood it seemed, sweating still the dew of his tears, cursing and reproving his whirling engine and toy in the unearthly terrifying grip in the water." I give these names to plumb an illustration of the cross-cultural figuration the entire party implicitly maintained. A subtle transfiguration draws them into carvings of wood resembling monkeys, spiders, snakes in hand or long-legged limb as they move in shadow and depth across memory to become "lifelike" in "appearance and spirit and energy."

It is true, as you say, that the horseman in the opening scene appears to be "shot" and to "hang" simultaneously in the air. The air or wind is "stretched and torn and coils and runs in an instant." It becomes "stiffened" rope and bullet. Later we discover that Donne, the horseman, may have "drowned." Three options of the way he died. This is important as it brings into play three lives he could have lived and which fiction should explore. I know that the view of science tends to be that we are all genetically coded, but I would suggest interior lives that touch nature and make us into *living* sculptures. Freedom therefore needs to be explored in depths beyond conventional linearities. A sculpture appears inanimate, ornamental, in its fixed lines, but it may have a psychical momentum within its stillness that makes it a piece of *living* art. Can a sculpture encompass the whole life or the whole death it presents? Would there not have to be "second deaths" and "second lives" in a fiction that seeks a wholeness beyond the violence that seems the inevitable and apparently absolute frame of human existence?

**FD'A** Donne's three lives work as a unique approach in your fiction that is highly textured and multidimensional. It contravenes a trend in fiction you characterized in a 1967 essay as the "novel of persuasion," which I understand to mean a novel heavily invested in the linear narrative, in a sequence of events relayed pictorially as a means of engaging a reader reputed to be terrified of stasis and "interiority" or reflection. The three planes of existence for Donne seem to mirror a necessary complexity you have invested in the notion of storytelling.

**WH** Donne is the brother of—and a stranger to—the I-narrator. This is confirmed in the I-narrator's namelessness, which reflects many names and heritages born of the mystery of Nature and Spirit. Donne's "three lives" is a unique approach, as you say, to a highly textured multidimensionality. The I-narrator *knows* him and does not know him. His "three lives" reflect a voyage, or voyages he may have made, in which little is accurately recorded. Even if there had been *apparently* accurate recordings there is much that would have been missed of his unorthodox, hidden, subconscious/unconscious diversions because of greed, lust for power, fear, dreams, emotions he himself is unable to express. All these constitute the "lives" one "lives." It is only by bringing them into quantum play that we approach—if nothing more—a possible transfiguration in the violent wastage of world events.

Thus it is not altogether astonishing, I would say, that Donne and his crew are part of a myth in which "their *living* names matched the names of a famous dead crew that had sunk in the rapids." The genuine possibility of remarkable myth—as profound and necessary in its changed form as Homeric and pre-Columbian myth—is present in Donne's "three lives." *Myth* is a term we have undervalued. *Myth* brings a dream of wholeness that cannot be taken for granted since it probes ceaselessly a material unconscious hiding much we need to know.

Let me give an example of hidden lives in world affairs. In America today there are many "colored" people who are designated "black" or "African." Whereas they are mixed with the West—with the so-called whites who represent the West—in blood and spirit. This is a fateful, hidden matter though we do not see it as such. It may be partly responsible for deadly, one-sided polarizations in cultures around the globe that see themselves similarly locked into racial investitures.

I am not suggesting that racial admixture is a solution to the world's grave problems. I am suggesting, however, that a *freedom* of diverse parts in Nature to blend into variant universals should be open in fiction and art.

Who, for instance, in our civilizational dilemmas would consider Legba of Haiti and Hephaestus of ancient Greece as cross-culturally and profoundly related? Both figures may deepen each other *psychically* and reveal a fixture of deceptions that may yield to a phenomenal regenerative truth through various roads of creative and re-creative complexity. Hephaestus—in his wounded technological unease—creates a deceptive armor of peace that Achilles wears for a battle with Hector of the Trojans. Legba is one-legged and stands *apparently* immune at the crossroads but sinks almost invisibly into the morass of Haitian affairs. They reach uneasily toward each other across the centuries to shed, by degrees, I would say, hard-and-fast notions of an absolute and invariant controlling ethos that bind them into ornamental fates.

Cross-culturality differs radically from multiculturality. There is no creative and re-creative sharing of dimensions in multiculturality. The strongest culture in multiculturality holds an umbrella over the rest, which have no alternative but to abide by the values that the strongest believe to be universal. Cross-culturality is an opening to a true and variant universality of a blend of parts we can never wholly encompass, though when we become aware of them we may ceaselessly strive for an open unity that they offer. In this quantum way we may forestall the tyranny of one-sided being.

**FD'A** Your British publisher, Faber and Faber, issued *The Guyana Quartet* in 1985, which comprised your first four novels from the early '60s. I wonder if for the sake of this interview you could extend that publishing package to a quintet that includes your fifth novel, *Heartland*. Would you say something about the story of the region in terms of its history as explored in your first five novels?

**WH** I shall begin with a quotation from *Palace of the Peacock*, the first novel in *The Guyana Quartet*, then discuss its relation to "the story of the region in terms of its history" in *Heartland*.

*DaSilva stared at the apparition his brother presented . . . Now he knew for the first true time the fetishes he and his companions had embraced. They were bound together in wishful substance . . . and self-destruction. Remove all this and weaken its appearance and its cruelty and they were finished. So Donne had died in the death of Wishrop. Jennings' primitive abstraction and slackening will was a reflection of the death of Cameron, Schomburgh had died with Carroll. And daSilva saw with dread his own sagging body's life like one who had adventured and lived on scraps of rumour that passed for the arrest of spiritual myth and the rediscovery of a new life.*

This passage speaks eloquently, I feel, for "control" that becomes "bondage" in which the members of the crew are helpless, they are tied together in a *psychical* web that makes them, in some instances, perverse and cruel and exploitative of each other. This bondage resembles a "spiritual myth and rediscovery of a new life." It is therefore partial, never absolute. It reveals implicit communities of fellowship. This throws light on a loss of control of the voyage upriver that the I-narrator—who plays, we may say, the role of "author"—suffers. He disappears entirely from the narrative. The I-narrator is nameless. Namelessness depicts a susceptibility to many names, many diverse heritages, which the I-narrator seeks in his quest for "wholeness." He returns to the narrative later after the death of the crew (which occurs in many cases in his absence from the narrative) and finds himself exercising another pattern of control, another intuition of wholeness. The currents of history, the events he has seen, the characters he has created, turn on him now and invoke new imaginative responses from him. Everything creates him anew as he once created it. This is the mystery of consciousness that brings different patterns of control in a fiction that seeks wholeness. The crew come alive again. They are drawn into a "second life" as they had known a "second death" before. This paradox in the "lives" of the crew—of which the I-narrator possesses but fragmentary indications—springs I feel from quantum unpredictability in language of which I knew nothing when I wrote *Palace* but which, across the years, I have seen to be native, I would say, to the fiction that I write.

"Quantum" brings a hand in fiction that challenges all conventional fixtures of control within the psyche of art. A "second death" and a "second life" are *incomplete* approaches to a wholeness that can never be seized but needs to be sought ceaselessly and requires an immersion in complex natures that we have bludgeoned into inanimate lifelessness save in "wilderness" areas of the globe.

The I-narrator finds, on his return to the narrative, that he has the "courage to make (his) first blind wooden step. Like the step of the tree in the distance. (His) feet were truly alive as were his dreaming shoulder and eye." This rare confession in a Dreaming man may tell perhaps of *incompleteness* in all principles of control one exercises. What can we know of "knowledge"—which is human and fallible—when we restrict "knowing" to a closure of learning in senses-in-non-senses? Do we not miss volumes when we think we have caught existence in a fixed or linear pattern?

In taking up *Heartland*, I shall touch on *The Far Journey of Oudin*, the second novel of the series. This will give us some idea of the "history" of which you ask.

Stevenson, in *Heartland*, comes to the Cuyuni forests disoriented and broken within himself. His business world has crashed. The woman Maria, whom he loves, has brought him close to a charge of conspiracy, which he narrowly averts when his father dies, a death in which he is unwittingly involved. He may conventionally be described within the agencies he has known: machinery, television, cars, telephones, etc., that have clothed him successfully in the prosperity in which he lived in the city. But now that so much has crashed and opened a wound he never saw before, he is imbued with startling memories of the machine as a struggling limb he must now feel for the first time like a stilted rock within symptoms of a rising subconscious consciousness. He is, with vagueness yet a certain clarity, aware of himself as experiencing "the heights of intoxicated limbs and suffering an acute fall into the void." He comes upon daSilva from *Palace*—of which he knows but little—and finds him occupying reserves of shared mindscapes in a Dream. It is a many-sided Dream, one aspect of which tells of the first arrivals from another world who stepped on the shores of Guyana, before it possessed a name, Portuguese sailors who may have known the Spanish conquistadores. DaSilva is of Portuguese descent. And, as a consequence, there dawns on him what he calls "the great conquest" whose symbols may still rule the intoxicated spirit of the Americas bent on conquest by technology.

He meets daSilva when he arrives at his landing in the Cuyuni. "The bones in (daSilva's) face were like splinters and the flesh over each fragile support was turning into grey animated newspaper." Flesh like limbs is the substance of memory. Not long after, in a journey around the Kamaria portage, around the falls, he comes upon daSilva in a ravine of precipitous descent to which he is guided by the chattering of a monkey "signalling and wiping his comic sad eyes in the bush." Here it is he sees himself precariously alive in daSilva's dead body, "so changed in twenty-four hours it could have been Kaiser or Cameron or *Stevenson himself*."

Who is Kaiser? Kaiser was consumed by fire in *The Far Journey*. He is an element of paradox "versed in the art of how to withstand the crack of doom." Stevenson may have heard of such a fire and the eruption of someone in the bush resembling Kaiser stirs his imagination into a "wholeness" of tragic proportions pointing still beyond itself, beyond the precipice of conquest, into tenuous antecedents animal and human. Such antecedents may be known to technical or mechanical science but are unknown in fictions of art, which should feel their way beyond the stasis of practical, one-sided language.

Heartland is a *fiction*, I feel, of *inexplicable* truth. Stevenson seeks to see through the violence of centuries. He is confused and skeptical. Nothing he thinks or says can be taken for granted. He mourns for the woman whom he loves. He is aware of himself like a clock of death that holds "diminutive hands" that are his.

*Stevenson dreamt he arose and approached his own chained diminutive hands on the wall. He stood within the false, uneasy circle of light spread by the lantern on the floor, to unhook the clock and begin winding the spring, listening to the startled conscientious sound time made anew, like the wavering crunching of a hard dry biscuit or metallic crust.*

FD'A  *When one dreams one dreams alone. When one writes a book one is alone. The characters one re-creates may have died, or may have vanished into some other country, so one invokes them as "live absences," absences susceptible to being painted into life, sculpted into life, absences that may arise in carvings out of the ground, from dust, from the wood of a tree, the rain of a cloud: paintings and sculptures that are so mysteriously potent in one's book of dreams that they seem to paint one (as one paints them), to sculpt one (as one sculpts them), and in this mutual and phenomenal hollowness of self one and they become fossil stepping-stones into the mystery of inner space.*

(From *The Four Banks of the River of Space*)

This passage suggests a particular species of fiction, and an approach to writing character in fiction that is highly invested in a spirit world or a world shadowing the one we see, an investment in an intuitive world, if intuition can be seen to have a double function both as water—divine that is, instrument, and the thing sought by it. You seem to suggest here for writers an approach to creativity that, if obeyed, should alter the result or outcome of what is written because of the apparent symbiotic nature of the undertaking.

WH  Perhaps I have anticipated this question in my comments on quantum *unpredictability*. I had not fully realized, consciously realized, the unpredictability that is intuitively, shall I say, at work in the fiction I write, even when I wrote *The Four Banks of the River of Space*. Yet it is there in "paintings and sculptures that paint and sculpt one as one sculpts them" in one's "book of dreams."

This, I know, causes difficulties with readers who are accustomed to one mood or principle of control.

I can only say that all intuitions are partial and that they give way to unforeseen impulses but that they retain a shared foundation—diminishing perhaps, growing perhaps—that I have called "the mystery of inner space." "Absence" and "presence" are shared beneath the apparent loss of a guiding "author" who returns—in a changed form—later. I have discussed this already in approaches to "wholeness."

I feel all this brings us closer to a creativity that could alter, as you say, the outcome of writing through a variant symbiosis.

FD'A *A great magical web born of the music of the elements is how one may respond perhaps to a detailed map of Guyana seen rotating in space with its numerous etched rivers, numerous lines and tributaries, interior rivers, coastal rivers, the arteries of God's spider. Guyana is derived from an Amerindian root word, which means "land of waters." The spirit-bone of water that sings in the dense, interior rain forests is as invaluable a resource in the coastal savannahs which have long been subject to drought as to floodwaters that stretched like a sea from coastal river to coastal river yet remained unharnessed and wasted; subject also to the rapacity of moneylenders, miserable loans, inflated interest.*

(From "A Note on the Genesis of the Guyana Quartet," in *The Guyana Quartet*)

Place as outlined here is a fully fledged character, rather than portrayed as symbolic or personified or pressed into service as metaphor (this is not to discount the three, since metaphor, symbol, and personification may be attributed to a successful character portrait). The landscape is not a backdrop. It is not passive. It exerts force and influence. The idea of a web that combines place and elements and stitches space together suggests fragility, vulnerability, and enormous strength, omnipresence. The perspective relates things to each other but each thing seen in isolation makes it vulnerable to misuse, squander. Does the secret of a more fruitful relation between writer and place or explorer and place have to do with perspective, with how the place is viewed, or is more required of the writer and explorer? I am thinking of the representation of place in your fiction, Guyana's interior in particular, and how your way of talking about the place, your perspective, appears to have been radicalized by the encounter and interaction with place, a notion perhaps of form emerging out of content.

WH When I speak of "music"—as in the quotation you raise—I am thinking of "wordless music," which brings an organ of animation within spaces in the dumb images we impose on nature everywhere. Such spaces are sparked into being and into "double meanings." They have vulnerability and fragility, yet, *through* such vulnerability, such holed transparency, they touch on strength and omnipresence between characters—normally polarized and wholly separate—participating creatively and re-creatively in each other's fates and freedoms. The language of conventional, linear fiction, which seems so strong, becomes an illusion and is broken by quantum holes that instantaneously make two penetrations or holes where one alone is expected. *The "double meanings" may be said, in a numinous sense, to spring from a "music" or a rhythm that awakens spaces within passivities we take for granted.*

Does the expression "land of waters" relate to a pre-Columbian complex we have long forgotten, or never understood, in our violations of ancient American civilizations?

Whether so or not, it summons us into an acute eye, an acute ear, beyond mere intellectuality, to listen for and to see "the land moving and capable of unconsidered arts in moved or moving rocks and shells and earth," implying in its rhythm that "the waters are still though in a web of rotating space."

Such paradoxes in variant symbiosis may assist us to harness the *living* waters in preparation for the dry, cracked face of drought that the earth wears, and it may help us to anticipate coming catastrophes from sea and river.

FD'A  In your new novel you introduce the idea of the "fire that does not burn." This strikes me first as a Christian emblem, the burning bush that instructs Moses not to sacrifice his son; second, as a revision of two fire-related myths, the myth of Prometheus, whose act of theft from the gods brought humanity a necessary lease into self and scientific inquiry, and the myth of the Phoenix, born out of fire, with fire as renewal; and, third, as a fictional process of illumination with the story as fire and its heat as ameliorating of the soul rather than as scorching of it.

WH  In *The Mask of the Beggar*, "the fire that burns yet does not burn" certainly has a Promethean aspect but is very significantly concerned with the enigma of the furies. Here is a quotation from the novel:

*What is art? What knowledge do we truly have of implements that tell us of the riddles of the past? A Ship of fire, a Pen or Brush of fire, fire that is not fire, may be an atmospheric trick or it may tell of furies, modulated, toned down, on planet Earth. It may tell of Venus that is an unbearable furnace in the Sky. Venus exists across distances from Earth we do not psychically understand. Such distances are close in psyche and yet faraway as a frail sunflower bobbing and burning on a wave. How close is China to South America, how far away from each other are these planetary waving continents in an Ocean of Space? Is inner peace the material benign raised into complacent hardness—when we are pulled into explosions of the Self in one another—or is it a voyage into spiritual deprivations we have amassed that bring us back to contemplate a corridor in the Beggar's mask that remains a subtle opening into the origins of meaning within the tone and temper of the furies?*

"The Beggar's mask" at the end of the quotation is Odysseus's mask, which he wore as a disguise on his return to the kingdom of Ithaca. It is changed, however, into a mask with holes and subtle openings through which reappear immigrants who would seem like his drowned crew who died on their way back to Ithaca from burning Troy, burning like a fury.

All this points to "the origins of meaning within the tone and temper of the furies."

Venus was and still is regarded as the planet of benign, invariant, or hard love though science knows technologically that it is an "unbearable furnace." We also know mechanically and technically but it is difficult for us to feel this creatively as one penetration of Space with a quantum *other* bringing unusual translations in depth and range on Earth.

We have traveled, it would seem, *psychically* from Venus to Earth but we have not yet learned that Earth exists as a modulated, toned-down version of the furies in Space and in ourselves. As a consequence China and South America, which have exchanged immigrants, become symbols of conflict between continents that may be translated into "planets" "in an Ocean of Space." In *The Mask of the Beggar* such "planets" become furies we need to read creatively in depth and range, or else it is possible that we could bomb each other in the future, fire meeting fire without a modulation, as Odysseus departed from Troy and left Troy in flames.

# Bernard-Henri Lévy
# and Frederic Tuten

BERNARD-HENRI LÉVY was born in Béni Saf, Algeria, in 1948. He is the author of many books, including works of philosophy, fiction, and biography. Recent titles include *American Vertigo: Traveling America in the Footsteps of Tocqueville*; *Left in Dark Times: A Stand Against the New Barbarism*; and, with Michel Houellebecq, *Public Enemies: Dueling Writers Take on Each Other and the World*. Lévy is a graduate of École Normale Supérieure and the founder of the Nouveaux Philosophes.

FREDERIC TUTEN was born in the Bronx, New York, in 1936. He is the author of the novels *The Adventures of Mao on the Long March*; *Tallien: A Brief Romance*; *Tintin in the New World*; *Van Gogh's Bad Café*; and *The Green Hour*. A graduate of New York University, Tuten cofounded the graduate program in creative writing at the City College of New York. He is a recipient of a Guggenheim Fellowship as well as an American Academy of Arts and Letters Award for Distinguished Writing from the American Academy of Arts and Letters. He teaches classes on experimental writing at The New School and lives in New York City.

*Lévy's responses translated by Jeanine Herman.*

*January 18*

Dear Bernard-Henri Lévy,

First, to say what a pleasure to meet you last week for the first time and to be able to tell you face to face how much I had enjoyed of what I had then incompletely read of *American Vertigo*. I must confess, I was unaware of what complexity of discussion and argument, of provocative analysis of the American experience lay ahead, having assumed the book was much on the order of the opening hundred or so pages: that is, a personal narrative and record of a journey through America more or less in de Tocqueville's footsteps. I was taken by the energy of your prose, by the vivid cameos of American life along your journey's path. I thought: This is a passionate journey of a man enamored with America, a journey with hints of Whitman's and Kerouac's, above all with their love of the mad originality of this vast and varied place, this circus of America.

A circus with prisons, the prison being the original consideration for Tocqueville's investigation of American life, and to which you give significant attention and reflection, visiting such disparate places as Rikers Island and Guantanamo, with stops along the way to Angola, Louisiana, a place Kafka would have found agonizingly, spiritually familiar. As you say, prisons everywhere are bad, but there is a unique quality to those privatized ones where the idea of rehabilitation vanishes and the human soul is replaced by its value as profit and loss. Let me digress and add a little item to your survey of prisons. Today a murderer in a wheelchair, blind, with diabetes, age seventy-six, was given a lethal injection in prison. This you may one day cite as an example of the compassion of the penal system and capital punishment, a mercy killing, if you will.

From prison to torture is a natural step. And perhaps nothing in your book did I find so moving as your chagrin at the recent American debate on whether to use torture in the defense of national interest. A debate unworthy of this nation, unworthy of being brought forth as a topic of discussion, let alone one for civilized consideration. You find it noteworthy and symptomatic of the health of our society, however, that revelations about the "extraordinary renditions"—the outsourcing of torture to centers abroad—and other such horrors were revealed in the press and to the public as quickly as they were; unlike, say, the way the French press was kept from revealing the facts of torture during the Algerian war. Yes. But let us not forget that one of our leaders made the case against the torture in Iraq as one of the reasons for our going there. Or that we tacitly approved of torture in Brazil, Chile, and Argentina during the Cold War period—to make democracy safe.

In spite of all the darkness you see around us, you refer to a spiritual spine or line, represented by such figures as Emerson and Thoreau, Washington and Kennedy running through our culture and speaking for the best and most noble of what we have been and what we still may be. But, perhaps, Bernard, what you see is only a spiritual glow from the past, the light of another America, like the light that comes from a distant star long dead.

—FT

*January 27*

No, dear Frederic, it's not a question of "compensation." And I don't believe that this lifeline, this light that I have ceaselessly invoked because, in fact, I felt its diffuse and vague presence, I don't think that it is comparable to the light of dead stars.

I really believe that American democracy is alive. I agree that it is in crisis. I agree that it is being led by poor shepherds. I also think, as Tocqueville said very well, that the margin between democracy and tyranny is narrow and that it is becoming even more narrow and more fragile. But I feel democracy to be alive, nevertheless. Vibrant. I feel it continuing to inspire if not your institutions then at least your civil society; and this famous fabric of "associations" that Tocqueville emphasized, was, in relation to Europe, one of its most original features.

I agree that the system is sometimes defective, but grant me that its wellsprings are healthy.

Some examples are necessary, and not just a declaration of principle.

The Los Angeles women who lobbied to prevent the construction of a Wal-Mart in their neighborhood, and who had, last I heard, succeeded against all odds. Big, bad Wal-Mart, monster, crusher of salaries and creator of commercial deserts. The embodiment of this evil market, this capitalism without virtue, the "sociopolitical obesity" that weighs on American democracy and is a source of the growing hubris of the current administration. Well, it didn't get the last word. Here were three women who remembered the 1960s slogan that "small is beautiful," and small won out over the Mall. Here we have a post-Tocquevillian association of women of color, and they beat back the monster—showing that, when the people join forces, and really want it, they still have the last word.

Next, homeschooling, to which I devote a short chapter while passing through Texas, and which is unthinkable in France. We have, in France, an educational system that is scarcely faring any better than America's, but we cross our arms and remain passive. And, in any case, the very idea of educating your children at home, of extracting them from these idiotic mainstream values and saving them from disaster is forbidden by law. Here, in the United States, you have the possibility of citizens taking control of their children's destiny. In short, you have the option of resistance to programmed idiocy: "The system wants to die; well, let it die, if it wants to, but it will be without us and, above all, without our children." I at first wondered, with the pathetic remnants of my Jacobin temperament, if this way of doing without the State, of saving oneself by deserting the field of collective struggle, was not a bit reactionary, but today, on the contrary, I think that here we have a real example of democratic vitality. People on the Right *and* the Left, religious types but also atheists, people of all sorts whose only real line is to *not* resign themselves to the programmed inevitability of mental stultification are the sign that morale is not broken.

Or take Katrina. It's one of the book's chapters to which I attach the most importance. There is this revelation with Katrina of the continent of American poverty, and the fact that the State, whether local or federal, is utterly failing in its duties. There is this idea of an anti-September 11 that, in contrast to the other, chose its dead, striking primarily the poor and the black. But look! There is also the extraordinary spectacle of the people reacting to this institutional deficiency by taking in hand the concrete organization of aid to the refugees fleeing New Orleans. Texas is not a particularly Democratic state, is it? And not a particularly liberal one, either. And yet the happy surprise of Katrina were these Texans opening the doors of their hospitals, schools, homes, opening their arms, their hearts, their wallets, in order to help, without concern for the political, social, religious, or, needless to say, ethnic differences of the poor people seeking shelter and simple comfort. And, say what you will, dear Frederic—that is a spirit of solidarity of the people that I'm not sure we would have had in France if a hurricane had struck Toulouse and the victims had tried to find refuge in Lille or Roubaix—and I won't even talk about what would happen if a catastrophe struck, say, Germany, and if victims tried to take refuge in France. That, for me, is another incontestable sign of democratic vitality.

There are scores of these examples in the book, and I've gathered so many since. But one has to show some restraint.

And it's not a question of falling into some sort of populist opposition between a "real" America that has remained healthy and virtuous versus an "official" America that, left and right alike, has turned its back on its values: in France we're familiar with that old refrain, and I certainly do not want to say such a thing. But to recognize that the America of the pilgrims and the Founding Fathers, of Thoreau and Emerson, the America analyzed and celebrated by Tocqueville himself with his glorification of the famous "associations," to recognize that all that is still alive, that it is the true resource of your system and the chance for your future, what harm is there in that? Is it overly optimistic to point out these features everywhere?

It's true; I have hope. The American dream seems to me to be of a nature to orient your future and ours.

—BHL


*January 30*

Dear Bernard,

Here I am again and wondering a few things, actually more than just a few. Your book was commissioned by the *Atlantic Monthly*, but I wonder why you agreed—or better yet, why you wanted to write about America at all. Some of my older French friends have a tender regard for us no matter what we do here and abroad; they lived through the Occupation and appreciate our role in chasing out the Nazis. Henceforth, America is always the place of the Good and the Just, a zany place, peopled with good intentions. Little can persuade them to feel otherwise. But you come from a wholly different generation, one born to an almost knee-jerk suspicion of America and its motives. To which you have had a counter reaction, and are closer to the postwar generation than you are to your own. Do I assume correctly?

Let me approach you and why you wrote your book in another way. When we met, you asked me if I loved France. Yes, I said, very much. When I was a very young man—until yesterday—when I was a boy in the Bronx, I dreamed of Paris, the one I knew from films like *An American in Paris*, where, at fifteen, I learned that I could live above a café and be a painter and meet a wonderful French girl who would live with me in that same little place above the café. As for money, the film and other sources of such myths, showed me that the French did not care for money but cared for, appreciated, love, art, and artists.

The pathetic thing is that against all reality, I still half subscribe to that myth, as well to others based on the beauty of the intentions of the French Revolution and the utopian nobility of the Paris Commune. Are you not a little like me, loving not the place, America, as it is, but loving it—against all realities—as a myth and for its myth?

—FT


*February 9*

You're partly right, my dear Frederic.

I like what you say, so amusingly, about your relationship with France. And, no doubt, there is an element of myth, or dream, in the way I see the real America of today: a motley assemblage of Kennedy; Ellis Island; Martin Luther King's dream; the civil rights struggle; Daniel Pearl and Norman Mailer, combined; the Jews of Brooklyn seen as characters out of Isaac Bashevis Singer; the hero Roosevelt; the great president Clinton; the famous American optimism that is perhaps, deep down, nothing more than another cliché that I am swept away by; New Orleans—yes, my love song to New Orleans.

I do not agree with what you assume about my generation—basically, the baby boomers born after the Second World War—and their relationship with the reality of your country. And I would like to make two observations in this regard that are—how should I say it—biographical-political in nature.

First observation. The memory of the Second World War and Nazism. The idea, as you say, of the Americans as liberators of Europe. Of course, this was initially the previous generation's affair. But how can one deny that it was also ours? How can we pretend that we, the French after Vichy, and especially the French and the Jews born after the Shoah—and thus, in a certain way, miraculously spared from a disaster that had aspired to nothing less than preventing our births—how can we pretend that we escaped the great beneficent shadow of the American army helping to destroy Hitler's killing machine? My father was liberated early on. At eighteen, he joined the ranks of the Spanish Republic to fight in the Spanish Civil War, then, immediately afterward, he volunteered to fight against Germany, then, after the defeat, he fought in the Free French Forces—in Africa, Monte Cassino, the liberation of Paris, etc. So this idea of a liberating and antifascist America, that even before the war, starting with the terrible '30s, had been a refuge for so many antifascists and for Jews fleeing the coming catastrophe, and writers, and artists—that was one of the first things I remember being taught by my father. I grew up with this legend. Not to mention my dear mother, who until the end of her life, left every summer with a girlfriend to spend a few weeks of vacation in America, always a new city, a new state, in order to discover more about the country that she adored and to which she felt she owed everything. You ask me what led me to accept *The Atlantic*'s and Cullen Murphy's proposal. Well, perhaps this, too, a discreet homage (though, now that I'm writing to you about it, a bit less discreet!) to a beloved mother who was crazy about America and who took this journey before me, who in a way "located" it for me, and in whose footsteps I am simply following, as I am following in Tocqueville's. Anyway, all this to say one can't simplify generational matters, and contagion, in this case, prevailed over the gap. Don't forget, by the way, how in even the most left-ist among us, in the most enraged, the most radical, and especially in the Maoists, the schema of the fascism-versus-antifascism opposition continued, until May '68, to structure our vision of the world and the struggles we led within it. Don't forget how so many of us hallucinated that we were the partisans of a great, new, antifascist war that was the fulfillment of the one our elders had waged. This vision of things, whether we like it or not, could only imply an enchanted vision of America, whether as memory, nostalgia, or, as you say, myth. It could not make us what the modern inheritors of this leftist movement have, alas, become—namely, enraged anti-Americans.

Perhaps you will say that the American army at the time, the army of the Vietnam War and its crimes, the army we see in Chris Marker's *Le Fond de l'air est rouge*, napalming the civilian populations, took on, in our ideological bestiary, precisely the role of the armies it had once defeated. Well, yes and no. I think that we had—and this is my second observation—*anti*-anti-American defenders that are exactly what our heirs on the extreme left today lack. I will take my own case. I don't know if this will apply to all the young men and women of that time, but for a number of us it was an unimpeachable and precocious certainty. Anti-Americanism was politically to the left, fine. In the political language, it was called anti-imperialism, okay. But for anyone who had not only an ear but a memory, a more specific idea of the ideological history of France, and especially for anyone who had grown up in the familial tradition that I just described, there were cultural sources, ideological and philosophical dynasties, of anti-Americanism that had absolutely nothing to do with the left. It came from the other side. It smelled not only of the right but of the French far right of the '50s, the '30s, and even before that. It reeked, if you prefer, of what we hated the most in the world, namely Pétainism—that mixture of racism, anti-Semitism, contorted nationalism, excessive patriotism, hatred of democracy and cosmopolitanism, phobia of the Rousseauist "social contract," the idea of a community founded on a pure "act of will," a "credo," which the Pétainists always vaguely felt that America—real or dreamed, it doesn't matter—was the first and, moreover, the only incarnation. I wrote that twenty-five years ago, in a book called *L'Idéologie française*, whose last pages dealt with this matter of anti-Americanism and its genealogy; I demonstrated that this old French passion had only very belatedly migrated into the discourse of the left and that its real birthplace was to be found rather in Drieu La Rochelle, Brasillach, the Maurrassiens [*Eds. note: Charles Maurras, French writer and principal thinker of the reactionary Action Française, counter-revolutionary movement; anti-Semitic monarchist*], even Barrès—our long and fetid national tradition of Anglophobia. But all this, which would eventually become a book, was something I always felt in some vague way. I was never really anti-American, just as I was never really anti-Zionist. I belong to a generation who felt, very early on, that anti-Americanism in Europe always had a connection to fascism.

Now that does not prevent me from seeing, or at least trying to see, the America of today as it is. Nor from talking to my American friends about everything in America that is unworthy of this idea that I will never weary of contrasting with antagonistic ideas that the anti-Americans hold. I speak to them of their atrocious prisons. I speak to them of their absurd and deadly malls. Of their dubious gun fairs. I talk to them about the death penalty, unacceptable in a large democracy. I speak to them about Guantanamo, where I had a chance to work for a few days and which I left convinced was, though certainly not the gulag, nevertheless a disgrace. I speak to them, you're right, of this ignoble debate on the conditions in which the use of torture could be justified. I speak to them about the massacre of the Indians and the fact that a gaping wound will remain in the flank of the nation until a real place of mourning and remembrance, a sort of Yad Vashem of the suffering of the first inhabitants of the country, is dedicated to them. I even talk to them about Mount Rushmore, this monument that is so emblematic of American democracy and about which I would nevertheless say: 1) it seems placed there as a colossal provocation, on a site that, for the Indian communities, was one of the most sacred in the country; 2) the sculptor of these icons is a former member of the Ku Klux Klan who apparently never renounced the ideas of his youth; 3) that it is called "Rushmore" after a filthy lawyer, a thief, employed by the great gold seekers and entrusted with finding legal ways to expropriate Indian landowners of their land at the cheapest cost. But all right. The little detail that changes everything and that I am grateful you have seen is that all of this proceeds from this fundamental love of America and the American people. I think that one cannot criticize America unless one is animated by a sincere love of its people and its Idea.

—BHL


*February 14*

My dear Bernard,

I've read your last two letters. My initial response was to open my window and sing the National Anthem. But now I'm in a cooler mood. Not that I have cooled to the intensity of your convictions or to your warmth for America in principle or America in the person of its generous and open-hearted good people, but I am reminded that there were good people, after all, in Nazi Germany, in Fascist Italy, in Vichy France.

In a passage in your book, you ask why Americans have not responded with a forceful voice to the issue of torture and its outsourcing, to the issue of the systematic encroachments on our civil liberties. Why do Americans not see that allowing these encroachments is "like inserting a worm into fruit, or a virus into a computer program? Who among them is fully conscious that, for America as for any democracy, this is the source of a crisis that could lead anywhere?" A good question and one that strikes at the core of your optimism, your hope that the great progressive American tradition not only shall endure but that it shall prevail.

Allow me for a moment, as you did, to indulge in the autobiographical.

Like yours, my father was an antifascist. He was a radical Southerner, who believed, as many of his Depression-era generation did, that America would one day undergo a great social transformation, in whose wake would come justice and equality. Like yours, my mother—the first-born in a Sicilian family—loved America. Like you, I, too, love this country. Perhaps in no other place in the world but America would I have had the chance to rise out of dire poverty and be allowed to live the life of a writer and a professor. America: The fair shake. America: The ever-evolving to the Good. America: Freedom.

Today, in a country cowed into the acquiescence of the removal of its freedoms because of the fear of an external threat, people do speak out, but there is a sense of pointlessness and futility in doing so. Sadly, the intelligentsia speaks only to itself, as it probably always has. It may have seemed different during the Vietnam period, but I suspect that those protesting voices of the intelligentsia were effective, to the extent as they were at all, because of the popular consensus against the war. I hope, as I am sure you do, that the natural resistance of Americans to tyranny will overcome their fears generated and propagated by official lies.

Let me confess to my chagrin in not finding a way to give voice against the growing darkening of America today.

So, mon cher ami, your book further points to the distance between me and your dreams—our dreams and my reality.

—FT


*February 16*

Dear, dear Frederic,

It is my turn, in reading you, to want to rush to the window. Not to sing the American anthem, but to breathe some air after the apocalyptic tableau that you paint of your country. I agree, of course, with what you say about the liberties that this government is taking with liberties. I, too, think this must be taken very seriously—the Patriot Act, wiretapping, the FBI's systematic surveillance of the Internet and all the rest. But without playing devil's advocate, would you allow me to observe that the Patriot Act, as far as I know, is something temporary? That it raised a spectacular collective protest all over the country? That the Administration met with the liveliest resistance when it tried to pass its "Patriot Act II"? Must I remind you that there were *Republicans* in the Senate, in the name of the libertarian tradition that is theirs, and that, in spite of the diversions, remains alive—who oppose the perpetuation of an arrangement that they know in the long run can only go against the sacrosanct Bill of Rights? Must I remind you that both the big newspapers and the television networks, in principle subject to the big lobbies of Faith, Money, and Authority, reacted with astonishing velocity to Seymour Hersh's revelations, two years ago, of the abuses of Iraqis at Abu Ghraib? And the matter of special prisons? And the question of Guantanamo? And this real public debate that, whatever we have to say about it, is traversing the country, regarding these rights-less zones, zones indeed of pure illegality, authorized by the "War on Terror"? All that is not the sign of tyranny setting in. We know in France what tyrannical temptation can be. During the Algerian War and afterward, we knew the temptation of stifling freedoms and the truth and the press. And from this point of view, believe me: a country that, to take the case of Abu Ghraib once again and the positive virus of truth that seized the media, including Fox News, a country that was able in forty-eight hours to take a path that has taken us forty-eight years to still not take regarding the barbarous acts committed by the French army before General de Gaulle's return to power—a country like this may be in crisis, unhealthy, seized by vertigo, etc., but it is not a "fascist" country, and it is not a "tyranny."

I have a hypothesis in the book. I was in Austin, Texas, the day of Bush's second victory, as a guest in a class that Paul Burka teaches on Tocqueville. I gradually noticed that the majority of students before me, if they were old enough to vote, voted against the president and, on questions like abortion, gay marriage, creationism, indeed, the death penalty, took positions contrary to his. At that moment, it seemed that the wave of conservative moral values that seemed to set souls ablaze in the final days of the campaign, this bizarre and bizarrely desperate fever to advocate the return to a fundamental order that modernity was thought to have beaten and condemned—all of that could perhaps be read completely in the opposite way: as the last hurrah of a very old conservative party that knows that the good old days will never return; that the youth have swung to the good side of the great cultural American revolution; and that it is time, therefore, for the counter-revolutionary forces to load their final salvo. That was my impression, that day in Austin. But it was, even more, the feeling that struck me a few days later as I went across true Southern states like Tennessee, Arkansas, and especially Alabama. Is this the South? The old southern culture, this quail-hunting party whose rituals are still there but are empty, deprived of meaning? Atlanta, this black and prosperous city where there are no longer any traces of Rhett Butler or Scarlett O'Hara? And what about racism? Where did it go, this open anti-black racism that, as a drugged and prejudiced Frenchman, I thought was part and parcel of the most deep-seated mentality of the deep South? I discovered that it had become, as in the rest of the country, if not minor, then at least unsayable—thanks to Morris Dees, who chased fascists from Montgomery, thanks to Jim Carrier, historiographer of the great antiracist struggles of thirty years ago. Something had occurred that cannot be erased. And the current wave of conservatism should not make us forget the much longer wave that started with Rosa Parks, Martin Luther King, et al., and that has durably changed the cultural face and landscape of the country.

So now, of course, there is the other question, concerning the lifelessness of public opinion today and especially that of the intellectual and political left, which I willingly agree is not rising to the level of its glorious elders.

There is something troubling, for a French intellectual, in this spectacle of a liberal camp so timorous in the face of the great, burning questions that should concern it. I will spare you the most pathetic moments of my submersion into the depths of the supposed new American left, my encounters with these holdovers of the Clinton era, more puritan than the most puritan, or with those Hillaryans who answer the question of how they count on winning the battle of ideas by speaking of the need to first win the battle of funding. What of creationism and the battle that must be led, in the name of the heritage of the Enlightenment, against the crooks who seek to impose the teaching of "intelligent design" as a "second" theory? What of the welfare state? The growth, everywhere, of areas of poverty? What of the pure scandal that is the presence of the death penalty, the keystone of the American penal system? And how can it be that there are no longer any great voices to rise up against this civilized barbarism, unworthy of a great democracy? The most common response is that public opinion would be against it. First of all, that is not an answer. There was a time when the American intelligentsia could take unpopular positions against the current. And, besides, I am not at all sure that the heartland is so definitively set against the idea of revisiting the matter of the death penalty. (Having discussed the topic dozens of times with people I came across in my travels, having spoken with conservatives aware of the numerous legal errors recognized by the courts, having discussed with Christians that it seemed problematic for a Christian to consent to human life's being at the mercy of anyone but God; I get the sense that America is more or less in the situation we in France were exactly twenty-five years ago, when a candidate, who then became the President of the Republic, courageously decided to try to abolish it, and did.) It is among politicians terrified by the thought of attempting the least deviation and raising their voices, it is in these think tanks, supposedly suppliers of ideas but who do not seem to know their country very well, it is among the intellectuals that there is, very clearly, a problem, and that problem must be not only raised but resolved. Let's call it a treason of the intellectuals. Let's say there is a new treason of intellectuals with American colors. We, the French, know the phenomenon. We are even sort of experts in it. And therefore we're prepared, if necessary, to share our expertise with you. But then, friends, it's your turn. And, this time, it's essential that you play.

—BHL

# Wayne Koestenbaum and Kenneth Goldsmith

WAYNE KOESTENBAUM was born in San Jose, California, in 1958. A graduate of Harvard University, Johns Hopkins University, and Princeton University, where he received his PhD, Koestenbaum is the author of numerous books of fiction, criticism, and poetry, including *Blue Stranger with Mosaic Background*, *Ode to Anna Moffo and Other Poems*, *Hotel Theory*, *Humiliation*, and *My 1980s and Other Essays*. Koestenbaum received a Whiting Writers' Award in 1994. He has taught English at Yale and painting at the Yale School of Art. He is a Distinguished Professor of English at the CUNY Graduate Center and lives in New York City.

KENNETH GOLDSMITH was born in Freeport, New York, in 1961. He is the author of numerous books, including *Day*, *The Weather*, *Soliloquy*, and *Fidget*, in which he transcribed every movement his body made over a 13-hour period. A graduate of the Rhode Island School of Design, Goldsmith teaches at the University of Pennsylvania and was the Museum of Modern Art's first Poet Laureate. He is the founder of UbuWeb and the coeditor of *Against Expression: An Anthology of Conceptual Writing*. He lives in New York City.

**WAYNE KOESTENBAUM**  I love your library. I had forgotten the precision and beauty of your collection. It's just unbelievable.

**KENNETH GOLDSMITH**  I only get one bookshelf here in the city so for anything new that comes in, a whole bunch of books have to go out to make room. I'm such a collector and hoarder that if Cheryl [Donegan] didn't make this rule, this place would be filled with so many books that you couldn't move.

**WK**  Do the discards go to the country?

**KG**  Nothing gets sold.

**WK**  I salute that retentiveness.

**KG**  I can't, because the collection is the trace of my intellectual life. As a kid I would go into new phases with records, and each time I entered a new one, I would sell the rest of my records. Eventually I ended up having to buy them all back.

**WK**  You've learned your lesson.

**KG**  Let me ask you a question here since I'm interviewing you. If this were your bookshelf, what would go?

**WK**  I don't think you have books as low as my low books go.

**KG**  You wouldn't have the Abbie Hoffman collection here.

**WK**  That's not low, though. I wouldn't have Abbie Hoffman because I lack the kind of street cred or lobby cred to earn the right to own Hoffman.

**KG**  Those are some of my very favorite things in the world. (*Points at an author photo in one of the books.*) Look at this. Is Abbie Hoffman cute?

**WK**  Yeah, he's really cute. Just my type. Berkeley radical. Polymorphous perversity.

**KG**  But totally Jewish. Come on, you don't think that's sexy? (*laughter*) In *Humiliation*, you talk about Woodstock and the hippies.

WK  I couldn't have gone to Woodstock because I'm not fit to be a nudist.

KG  (*laughter*) I know.

WK  Okay, let me think of a title I own that you would never go near. I have a poetry library that I started when I became a poet, in 1981.

KG  When you were a Yale Younger Poet?

WK  Never. I entered the Yale Younger Poets contest in 1983 with my first manuscript of poems—called "Fifty Sonnets," which tells you something—and I got a tiny rejection note that said, "Accomplished manuscript." My library is the library of someone who would live on that praise for two years and who would write a book called "Fifty Sonnets."

KG  My first book was called *73 Poems*.

WK  Very different lineage.

KG  I took the title from E. E. Cummings. Where did you take your title from?

WK  Nowhere.

KG  Cummings wrote a really beautiful book called *73 Poems*. Are you a Cummings fan?

WK  I'm not, actually. Not because I don't like him, just because I've never crossed the street to taste him.

KG  How did you miss Cummings?

WK  How did you find Cummings?

KG  Through concrete poetry and visual typography. Cage actually set a Cummings piece to music. So Cummings is in my lineage.

WK  But Cummings has not received the full recuperation and renovation that others of his era have.

KG  Well, he was a horrible man. He was a bad anti-Semite and a grouch—

WK   —Right, not a good anti-Semite. Not a charming one.

KG  Unlike Ezra Pound.

WK  Exactly; a charismatic anti-Semite.

KG  We still care about Pound, but we don't care about Cummings.

WK  He just fell through the cracks. When I was coming of age, no one talked about him.

KG  But when you were coming of age, nobody talked about modernism.

WK  I never came of age, that's part of the problem.

KG  But, seriously, nobody talked about modernism.

WK  They did, actually. I wrote my undergraduate thesis on Ezra Pound. And I read *The Maximus Poems* in a course in college.

KG  Really? At Harvard they were teaching Olson?

WK  Olson is canonical. He has more fans than Wallace Stevens.

KG  They both have a lot more fans than we do. (*laughter*) Speaking of which, I didn't know that you were painting!

WK  It's the new thing.

KG  When did that start?

WK  On September 19, 2010.

KG  (*laughter*) Stop that!

WK  Why is that funny, because I know the day?

KG  Yeah.

WK  It was the day before my birthday, and I was walking by Utrecht Art Supplies. I had had a dream about drawing with a fountain pen—I was writing, but the lines weren't words. So I bought watercolor pencils and played with those for a day, and the next day I bought a watercolor set, and the next day I bought some gouache. Now I've graduated to DaVinci Artist Supply; I haven't gone near Pearl or the real temples.

KG It all begins with dreams, doesn't it?

WK Yeah.

KG We had a talk a while ago about the importance of dreams—which I don't pay any attention to—and you told me that I should. You lectured me on the importance of Freud and convincingly applied the whole thing to Warhol.

WK Andy's outsides are insides. And you are so totally open to external information that it becomes your unconscious. Or, rather, you're not imperialist toward the noise of the world. You are receptive and porous, so the world becomes your unconscious. I do not let in the world.

KG I feel the total opposite. I move through the world but repel it. You, on the other hand, are completely permeable. Unlike Warhol, though, who also let things pass through, things go through your skin and get stuck in your body. I realized that, having spent so much time with your new books. Your body absorbs—that's a difference.

WK And Warhol is right in between because he takes in everything and keeps it, but he also pretends to move through the world with a body-suited fluidity and impermeability. I'm influenced by surrealism and psychoanalysis; to both of those forces, you seem immune. We dive into aesthetic history at different moments: it's as if you started in the late '60s and I started in the '50s.

KG In a lot of ways your practice is informed by the bodily celebration of the '70s, not the '50s. I think you like to construct yourself as carrying the repression of the '50s. Everything you're doing is hinging between total abandonment and total repression all the time. You're not *just* '50s, but you're also not '70s either. There's also this wild awareness. Do you exist without self-consciousness?

WK No, I don't, but when I say the '50s I don't think I mean *that* '50s. I actually mean the '50s of Rauschenberg, Twombly, and Joan

Mitchell. Drink was a big part of that era. These artists externalized their internal landscapes and transformed psychic matter into urban phantasmagoria.

KG  Oh, I get it. I was thinking of a buttoned-down '50s repression.

WK  Rauschenberg et al. are in dialogue with the buttoned-down, but I'm most interested in their bold decision, in the '50s, to perform certain import-export acts. Those acts of subterfuge are behind what you do, but you don't dwell on the glee or the sense of personal liberation that accrues from textual sampling.

KG  And your glee is about getting away with something from the culture at large. My glee is more about tweaking the noses of those who profess themselves to be ultraliberal, by testing their limit. I'm surrounded by so many people who think and feel the way that I do, who are so accepting, that I wonder how can I push those buttons a bit further.

WK  We both are outlaws in different ways. I stage my sense of outlaw behavior within the proscenium of aesthetics, so my stances refer to laws that don't exist anymore. I disobey laws that no longer exist, but I acquire the full quotient of glee and abjection that comes from feeling as if I were still living in a police state. You are actually dangerous. You're trying to change the paradigm of aesthetic practice altogether, in a way that is iconoclastic and desecrating.

KG  Weird, I think one of the most viewed things of yours were the vignettes of *Humiliation* on the Internet where you answered "Dear Wayne" letters by people writing you about how to handle their humiliating experiences.

WK  Definitely more people saw those than ever read any book of mine— that fact is either sad or great. Actually, it's not sad in the least, it's shocking.

KG  I actually feel like *The Anatomy of Harpo Marx* is the closest our works have ever come together while still being completely different. For example, if I were to have written that book, which I actually may do because I was so inspired by it, I would have watched the identical things that you did but then simply narrated all of Harpo's body movements, without any interpolation, any subjectivity, any historical or biographical references—I may actually do that and dedicate the book to you. The obsession in your book is intense, unexpected. This is a totally different book for you. It's funny that University of California Press put it out instead of Turtle Point, your poetry publishers. In a way, it's a work of conceptual poetry. All of your books intimidate me in different ways, but this one is a new note of intimidation. It's so dense and obsessive that it verges on the unreadable, which I mean in a good way. I think it's a work of conceptual literature, the likes of which you've never really done before.

**WK**  You know? It was indirectly, and probably very directly, influenced by you.

**KG**  I really feel that, but there's an exhaustion in the book, scene after scene of the movies in which Harpo appeared, each described in great detail. It's an absolutely insane project.

**WK**  The first version of it was like fifteen hundred pages.

**KG**  (*laughter*)

**WK**  And the pictures were large, not thumbnail-sized. I had taken the original pictures with a digital camera from my computer screen, so they were blurry. They were actual photos. I did not use screen grabs.

**KG**  Let me ask you a question, now that you're a visual artist: Could you see your blurry original photographs being blown up and put on the wall as artworks of yours?

**WK**  I don't know if I would be interested in the spectacle of such an installation, but when I was making those photographs I understood that these were art acts and that the writing was merely supplementary. The real feat was taking the photo. To allow that practice to enter my world, I was forced to describe the photos, but that gesture of description was extra. The moment of arrival was when I chose the image and I took the picture.

**KG**  That's a classic act of Pictures Generation appropriation.

**WK**  Yeah, it's totally Pictures Generation. That was the Kenny part of it, if I may.

**KG**  Maybe not me. Let's call it the Richard Prince part of it.

**WK** Right, but in a literary context I would much rather have it be Kenny than Richard Prince.

**KG** The cover image of *The Anatomy of Harpo Marx* is really weird.

**WK** What was weird?

**KG** Well, it looks contemporary. I thought it was from a Kalup Linzy piece.

**WK** I knew you were going to say Kalup Linzy.

**KG** It's about the most perfect cover.

**WK** I'm not just flattering you; the book is situated in our friendship and what I've learned from you. Seriously. You pay a seemingly useless and counterproductive amount of attention to transcription, and you enter a space of boredom and deadness, but the concept that you're serving redeems everything. In a Kennyesque gesture, I decided to write my longest, most ambitious, and exegetically rigorous book about an actor who never spoke onscreen.

**KG** When you had told me that you were doing the book, I had imagined a really different one, more along *Jackie Under My Skin.* This is—

**WK** —A friendly book.

**KG** Well, *Humiliation* is super friendly. But *Harpo* is barbarous—it seems like it's going to be fun and then you get into it and it's got the weight of art.

**WK** Yeah, it's my Rosalind Krauss. My *Optical Unconscious.* When I taught a Walter Benjamin course I realized he's *really* slow. And, I mean, there's nothing I love more than your *sprechstimme* performances of his essays—or is it Adorno's?—to Erik Satie.

**KG** (*laughter*) Adorno's.

**WK** If there were one reason to love you, just one, it would have to be because of those performances. They are priceless works of art! Anyway, as I slogged through Benjamin—and he's easier than Adorno—I thought, Okay, that's the space that these thinkers claim, that you read a sentence and you stop, and then you read another sentence and stop, and so on—it's an arduousness that's somehow ethically informed by the Holocaust. You *have* to pay this much attention because of the six million. That's the threat beneath it all. So, similarly—forgive the obscenity of this comparison— because of the six million you have to follow every sentence of *The Anatomy of Harpo Marx*, because if you don't care about Harpo's dead body then you are desecrating the six million.

**KG** Wow.

**WK** And so I would take on a Germanic style of great, condensed sentences and just do a crazy thing, because they never would have allowed themselves the leap into popular culture.

**KG** Popular culture but, even more, autobiography.

**WK** Right.

**KG** For me, reading the Harpo book was a door into your past. There's so much about your parents, and so much about your relationship to Judaism, to your body jazz, Truffaut, Fatty Arbuckle, and a million other tangents. What happens is a swerve: you make a proposition here—"Record and analyze the body of Harpo Marx in every onscreen appearance he makes throughout his career"—and then you break it, subjectify it, and personalize it in ways that we only dream, say, Benjamin or Adorno would've done. We love them now, but we would love them much more had they gone off and talked about their mothers' underwear!

**WK** Before I wrote *Harpo* I wanted to write a book called "Walter Benjamin's Body," and it would talk about the diaper-load look he has—

**KG** (*laughter*)

**WK** It's true, he has diaper face! What did he smell like? His slow walk. I wanted to write about how the details of his body inform his work; I wanted to pay attention to the body of a slow thinker.

**KG** So here we are, seventy-five years later, reading your book, and people are trying to do the same deconstruction—or reconstruction, I should say—of you. There it all is: Wayne's deep insides and his body, clearly. Boy, do we know about his body! So what would be the parallel path, the interpretive path, of decoding when the body, subjectivity, and interiority are completely present?

**WK** I'm imagining that seventy-five years from now there will be a way of looking at literature that understands words as mouth objects, a way of reading that is not stuck on issues of history, theme, content, figuration—a reading practice that has a much more radically material, and even scientifically rigorous, understanding of the flows and weights of words and how they connect to historical, physical, chemical, and mental processes. And so my language, anything I ventriloquize as a literary movement or identity politics, will mean nothing. Instead, the issues will be: How many times did I use the word *indefatigable*? What is the weight and history and sound of *indefatigable*? How many people in 1985 used the word *indefatigable*? Just a weird topographic analysis of my language. That's the way I write, actually. I use autobiography because I need *something* to write down. And I need to interpret, so I'll interpret the loaf of bread and I'll talk about the breads of my earlier life, but that's just because writing requires a material subject. The process is kind of Agnes Martinesque—all about texture and very close, dull investigation of verbal surfaces.

**KG** So you feel that autobiography and interiority will ultimately fall off? Are they an apparatus?

**WK** Right. An apparatus in the same way as dialogue in screwball comedy or suspense in Hitchcock is. Autobiography is my apparatus, my vehicle; my real activity is words and sentences and the psychological and historical positions that they embody. That said, I do also believe in the unity of a human life and particularly in how artists' lives—how they behave—all fit together in a fascinating way that can only be seen in retrospect. How they dress, whom they know, the whole picture. I look forward to being that object of scrutiny for five people in some archive. Not nearly as sexy as Arthur Cravan or Paul Thek. What's interesting about Paul Thek, though, is not any particular work he made. It's his entire vision of how a body moves through space and sex and history, and the artifacts that he deposits along the way.

**KG** When you're writing, do you apply those types of narratives or models to your own trajectory?

**WK** Secretly, yeah. Often in a somewhat nondemonstrative, local, aesthetic way, having to do with length of sentence, kind of tone, dimensions of project.

**KG** Clothing?

WK  Clothing. Style—whether it's written longhand in notebooks, whether I'm using the digital camera, whether I'm typing, collaging, cutting-up, playing N+7 . . .

KG  But this is not what you're saying. You're going back to the practice, but then you are talking about the kind of life—the clothes, the food, the smell. You're saying, "Let's talk about Benjamin's body, we don't need to talk about the words"; or, "Let's talk about the mystique of Cravan and Paul Thek." We're not really talking about the words there, but when you begin to talk about your own practice, it does drift back to an analytical, you know, a purely Apollonian—

WK  —Yeah, I'm kind of Apollonian, because I have not mastered the art of friendship. When I think about the artists' lives that are interesting, I have had, to some extent, an unfortunate notion—from never having gone to art school—that socializing and practice are somewhat separate.

KG  Really?

WK  Your work shows the imprint of having gone to art school. You understand that interpersonal behavior determines aesthetic protocol.

KG  It's an interesting point. Having come through an art education and now teaching English, here's what I've learned: English students function from the neck up; they don't have bodies, they just have heads.

WK  Oh, that's pathetic.

KG  And art students function from the neck down—they don't have heads, they just have bodies. And they're distrustful of heads. In the same way a literature student is distrustful of the body. After class the English students drift off, nothing happens. After class in art school, everyone goes dancing and gets drunk.

WK  It's frightening. So what do you do, pedagogically?

KG  How do I join the two? Well, an English student, by doing something very dull, would be forced to confront the body. For instance, retyping things, he will be forced to notice the body, because the body is actually a really important part of writing. I don't have to teach art students, so actually my job is much easier. I have very smart literature students, like you do, and my job is to make them dumber, you know? It's a little downhill push.

WK  Oh, I can't wait to hear you say that at the fundraiser at UPenn: Professor Goldsmith speaks to the donors about what he's contributing to the student body!

KG  (*Looks at flowers.*) These are really beautiful.

WK  I love peonies.

KG  You want to hear something really funny about flowers? I'm doing a collaboration with John Ashbery.

WK  You are? How exciting!

KG  I'm doing tapestries with him. It's an uncreative writing project. I have been given the run of his notebooks—all the stuff from which the poems are culled—and am editing them as whole thoughts, pre-Ashbery process. They're really amazing. Then I'm going to be laying them out as visual or concrete poems.

WK  Oh my God!

KG  I've been bringing John and David flowers to their apartment on Ninth Avenue. And it's become this kind of game, because every time I go over there I have to keep upping the flower ante—we started with these beautiful mums and now we're into tropical things.

WK  So tell me, what is a tapestry?

KG  We're creating Flemish tapestries together. We're sending them off to Belgium and someone is going to make very large-scale Flemish tapestries. Do you like Ashbery?

WK  I worship him.

KG  Was he a huge influence on you?

WK  Bigger than Warhol, by far.

KG  Tell me about that.

WK  Well, I discovered him earlier. He's one of the only idols of mine whom I've ever met who hasn't disappointed me. I mean, you knew John Cage and I never did, but I feel about Ashbery the way I imagine you feel about Cage. I also worshipped Cage, but I don't take as much from him as I do from Ashbery. Ashbery combines a rarified and supremely sophisticated sensibility, perfect taste in literature and art, and a receptivity to the entire linguistic cosmos.

KG  I'm going to get you something. (*Leaves and reenters room.*) These are the things we're working from—fragments from John's desktop from mid-2010 to the end of 2011.

And these are our notes. He wakes up in the middle of the night in a dream and keeps them by the side of the bed; he scribbles them down and they get kind of tossed up into the poems.

WK  There is no Parnassus to me higher than this.

KG  I thought you would get a kick out of it.

WK  This is everything I care about—it's Paul Thek's *Susan Lecturing on Neitzsche* [sic], Martin Kippenberger. But it's also Emily Dickinson and Jonathan Edwards's mystical, crazy writing, and Charles Peirce's philosophical practice.

KG  Can you read anything here? What does it say?

WK  "The Devonshire, the earwigs used to fall in the tea on Sunday evenings. Come down on my head, gallons of earth bump infernos. Extended around Christmas time they'll just use it."

KG  Isn't it great?

WK  You know what this proves that I didn't understand before? That his work doesn't come from a continuous fountain. His interviews imply that there's this kind of wellspring of language that is inside him that bubbles up when he's seated at the typewriter, but, I mean, he's a collage artist, working from tidbits he generates at all times of day and night, in and out of bed, asleep and awake! That's really inspiring.

KG Isn't that interesting. Now, I don't feel the same way about Ashbery as you do, which maybe makes it easier for me to be able to work with him. He's not a figure like Cage is for me.

WK Ashbery renovated a tradition of American poetry that includes everything from Walt Whitman to Marianne Moore and Laura Riding. He brought something of Cage and Warhol into literature but with a kind of Scriabinesque or Debussyan sense of deep mandarin mystical atmosphere—an attentiveness to nuance, room-tone, haze . . .

KG I'm curious about your use of the word *American*.

WK That's so English program of me. Pretend that I didn't say it.

KG I'm really curious about that. How important is that to you?

WK I was thinking of Susan Howe's *The Birth-mark*, the lineage of American wilderness and innovation going back to the Puritans and Jonathan Edwards and Thoreau. Ashbery is part of that autodidactic wildness.

KG Where do you situate yourself in that tradition?

WK I am so provincial: San Jose, California. Did not go to Europe until I was twenty-five. Had a very sketchy high school education, I'm not bilingual in any reasonable way, I could go on . . . That's my Larry Clark dossier of who I really am. I am *that* kind of American. Even though I live in New York, and though Paris seems to float through me and out my mouth, I'm not cosmopolitan.

KG But what about your own writing? Do you situate it somehow in American tradition?

WK Yeah, I do. I poach from the biggies—Dickinson, Whitman, Ashbery, Stein—but I also learnt from Michel Leiris. Most things I do on the page I wouldn't have done if I hadn't read Leiris and Roland Barthes. Do you feel American?

KG No, because I feel digital and global. I was just reading that Jerry Saltz article "How to Make It in the Art World" in *New York Magazine* this week and it's so amazing to me that the entire article doesn't mention the Internet. It's so focused on New York; it's as if it were 1982, when *everything* was focused on New York. The world has changed so dramatically, even in the last ten years. I'm not really here that much; I'm traveling all over the world. Ubu is a global thing, it has nothing to do with New York. I teach in Philadelphia. I'm here as sort of a private citizen.

You often say that you don't travel very much, that every weekend you're up in the country. You say that your life is sort of prescribed, that you practice piano at a certain time every day. It's something that I really love about you—that you *live* in New York. I remember asking you once, "Wayne, what are you going to do this summer?" And you said, "I'm just going to stay in and practice piano."

**WK** If that's true, it comes from a sense that I'm not even in New York yet, that I'm still cresting toward arrival. I feel like this is the last episode of Fassbinder's *Berlin Alexanderplatz*, which takes place in some kind of dream disco-inferno space—that's my New York life. The twelve earlier episodes took place in San Jose maybe, in some drought space. Here in New York, I feel deeply invisible and posthumous, like the woman in *Our Town*, which I've actually never seen but I know that there's some young woman who comes back from the dead to visit her hometown one day. I feel like that person because I am aware of my mother's parents having grown up or lived here and my great-grandfather on the Lower East Side. That history is all still here, and then there's this weird phenomenon called Wayne, who is barely here, barely in a body, and he's just sitting on top of all this rubble.

**KG** Is that body distributed the way that I feel distributed, globally? You're *always* in the media. I can't tell you how many times I've showed the Warhol PBS film to my students. They're completely spellbound by you and feel like you're a bunch of pixels.

**WK** If that's true, it doesn't somatically influence me. It's an occasional payoff or lucky break, not a fact, a foundation, or a bedrock. However, I'd love to be translated into a lot of languages.

**KG** What's your most translated book?

**WK** I haven't been translated very much at all. I've appeared in German, Chinese, Spanish, French, Swedish—

**KG** Yes, I can see you haven't been translated at all.

WK  Only five languages, though! That's not global. Global would be one of these schlocky fiction writers whose books have been translated into twenty-five languages. That would be so fun! I would just sit there in my hot tub all day looking at my translated books.

# Rachel Kushner
# and Hari Kunzru

RACHEL KUSHNER was born in Eugene, Oregon, in 1968. She is the author of the novels *Telex from Cuba* and *The Flamethrowers*, both of which were nominated for the National Book Award. She has been shortlisted for the Folio Prize, longlisted for the Baileys Women's Prize for Fiction, and is the recipient of a Guggenheim Fellowship. A graduate of the University of California, Berkeley, and Columbia University, where she earned her MFA in creative writing, Kushner also served as editor at *Grand Street Magazine*, *BOMB* and *Soft Targets*. She lives in Los Angeles.

HARI KUNZRU was born in London, England, in 1969. He is the author of several books, including the novels *The Impressionist*, *Gods Without Men*, and *Transmission*, which was a *New York Times* Notable Book of the Year. He studied at Wadham College, University of Oxford, and Warwick University. He has been named a Best Young British Novelist by *Granta*, and awarded a Somerset Maugham Award and a Betty Trask Award. His work has been translated into twenty languages. He was a 2008 Cullman Fellow at the New York Public Library and is the recipient of a Guggenheim Fellowship. He lives in New York City.

**HARI KUNZRU**  So what's your story about how you got from being born to publishing a novel?

**RACHEL KUSHNER**  It would be something if I had a one-sentence answer to that, right? My parents were beatniks who had a lot of books around the house, and it was instilled in me that I was going to be a writer of some kind from a young age. So I did what was expected of me, which is a bit lame, but there you have it: I have much more admiration for sui generis people who come from homes that don't respect art. My trajectory did, however, have deviations to it. I ended up studying political economy at UC Berkeley, rather than English. I was politicized. I was sixteen when I went to college and I had an anti-authority outlook and personality, and I couldn't imagine going into academia and having a job. Eventually I realized that the only thing I was suited to was the novel, because it was the one project that could answer to my various interests, incorporate all the different aspects of life that I care about. After college I lived in San Francisco, a few "remedial years" that followed my accelerated education. I worked at nightclubs, rode a Moto Guzzi, and then finally got bored with that scene and wanted to be serious about writing. At twenty-six I enrolled in the fiction program at Columbia. I didn't get the idea for my first novel, *Telex from Cuba*, until *after* I had finished my MFA. Then it took me six years to write it.

**HK**  So your first interest in fiction as a project has to do with a way of talking about the complexity of the world that other disciplines don't capture. That's similar to my sense of why I do it. It allows me to connect lots of things together in a way that is not legitimate academically. That leads us both to these heavily researched books. Talk me through how the research sits alongside the writing.

**RK**  Yes—"the complexity of the world." My whole trajectory as a novelist is maybe about finding the form and through line of a constructed world that can hold in it what I really think about . . . everything. With *Telex*, it was funny to realize that I'd come full circle to write a book that took as its fictional context a mid-twentieth-century national liberation movement and American dominance. My emphasis in college had been American foreign policy in Latin America. Suddenly there I was doing all this research into the Cuban Revolution and the role the Americans played in their quasi-colonial society there. But I was new at figuring out how to balance research with the very delicate mechanism of character, the organic unity of fiction. I did a lot of research and then I had to de-cathect from it in order to actually write the novel. With my new novel, *The Flamethrowers*, I was merging different fields I sensed were connected, but not in overt ways. I did some research, but the various strands of the book were mostly realms I'd learned about over the years just by personal interest.

HK  You probably already had the '70s art world, the bikes, and Italy down in some sense.

RK  I lived in Italy as an exchange student when I was eighteen, in the crass and conservative era that, as a reaction to the radical '70s, paved the way for Berlusconi. I was astonished to learn that Italy almost had a revolution in the 1970s. Through my husband I got introduced to the Autonomists—he has written about that milieu. We know people who had been involved with that movement, and it seemed like it was ripe to be made into fiction, partly because of renewed interest. But it's also very dramatic and complex, and full of intrigue that seems right for the novel. There is a darker armed side. There's this great reader that Semiotext(e) reprinted that was originally published in 1980—

HK  (*Holds up the book.*)

RK  Exactly. I don't claim to be an expert on Autonomia, I should say, especially the theoretical origins. As a fiction writer, in any case, I wanted to understand aspects of the movement that cannot be fully apprehended from reading about it. It was important to go to Italy and talk to people and get them to explain things to me—the difference between Autonomia as an open movement and the much more clandestine armed movements in Italy at that time, for instance. Did they overlap? There are a lot of gray areas that you won't ever hear about without someone talking off the record.

HK  When I was researching *My Revolutions*, I realized that, being a novelist, I wasn't going to be able to represent anybody's political stance in a way that was accurate or faithful to some way they'd want to be represented. There were issues, you know—people had done things that are illegal, people's lives had been very much changed by their participation in social movements . . . I decided not to do interviews even though there were people I could easily have gone to. I was spending a lot of days in a squatted café near my house, which had been occupied as part of a local antigentrification campaign. At the time I was researching the Angry Brigade [1970s UK terrorist group], and I realized one of the guys in the café with me was one of the people I'd been obsessively reading about. I knew every publicly available fact about him, and I had this issue: Should I confess that I was doing this work? I ended up scrupulously not mentioning it to him and never talking to him about the past until the book was finished. Then I took him for a drink and came clean. Thank goodness I did, because he would have been suspicious of my motives otherwise. How did you approach people when you're basically saying, "I'm going to confect a set of stories around what you tell me"?

RK  Perhaps optimistically or foolishly I always told people that I was writing a novel—it was probably a defensive measure, because it meant I was just a kind of dreamer type who was not expected to have an expert's grasp of the minor but absolute differences among various groups or theoretical strands. People in Italy were not so inhibited by the idea that I was interested in Autonomia for the purposes of confecting stories, as you say. Maybe because the general sense among those who care about it in Italy is that the history of Autonomia has not been told of nearly enough, especially there. Some people's silence is a kind of information, too. One learns to interpret doublespeak. Mario Moretti of the Red Brigades [who went to prison for the kidnapping and subsequent murder of the former prime minister Aldo Moro] has never given a straight answer, for instance. I didn't interview him—there's a book-length interview done by Carla Mosca and Rossana Rossanda, where he turns the tables on them and speaks in this persuasively ambiguous way. I think I learned from that. Sometimes you have to pretend to understand, even when you don't, in order to have any purchase. You have to nod and agree when someone's being cryptic, go back later and try to parse what they said.

HK  People often, in my experience, talk in generalities rather than saying, "On a certain day somebody picked up a certain package . . . "

RK  Yeah, totally. Moretti and the other Red Brigades leader, Renato Curcio, talk like priests, in poetic aphorisms, and they neither confess nor regret nor ask for any redemption.

HK  I suppose most of the people who are interested in talking about this end up in a sort of basement-dweller headspace about who took what line at what meeting, you know. As a novelist, what do you feel the approach of writing fiction brings? What does the novelist bring to that situation?

RK  Cliché? Crude oversimplification? And melodrama, of course. Also sex and humor, hopefully. But seriously, a couple of things come to mind. There is this line from Cheever's journals: "I think that the task of the American writer is not to describe the misgivings of a woman taken in adultery as she looks out of a window at the rain but to describe four hundred people under the lights reaching for a foul ball." A challenge taken up by DeLillo, of course, in *Underworld* and echoed, earlier, in *Mao II*. I think it's perfectly legitimate for the novel to attempt to capture the sense of a large-scale event, of lots of people being involved in a political moment, an art movement, a march, a kind of collective aesthetic or illegality, by something like electricity or feeling. But the novel is also pretty effective at bringing the individual experience into relief precisely because of what you say: The novelist isn't fixing little embattled splices of historical accuracy, fighting old battles, or offering an anarchist cookbook but instead is trying to recreate a feel and texture of a time. There is a great Italian novel about Autonomia by Nanni Balestrini called *The Unseen*—

HK Which I read for the first time very recently and admired. It's a wonderful novel. I'm hoping they'll translate some more of his work; there's not very much available.

RK There's an earlier novel by him called *Vogliamo tutto* (*We Want Everything*) about the "Hot Autumn" of 1969. *The Unseen* is a potent example of what can be done in fiction with this specific history. Balestrini based it on the oral history of Sergio Bianchi, who lived the experience that the book outlines. So it's fiction and also probably nonfiction, but it's written like literature and so it becomes irrelevant, in a way, whether its details follow a real life or an imagined one. Does it say something true of the time? Does it utilize history in a meaningful way? Those are the salient issues to me. The novel puts people in motion and, in that, tries to render invisible things visible and deal with questions that don't have easy answers. I think fiction is a space in which you can use naïveté to bump up against ambiguities.

HK Which is a structure you've used in both novels. There's a sense of an innocent or several innocents being inducted into some space of political experience. Either they're the kids of the American managers experiencing the Cuban revolution or the young American woman getting involved in Autonomia. Are you a political writer? What would that phrase mean?

RK I am a bit hesitant to use that phrase even though yes, sure, maybe I am. But I qualify. The polemical work is not a work of art; it's something lower. It doesn't transcend its objective to influence and explain.

HK It's instrumentalized writing.

RK Precisely. The novel ideally is not reducible to the political. It's a journey toward meaning that transcends the frame of politics. *Blood Meridian*— just to think of a great novel that traverses the political—is not simply a book about the violent policies of the American government paying out for scalps on the Western frontier. It takes up subject matter that is inescapably political, but it builds of systemic violence a work that comes to rest only in the territory of art, where the thing built is so elegant and strange that it cannot be justified or even really explained.

HK I always get muddled between intention and effect. The author's intention is never visible in a text—we know this as good poststructuralists. Also, we can read anything politically; we can read things that are silent about political issues against the grain. Maybe *engagé* is a useful word. I think the novel has to hold things open rather than close things down or collapse things onto a single polemic point of view.

RK I always thought I aspired to that engagé tradition, but Sartre's conception of the novel was not a model for me. I find Céline, his foe, much more attractive as a writer in his disregard for an obligation to the common good and for his searing high style. I prefer to read the despicable stylists, but I am not like them in the most crucial of ways. I love people instead of hate them. I care about struggle. Yet I also sort of detest the idea of moral fiction.

Back to this matter of politics: If the novelistic canvas is the broader scope, in terms of time, diachronically, and also in terms of society's classes and milieus, the novel is inevitably going to be to some degree political. I tend to write in the broader scope, so my work, in the sense of subject matter, is political. But the political also inheres in the very basic matter of "character" and cannot really be avoided by those who keep their fiction to the house and the yard, so to speak, even by writers who think they are avoiding it. Character is sometimes talked about in these pious terms of timeless, essential human traits, but people are bundles of meaning that relate to the time in which they live, their race, their class . . . It's like this quote in an interview with you when *Gods Without Men* came out. You rhetorically ask, in reference to people living in these tiny towns in the desert with one gas station, "What is your outlook, if that is your milieu?" I love that question not only because it makes clear that understanding their outlook is imperative to you, but also because implicit in it is the fact that outlook is shaped by milieu. And *milieu* is shaped by structure, history. Who is Emma Bovary if the reader ignores Flaubert's utter disdain for the petite bourgeoisie? This idea that you can get to intrinsic qualities that transcend time or politics or class is a naïve by-product of liberal humanism.

HK It's the most highly ideological position imaginable, isn't it? Despite all the many troubles with this model, I've always been very interested in the old '70s project of linking Freud and Marx—this notion that your subjectivity is in some way constructed by large social forces. That's certainly there in my project as a novelist.

This is a kind of back-route into this question of the art world. The tools you and I are using to interrogate these things are in some ways the tools of the traditional novel. We make plots and we put characters in those plots. I've noticed there's a disjunction between the conversations that are going on in contemporary art and the conversations that are going on in fiction, at least English-language fiction. In some ways, I'm much more engaged in the cultural conversations of contemporary art. They're reading the books I'm interested in. There's a way of talking that I find congenial. You're one of the very few people that seem to exist in both worlds. How do you see that divide?

RK There *is* such a divide. Lynne Tillman and Wayne Koestenbaum always seemed like heroes to me because they are intellectually engaged writers who thrive in the art world. When I moved to New York to get an MFA, I found there weren't commonalities that aspiring writers circled around that could connect us as a group of people. I hung out with artists, not writers. They had one common discourse, and it was rich—it incorporated a lot of ideas, and they really cared about art, philosophy, music, all kinds of culture. They wanted to stay up late talking about Freud and Lacan (via Žižek, it was the late 1990s), Brian Eno, Benjamin Buchloh, the question of politics in art . . . The writers I knew then, from school, didn't have one set of discursive connections. There were some overlaps in what fiction people read—Jane Austen or, say, Barthelme, more hip, you know—but that's not a position in the world. And so I hung around with artists and read what they read and participated in their conversations, even the gossip about the market context and the power hierarchies that are so endemic to the art world, which is sometimes interesting if you get to be a voyeur, like I was, and aren't scrapping for a place at the table. All that said, you address a funny contradiction: The art world is all change and reflexivity and the dematerialization of forms, while the novel is stiff, fairly unchanging, and conservative as a form. There is a divide between the way the avant-garde works in art and the way that it works in fiction. In art the search for ever-newness continues to be the paradigm of what's valid. This is not the case with the novel. For whatever reason, none of the postmodern experiments in fiction really "succeeded" to the degree that they one-upped everything. The novel is somehow not on that axis; it keeps being recognizable.

HK It comes down to this: there's something about the novel that will never be fully assimilated into the modernist project. Novels are messy. They are always embarrassing, to a certain degree. They can never be hermetic in the way that Malevich is hermetic. Words refer. Novels are baggy monsters. What you say about the new is important. Approaching fiction as a modernist is still the most interesting thing to do, but many people who present themselves as being committed to modernism end up identifying with an extremely conservative mid-twentieth-century notion of formal experiment. Then they realize that the conditions of 1979 no longer pertain, declare literature over, and play in the ruins. That's fine, but I don't have that feeling of belatedness. The new seems to be breaking over our heads.

RK Proust's novels were different from their forebears in some very subtle ways, and those shifts are still worth paying attention to and studying. I'd love to read a contemporary novel that ingenious; while the New Novel, important as it is to a twentieth-century history, is not fresh in the same way, cannot be an enabling guide. Novels have emotional content. It's hard to negate that totally and still get a work of meaning, which is maybe why *Jealousy* is the only Robbe-Grillet novel I can truly relate to. In art, an emotionless work can utterly be done, of course. Pleasure and being enchanted, transfixed, is often purely intellectual in contemporary art, but it's hard to imagine a successfully original novel that has no emotional gravity, that is subtended only by idea.

HK You've also made the art world a context for your fiction. I wonder if you have anything to say as to why there are so few good art-world novels?

RK I hadn't thought much about a lack of good art-world novels, somehow. I wanted to write one because the 1970s in the art world have a particular, slightly romantic glow. For me it was a time when nobody had any money and people could take over spaces and live in Manhattan and be poor and adventurous. It was the merging of art and life, to put it too simply. It was also the point at which the manufacturing age was coming to a close and artists were moving into former factories and warehouses, harbingers of change—

HK Before it became revealed as the probe head of gentrification.

RK Indeed. Back to the question of good art novels—it's true there aren't many. *The Recognitions* by William Gaddis is pretty astonishing in terms of his understanding of certain aspects of painting and the secondary market. His details are spot-on. There are certainly novels now in which the characters go to gallery openings—

HK Right, it's a social landscape rather than actually taking the work seriously.

RK Yeah, a setting in which novelistic intrigues—love and power—can take place. The art world is a very particular place, and, like I said, what drew me socially was that it had a fully intact discourse. It's hard to write about that discourse as fiction; it has to be done in a way that is not insular.

HK And hard to write without jargon, I suppose.

RK Another problem in making fiction about the art world is that it doesn't really work to create fictional artworks and describe them. It comes off as precious. I kept that to a minimum in my novel. What I wanted to reference from real life were not art objects but gestures and attitudes—a way of parsing the culture of advertising, for instance, the way the Pictures Generation artists took John Berger and Marshall McLuhan and accelerated their ideas. You had this very deft shorthand in artworks whose humor had to do with an understanding of how images work.

HK Richard Prince's entire career is based on making deft gags about just that, isn't it?

RK Yeah, he was an inspiration to me. I named a character after John Dogg, an alter ego of his.

HK There's a '93 *Paris Review* interview with DeLillo where he says, "I construct sentences." And then he goes on to say, "There's a rhythm I hear that drives me through a sentence. And the words typed on the white page have a sculptural quality. One syllable too many [ . . . ] I look for another word. There's always another word that means nearly the same thing, and if it doesn't then I'll consider altering the meaning of a sentence to keep the rhythm. [ . . . ] I'm completely willing to let language press meaning upon me." A lot of the pleasure for me in making work is on this level of constructing sentences. Talk to me about how you actually make sentences.

RK  There's that line in *Mao II* where Bill Gray says, "I'm a sentence-maker, like a donut-maker only slower." In that quote you read from the *Paris Review*, he makes his process sound much more runic than its effect. One of the magical things about DeLillo's sentences is that he is letting you know in the very tissue of the sentence, in its cadence, that he's *right there*. He is letting you know he's alive to meaning and experience and, most importantly, that he's in on the joke.

For me, the sentence is the fundamental integer. But there is an ebb and flow in density, and the rhythms change. Tone is a ruling condition of possibility of life on planet fiction—every sentence must embed and embody a very particular tone and also further it, propel it. The sentence has to be doing something hidden, or coy, or openly funny, or odd. I use different tones in *The Flamethrowers*, so different parts of the book have different densities of sentence. Some of it is more conversational, while some of it is more thoroughly ruled by the language, which then creates the meaning rather than the reverse. I loved the phrase "the trembling of the leaves" and wrote a chapter based around what that image evoked (it's actually a mistranslation—mine—of the name of Renato Curcio's press, Sensibili alle foglie). In the parts that are more conversational, one of the fun challenges is to make people speak in the way that only people in this book speak: What is that global condition, or tone, which allows each voice to be different but gathers them all as distinctly belonging only in a particular novel? I couldn't tell you, but I know when it's there and when it's not there.

HK  Do you have any formal or informal rules on the level of the sentence? Do you have rhythms, like ta-tum-ta-tum-ta-tum? Is there anything you can point to which could be the reason to strike out a sentence and start again or the reason to be pleased?

RK  It's really intuitive, that rhythm, for me. It's like music: you know when you hit an infelicity, and you fix it. Reason to strike out a sentence? If it's not needed. I love to delete; I pare back a lot. Strangely the really early sentences that I make, like in notebooks, that I know I want to use, the ones that become like images in the mind around which to build something, those often remain. The only formal rule in fiction that I have is the reversal, as I think of it. If somebody reacts in a particular way or says something that's logical and expected, then I make them say the exact opposite thing to—

HK  —move it on, yeah.

RK But in terms of the structure of the sentence and cadence, no. Maybe I should have formal rules, but I don't, really. They change.

**HK** My main guide for what's working in a piece of fiction is "Am I having fun doing it?" And that seems, in a reasonably straightforward way, to translate onto the page—if I'm not having fun making it, why should anybody have fun reading it? But I'm beginning to suspect at this stage that there are things I enjoy doing as a writer that as a reader I might not appreciate in the same way. Is pleasure your main guide for what's working for you?

**RK** A very particular kind of pleasure, born under the domain of tone. The tone tells me in some deep unconscious way how to build the cadence of the sentence and the kinds of words to use. Also, the writing has got to have this kind of energy where I think I'm onto something and I've figured out a track in the language to keep me onto that thing.

Is there a divide between the author's and the reader's pleasure? I'm keen on a type of writing where I can feel the pleasure of the author. It's about the authors' lightly handled awareness that they are, at least for a moment, doing something. Breaking through, somehow.

**HK** I've only really got one more area that I wanted to cover, which is sexual self-presentation. Hiding in the corner of *Telex from Cuba* is Rachel K, who is the desired female, the seducer of powerful men. There's also a lot of stuff in *The Flamethrowers* about attempting to be a full subject as a woman, as opposed to being the "chick," the "plus one." There's also a passage about *Behind the Green Door*, the porn movie. You seem very interested in the experience of women who perform this erotic self-presentation and the tension around it.

**RK** If my analyst were in the room, he'd laugh—or just sigh, maybe. I am indeed interested in the tension between being a subject and being an object, an irreconcilable state of existence known as "womanhood." If we are all wandering around in the vestiges of courtly love, then desire is really the pursuit of finding a way to sustain desire rather than the capture of a love object. Love's true object is absence. Women, in this game, must be alluring but not obtainable. A woman on a poster, Marilyn Chambers, for instance, is alluring and not obtainable. A girl with no loyalties, like the character you mention from *Telex from Cuba* (who, incidentally, was based on a real historical figure—Rachel K, a call girl found murdered and posthumously upheld as a victim/symbol of the late decadence of the Machado regime), is not obtainable by any of the men around her. She slips out of grasp, which in that novel was for me a rumination on, if not a solution to, the "female" problem. She's an object, to be sure—but she cannot be fixed as such, she's ungraspable on account of a seditious streak. There is a question that, for me, is not answerable: Does the object have more agency due to the power she has over men? Or is the subject more emancipated, while forgoing what men wish her to be? I don't want a lecture about female agency. It's a form of interior contemplation that I am trying to honestly render in fiction.

I admire Clarice Lispector for her total commitment to glamour, which seems to have nothing to do with her fierce intellectual drives. They are not at cross-purposes. She puts on full makeup and reads Spinoza. Do you have to be a Ukrainian Jew living in the Copacabana in the 1960s to enjoy the luxury of such a synthesis? I don't think so, actually. Everyone knows that you cannot deny the question of sex, which is to say, the issue of objecthood. Real emancipation may incorporate the power of objectification. Or it will be rethought, possibly even dispensing with gender finally and altogether, and go by a new name.

# Ben Lerner
# and Adam Fitzgerald

BEN LERNER was born in Topeka, Kansas in 1979. A poet, novelist, and critic, he is the author of *The Lichtenberg Figures* and *Angle of Yaw*, a finalist for the National Book Award. Lerner's first novel, *Leaving the Atocha Station* won the Believer Book Award and was a finalist for the *Los Angeles Times* Book Prize for first fiction and the New York Public Library's Young Lions Fiction Award. A graduate of Brown University, Lerner has taught at California College of the Arts, the University of Pittsburgh, and in 2010 joined the faculty of the MFA program at Brooklyn College.

ADAM FITZGERALD was born in New York City in 1983. He is the author of *The Late Parade*. A graduate of Boston University and Columbia University, he is the founding editor of the poetry journal *Maggy* and contributing editor for *The American Reader*. He teaches at Rutgers University, The New School, and New York University. He lives in New York City.

# BEN LERNER AND ADAM FITZGERALD

**ADAM FITZGERALD** When John Ashbery told me he was reading your novel and how good it was, I was expecting almost anything—perhaps something a tad Language-ey, or something in the vein of *Three Poems*." That is, a book ostensibly experimental. I was surprised. Not to say that your new novel isn't a thought-bomb in its own (dis)quiet way, but the surface style is undisturbed, placid, a novel about poets and poetry but in no way is it "Young Poet does The Big Novel" (that sounds pornographic). Adam Gordon—soon seen by the reader as a version of someone who might resemble you, the author—is a young, post-graduate Fulbright scholar, spending time in Spain under the pretense of studying literary responses to the Spanish Civil War. He's an Ashbery and Lorca devotee. He's from Kansas, has published poems, has Gchats with friends who share the names of Ben Lerner's "real life" friends. Though that can of worms wasn't what captivated me at first—I found it sneakily provocative considering the work opens with an extended questioning of the possibility that art in our contemporary context can ever be properly "authentic."

I found myself entranced by the elegance of your prose: its sharp, crisp syntax that can widen out to capture the self-conscious thinking of a young, self-conscious writer. It also can accommodate a kind of American elision in phrasing, a vernacular way of being, that is immediate and—for lack of a better word—"believable" given the artful, combed quality the sentences have. So when did you decide to work out some of *your* experience of poetics, of Spain, in the form of a "straight-faced" novel?

**BEN LERNER** I was surprised—as you were—to find I had written a novel with a largely undisturbed surface, or whose disturbances don't disturb the narrative, a "real" novel, not a "poet's novel." That's the sense in which I can think of it as "straight-faced"; in many other ways it's bizarre. I had never written any sustained narrative prose before and I assumed if I tried to write a novel it would become one of the two kinds of books I think we mean by "poet's novel": either a lyrically charged text in which the signifier keeps overwhelming the signified or a more Ashbery-like (or de Chirico or Pasternak-like) drama of evaporating content, a kind of syntactic engine in which language dematerializes as *if* into narrative but the narrative itself is more of a motion than a meaning. Adam Gordon, the protagonist of my novel, prefers this second kind of prose: "I came to realize that far more important to me than any plot or conventional sense was the sheer directionality I felt while reading prose, the texture of time as it passed, life's white machine. Even in the most dramatic scenes, when Natasha is suddenly beside him or whatever, what moved me most was less the pathos of the reunion and his passing than the action of prepositions, conjunctions, etc.; the sweep of predication was more compelling than the predicated." He reads—or claims to read—even the most narrative and canonical novels as "poet's novels."

Part of what was exciting and unnerving about writing this book was moving away from enactment—say, writing a sentence in which the dissolution of the predicate in the sweep of predication is brought about—toward something closer to description: a critical and narrative account of such phenomena and the way they spread out from the aesthetic to other domains of experience. This movement from enactment toward description was new to me because, following Olson (and many others), I think of poetry as requiring exactly the opposite, as characterized by the attempt to create structures in which content is sedimented so that the poem becomes (or ironizes) an experience prose might just describe. Of course it's never all or nothing, and producing a first-person narrator through the action of his thinking is a kind of formal enactment, but I mean that a refusal of both poles of the "poet's novel" was necessary in order to produce a world in which a character can experience, among other things, those poles themselves.

**AF**  One of the local effects I observed and felt smartly carried the book throughout could be summed up by your marvelous use of the word "or," which has a solemn grammatical function from Mallarmé to Derrida in trying to rethink ontology through an existential awareness and demonstration of lexical instability (cue apophatic poetics). Less pedantically, your speaker's frustrated fluency in Spanish keeps him in a space where people are possibly saying *this* OR *that*, sometimes with hilarious or then again rather grave consequences. Adam misunderstands his interlocutors, they misunderstand him about mundane matters as well as heavier subjects like sexual desire, and the proper etiquette for grieving. This device of the OR (can I call it that?) impresses me because it so accurately encapsulates travelers' panicked need for constant self-improvisation, but also because I found it telling me something how you, the writer, view the nature of communication itself.

As Harold Bloom's always harping in regard to Shakespeare's characters—us humans are never having the same conversation, we're lost in the labyrinth of perpetual mishearing of one another, yet the great hope in this isolation is—how successfully? at what costs?—to recognize and realize our innermost selves. I wondered about our narrator throughout: isn't he doing *just* that, overhearing his own private language, and diabolically, at times, trying to manipulate the world for intimacy, attention, sex, what have you. I don't mean to sound judgmental, except Gordon's criticality of everything and everyone is infectious—and his transparency as a flawed, slightly deranged, charismatic, pathetic, vain poet stems from the same ability to creatively sustain our adolescent myth that maybe we poets never want to outgrow. Maybe what makes for a solipsistic or narcissistic "adult" also allows for a continuation of poetry, that argument with self.

BL  Yes, "or" is an important word in the book, especially in those scenes where Adam Gordon can't tell if he's following the Spanish of an interlocutor, and so, instead of simply failing to understand, understands more than one possible meaning at a time. He "understands in chords," as he puts it. I can relate to this; even in a long conversation in Spanish, I'm often unsure if I'm responding to what the other person actually said—that I haven't mistaken, say, "time" for "weather"—and this probably encourages me to respond with abstractions that can accommodate either possibility. And I agree with Bloom that this isn't just characteristic of speaking a foreign language, but also typical of exchanges in your native language, as one can never be sure what meanings lurk behind the literal, and as one often finds oneself trying to respond to an array of possible implications simultaneously, intended or projected. Adam tries to exploit this indeterminacy in his own speech; he speaks willfully fragmented Spanish with Isabel, for example, because he believes she intuits from those fragments depths of intelligence he doesn't actually possess.

The way that Adam experiences his incompetence as ambiguity or polysemy in Spanish conversation parallels in many ways his thinking about art. He is obsessed with this binary of the virtual and the actual, terminology I stole from Allen Grossman. He is interested in the gap between actual artworks and the claims made on their behalf, and finds art and poetry most beautiful when encountered in a virtual form: "I tended to find lines of poetry beautiful only when I encountered them quoted in prose, in the essays my professors had assigned in college, where the line breaks were replaced with slashes, so that what was communicated was less a particular poem than the echo of poetic possibility." Hearing a Spanish sentence as $X$ or $Y$ allows him to keep his exchanges from becoming actual, to keep them in the realm of the virtual. It's worth noting that the virgule we use to represent a line break in prose is the same glyph we use to indicate alternatives, the "either / or." Whenever I read Olson's "The Kingfishers" I find myself viewing that first line ("What does not change / is the will to change") both as a virtual line break and as indicating alternatives (choose what does not change *or* choose the will to change).

One strange effect of "Adam's" investment in the virtuality of "or" is that learning Spanish, or admitting that he's achieved a workable fluency, becomes a kind of limit for his relationships and the identity he's projected in Spain. He's often worried that he's failed to understand, but as the book goes on, he's perhaps even more worried that he's been understood: that Isabel or Teresa know what he *actually* said and so stop experiencing his statements of having the "echo of poetic possibility." This is one domain where Adam's aestheticization of experience gets him in trouble. But it's an extreme case of something I think we all do. Certainly I've known couples whose relationship seemed to depend on their not speaking each other's language; expats who have dumped (or been dumped by) their significant other as soon as they could understand the significance of each other's sentences without the glimmer of the virtual. So if you stay in Italy or bring someone back you might want to develop a sustainable strategy for defeating actuality.

Maybe literature is a way we work against fluency, a way of creating a language within the language where the experience of "/" is protected from actuality. *Virgule* comes from *virga*—which means *rod* in Latin and in English refers to rain that evaporates before it reaches the ground. That's a nice figure, I think, for the virtual: wisps of precipitation that never arrive. (Does this have something to do with the etymology of Viagra?)

**AF** Let's talk about the book's space for language-as-place more. That "Lost in Translation" topos that situates not only what can possibly happen narratively—Adam's two opposing and competing female interests; the novel's opening in a museum; its closing in the aftermath of the 2004 Madrid bombings—but also the sizable materials for the author / narrator's reflections on poetry, sex, grief, drugs and more.

I'm thinking first of the aphasia that attends the constant extrasensory attention to random, minuscule details—from the shape of European toilets or plugs, to meatier matters like the fog of literality that infuses each communication's promise, and encounter. One thinks of that striking phrase from Wittgenstein—"The silent adjustments to understand colloquial language are enormously complicated." Jeez, ain't that the truth. Being a foreigner doesn't so much isolate you from asking for the Internet or how to find the discotheque with sexier people. But it does show you that aside from all the words you don't recognize, it's the intonations and languages-within-languages that you're inherently, well, excluded from.

**BL** There is a lot of "silent adjusting" in the book, especially of the face: Adam has a particular look he wears around more attractive people to make his "insufficiencies appear chosen, to give [his] unstylish hair, clothes, etc., the force of protest." He has a particular expression of disdain for other tourists, involving his eyebrows. Teresa is particularly good (he thinks) at tactically modulating facial expressions: "Her face was formidable; it seemed by turns very young and very old; when she opened her eyes wide, she looked like a child, and when she squinted them in concentration, the tiny wrinkles at their outer corners made her seem worldly, wise. Because she could instantly look younger or older, more innocent or experienced than she was, she could parry whatever speech was addressed to her," and so on. The novel tends to describe the expressive machinations of the face more than it describes the attributes of the face itself. It talks a lot about Teresa's eyes, for example, but never mentions their color. The book includes a fragment of a black and white photograph of Maria Schneider taken on the set of *The Passenger*, a movie Adam has never seen; Teresa is said by another character to resemble her. The photograph is not only colorless, but it's cropped so as to exclude the eyes, the feature of Teresa's face that's most often "adjusting." So the novel stays silent about the crucial mechanisms of silent adjustment by refusing to attempt to produce an image of these complexes (faces) that communicate visually. And the significance of these communicative strategies is, as you say, heightened because "Adam" can't take the verbal for granted in Spain.

I am going on about all of this (and pirating Wittgenstein's phrase) because I want to say that a formal problem of translation underlies all the other thematic problems of translation in the book, and that's the question of how prose translates or fails to translate into images, how an optical realism is achieved or purposefully frustrated. The novel's silence about certain elements of exposition and detail and its inclusion of photographs—that are never illustrative in any straightforward way, but always contain the promise of the illustrative—inscribes what you called the "'Lost in Translation' topos" into the structure of the book. I know this is a strange and tangential way to answer your question, but I think the relation of prose to the optical is in an important parallel to the relation of the verbal to the nonverbal within the novel.

**AF** There's a neat ode to John Ashbery in the middle of the book when Adam explains in typical hyper-articulate fashion what he finds so prepossessing about Ashbery's work, which he claims as one of the truly important corpuses of contemporary literature.

So, say something about John Ashbery's *The Tennis Court Oath* (1962). That book, as we know, was written in the middle of his time in Paris (1956–1966). It signals a departure from the Audenesque classicalism of *Some Trees* toward a radical engagement with collage and American colloquialism. The poems are unique not only for their rampant cubism but a newer, more assured mournful tonality, I think. In a way, isn't *Leaving the Atocha Station* a prolonged essay on what its title alludes to, a re-envisioning of the Ashbery-in-Paris narrative by your novelist's protagonist, but also, by you?

What of course seems different is that eruption of the political within the framework of aesthetic liberation that Ashbery's work, and *The Tennis Court Oath* in particular, signifies. But the title does more than wink at a seminal book for American poetics (especially for LangPo, East and West coast inventors and researchers); the title—given your novel's trajectory—reorients it. That is, Atocha is also the station of the 2004 Madrid bombings—and while your work begins with your young narrator *inside* a museum, meditating on the possibility of profundity in any contemporary setting, it soon opens outwards onto a global stage. I'm interested, as you can see, therefore, how "Atocha" is, perhaps more than an allusion, a pun— one side of the coin, Ashberyian aesthetics, and its lineage of aesthetic free-play; the other side of the coin, a repoliticization of language given 9/11 and terrorism, as in your previous books' engagement between form and protest.

BL  I like your observation about the way the title evokes Ashbery's own time abroad—and the strange work that arose from his being outside of English. Adam Gordon's poems are collages, although not nearly as interesting as Ashbery's, and I think it's reasonable to speculate that both Gordon and Ashbery are drawn toward a sense of language as assemblage in part because they're living outside of English. And I think you're also correct that the title here evokes the aesthetic and the political and the troubled relation between them. The title names the site of the tragedy only to "leave" it; is there a turning away from the political toward poetry? Or is what's being left the poem—the virtual Atocha station of poetry—for a place made actual by the irruption of the historical real?

Chris Nealon has a beautiful reading of Ashbery's poetry (of the '70s) in *The Matter of Capital* as staging a kind of "wandering away" from crisis, what he calls Ashbery's "optional apocalypse"—an embracing of the minority of the poet as a way of dealing with the guilt of being part of the American hegemon but without any real power to change it. Adam Gordon does a lot of wandering away—most notably during the protests—and he also articulates his commitment to the arts through series of negations about their political efficacy:

*. . . I tried hard to imagine . . . how my poems could be said meaningfully to bear on the deliberate and systematic destruction of a people or a planet, the abolition of classes, or in any sense constitute a significant political intervention. I tried hard to imagine my poems or any poems as machines that could make things happen, changing the government or the economy or even their language, the body or its*

*sensorium, but I could not imagine this, could not even imagine imagining it. And yet when I imagined the total victory of those other things over poetry, when I imagined, with a sinking feeling, a world without even the terrible excuses for poems that kept faith with the virtual possibilities of the medium . . . then I intuited an inestimable loss, a loss not of artworks but of art, and therefore infinite, the total triumph of the actual, and I realized that, in such a world, I would swallow a bottle of white pills.*

Gordon isn't a modernist (or a Language poet, for that matter) who believes in the traditional vanguard dream of a poetry that can overcome the difference between art and life and directly intervene in history, although later in the book he will evoke that fantasy. But that's not to say the position he's articulating here is apolitical, exactly: I think he's saying that the arts preserve the possibility of alterity precisely by enabling us to experience a desire for something other than the given, by allowing us to wander away from official reality, to experience our own agency. This is at least compatible with one of Ashbery's few statements on the relation between poetry and politics: "All poetry is against war and in favor of life, or else it isn't poetry, and it stops being poetry when it is forced into the mold of a particular program. Poetry is poetry. Protest is protest. I believe in both forms of action" (in *The Nation*, May '67).

The scene where the novel discusses Ashbery's poems at length and tries to account for how they produce an intensification of life by enabling an immediate experience of mediacy—by making us conscious of our reading as we read, by compelling us to attend to our attention—takes place when he is literally leaving the Atocha Station by train for Granada with Isabel. But that's before the bombing. I think the book ultimately leaves open the question of whether or not the attacks change his position about the relationship between poetry and politics, the virtual and the actual. It's certainly not a question I can answer.

# Sam Lipsyte
# and Christopher Sorrentino

SAM LIPSYTE  was born in New York City in 1968. He is the author of the story collections *Venus Drive* and *The Fun Parts*, and the novels *The Subject Steve*, *The Ask*, and *Home Land*, which was a *New York Times* Notable Book and received the first annual Believer Book Award. He is the recipient of a Guggenheim Fellowship. He lives in New York City and teaches at Columbia University.

CHRISTOPHER SORRENTINO  was born in New York City in 1963. He is the author of five books, including *Sound on Sound*, *Death Wish*, and *Trance*, which was a finalist for the National Book Award. He has been the recipient of fellowships from the Lannan Foundation and the New York Foundation for the Arts. He has taught at Columbia University, The New School, Fairleigh Dickinson University, and the Unterberg Poetry Center of the 92nd Street Y, where he is a core faculty member. He lives in New York City.

# SAM LIPSYTE AND CHRISTOPHER SORRENTINO

**CHRISTOPHER SORRENTINO**  There are ways that a writer can be pigeonholed. For example, you're routinely referred to as a "satirist." Do you think of yourself that way?

**SAM LIPSYTE**  No, not necessarily. There's a kind of pure satire that sustains itself and never breaks into other modes and I don't see myself trying to accomplish that. Maybe I have a worldview that values the satirical approach but it always felt reductive to call it just satire. People might think that I'm blowing something out of proportion, when in fact I feel that I'm working in a more realistic mode. In *Home Land*, for example, Lewis Miner perpetrates satire in his descriptions of his life, but the external action is perhaps not so satirical.

**CS**  Your books are in the first person, including nearly all of the stories in *Venus Drive*. What has attracted you to that voicing, and how do you think you've sustained its use without seeming mannered? Some writers settle into a comfort zone; not you—Milo Burke's voice is not Lewis Miner's, which isn't Steve's, which isn't that of any of the narrators of *Venus Drive*.

**SL**  First person initially allowed me to get where I wanted to go; I stumbled a lot in third person. There were earlier drafts of *The Ask* where I was experimenting with third person. I guess I'm very interested in the performative aspect of first person, in inhabiting roles and voices that have particular tics, particular syntactical inclinations, that do different things with the language. I see infinite variety in first person.

**CS**  Despite that infinite variety—and coming back to the pigeonholing—reviewers often, especially with *Home Land*, have identified you with your narrators.

**SL**  Being pigeonholed is better than having no hole at all. But one's job is to squeeze out of it. I concede there are often elements in the work that lead people to assign a lot of the values or incidents to me. But people approach this question in different ways. There's a story in *Venus Drive* called "Old Soul" and in it a character who's pretty messed up goes to see his sister, who's in the hospital dying of cancer. She's in a coma, and at a certain point he puts his hand between her legs. A very tender moment. After the book came out my own sister who, you know, has had no medical problems that I know about, said to me, "Well, I read that story and I found it a little disturbing when *you* put your finger in the sister." I found that very interesting. If it's comfortable for people to think that they're reading a first-person account of somebody's experience, they will. We live in a culture that encourages the tell-all . . . that's a so-called comfort zone for people. Strangely, it's within the comfort zone to know that the writer actually did murder somebody . . .

CS  What's striking about your books is the degree to which we can—outside anything even similar to our own context—identify with some dark thing that the narrator is saying or feeling or doing.

SL  Right, and I'm hoping for that to happen. I'm not innocent: I certainly am aware of the possibility of that kind of identification occurring, both with the characters, and to some extent, me, the author. I've had experiences where people have met me after reading my work and, you know, when they see this friendly, schlumpy guy, they're very disappointed.

CS  What do they want you to be?

SL  I think they assume I'm going to come in snarling and maybe throw some objects around the room while I clutch a bottle of Jack Daniels and say inappropriate things at all times.

CS  I wouldn't say that you haven't lived up to my expectations. (*laughter*) I've never actually confused you with anybody in your work, but I certainly can hear you in it.

SL  Yeah, I feel the same way reading your books, I mean, there's no way around that. Even if you're writing a novel of fifteenth-century Venice, somehow your syntax is going to bleed through.

CS  Please agree or disagree with this statement: the comic author has trouble being taken seriously in a literary culture that seems to value serious, even self-important, books.

SL  So I have to say true or false? The comic novel presents ideas but undercuts them in ways that make it hard for book critics to talk about it. With novels that present ideas with complexity, it's the same problem.

CS  It does seem as if the undercutting of ideas denies the possibility of there being a fixed answer to any question that's raised. Also, comic writing privileges language in a way that a book that's trying to be earnest may dispense with. You don't get the sense that Flann O'Brien, or Joseph Heller for that matter, was all that interested in presenting an argument point by point.

SL True.

CS Which strikes me as a very pure way of writing. I was sitting on a panel with a guy judging an award, and his defense of a book he wanted to short-list was that it was okay if it took a careless approach to language because that wasn't a priority for every writer. That's the opposite of your approach. Going through your work I didn't find very many sentences that are strictly functional—nearly each of them has a pop to it, and even your harsher critics seem to recognize that.

SL I've always thought of each sentence as an opportunity to do something. Sure, it should move the book forward, but that doesn't mean it can't do other things while it's there taking up space killing a very small part of a tree.

CS Sometimes critics say that your work is almost all style and little substance, or that the story isn't front and center. I don't think that "the story" is the point of your books.

SL No story; stories, yes. I'm more interested in a swirl of stories and lives and outrages rather than one simple illustration of, say, the notion that inequality is evil. I'm interested in how those ideas live with us in our daily humiliations rather than in propping up some large placard and trying to carry it forward with functional sentences. This kind of work that we're talking about does rely on language. It's not staking its authority on something outside of the book: "I lived through this," "I researched this for many years." It's an improvisatory dance and you have to think of language as your primary way of performing it.

CS We were talking before we started taping about Richard Powers: he delves into neuroscience, the history of the multinational corporation, or the workings of a pediatric oncology ward, and then dramatizes the data, putting it in the mouths of his characters. For you, it's not necessary to explain in *The Ask* how it is that capitalism operates to get a severe sense of its effects.

SL At a certain point in history the novel was a narrative vehicle for information about how societies worked. Now we live in such a technological age it's often a vehicle for ideas about science or technology. But I've often thought there are lots of wonderful nonfiction books to read on these subjects.

CS There's this persistent idea that a novel must have a kind of use that we can put it to. Even good books tend to be criticized that way. The reviewer reduces it to an argument: "a scathing moral portrait," "a devastating critique of postmodernity," or what have you.

**SL** But I think the job of the novel is to make you *feel* those things. A scathing moral critique is neither here nor there if one isn't made to feel the effects of these forces.

**CS** Reading *The Ask* after rereading your other books it struck me that much more seems to be at stake for Milo Burke. He's older than your previous protagonists, on the verge of middle age, he's married, he has a child, and he's trenchantly aware of his various failures—he's an unsuccessful painter, he's unemployed, his family is starting to come apart. You do feel all the ways that his life has been a bust, despite a middle-class foothold in the world. Is this sense of more being at stake something that's come to you due to your own experiences as a fortyish married guy with kids?

**SL** The autobiographical element tends to be more emotional than rigged to the facts; things aren't made up wholesale here, but they're grafted on to other things and mutated—you know what I'm talking about because you do this too. I wrote this in the wake of having children, working at a university, being someone in the arts. There's nothing in the book that's really my life except all of it. (*laughter*)

**CS** Compare Milo to Lewis Miner in *Home Land*. Lewis is awash in a certain kind of failure, but his troubles seem low impact in a lot of ways, and in the end, the book is shot through with ragged hope.

**SL** I'd say Lewis is still in some sort of bubble. And there is hope there. Though I think there's a kind of hope for persisting in the human at the end of *The Ask* . . .

**CS** It's not exactly Faulknerian, Nobel-speech kind of endurance, though. Milo has come down in a way that strikes fear in the bones of a reader like me.

**SL** I was trying to find a way to distill that fear.

**CS** It's not territory that you've explored before. *The Ask* is explicit in its depiction of regular people's relationships with power and money. It suggests that that relationship is entirely exploitative, and that, consequently, the lives of average people are impoverished in ways that go far beyond their lack of money and influence. Big "systems novels" like those of Gaddis and Pynchon explore this idea of life as a rigged game—you really distill it. I admire how you isolated that sense of some aspects of life simply being out of one's hands—it's a way of being that doesn't intrude into the lives of the characters in *Home Land*, or even in *The Subject Steve*, a book about complete loss of control.

SL  When I was writing *The Ask* I was feeling those pressures, and seeing them in people around me. For a character like Lewis Miner they're more abstract and his outrages are almost romantic.

CS  And Milo Burke is not; the romance has been bled out of him. He's constantly self-lacerating, he divulges all of his fantasies of being a successful painter, confesses to conducting imaginary interviews with himself for art magazines, imagines NPR speaking about him in hushed tones. But there's nothing cute about it. It's angry. There are a lot of shades of gray in the book.

SL  What felt dangerous to me in an exhilarating way was that I knew Milo wouldn't be entirely loveable. There's a kind of teddy-bear quality to Lewis Miner that works for *Home Land*. Milo also has the kinds of conflict and turmoil that we can connect to, but you begin to realize empathy does not always feel nice. It can be shocking.

CS  And Purdy Stewart, the "ask" of the title, is presented as a nominal villain. But we discover that he isn't really a bad man.

SL  No, he's not a bad guy . . .

CS  Most of the hostility that we're urged to feel toward him exists entirely in Milo's head, and Milo's very ambivalent about it himself.

SL  It goes back to what you were saying about the pressures of not having money and power. Possibly it makes you a little more of a shit when you know the object of your ire, who doesn't feel those kinds of pressures in the same way, is free to be a good guy. A lot of Milo's anger is linked to his fantasy of what it would be to have that kind of wealth.

CS  But I got the sense that, despite his wealth, Purdy's just as trapped in the game as Milo.

SL  Yeah, he's got his gilded cage.

**CS** We see Lewis Miner only by himself and with his friend Gary, but with Milo you create a son, along with the ambivalence that we have toward having children, a marriage, and his anguish that it's coming apart at the seams. Through his wife Maura you also give us a sense of what it's actually like to live with a guy like Milo.

**SL** I became interested in Maura and how she could even stomach some of Milo's bitterness: even if it is somewhat understandable, it's still this horrible cloud that she has to live in and under.

**CS** Milo's good at disguising that from us; we don't necessarily see it unless another character points it out. Somewhere in the book someone says something to Milo like, "You take self-pity to new heights." That's where it struck me that it's hard to get behind him.

**SL** I hope people get behind the book more than behind the characters. They don't even exist anyway. We don't necessarily have to fall in love with a character to be fascinated by his plight, and to take pleasure in the language. I'm just trying to reclaim the readers you've been driving away this entire interview by talking about what an absolute shit my main character is.

**CS** (*laughter*) More like somebody who's not idealized in any way.

**SL** I'd say he's more like somebody you know. And I think that, partially, it's about how he comes to see himself throughout this crisis, about whether he fails or succeeds in the immediacy of the narrative.

**CS** Milo's failings and frustrations are amplified in the character of Don Charbonneau, Purdy's illegitimate son, whose state of mind Purdy wants Milo to ascertain as a condition of the "ask." Don's lost his legs in Iraq and has given himself over to both bitterness and extorting money from Purdy. All of Milo's flaws—anger, bitterness, disappointment, envy—are present to a much greater degree in Don.

**SL** The difference is that in certain ways, Don has earned it. That's why I decided to veer a bit at the end of the book: to put Milo's plight in some perspective.

**CS** Don punctuates the abstraction of the war in Iraq, at least as it relates to a world of middle-class worries and upper-class dramas. The book spends a lot of time in a world of oblivious comfort. It opens with Horace, Milo's coworker, casually fulminating about the death of the American empire, immediately after which Milo loses his job following a meaningless confrontation with a spoiled student. Don reminds us that people are dying to further the goals of American empire—there are actual life-and-death issues beyond the bubble of that world.

SL  Yes, I agree with that.

CS  *The Ask* is your first book to be set entirely in New York, a complicated target of satire.

SL  Although we're not sure if I'm a satirist, so it's okay . . .

CS  It's a complicated object of contemplation. You've put in time riffing on a suburban landscape that at this point is enshrined in a state of self-satirization. You could argue that lots of the things that exist in big cities are equally fatuous, but you aim at some formidably complex targets: universities, the art world, progressive preschooling, fabulous wealth. Does it seem to you that such things, whether a tacky event space in Northern Jersey or a trendy Manhattan birthing center that serves up colostrum shakes, all flow from the same American font?

SL  I'm beginning to understand that they must, because I've had a hard time occasionally with foreign publishers who don't understand what I'm writing about. With *Home Land*, some of them passed saying, "Nope, none of the people in our country will understand what a high school reunion is." I've traveled, but my source texts tend to be American. I didn't spend a lot of time in *Home Land* making fun of the mall because, as you said, it's self-satirizing at this point. Whether it's the mall, contemporary marriage, or the university, I'm conscious of not just standing outside of it and making fun. I find characters tied to them in some desperate way. These places, these notions, these relations have consequences for the characters, their absurdities need to be pointed out by people who are in the throes of experiencing them.

CS  I was thinking about that indie sensibility that takes as its rubric "everything sucks."

SL  Right, that kind of quirky, outsider stance seems too safe to me.

CS  I find it simultaneously safe and vastly insulting. Fish-in-a-barrel tactics.

313

**SL** That stance has been absorbed by the corporate culture anyway. And it's disseminated everywhere. Everybody in Starbucks thinks Starbucks is stupid. This is old news, but the great revolution of the '90s was creating a consumer who could see himself as a rebel outside of this machine yet *still* consume its products. That kind of glib, judgmental stance. It doesn't quite seem to say Ikea sucks and Starbucks sucks so let's all live in a commune or let's redistribute the wealth or, you know, let's get some better coffee.

**CS** Money itself is foregrounded in *The Ask*: where it goes, what it does, what happens when it's not available.

**SL** Yes. What's that Bresson movie where they follow the money?

**CS** *L'Argent.*

**SL** In *The Ask* following the money is not about revealing its insidious trail (lots of great journalism does that) but about seeing how people are tied emotionally, spiritually, to the economic model we're living under. What kind of giant and tiny struggles and concessions go on daily. It's partly the proximity of these two different-sized struggles that produces the comedy.

**CS** You convey the way that model warps people. Milo's preschool son says miniaturized versions of what a working adult might be expected to say, you refer to Maura sitting at the kitchen table, doing what you call "the work before the work." Milo's co-worker, Horace, a hipster kid, lives in Williamsburg in one of those cages for kids who can't afford actual apartments: starter habitats. And he's serious about his career!

**SL** He's not a slacker, for sure, he's a young man on the go.

**CS** The Michael J. Fox character in *Family Ties*, realized twenty years later. Let's talk about your influences. What excited you when you first started reading like a writer?

**SL** There was no switch flip that then had me reading as a writer. I stumbled into it. In my late teens I was writing dreck, but wanting it to be good. I started to take notice of the way people who were good with language were writing fiction in America: Don DeLillo, Robert Stone, Barry Hannah was a revelation, Stanley Elkin I immediately fell in love with. You absorb these incredible rhythms and tones and you hope that by dint of some alchemy they emerge from you in a way that at least doesn't seem derived from one person.

**CS** The writers you've mentioned all have singular approaches to storytelling per se. You can savor them by taking a book off the shelf and opening it at random.

**SL** Any book that's worth reading, you should be able to open it anywhere and find you can recognize some authority or magic going on that has the possibility of enthralling you. One can argue about what constitutes a story, but those books all have movement.

**CS** It's movement, but plot isn't going to get in the way of the writing.

**SL** No, and plot doesn't get in the way of the story, either. (*laughter*)

**CS** Take Elkin, one of the most digressive writers you could have named— once he gets his teeth into something, he'll follow it for as long as it takes before finally veering back onto what an impatient reader might think of as the track.

**SL** Right. But the track is not for staying on, it's for leaping off and then returning to. The notion of the page-turner always seemed foreign to me. I don't want to be sitting on the edge of my seat waiting to find out what happened next. I want to be falling off my seat in ecstatic pain because of what language and consciousness are doing on the page. With *The Ask*, the plot may not be up to Grisham standards, but I'm certainly trying to achieve a sense of hurtling that I think all good books have—maybe not toward a plot point, but toward something more devastating.

**CS** I wouldn't say of the influences we've mentioned that they've bled their work dry of feeling to execute some formal requirement, though. That leads me to a question I wanted to ask.

**SL** Do I have to say true or false?

**CS** There's a passage in *The Ask* where Milo likens himself to a figure in Hopper's *Nighthawks*, and he mentions how, as a painter, he'd always described it in terms of "the stark play of shadow and light." This is a perfectly appropriate way of looking at Hopper's work, but then Milo says, "to be the fucker on the stool is another kind of stark entirely." It's a funny line, a throwaway almost, but it strikes me as an encapsulation of the burden of writers working today. Yeah, we're concerned with form, with language, with allusiveness and scaffolding—the legacy of modernist and postmodernist writing—but a lot of us also want, to a degree maybe not countenanced by more playful antecedents, to get at the starkness of being "the fucker on the stool." That seems like the project David Foster Wallace was working on for his entire career: getting at that, at how the methods of getting at it sometimes work at cross-purposes to the goal.

**SL** The various ways to approach prose composition, to play, left to us by modernism and postmodernism are important. Maybe it's something in the culture, but those differences now seem beside the point. We have a certain freedom that comes from mattering less, a freedom to use tools from prior texts, but not feel wedded to a certain camp. I'm drawn to many strategies and devices often from previously opposed camps. They all seem to have a common end, which is to give a reader some insight into his or her own fucker-on-the-stooldom.

**CS** The anxiety of influence isn't the factor it once was. To writers of an earlier generation borrowing had to be bracketed in enormous quotation marks, or sublimated and disguised, to make it plain that this was a form of parody. Writers around our age and younger think of the people we grew up reading as useful predecessors to be drawn from unselfconsciously.

**SL** I agree. I think that it has something to do with a diminishment in the entire field—not necessarily in quality, but in the way it matters to people in general.

**CS** As ever, the important books often were being published in a small way. Writers like you and me are going to return to being published in a smaller way, either by the trade houses that may end up subsidizing our work, or, perhaps more likely, by small presses.

**SL** Absolutely. It's going to become increasingly about small publishers. There have been times when the only music you really wanted to listen to was coming out on small independent labels. We're headed for that, especially given what's going on in big houses.

**CS** Also what's going on in the lives of readers. Even if book coverage reaches people, it seems irrelevant because it's only a *book*, as opposed to an *event.*

**SL** There's no pressure on people when they go to a cocktail party to have read the latest book by the leading literary lights the way there once was;

you're not even supposed to buy it anymore. You still have to have seen the movie or the HBO series. So far we've both been lucky enough to keep getting published, and *where* we get published may change, but if you're writing seriously good work, it's going to find a home. It's just not going to provide you with a home.

CS  You started with a small publisher, Open City Books, which published *Venus Drive*.

SL  It was an anomalous experience because it was the only book being published that year by the house, so I received the kind of attention that most writers don't experience from their publishers. It was great; when people talk about going back to the model of small publishers, it doesn't frighten me.

CS  After Open City you moved to Broadway Books. Notoriously, *The Subject Steve* was published on September 11, 2001. It's a book, as we said earlier, about loss of control, about death, and it's a very funny book, but not one you necessarily want to curl up with after a major terrorist act.

SL  It's not a consoling book.

CS  After that came *Home Land*, a different kind of notorious story. You delivered the manuscript to your agent, Ira Silverberg, and then what happened?

SL  Ira seemed excited and sent it out to a bunch of places and "no's" just kept coming for a long time.

CS  How many rejections, total?

SL  I don't know; we always keep increasing the number . . . somewhere around thirty-five. In the meantime it was published in the UK by Flamingo a year before it came out here. In the US, they kept citing the sales figures for *The Subject Steve* as a reason that they couldn't take a chance on *Home Land*. That was a dispiriting time; it made me wonder not about my writing, but about publishing. I'd have these strange phone conversations with editors who loved it but were convinced they wouldn't be able to sell it upstairs. Eventually, Lorin Stein at FSG was able to finagle some sort of deal whereby it would be published as a paperback original with Picador, but it would have an affiliation with FSG. If it was a total disaster, the blame would be less concentrated in any one place.

CS  But it ended up doing quite well.

SL  The amount of money that I was paid for it allowed it to earn out.

CS  That goes back to what we were saying about publishing with a different set of expectations.

SL  I was just thrilled that it was happening after all of that.

CS  And the lesson from all this *tsouris*?

SL  Learning how to think of these things as separate paths: there's your writing, and there's publishing, and occasionally they intersect, but mostly it's just about your writing.

# Ben Marcus
# and Courtney Eldridge

BEN MARCUS was born in Chicago, Illinois, in 1967. He is the author of several works of fiction, including *The Age of Wire and String*, *Notable American Women*, *The Flame Alphabet*, and *Leaving the Sea*, and is the editor of *The Anchor Book of New American Short Stories*. He received a BA in philosophy from New York University and an MFA from Brown University. He has been awarded a Guggenheim Fellowship, a National Endowment for the Arts Fellowship, the Berlin Prize, and a Whiting Writers' Award. A professor at Columbia University, he lives in New York City.

COURTNEY ELDRIDGE was born in Iowa City, Iowa. She is the author of *Unkempt*, a collection of short stories, and the novels *The Generosity of Women* and *Ghost Time*. She has received fellowships from the Edward F. Albee Foundation and the Ucross Foundation. Her writing has appeared in *McSweeney's*, *The New York Times Magazine*, *BOMB*, and elsewhere. She lives in Portland, Oregon.

# BEN MARCUS AND COURTNEY ELDRIDGE

**COURTNEY ELDRIDGE**  I thought I'd start with a pretty broad question. What's the state of the art, where are we today with the short story?

**BEN MARCUS**  There is an interesting melding of traditions going on in which distinctions between what used to be called experimental, traditional, realist, lyrical—all these different genres seem to be getting conflated.

**CE**  In a good way?

**BM**  In a way that I like. Writers seem to be feeling that various techniques are up for grabs, and you're not necessarily called a postmodern writer if you write self-reflectively or if your story performs strenuous formal leaps. Traditional writers are using techniques that would have been anathema to them twenty years ago. On the other hand, the trickier writers, the ones more interested in invention, seem to be looking to have a much deeper emotional effect in their stories. It's pretty exciting. Hard to keep up with all of it but there's some excellent work out there.

**CE**  Why does the short story seem to be the poor relation of literature? Why do people still go after the novel and shy away from the short story?

**BM**  Do you mean that people want to write the novel instead of short stories?

**CE**  Publishers are tentative with short story collections, to say the least.

**BM**  I agree, but I wonder if that commercial distinction really means that there is a distinction to be made in the larger culture of writing. Readers are reading just as many if not more short stories. Of course you're right that novels always sell better (which is never the best indication of what's interesting). I guess if that's what matters, then novels are more important. I don't see why there's a competition. They're distinct art forms and they're both important in different ways. Some of the most memorable books of the last fifteen years are collections of stories like George Saunders' book *CivilWarLand in Bad Decline*, or Denis Johnson's *Jesus' Son*. Short stories seem to have a bigger impact on younger writers, the sort of writers I might encounter when I teach. They're not arguing over whether Philip Roth is a better writer than Coetzee. They're talking about who the good story writers are. So I don't think the short story is the bastard cub of lit.

**CE** Which brings me to teaching. Where do you begin with your graduate students at Columbia? What do you say on the first day?

**BM** I try to stress how important it is, when you're asking for the attention of a reader, that you're doing the most intense, interesting, compelling, fascinating thing that you could possibly do. I focus on getting writers to recognize when they become bored while reading other people and why. And then why they might allow themselves that boredom when they're writing. Students want to give themselves permission that as readers they won't give to another writer. Graduate students in fiction are some of the least forgiving readers I have ever met. They tend to be very critical of almost everything.

**CE** Why do you think that is?

**BM** When I was that age, I wanted to denounce everything because I was terrified. For me, the easiest stance was to say it all sucked. I'm a little more lenient now that I've written books. The people that I hung out with in grad school weren't terrible people, but we did walk around shooting arrows at all the great writers.

**CE** It's an adolescent phase of a writer's life, isn't it?

**BM** I'm wary of saying that some new young MFA student's highly developed critical faculties are defensive, but mine were. In teaching, I'm interested in turning those critical faculties around. Teach people to read themselves the way they might read others. I try to promise them that I will be their most serious reader that term. I will read every word they write. I'll look at what their work is dreaming of being and help them get there.

**CE** Do you have your own personal canon that you teach?

**BM** No. I did at first. I would push the books that had really amazed me. But now when I look at a student's work in a workshop situation I might say, "This person would benefit by reading Eudora Welty or Grace Paley." Or with someone else I might say, "Read Dennis Cooper," because they're flirting with his territory, or they need to read their Burroughs before they do this. So I look at the writer's particular space and try to make suggestions that make sense for their interests.

**CE** As opposed to approaching the class on the whole?

BM: As opposed to saying, these are the good books that everyone has to read. I teach lit classes also. In those courses I do come up with a book list, but it's not necessarily a canon so much as a set of related ideas tied together by good books. I taught a course called Technologies of Heartbreak in which we looked at sad novels and tried to figure out how emotions of that degree were achieved in fiction. We examined questions of sentimentality, heightened drama and descriptions of emotional states. Books with really extreme grief, what they flirted with, and what they risked. Sometimes I'll teach a class because I'm interested in a larger issue, and this interest ideally should help me be a more engaged teacher.

CE  Can I ask who your favorite teacher was?

BM Yeah. Robert Coover. Far and away.

CE  Why? What about him really brought out the best in you?

BM I never had a creative writing class with him. But at the writing program I attended, Brown, he taught a course called Ancient Fictions which included the Bible and Homer's *Odyssey*, *Gilgamesh*, Ovid; early works of fiction. He was enormously erudite, generous, challenging, fascinating, filled with ideas. He didn't seem to mind when a student did really well, he was extremely supportive of a whole range of younger writers to an incredible degree.

CE  If teaching is learning, what is it that you're learning?

BM My students have an incredible litmus for insincerity, cliché, soft thinking. They'll catch me if I say anything that's half-assed in class. They're the toughest audience. The classroom is where we all have to do our very best thinking. I can't go in there and repeat a bunch of platitudes that sounded good when I heard them. What they teach me is to think on my feet and to never feel like I know anything, to always try to outsmart my easiest assumptions. Because as soon as that comfort settles in, some smart-ass in class is going to point out the nine ways I'm wrong.

CE  Do you leave class feeling dumb?

BM Oh yeah!

CE  In a good way?

**BM** In a good kind of hungry way. The community is challenging. Like, say, a group of friends who all get together and each tries to be funnier than the other, or smarter or wittier. Everyone's trying to perform for each other, which by itself could be annoying, but that's not all that's going on. The standards are high and there's a deep commitment to be interesting, to write well. There's the hope that that alone might lead to better writing because you've exercised your mind really hard for one or two hours.

**CE** How do you describe your writing to someone who doesn't know your work?

**BM** It's a horrible thing to have to do. I just wouldn't.

**CE** It's an awful question, isn't it. "What's your work like?"

**BM** "What do you write about?" I was once at this Four Seasons bat mitzvah. They have these incredible theme parties now.

**CE** They have DJs, don't they?

**BM** They have DJs. They had line dancing. They had these hot pants dancers. They got the dad of the bat mitzvah to stand up and sing. The line dancers were probably fifteen years old. And maybe religious rites of passage should be this blatantly sexual but . . . I was at the table with a bunch of old-timers and they had heard I was a writer. I had tried to keep that from them. They asked me the title of my book. At that point I had just published my first book and I said, "*The Age of Wire and String.*" And they said, "What? 'The Face of Wire in the Wings'?" I said, "No, *The Age of Wire and String.*" They said, "'Why the Caged Bird Sings'?" (*laughter*) I don't want to have to proselytize in order to describe it. If I'm trying to be nice I say, "I write about family." I used to be a smart aleck and when people asked me what I wrote about, I'd say, "I write about you, you and people like you. And I'm never wrong."

**CE** (*laughter*) When did you try to not be a smart aleck about it?

**BM** Well, for instance, my wife and I are living up in a little town in Maine this year.

**CE** Brooklin.

BM We have good friends who live here year-round and for months we kept from them that we write, not that they were dying to know. We have plenty of aspects of our identities that don't involve writing. It was just nice not to have to explain. I think my wife, who writes a little more readably, you could say, was better off maybe. I just felt, if they even got hold of one of my books, I'd be in big trouble. They would be embarrassed because they would not like it, or would not be able to read it. And we'd have to somehow talk about it. Sure enough, there's a little library here. I had to give a reading; some of them came. We've never talked about it since.

CE You write, you're an editor, you teach and you're married to a writer. What do you do to let off steam, get out of your head? Do you garden, do you cook?

BM Well. I've been building furniture.

CE Really?

BM Yeah. And I also love to cook. When we got to Maine, there was work that needed to be done on the house. So I started picking up some tools. The town is a boat-building town. Everybody is a master carpenter; it's a high-end skill. I've made friends with all kinds of people who have taught me stuff. Around here, people talk about clearing land, whom you buy your firewood from, or how to make a certain wood joint fit together properly.

CE But you like that because you're very interested in structure.

BM And I also like it because it's just two people talking about things that interest them. Also, I'm sensitive to the blowhard who talks about his writing all the time.

CE I guess it's good to be out of New York then.

BM A lot of my friends have a code *not* to say, "Oh, I really kicked ass on the page." There are some friends I love to talk about writing with, it's not as though I don't do it. Maybe just when I'm trying to have a little more fun and relax, it's nice not to talk about it. When you're doing it all day, it doesn't seem that necessary to talk about it.

CE Craftsmanship and wood. Inevitably it will bleed into your work.

**BM** I must have bought fifty or sixty woodworking books. My skills don't reflect that at all, and yet I have this library. I've read them all cover to cover, I reread them, I take them into the bathroom. I read them instead of fiction.

**CE** Do you enjoy the language of the books, the writing?

**BM** Yeah, I do, but I feel kind of on the tail end of my romance with the fictional uses of nonfiction. I've pretty much rubbed that idea into the dirt, had my fun with it. I used to more or less pick up any book of nonfiction and feel really inspired by how close it could be to being fiction if you tweaked it. I would read it as though it were fiction.

**CE** Which leads to mimicry.

**BM** Yeah, but it's also being available to a different component of language other than fictional narrative language. I don't have the exact, ready excitement about that idea anymore.

**CE** Writers think that other writers have this ability to sit down and get to work in a way that's not true at all. Many writers spend their time doing just about anything else, and then they finally get down to it because they've exhausted all of their options. What is your writing schedule, do you have any rituals around it?

**BM** Yeah, definitely. There are no interesting stories surrounding any of those subjects for me. If you can come downstairs and have gotten something done, it doesn't matter what you wore, what you drank when you were doing it, coffee or tea, pajamas or bathrobe. We have a new baby, my wife and I.

**CE** Congratulations.

**BM** Thank you.

**CE** Boy or girl?

**BM** It's a girl. Delia. A lot of people say, "Yeah, that's a cool name except you know, you have that problem because she cut off all of Samson's hair." She doesn't have a problem, that was Delilah.

**CE** How's the baby changing life and writing? Not to ask the obvious . . . but? (*laughter*)

BM Not at all. Before we had the baby, everyone we ran into was saying, "Dude, life as you know it will never be the same." We both got so resentful, this promise of change, it can come out as patronizing.

CE And?

BM It's true and it's not true. Change is incremental. It's fascinating and fun and really incredible to have a baby around.

CE How old is she now?

BM She's seven weeks.

CE Oh my gosh! Oh, she's a little thing. Are you guys sleeping?

BM Yeah, we're sleeping plenty. But we both said to ourselves that this summer with the new baby, we weren't going to try to do a ton of work. I think taking a little pressure off ourselves in fact has helped. We both work every day now already. It actually, in terms of work, focuses things. If I know I have a two-hour window, I don't just go and look up the history of ink on the Internet because I'm curious. I actually try to get some writing done.

CE Let's talk about the anthology, *The Anchor Book of New American Short Stories*. I'm curious how you began the editorial process. One of the stories, "This Is About the Body, the Mind, the Soul, the World, Time, and Fate," by Diane Williams dates back to 1988. Obviously you had a pretty wide net. You must have come to the table with certain stories in your mind.

BM I did, and the table got tipped over a bunch of times. I had a very different idea when I started and that was to put together an anthology of styles from direct to circuitous to realist to experimental, sci-fi, mystery—an anthropological selection of short stories with completely different styles that would highlight the range of languages we use to make fiction. But that would have involved including the bigger giants of American short fiction: Raymond Carver, Flannery O'Connor, Donald Barthelme, Joy Williams. It made no sense for me to be republishing those people. Does Raymond Carver need to be in another anthology? No. So the parameters kept changing, and you're right to point out that there are these discrepancies, which I worried about for months. Should I set firm timelines? Who gets in? Who gets left out, and why? In the end, I don't know if this was the right choice, but after I'd read these stories ten or fifteen times as I was trying to decide,

I copped out and scrapped any rigid way of looking at the book. In some sense, it's a reconciling book that takes the kind of storywriters who would never be in the same book and puts them together. I wanted to make a little bit of a dream book for somebody who's just starting to write fiction to see—

CE —What's possible?

BM Yeah, arrange the stuff that to me still seemed vital. The more I did this, the more I realized this is an extremely subjective book. For instance, if I put it together today, there are five or six writers I should have put in that I didn't.

CE Let's talk a little bit about its organization, how it came out in the end. I mean, it's kind of an impossible feat, don't you think?

BM There's also a concrete explanation and it comes back to teaching. Students ask what they should read. Like a lot of teachers, I develop course packets, a collection of things that I can never find in one anthology. Anthologies, including some that I really love, often represent a single artistic idea. Tobias Wolff's *Vintage Book of Contemporary American Short Stories* reinforces a single—granted, a big—artistic idea of short fiction, and in the intro, Wolff takes a potshot at what is called postmodern fiction. The anthologies that are supposedly more cutting-edge, whatever that is, go into a different ghetto. I wanted to make the sort of anthology that I could actually use in teaching, that would fulfill a variety of desires in a reader. There are some really eccentric stories in this book, but there are conventional ones as well. I was imagining the kind of reader who would be turned on by that. There are always younger readers who don't feel spoken to by the conventional ways that writers do things. Then they suddenly come across an author like Anne Carson and think, "This is so enabling, so interesting and fascinating, this is exactly the sort of thing that I'd like to try to do or try to push past." I wanted the anthology to have all of these little pockets of promise, all these little side alleys of provocation. And I also thought it would be pretty interesting to put stalwart realist stories right next to those pieces like Carson's or Joe Wenderoth's.

CE When you pick up an anthology, do you just open a page and start?

BM I probably look at the contributors. I might thumb through it. I like to read first sentences—

**CE** I do too, it's a habit I have at bookstores; picking up a book and reading the first sentence. Actually, this is what drew me into *The Age of Wire and String*; the sentences were unlike anything I'd ever read. Do you have a favorite first sentence? For example, I've always loved Amy Hempel's "My heart it stopped." Can you throw some at me—from the anthology? I think this relates to the point you made about not wasting a reader's time, not allowing boredom.

**BM** I'd like to think I don't have a specific requirement for what a first sentence should be, but at the least, of course, it should create desire for the second sentence, and so on. Provocations, and strong statements like Hempel's, are an obvious choice. But flat openers have their place, too, sentences not so obviously concerned with seduction. We don't necessarily want to get a deep kiss on the mouth right away. Something plain, without, say, the self-conscious grammar inversion of the Hempel sentence, could work just as well, because it would conceal the larger artistic project; it would be more reluctant than a self-conscious gesture. The mystery of artistic intent would play out more gradually. Does Hempel's deliberately clipped rhythm tie her to something for the rest of the story, commit her to a specific approach? Having read the whole story, I'd say it does, since the story is just as much, if not more, about acoustics and the sounds of sentences as it is about their meaning and we could have a happy argument about whether these things could, or should, even be separated. What I'm saying, though, is that the opening sentence does not necessarily have to grandstand an artistic project. It can be far humbler or modest, and still just as interesting to me.

But that said, I'll list a first sentence that has stuck with me, and this probably refutes everything I just said: This is Gary Lutz, from "People Shouldn't Have to be the Ones to Tell You": "He had a couple of grown daughters, disappointers, with regretted curiosities and the heavy venture of having once looked alive."

This is grammatically intact, easily parsable, but filled with the most complex rabbit holes. The phrase "regretted curiosities," by itself, could inspire an entire story. Here it's used as a character detail for two people—they regret the things they were curious about. An emotion is already created here, even though we're still in abstract territory. Earlier in the sentence, the daughters are called disappointers, and this too is beautifully loaded. It is the only thing we know about the "he" who starts the story that his daughters have disappointed him. But because they are defined as "disappointers," we can guess that they have disappointed others. This sounds heavy and bleak, but upon examination is really universal, or at least it's hard to imagine the reader who believes that he has not disappointed people.

So a connection is being made to the reader, and it's not a happy one. The closing line of the sentence, that the girls once looked alive, is horrible and amazing and puzzling. In theory, the girls could now be dead, but chances are they merely look dead, which seems somehow worse.

The danger with a sentence as rich as that, however, is when it encounters a reader who is looking more for the journalistic Ws, some basic info. This Lutz sentence tells us to slow down, that the pleasures of this story will be in the phrases, they will be hidden and clustered around punctuation, and a patient reader will be rewarded. Another kind of reader might zoom right by all the good stuff and end up finding no story there.

**CE** Ben, how has your work changed since your first book? Where do you think your work is headed?

**BM** I saw the apparent impenetrability of my first book as something that was a liability and was curious how to write exactly the way I wanted but to somehow make it less opaque, because readers matter to me. In some sense just telling a story, just announcing that something's going to happen can lessen everyone's anxieties when they're reading you. This isn't necessarily true for me, and yet there are a lot of pleasures in storytelling that I denied myself in the first book. So the second book, *Notable American Women*, was more narrative. Instead of portraying an enormous abstract world, I was interested in having a little bit more unity to the portrait I was making of a world and a set group of characters. A real, physical place and a real set of people. The first book could not really be reduced to that. And so in that sense, there was more legibility, but probably less poetry—a bit less interest in linguistic play in the second book.

**CE** More emotion?

**BM** I was trying for more emotion in the first book. The criticisms that stung the most were about its coldness. I just tried a different angle at emotion. It's something I can't imagine writing without. But to me it's an enormous challenge and problem. I can't write a conventional story where a kid's family gets molested by an elk and he ends the novel weeping. I take a lot of circuitous approaches to emotion, not as an effort of trickery, but so that I can get at it and make it feel genuine. I wanted that first book to be emotional, but it seems like a lot of people didn't see it that way.

**CE** What things do you like best about your work?

**BM** It's a constant struggle to make the sort of writing that I can feel is my own, something that comes out of a pretty deep place and is not a contrivance or a response to other writing. Writing presents this interesting challenge to work within the confines of grammar, sense, and narrative, and then still do all the artistic things that you're attracted to. That there are a handful of writers in the mode of storytelling who are being intensely creative and artistic and innovative is a miraculous event. A large bulk of writers are practitioners of established modes of storytelling. They can be fantastic to read, but their texts don't look like artistic advances to me. And certainly they don't have to be—I would imagine they're not even intended to be. But I like it when writing can do that without seeming like it's navel-gazing, forbidding, and impenetrable. Writing is in a hard place in that respect. A strange painting on a wall asks you to stand in front of it and get an impression of it, whereas a strange, weirdly unreadable novel asks something so much more and it's much harder to engage. So I get excited about writing when I think about the possibility of being artistically relevant without alienating lots of readers.

**CE** What are you working on right now?

**BM** I'm working on a bunch of short things and a novel. The novel is pretty much in its formative stages, so it's hard to talk about. I'm trying to find the sound, the voice of it. The book deals with a lot of deep allergies that the characters have to almost everything, and at the top of the list is language: people get sick when they speak. But I always have my conceptual ideas first and in a way they can become a bit of a problem because I need to find ways to make that world come to life in fiction. I always seem to feel like I have to reinvent the wheel and I can't just tell it as a story. So I'm still working on the form and the language part.

**CE** Was either of your books an easier birth?

**BM** My first book, *The Age of Wire and String*, probably came along more innocently and haphazardly, when I had no idea what a book was, and no real hope of publication. I had almost no notion of an audience and was writing purely to satisfy myself. But the willfully obscure elements of that book look somewhat easy to me in retrospect, at least when I compare that impulse to the unifying narrative I attempted in *Notable American Women*. And while I was slightly more worried about readability for that book, it's hardly a crowd pleaser. What I'm saying, I guess, is that I'm not really crazy about finding an easier birth for a book. The struggle and impossibility of bringing a book to life is what's attractive to me.

# Steven Millhauser
# and Jim Shepard

STEVEN MILLHAUSER was born in New York City in 1943. He is the author of numerous books, including *Edwin Mullhouse: The Life and Death of an American Writer, 1943-1954*; *Dangerous Laughter*, a *New York Times* Notable Book of the Year; *The Barnum Museum*; and *Martin Dressler: The Tale of an American Dreamer*, which won the Pulitzer Prize for Fiction. Millhauser lives in Saratoga Springs, New York and is a professor at Skidmore College.

JIM SHEPARD was born in Bridgeport, Connecticut, in 1956. His novels and short story collections include *Like You'd Understand, Anyway*, which was nominated for the National Book Award; *You Think That's Bad*; *Love and Hydrogen*; and *Project X*, which won the Massachusetts Book Award and the Alex Award. A graduate of Trinity College and Brown University, where he earned his MFA, Shepard teaches at Williams College and in the Warren Wilson MFA program, and lives in Williamstown, Massachusetts.

**JIM SHEPARD**  Perhaps as much as any American writer I can think of, you've been drawn to the novella. Are there aesthetic advantages and disadvantages peculiar to the form? Does it even have a form?

**STEVEN MILLHAUSER**  Is it possible not to be drawn to the novella? Everything about it is immensely seductive. It demands the rigor of treatment associated with the short story, while at the same time it offers a liberating sense of expansiveness, of widening spaces. And it strikes me as having real advantages over its jealous rivals, the short story and the novel. The challenge and glory of the short story lie exactly there, in its shortness. But shortness encourages certain effects and not others. It encourages, for instance, the close-up view, the revelatory detail, the single significant moment. In the little world of the story, many kinds of desirable effect are inherently impossible—say, the gradual elaboration of a psychology, the demonstration of change over time. Think of the slowly unfolding drama of self-delusion and self-discovery in *Death in Venice*—a short story would have to proceed very differently. As for novels: in their dark hearts, don't they long to be exhaustive? Novels are hungry, monstrous. Their apparent delicacy is deceptive—they want to devour the world.

The novella wants nothing to do with the immense, the encyclopedic, the all-conquering all-devouring prose epic, which strikes it as an army moving relentlessly across the land. Its desires are more intimate, more selective. And when it looks at the short story, to which it's secretly akin, it says, with a certain cruelty, No, not for me this admirably exquisite, elegant, refined?—perhaps overrefined?—delicately nuanced, perfect little world, whose perfection depends so much on artful exclusions. It says, Let me breathe! The attraction of the novella is that it lets the short story breathe. It invites the possibility of certain elaborations and complexities forbidden by a very short form, while at the same time it holds out the promise of formal perfection. It's enough to make a writer dizzy with exhilaration.

**JS**  And how do such characteristics impact the novella's form? Is it worth trying to talk about the peculiar nature of that form, or does that simply head us into the land of "There are as many forms as there are . . ." etc.?

**SM**  The novella isn't really a form at all. It's a length, and a very rough length at that (sixty to a hundred pages? Seventy-five to a hundred and twenty-five pages?). In this it's no different from the short story or the novel, which are frequently called "forms" but are in fact nothing but rough lengths. A true literary form exists only in the fixed poetic forms: the sonnet, the villanelle, the sestina, and so on. But having said that, I don't mean to suggest that nothing more can be said about the novella. Length invites certain kinds of treatment rather than others. Just as a very short length is likely to concentrate on a very short span of time (say, a crucial afternoon), in a tightly restricted space, with a very small number of characters, and an extensive length is likely to cover a great stretch of time, in a wide variety of settings, with many characters, so the novella length seems to me peculiarly well suited to following the curve of an action over a carefully restricted period of time, but one wider than that suited to the short story, in a small number of sharply defined spaces, with two, three or perhaps four characters. To be more precise than that is to risk insisting on proper behavior. But the novella is much too alive to be asked to behave properly. Compared to the short story, it's a length that hasn't even begun to be explored.

**JS** Part of the revelation of *Edwin Mullhouse* for many readers was its ability to render the intensity of attention involved in childhood perception: how certain objects, especially for children, become luminous, if not numinous. Does what you're doing—when it's going well—feel like aesthetic problem solving, or more exalted than that?

**SM** Hmmm: aesthetic problem solving. That sounds like the sort of thing a sly critic might wish to say about a book he particularly dislikes. Of course, there's no getting around it—one thing you relentlessly do when you write is solve aesthetic problems. But to leave it at that! No, when things are going well, the feeling I have is much more extravagant. It's the feeling that I'm at the absolute center of things, instead of off to one side—the feeling that the entire universe is streaming in on me. It's a feeling of strength, of terrifying health, of much-more-aliveness. It's the kind of feeling that probably should never be talked about, as if one were confessing to a shameful deed.

**JS** And is that a feeling that seems important in terms of understanding childhood?

**SM** Yes, so long as it's clear that, for me, childhood is above all a metaphor for a way of perceiving the world.

**JS** In that we're all, if we keep our eyes open, in the position of confronting barely apprehensible wonders?

**SM** Exactly.

**JS** Don Juan in "An Adventure of Don Juan," the second novella in *The King in the Tree*, longs for "a madness of desire, a journey into feeling so intense that he would ride through himself like a conqueror of unknown inner countries." Is that what fiction should enable?

**SM** I'm fanatically reluctant to say that fiction ought to do one thing rather than another. I do know what I want from fiction. I want it to exhilarate me, to unbind my eyes, to murder and resurrect me, to harm me in some fruitful way. But that said, yes, the journey into intense feeling and the conquest of unknown emotional territory is something fiction can make possible.

**JS** Your Don Juan also says of his host that "the irrepressible squire had a way of making you feel like a twelve-year-old boy following an adventurous fourteen-year-old brother." Is that also an ambition of your fiction?

**SM** Fiction is an adventure or it's nothing—nothing at all. What's an adventure? An invitation to wonder and danger. If what I write doesn't lead a reader into the woods, away from the main path, then it's a failure. Somebody else wrote it. I disown it.

**JS** Does that mean that your fiction is always in some ways a fiction of initiation?

**SM** I would never myself put it in those words. That is, I would never say to myself: Now I am writing a story about initiation, or Now I have written a story about initiation. But if you define "initiation" to mean more or less what I mean by adventure and the wayward path, then it must be true that in some ways my fiction is a fiction of initiation.

**JS** The narrator of "Revenge," the first novella, in her opening paragraph compares houses where doors open right into living rooms to "being introduced to some man at a party who right away throws his arm around your shoulders," and says she prefers instead "a little distance, thank you, a little formality." Do you find yourself making aesthetic choices with the same sort of preferences in mind?

**SM** Yes, I do. But words like "distance" and "formality" are easily misunderstood. To say I prefer distance isn't to say I prefer coldness, haughtiness, lack of feeling, deadness. In my view, it's precisely that "little distance" that permits genuine feeling to be expressed. My dislike of warm, cozy, chummy writing is that it always strikes me as fraudulent—a failure of feeling.

Passion, beauty, intensity—everything I care about in art—is made possible through the discipline of distance. Or to say it another way: Powerful feeling in art takes place only through the particular kind of distance known as form.

JS  Many of your works play off literary antecedents in affectionate and complicated ways. Does that mean you'll reread *The Romance of the Rose* or "The Cask of Amontillado" half thinking it might engender a story of your own? Or do you continually tell yourself you're just reading?

SM  It may be that I'm deluding myself, but I never have the sense of looking for inspiration in my lustful, wildly irresponsible reading. What I'm looking for, I think, is pleasure so extreme that it ought to be forbidden by law. As for the engendering of stories: that, for me, is a mystery I don't pretend to understand. I not only don't know what gives me the idea for a story, I don't even know whether it's proper to say that what comes to me is something that might be described as an "idea." It's more like a feeling, vague at first, that becomes sharper over time and expresses itself after a while in images and then in oppositions that might develop into proto-dramas. A murky business, at best. But once a story starts taking shape in my mind, if that's where it takes place—I think it takes place all over my body—then it's fed by everything in my experience that can feed it. And part of my experience is a mile-high mass of books, which I sometimes draw on deliberately to create certain effects. I'm reluctant to talk directly about my work, for fear of harming it with deadly explanations that I'm bound to regret, but let me try just a little. When I wrote *Edwin Mullhouse*, I made use of a number of models, such as Leon Edel's five-volume biography of Henry James, Nabokov's *Pale Fire* and Mann's *Doctor Faustus*. But to say that any of those books somehow engendered my own would be, I think, false. My book came from something deeper, more personal, more intimate, more ungraspable, more obscure than other people's books, though at the same time it was pleased to make use of those books in order to become itself, in order to give birth to itself. Books as midwives—maybe that's what I mean.

JS  Books as midwives makes sense. But when asking about how much your reading engendered in you, I didn't so much mean ideas as feelings: so much of your fiction seems to come from deeply personal responses to already-created worlds, to previous stories: Tristan and Isolde's, or Don Juan's, to cite the most recent examples. Is that another way of maintaining what you called that discipline of distance?

SM It's true that I sometimes make deliberate use of existing stories, though it's also true that I very often don't. Insofar as I do, it is, yes, one way of maintaining a necessary distance, for the paradoxical sake of closeness. But I think something else is also at work. When I make use of an existing story, I take pleasure in participating in something beyond myself that is much greater than myself, and equal pleasure in striking a variation. I take pleasure, you might say, in acknowledging the past and then sharply departing from it. And there is something to be said for releasing oneself from the obligations of relentless novelty; a certain kind of insistent originality is nothing but the attempt of mediocrity to appear interesting to itself.

JS Given your delight in wonders and your interest in the forbidden, does it surprise you that you haven't taken an even greater interest in monsters? The Lernean Hydra shows up in Don Juan, for example, but it's a special effect in a theme park.

SM Legitimate, bona fide monsters do in fact make occasional appearances in my work, but what interests me is something quite different. What interests me—not exclusively, but in relation to the monstrous—is the place where the familiar begins to turn strange. When things cease to be themselves, when they begin to turn into something else, which has no name—that is a region I'm always drawn to. This, I think, accounts for my interest in night scenes, in childhood, in bands of prowling adolescent girls, in underground and attic places, in obsession, in heightened states of awareness. In this sense, it might easily be argued that the wondrous and the monstrous are very much the same. My plan for Mr. Juan was to estrange him from his familiar world of loveless conquest and lead him toward the terrifying world of genuine feeling.

JS So is the stress on "terrifying" intended to crucially complicate the novella's overall design as a moral fable? Or would you claim that it has only the shape and not the intent of a moral fable?

SM If I hear a piece of writing described as a moral fable, my instinct is to head for the hills. I'll never admit to having written one myself. But let's say that, by some oversight on my part, a moral fable did slip out. In that case, then yes, the design is crucially complicated through the new discovery of feeling. Don Juan's fate isn't to be punished for sin, but to be led—or shall we say initiated?—into human feeling. To put it somewhat differently: In traditional Don Juan stories, the hero is punished by hellfire. Here, his fiery punishment is unrequited love. Meanwhile the underworld becomes, as you wittily put it, only a theme park.

**JS** The "head for the hills" disclaimer is one very similar to Nabokov's, but like Nabokov's, it's a claim that's easily misunderstood. Would you resist the notion that your work promotes or valorizes certain values—such as an exalted tenderness—while repudiating others, like cruelty?

**SM** I do resist the notion, even though it may well be true. I resist it because when I write I have the sense that what compels me isn't the promotion of certain values, but something else—the working out of a harmony, the completion of a necessary design. This may be just another way of insisting that the values that belong to art are aesthetic. Exactly how moral values fit in is for a trained philosopher to say.

**JS** Two of the three novellas feature obsessional preoccupations with betrayal (three of the three, if we imagine Don Juan as feeling as if he's betrayed himself), and betrayal can be understood as a darker, and more intensely felt, version of that fundamental moment you were describing earlier when the familiar begins to turn strange. Are you drawn to betrayal for its potential to generate that "inner riot of grief" in a way that's more charged and divided against itself than other kinds of grief—say, the death of a loved one—would be?

**SM** I don't know exactly why I'm drawn to the notion of betrayal, though your explanation of it makes good sense to me. I like things that cut deep. And I'm attracted to opposites. Betrayal is the dark other side of friendship and love—it's, if you like, the monster that friendship and love are always threatened by.

**JS** Did you have fun with the chatty/colloquial voice narrating "Revenge"? I'm thinking of the playfulness in all those radio-like moments such as "Mmm, that's good. That's very good. Tea calms me."

**SM** Yes, I enjoyed that voice, which one day began speaking to me like a troubled stranger on a street corner. It's almost as if all I had to do was write down what was being whispered in my ear. Her playfulness exhilarated me. Who knows where she came from? The whole story strikes me as an unlikely, uncharacteristic one for me to have written, and I'm pleased by anything in myself that strikes me as not myself.

**JS** Jeffrey Eugenides has remarked that his generation of writers grew up backwards: weaned on modernism and fabulism and then working their way back to the great nineteenth-century masters of realism. Was your experience anything like that?

**SM** Not at all. Or rather, not exactly, and therefore not at all.

What troubles me about such a formulation is that it seems to imply a dismissal of modernism and fabulism—those decadent, questionable pastimes—and a retreat, with a great sigh of relief, into the arms of dear old realism. But the great modernists, including Kafka, are all supremely gifted masters of realism. To experience the modernists—I'm speaking specifically of Joyce, Kafka, Mann and Proust, though it applies to lesser figures like Musil and Gide and Woolf—is to experience the shock of realism, along with the shock of what undermines it or transcends it. To work your way back to the great nineteenth-century masters of realism from the astonishing heights of twentieth-century modernism is to experience a past that, however noble and admirable it may be, has already been questioned and challenged and, as I see it, vitally transformed.

As for me, I revere the great realist masters and am drowned in their work. I turn to Chekhov and the maligned but superb Maupassant far more than I turn to Kafka and Bruno Schulz. But I read them, always, with the sense that they brilliantly exhausted a method, a way of looking at the world, and that another way must be found. I read them, in short, as they were read by the very writers who directly inherited their work and turned it into something boldly new. The problem, as I see it, isn't to choose between two opposed methods—the method of nineteenth-century realism, on the one hand, and the method, as if there were one, of modernism/fabulism on the other—but to write something that pays homage to whatever in the past is richest and most alive, while it sets forth on its own wayward journey.

Something must be wrong with me, I think I'm beginning to enjoy this. Well, fire away.

**JS** I want to get back for a moment to your nice notion of wanting fiction to unbind your eyes. Is the implication that we might fathom ourselves more fully if we direct a more perfect attention to those unexpected things around us? (I'm thinking of a remark like Hemingway's: "A hard light thrown on objects softly illuminates the beholder.") Or does it have more to do with the giving of one's self that's involved in perceiving: as in Simone Weil's formulation that attention is the rarest and purest form of generosity?

SM I like both those suggestions, but what I meant was much simpler, much less . . . interesting. I meant that the world is there, presenting itself to us ceaselessly, and yet it remains largely invisible. I remember being struck by a passage in a philosophy book that pointed out how no object is completely present to sight. If you look at a cube, you can see only three sides. The passage went on to distinguish seeing from imagining—in imagination, I immediately apprehend all six sides—but for me the simple fact that objects don't reveal themselves completely to sight became a symbol of the general invisibility of the world. Even the three visible sides of a cube are barely visible if, when it hits your sight, you happen to be meditating on the murder of your wife's lover. And what about hollow cubes, like houses, that contain invisible spaces, filled with unseen things that we can only guess at? To say nothing of cubes that once were there and are there no longer. We walk through a world continually disappearing from view. One thing fiction does is restore the hidden and vanishing world. It makes the blind see. It gives us the mystic's vision: the universe in a grain of sand (not a bad definition of the short story, by the way). That's what I meant when I said that I want fiction to unbind my eyes.

JS I like the wistfulness of "We walk through a world continually disappearing from view," as well as the consolation inherent in the notion that fiction restores some of that loss. And I've always loved the quiet comedy in your work. It seems to depend on a sobriety of tone, often in the seemingly straightforward presentation of the impenetrably mysterious. Isn't there something inescapably comic about our relation to the cube, as you've just described it? Potentially comic?

SM I hadn't really thought of it that way before, but as you say it, I'm immediately struck by the comedy of the cube. I imagine some earnest soul eager to see the other three sides: he turns the cube, discovers the missing sides, and suddenly realizes that he's concealed the original three, which he desperately longs to see again. He turns the cube, faster and faster; finally, in rage, he picks up a hammer and shatters the cube. The lust for knowledge, for vision, for memory, for penetrating the impenetrable—all this noble longing hovers on the edge of the comic. You remember those old toys in Cracker Jack boxes—or am I inventing them? One slight turn of the wrist, and the clown's glum mouth becomes a smile.

JS We're almost out of space, or time. So: whether we like it or not, there are some matters about the Writer Himself that need to be at least gestured toward when one is doing an interview like this. Here are four of those sorts of questions, for you to evade or deflect as you please.

**SM** Phew.

**JS**  First: *The King in the Tree* is your tenth (!) book. In many ways I assume you feel yourself to be the same writer who delivered *Edwin Mullhouse* to Knopf. But are there any aspects of that guy that you miss?

**SM** I have the belief that I carry around in myself all stages of myself simultaneously. I don't outgrow myself, I merely add on. In that sense, he's still with me, whoever he is, or was. I don't miss him, or any of them. They're here.

**JS**  Second: Do you have a horror of the hands-on editor? At what point do you want other opinions? And from whom do you want them? Does anyone else read your work in its early stages?

**SM** I once read a biography of Robert Lowell, who was quoted as saying something like: "A good critic is someone who loves your work but doesn't like all of it." Bravo. I've always shown my work to a small number of friends, who are in sympathy with what I do but are willing to say that they don't like this or that. I show only work that seems to me final. If they're right, I change it. When it comes to editors, my feeling is basically: Take it or leave it, kiddo. In general, I feel immense gratitude to anyone, even an editor, who points out to me a blunder of any kind. An editor once suggested that I change the fate of a character. I was not grateful.

**JS**  You've always kept your distance from that part of the writer's life in America that doesn't involve writing: judging contests, going to conferences, etc. Was that distance changed in any way by receiving the Pulitzer Prize for *Martin Dressler*? Has it been changed by teaching?

**SM** Prizes have always struck me as extremely arbitrary. The one you mentioned—what was it called again?—somehow appeared, but I could just as easily have been arrested and shot for the crime of fiction. As for teaching: the difficulty for me is that I'm essentially a person who likes silence, and teaching is talk. I now talk more—a bad sign, surely.

**JS**  And finally: this may represent your only opportunity to reminisce about your hometown of Stratford, Connecticut, in an interview with a fellow native. Any biographical tidbits, fictional or otherwise, that you'd like to relate? Any horrors or delights you'd like to revisit? What was it like growing up there?

SM Everything I had to say about Stratford is in my first novel, though in a fractured, splintered, meticulously distorted way. But there are two things that your question brings to mind, as a kind of legacy from those years. One is the sweetness in my ear of Italian and Slavic surnames. My father was a teacher, at the then-brand-new University of Bridgeport (we had moved to Stratford from my original home, in Brooklyn, when I was four), and his salary and my mother's (she taught first grade) brought in only enough to permit us to live in a working-class neighborhood. My friends and classmates all had names like Zielski, Stoccatore, Saksa, Mancini, Pavluvcik, Ciccarelli, Leitkowski, Cerino, DiCicio, Politano, Recupido. Names like these, as sheer sounds, have the power to move me like chords struck on an old piano. The other thing that springs to mind is more difficult to express. It's the sense, given to me by growing up in that neighborhood, in that town, of what an American small-town street feels like and smells like, what kitchens and cellars and attics are like, what roadside weeds and telephone poles are like. There's plenty I don't know about American life, but those things are mine.

# Álvaro Mutis and Francisco Goldman

ÁLVARO MUTIS (1923–2013) was born in Bogotá, Colombia, and lived most of his life in Mexico. A poet and prose writer, Mutis is the author of *The Snow of the Admiral* and *The Adventures and Misadventures of Maqroll*. For his work, Mutis won the Premio Xavier Villaurrutia, the Premio Príncipe de Asturias, the Premio Reina Sofía de Poesía, the Miguel de Cervantes Prize, and the Neustadt International Prize for Literature.

FRANCISCO GOLDMAN was born in Boston, Massachusetts, in 1954. He is a journalist, critic, and novelist. He is the author of *The Ordinary Seaman*, *The Divine Husband*, and *Say Her Name*. For his work, Goldman has twice been a finalist for the PEN/Faulkner Award and the *Los Angeles Times* Book Prize; he has also been shortlisted for the International IMPAC Dublin Literary Award. He won the Sue Kaufman Prize for First Fiction for his novel *The Long Night of White Chickens*. A Guggenheim Fellow, Goldman is an Allen K. Smith Professor of Literature and Creative Writing at Trinity College. He lives in Brooklyn, New York and Mexico City.

*Translated by Marina Harss.*

**FRANCISCO GOLDMAN**  Alvaro, I have always had the impression that if I were to tell you a story about Maqroll, one I heard, say, from a ship captain in Veracruz, who'd supposedly been with Maqroll last year, you would believe it. In other words, sometimes it seems to me that you are as surprised and curious about the fortunes of Maqroll as any of his fictional friends. How have you developed this wonderful character over time?

**ÁLVARO MUTIS**  Well, Maqroll has been with me since I wrote my first poems, when I was nineteen, and I'll tell you what happened. I had written a series of poems and all of them had the voice of a person who had lived and had experienced things that I had not experienced at nineteen; I hadn't experienced anything then, you see. So I thought that this character would be very useful for my poetry. And during the forty years in which I wrote poetry he did turn out to be quite useful and he came with me when I started writing novels, which wasn't my original intention. My intention was to continue to explore the same themes in narrative prose that I had developed in my poetry, to talk about the landscapes of sensation and about my notion of man and of the world. I wanted to translate all of this into a narrative rhythm. And Maqroll helped me do this; he accompanies me. However, we are no longer side by side, but face to face. So Maqroll doesn't surprise me too much, but he does torment me and keep me company. He is more and more himself, and less my creation, because as I write novels, I load him up with experiences and actions and places that I don't know but that he of course does. And so he has become a person with whom I must be cautious. I'll give you an example: The other day, in the novel that I'm working on now, I thought, I'll have him board a ship in Morocco that is carrying phosphates, which are highly explosive and very dangerous. Would you believe I could actually hear Maqroll saying to me, "Hold on—don't be a fool! I can't be in Morocco! In Morocco, I'm wanted by the police for that business with the rugs in *Abdul Bashur, Dreamer of Ships*." "So, where should he board the ship then?" "In Tunisia." "All right then, Tunisia." This is my relationship with Maqroll. And I'll tell you something else, *The Snow of the Admiral* as well as several of my other books have come out in Turkish, a language Maqroll speaks fluently. I swear that sometimes when I hold that Turkish edition in my hand, I think, I have to show this to Maqroll. (*laughter*) So this is my relationship with him. In my poetry, he no longer appears, because my poetry has gone in other directions, on other paths where I don't need his help.

**FG**  You've written eight novellas about Maqroll in less than a decade. When you wrote the first one, did you know there would be others?

**ÁM** No, no. I was editing a text that I thought was a prose poem entitled *The Snow of the Admiral* and then one day I read it in a French translation about to be published and I said to myself, This isn't a prose poem, this is a piece of a novel I'm going to write. With a great sense of fatigue I said, I'm going to finish this story. I sat down and started to tell more, and more, and more, and when I had about three hundred pages, I edited it. I sent it to Carmen Balcells, my literary agent. I said to her, "Here. I don't know what the hell this is." And she called me three days later and said, "It's going to be published by Alianza Editorial. It's a wonderful novel and I love it." My response was, "But wait a minute, it's not a novel." And she said, "That's not up to you, it's up to me and your readers," and that was that.

**FG** Something very important in your novels is the sense of place. It's clear that you love the ocean, the desert, the jungle, especially as spaces to be traveled through. What do these settings mean to you?

**ÁM** Well, this is really something that comes out of my own life. I traveled with my family from the age of two. We went to Brussels. My father was in the Colombian diplomatic service and we were there for nine years. We traveled to Colombia by sea for vacations. Those trips were wonderful for me. They were like an extended holiday, because on a ship you are not responsible for anything. All you have to do is coexist with the sea and its life and watch it all go by. And again, when I worked for Standard Oil as Colombian head of public relations for five years, I traveled on oil tankers and had interesting experiences and met extremely curious people, many of whom appear in my novellas. So I loved traveling and moving around. And interestingly, without actively trying, I have always had jobs that forced me to move around. For over twenty-three years, I worked for Twentieth Century Fox and then Columbia Pictures as sales manager for the television division in Latin America, selling sitcoms and specials and made-for-TV movies. And I went from capital to capital to capital: Guatemala, Honduras, Nicaragua, Costa Rica, to Chile and back through Argentina, Brazil, Venezuela, Puerto Rico and then back to Los Angeles. So my life became a long trip and I met thousands of people, in all different kinds of situations. And this was like a continuation of what I had experienced as a child. In this way I lost the sense of belonging to a particular country. I know that I am Colombian and will be until I die, and there are landscapes in Colombia that I love and am fascinated by, and they appear in my poetry, but I don't feel a commitment to any one country because, after all, I'm just passing through.

FG  And that's why there's a real sense of the experience of the working life in your books, something that is rare in contemporary literature.

ÁM  That's because of a reality that I think is important: I have never lived from my literary vocation. I have always worked in fields that have nothing to do with the literary life. I have never worked at a newspaper or at a magazine. It's not that I am against it, it's simply the way my life has been. So, I started studying poetry, then fiction, and meanwhile my work was completely unrelated to that. But the reason why I know the jungle, for example, is that I accompanied geologists from Standard Oil who were searching for oil—which does exist in the jungle, although it's complicated and expensive to extract; I was there in case they had problems with the army, among other things.

FG  The Belgian engineer in *Un Bel Morir* is such a sinister and odd character. The reader gets the feeling that you must have known and worked with people like him.

ÁM  Absolutely; that was when I was working in aviation; I was the public relations person for the airline that later became Avianca. I had to go to accident sites and even help remove bodies from the wreckage and be present when the bodies were identified. And then face the press and the families, and—well, you can imagine. These were very difficult, hard things. And I have made my life doing them. Now I am retired and I have a pension from Columbia Pictures.

FG  When people talk about Maqroll, they think of hopelessness. Is this his existential condition, or is it political, or psychological?

ÁM  No, that is something that comes from me. Remember—something you, as a novelist, know as well as I: all of the characters created by a writer contain bits and pieces and moments of the writer. I've never been involved in politics. I've never voted. I have never believed and have no faith in the intentions of a man who wants to make life better for all men. I think this just leads to concentration camps and Stalinist purges, the Inquisition and all of that horror. I believe that man is a species one should be very suspicious of. Now, I have no bitterness, but I am not going to change things, and I don't want to change them. I accept them as they are, and that is how I live. So, it is natural that Maqroll, without being my exact reflection—which he is not at all—should have my hopeless view of the world.

**FG** On the other hand, not only I but other people have noted that Maqroll is like your opposite; you have such love for life, and you are known for your radiant disposition and your generosity.

**ÁM** (*laughter*) Well, people have said that to me before, but of course, I never meant to create a character that was my reflection. I am interested in a man with a tendency to dismantle formulas—not a revolutionary, but someone who breaks down established, conventional formulas. A man who is capable at times of great violence, and who pushes this violence to its full, brutal, tragic end. This is not me, but I can imagine that someone who thinks the way I do about the world could be this way. Maqroll lives by a rule that is stated in one of the novels, I can't remember which; it is his dictum: never try to change or modify what destiny puts in your path, and never try to judge things.

**FG** A fascinating aspect of Maqroll is the strange books that he's always reading: the memoirs and biographies of kings, of Saint Francis of Assisi and so on. Can you tell me a little bit about this?

**ÁM** Maqroll exhibits something which, in part, could have happened to me. I read almost as much history as literature, maybe more, and I always have since I was a child. The first books I read in my father's library, in French, were history books. So, what happens? I think that when a man like Maqroll reads Chateaubriand's *Mémoires d'outre-tombe*, or the memoirs of the Cardinal de Retz, he puts himself in their places and asks himself what he would have done if, and oh yes, that's how it was, yes I see. His curiosity about the past helps him to live the present. And why? Because the present becomes not something that just crashes over you, but rather when he hears about the terrible things happening in Kosovo he says, "Hold on, this same thing happened in Spain, in Granada, at the end of the Reconquista."

**FG** Maqroll has a very poetic sense of the past.

**ÁM** Because what the past says to us is that humans do not change. And this is a very good thing to know. Through his reading, Maqroll realizes that we remain the same.

**FG** Speaking of Saint Francis, there is a sense of renunciation about Maqroll.

**ÁM** Yes, radical renunciation. But he, unlike Saint Francis, does not want to make this renunciation into a regimen for others or for a community. He says no to things precisely because of his philosophy of not trying to change anyone—each person is the way he is and that's it. Now, if I were to load up on—as Maqroll would say—luxury items and objects, and these objects were to define me, I would be forced to stay still, not move. This doesn't suit me; I don't need anything.

FG  Maqroll and his friends always have schemes that are supposed to make them lots of money and always fail. If one of these schemes had made him rich, what would have happened to him?

ÁM  But Frank, he already made Ilona so angry when they won all that money in the business about the rugs. And all Maqroll wants to do is give his check to Abdul so he can buy the tramp steamer he has been dreaming of. So, money never stays in his hands, it always slips through his fingers.

FG  Another important theme in your books is love. In *Un Bel Morir* you say that love has many faces and many masks, and that we use that word to describe many different things. The last stop of the tramp steamer is that rare thing: a novel of romantic love between two mature adults. Do these late loves happen in real life?

ÁM  They do happen. Maqroll demonstrates this in his love affair with Amparo Maria and then with the other woman, the one who works at a café, Doña Estela. He has a great admiration for women and he realizes that they see much more deeply than we men do, and know much more than we do, and that the best thing is to listen to them and do as they say. He always creates a sense of complicity with the person he loves. He thinks, We are together, but with no obligations—we won't get married or enter into a bourgeois lifestyle. I love you deeply, and whenever we meet we will be together, because it is wonderful to have a relationship with someone who is my accomplice, and someone who feels no sense of obligation towards me. So that is his attitude, and if women sustain him and love him, why is that? Because he is not obliging them to do anything—he's leaving the next day, or will be arriving the day after. He is their friend, their accomplice. There is a basic friendship in love that I do believe exists.

FG  Is there anything in this world as beautiful as a tramp steamer?

ÁM  (*laughter*) No, there isn't . . . well, not anymore. You know, when I see one, and I see them often when I travel, it brings tears to my eyes. The other day my wife and I saw a tramp steamer on a beach in Miami. There was no one around, and they were just letting it go to pieces on a part of the beach where it didn't matter. It made me want to raise some money and get the poor thing out of there, so it could live.

**FG** Flannery O'Connor once said that for her it was impossible to read a page of Conrad without feeling an urge to write, though, of course, there are no boats in her books. It is a commonplace to say that you are influenced by Conrad because you both write about boats. What do we mean when we talk about influences?

**ÁM** Well, a real influence. You know who is my greatest literary influence? Charles Dickens. Why? A real influence is an author who communicates an energy and a great desire to tell a story, and it isn't that you want to write like Dickens, but rather that when you read Dickens, you feel an imaginative energy that you use to your own ends. In other words, you're not going to write *Oliver Twist*. Dickens has an impressive imagination for situations, characters, places, corners. There are corners of his Dombey that I swear I've been to. I have read all of Conrad. I admire him enormously, and it has never occurred to me in the seven novels that I have written to do anything that bears any relation to Conrad. So people tell me, as if it went without saying, that *The Snow of the Admiral* is like *Heart of Darkness*, because a boat travels up a river. Well, I've traveled up that river, not in a beat-up boat, but in a nice one with engineers and such over the course of fifteen or twenty days, and I know what it's like. So, I put Maqroll there, not thinking of Conrad, but of myself. If someone like Dickens, or someone completely different, such as Proust, who gives you an impression of the interior of life, helps you when you are sitting in front of the typewriter and gives you a kind of compass in your writing, then you can use that influence to write whatever you want to.

**FG** I have to ask you this, warning you in advance that in the United States people have no sense of humor about political issues and that you have to be careful with these subjects, but you have a reputation for responding to political questions with impertinence, often hilariously. Some people even say that you are a monarchist, and at times you've been very hard on democracy. So, are you really a monarchist?

**ÁM** Look, people think that when I say that I am monarchic I mean that what I want is a kingdom of Nicaragua, a kingdom of Honduras, a kingdom of Paraguay. Monarchy is a thing of the past, and a government with divine right and absolute power like that of Louis XIV or Charlemagne is the last thing I would want. In this day and age, something like that is impossible. The kind of monarchy that I am dreaming of does not exist. I agree with Borges when he said that democracy is "a deception of statistics," I think that it is something that does not work, and we see it failing all the time. Something that we must keep in mind is that one of the most sinister characters, the most sick and diabolical murderers, Adolf Hitler, was voted chancellor of the German Reich by a majority. So, I say, like Ortega y Gassett, that when a lot of people agree about something, it's either a stupid idea or a beautiful woman. Dictatorships, which I detest, especially these military dictatorships in Latin America, have had enormous popular support. I saw the Plaza de Mayo full of people yelling "Perón! Perón!" and it filled me with disgust, but that's how it was. So, one must be careful with the application of the formula. But I don't mean to frighten anyone. As I don't follow politics, I have never voted, and the most recent political event that really preoccupies me and which I am still struggling to accept is the fall of Byzantium at the hand of the Turks in 1453.

FG  Even so, you have had close friends among the Latin American writers, who tend to be very politicized.

ÁM  With my closest friends who belong solidly to the Left, we never discuss such things. We talk about literature and life and our friends, and furthermore, it does not interest me to talk about politics.

FG  And with your friends on the Right?

ÁM  Well, with the people on the Right, I have greater reservations, I am more careful. The Right is quite sinister. The power of money is terrible.

FG  Although you are thought of as apolitical, in your works there is a great sense of the lives of poor people, the vulnerability of poverty, and you portray the arbitrary and corrupt violence of the military.

ÁM  Which is horrible and infernal.

FG  Even though you've lived in Mexico for forty-three years, Mexico never appears in your novels.

ÁM  (*laughter*) That's strange, isn't it? Well, you know, it's not planned, it's not that I don't want Mexico to appear.

**FG** Sometimes, you need to make the place where you live into a kind of neutral zone.

**ÁM** Yes, that's true. I've lived here for forty-three years. No print or radio journalist has ever asked me to speak or write about Mexico in any particular way. I have always said what I wanted, and here I am.

**FG** How did you come to Mexico?

**ÁM** I came here because of a terrible problem. When I was working for Standard Oil, I managed a sum of money that was destined for charity and social programs, and I used that money to help some friends who were in danger under the military dictatorship and I also spent the money on parties for journalists and friends. There was an investigation, and a lawyer friend of mine told me, "You have to leave—if possible, today or tomorrow." So I flew to Panama, and from there I decided to go to Mexico. I had been in Mexico in '53 and loved it, so I settled down there. Then there was a trial, and the Colombian military government asked the Mexican government to extradite me. The Mexican government, in accordance with an international agreement to monitor people whose extradition has been requested, put me in a jail in Lecumberri for fifteen months. And then the government of Rojas Pinilla fell, my trial was dropped, and I was set free. And now I've gone back to Colombia several times.

**FG** And your time in Lecumberri was a tremendous experience.

**ÁM** Yes. That experience was truly an influence, much more so than Conrad or anyone else they care to name! (*laughter*) Because in a place such as that, one experiences situations that are extreme and absolute.

**FG** You were not a privileged prisoner.

**ÁM** No, not at all. I worked like everyone else. In those days, the jail was managed by the prisoners, who were divided into wards. I was the head of a ward, which was a huge responsibility—but not a privilege. There is one thing that I learned in prison, that I passed on to Maqroll, and that is that you don't judge others, you don't say, "That guy committed a terrible crime against his family, so I can't be his friend." In a place like that one coexists because the judging is done on the outside. This is vital, because in there, the density of human relations is absolute.

FG  After you left, did you have any contact with the other prisoners?

ÁM  Yes, in fact the other day I had an experience that is worth recounting here. I went into a big department store here, a very famous one, and one of the security guards came up to me and said, "Hello boss, how are you doing?" He had been a thief. He broke into people's houses and assaulted and robbed them. He said, "I changed my name and came over here to offer my services." And I said to him, "They were smart to hire you, because no one is going to get away with stealing even a bottle of talcum powder with you around!"

FG  Is it true that Luis Buñuel would bring you bread when he came to visit you in prison?

ÁM  He didn't bring me bread, I gave *him* bread when he came, because in the prison we had a bakery that made baguettes like in France, really delicious. Because that jail was founded by Don Porfirio Díaz (president of Mexico in the late nineteenth century), who was a real Francophile, it had certain French norms for food and other things. The bakery was very good, and Luis, who was a close friend, would come and visit and I would give him a croissant or a baguette and he would leave impressed. He said to me once, "You know, my friend, I think the real reason I come here is for the bread."

FG  In those days your friends in Mexico included Botero, Gabriel García Márquez, Paz and Carlos Fuentes, right?

ÁM  When I came to Mexico, the first thing I did was look for Octavio Paz, who had said some very generous things about my poetry. I met him, and he was working with Fuentes in foreign relations. We became friends. Then, Botero was living here; we had been good friends in Colombia and I had helped him come to Mexico for family reasons. It was an interesting time. We were all young. Gabriel García Márquez and I have known each other for fifty-one years. We met in Barranquilla and our friendship has been very solid, without any cracks or fissures. I feel a great fondness for him, and we have shared wonderful and also difficult times. We love each other and have never had a disagreement. There is not the slightest shadow in our friendship; it is pure affection and love.

FG  You told me a story once that I think is brilliant, about the friendship between you and Gabriel García Márquez. It dates from the time when he was writing *One Hundred Years of Solitude.* Do you remember it?

ÁM  The amazing thing with Gabo is that Gabo, when I met him, was twenty-one or twenty-two, but he was already a fully formed writer. Gabo has never lived an instant without his typewriter; writing is his destiny. What happened was that he would tell me about the book, and he would tell me about things that he was thinking about, but didn't end up in the book. I would tell our friends, "Listen, Gabo is writing a novel in which a man does this, this, and this." And then, when I read the book, it was a completely different book than the one we'd been talking about.

FG  When you turned seventy-four they honored you in the Bellas Artes opera house. It was really moving, especially when Gabo spoke. He said that the reason your friendship has survived is because you once made a pact never to speak about one another to the press. But that he was there because you'd broken that pact by announcing publicly that you didn't like the barber he'd recommended to you.

ÁM  Yes, that's right. (*laughter*) That was when I turned sixty, and President Betancourt decided to give a dinner in my honor at the president's palace. My hair was a mess, and I needed a hairdresser fast. Gabo told me he had a wonderful barber, and so I went to him but he left my hair looking like yours [nearly a crew cut]. So then, when I had to speak, I talked about Gabo, and said, "And regarding this haircut, I would like you all to know that I am not responsible, but the one who is is right here: my friend García Márquez, who recommended the barber." This was broadcast on television. And the barber complained to García Márquez.

FG  That's how you planned it. I remember the day I met you and you were already saying that he was aboard a ship carrying phosphates and everyone was saying "no, don't do it!"

ÁM  But I know how to get him off the ship before it blows up.

FG  And coming back to Maqroll . . . are you working on another novel?

ÁM  Yes. I just keep working and thinking, I don't take notes or make outlines, and then one day I just sit down and start to write. So, one of these days I'll sit down and write this one. I need to be careful because this time Maqroll's life will be in danger. I have already tried to kill him three times and I just haven't been able to do it. A French writer said to me once, "Don't keep trying to kill Maqroll, he's going to die with you."

FG: What is your opinion of so-called magic realism?

ÁM   What happens is that critics invent these words, if you know what I mean. Authentic magic realism is José Saramago's *El memorial del convento*, or the work of German Romantics like E. T. A. Hoffmann. But basically, magic realism is just an easy way for critics in the United States and Europe to think about Latin American literature. My books have been described this way and there's nothing magic realist about them. A book like *One Hundred Years of Solitude* is a work that presents an extraordinary universe made up of magic and truth and horror and sadness . . . one can just simplify all of that and call it magical realism.

FG   If you could travel with Maqroll to any period, which would it be?

ÁM   The eighteenth century. Casanova and I would have been friends. I would have been friends with the Prince de Ligne and I would have lived in Paris and Venice. I'd take the elegant life, the brilliant prose, like Voltaire— each time you read him you realize that he's the real thing. And that is where my interest in the eighteenth century ends; once they get to the French Revolution and the horror and saving of mankind, that's where I exit.

# Sharon Olds
# and Amy Hempel

SHARON OLDS was born in San Francisco, California, in 1942. Olds has published numerous collections of poetry, including *The Dead and the Living*, which received the National Book Critics Circle Award, *Stag's Leap*, which received the Pulitzer Prize and the T. S. Eliot Prize, and *The Father*, which was shortlisted for the T. S. Eliot Prize and was a finalist for the National Book Critics Circle Award. A graduate of Stanford University and Columbia University, Olds held the position of New York State Poet Laureate from 1998 to 2000, and currently teaches poetry workshops at New York University. She lives in New Hampshire and New York City.

AMY HEMPEL was born in Chicago, Illinois, in 1951. She is the author of five books, including *At the Gates of the Animal Kingdom*, *Tumble Home*, and *The Dog of the Marriage*. She is a recipient of the Hobson Award and a Guggenheim Fellowship. She won the Ambassador Book Award for her *Collected Stories*, which was also named one of *The New York Times'* ten best books of the year. She teaches creative writing at Bennington College and Harvard University and lives in New York City.

**AMY HEMPEL**  All of the poems in your last book had to do with the death of an alcoholic father—approaching his death, the fact of it, and the aftermath. Richard Howard said that you've never lost sight of the narrative of feelings: "Very few poets understand this, that feelings do not just exist, but have a trajectory of their own." In the father poems, the trajectory of feelings runs from the early angry ones to the more compassionate. In your new book, the father is nearly absent. Have you said everything you can say about that father?

**SHARON OLDS**  No, no. I guess in the last year I've written fewer father poems than in the year before that but I guess each one of us has a handful of subjects we go back to over and over. We don't choose who our muses are.

**AH**  In "The Swimming Race" from *The Wellspring*, a father is smiling at his daughter who is coming in last in the race, and I got a twinge because his smile, you write, is "almost without meanness."

**SO**  Funny what we don't think of, we're just going on writing! Does it seem self-pitying? No? I like to be accurate—"almost without meanness." It seems true. As we get older, we see the old things in a new light, don't you think? I expect I will be writing about the same things all my life.

**AH**  In addition to *The Wellspring*, you've been assembling a collection of World War II poems. What prompts you to move from "private" poems to public—you wrote once about Christa McAuliffe in the shuttle Challenger, and you've written other poems about things you weren't a part of, but that moved you.

**SO**  Right. I wish I could do that better. I wish I did that more. I love and respect work that can do that. The number of poems I write that are what I call *apparently* very personal—more of them seem to me to work as poems. I write a lot of poems that aren't personal, but they aren't free to play in the same way—maybe because I'm in awe of lives that aren't mine, I can't be playful, maybe I get frozen in wonder, and ignorance.

**AH**  How would one of your "public" poems start?

**SO**  Once on a front page I saw a picture of a child, a girl of about eight, smiling, with buck teeth, and next to her a picture of her diary in a fireman's blackened glove. I went home and cursed. Then maybe I made supper and was still cursing. And the next day, a sentence began to take shape about how they shouldn't publish her diary on the front page of the paper when she died in a fire, and maybe the next day I realized that over and over I was saying the same sentence to myself, and the day after that I realized it might be a first line. In the old days, I would've said, You stay away from her—you have no right to talk about her, you don't know her.

AH And her suffering isn't available to you?

SO Some imagined sense of it is. But I ask myself, as with the World War II poems: How strong does your craft have to be to handle things that are none of your business? I was very bold with other people's business when I was getting started as a writer. I didn't seem to think that I had no right to just clomp in wherever I wanted to go. I thought that I could make my own rules.

AH What changed that?

SO I don't know how it happened, I began to see myself as a bit of a sociopath that way. But in the writing of *The Wellspring*, I learned an awful lot about where I could step and where, maybe, I shouldn't step. I look with alarm at this writer I was who was just not going to stop for anyone or anything.

AH But don't you think that's necessary at the start, that chutzpah, or blithe spirit?

SO Well, when our subjects are much younger than we are, we have a responsibility to protect them. And, you know, when people would say, Oh, you're so brave! I would think: Oh, goody—I'm brave! And then later I thought, It's not brave, it's just that I wasn't loyal.

AH That makes me think of your famous "Spectrum of Loyalty and Betrayal," of the consequences of going too much in one direction or in the other.

SO Right. How does that go?—it's almost like a spectrum of identity, who one is in relation to other people. Let's just use us at this table. If what you write about me is only what I would want you to write, what would agree with my picture of myself, I'd be comfortable with that, but then you're not very free as a writer. Of course, in certain kinds of Christian thought, thoughts are actions, so if you even *think* something about your subject that they wouldn't want you to, you're disloyal. And if you are ultimately purely loyal to your subject, you're *silent*. And it's almost like a form of suicide, certainly for a writer. There's loyalty to the other and none to the self. But then, at the other end, if you tell secrets, and names, then other people are in danger the way you're in danger if you have to be silent. It could be a kind of spiritual murder. I mean—where on the spectrum of loyalty and betrayal does song begin? And where does it end? I think each writer has to decide this over and over.

AH And you would place yourself—

SO I've moved. People used to ask me, "How can you do this?" And I'd think to myself, I like doing this. (*laughter*) But then I realized that people who have a passionate sense of loyalties learned it; they *learned loyalty*. They don't want to break certain taboos because it would hurt their heart to imagine how it might make someone else feel . . . And you're alone when you're writing, and at that point, hopefully, you're not thinking, What would someone think of me for doing this? Strong forces are at work, like if you're on a raft, *and* you're rowing, *and* the river is rushing, *and* you need to get to the other side, *and* you're being pulled under a bridge; you're feeling a shadow crossing, you're not really thinking, What is playing on the radio on shore? You are, to an extent, *in extremis*.

AH Have you held something back from publication that you thought was a successful poem?

SO All the time!

AH I want to quote from a friend and fan of yours, the religious historian Elaine Pagels. She calls it "a great moral discipline," your willingness to stay and see the things most of us would instinctively turn away from.

SO I might say I'm compelled. It seems to follow need and pleasure and compulsion more than moral discipline.

AH Well, it ties into the bravery question, and you don't think what you do is so brave.

SO To me, being brave means that you do something that you don't want to do, because you have to—for someone else, probably.

**AH** I read an interview you gave in England where you said that your poems form in your lungs?

**SO** I'm pretty mixed up about how everything works. I have primitive notions about science and the body. I don't think of a thought as being in my head. I find that idea really distressing—my head is too small! I feel as if my mind occurs in the space as far as my eye can see. My mind stretches to California if I think of someone I love, and it goes uptown and cross-town, so my mind is also my heart. But I don't really have a mind, I don't really *think*. Do you ever sit down and *think thoughts*?

**AH** Can't say I do. And yet you have degrees from Stanford and Columbia, a PhD in American Literature, you've been Director of the Creative Writing Program at NYU—these are all very brainy things, but what's moving your poems is not in your head, it doesn't seem. Not to say they don't get ideas across, but that's not where they start.

**SO** They're not in the front part of the brain. They're more in the body. And the senses, and imagery, and the story. Many poets are storytellers as well as singers, who want to preserve, record, create, put together (where we can see it) a little version of something human.

**AH** You've said that "Writing poems moves us past where we were when we sat down to write them." Sounds like you're talking about catharsis. Is that valuable to the poet? The reader?

**SO** Well, when I read someone's poem where that's happening, it's very valuable to me, it tells me about another life, it expands my experience.

**AH** You also said one purpose of a poem is to cause another poem to be written. Does that work for you and for somebody reading your work?

**SO** I would think so. I often write poems after I've read poems. What I was thinking was that if you have a story all ready to be written and you don't write it, maybe the next one won't come down the chute. Was it Bill Matthews who said that we *need* to write our bad poems, because if we don't write them, how will we get to the next one, which might be a good one? But of course, what you say is also true, that we inspire each other.

**AH** One of your former students told me that the most valuable thing she got from your teaching was your ability to point out "poems that stop just where they should begin."

SO I learned this from Galway Kinnell. In his craft lecture one year, he pointed out that the last line of many poems is the best one. But what happens is, we're so relieved to have got to something that we think it's the end, and we stop. But if we would keep going from *there* . . .

AH You teach at Squaw Valley most summers, and I heard you also teach writing on canoe trips?

SO Yes, week-long poetry workshops for women in the wilderness—in canoes. Beverly Antaeus, in Santa Fe, runs trips all over the world. June '96 will be my fourth year. People write new poems, and—depending on how many times we move camp—we have a workshop about every two days. And we're completely alone, in the wilderness.

AH Do you find canoeing and poetry compatible?

SO Learning about craft on the river, and in camp, and in poetry, works together—I also find the challenge and the fear of being in the wilderness very stimulating! I was a bow in the beginning because I didn't know how to paddle. It's like the Girl Scouts, like "flying up." Also the chance to hear all the other voices moves one forward.

AH This goes back to your visceral sense of where poems form. The first time we met, you did something I'll never forget. You looked out of the window of the restaurant at an ordinary brick building and described the building like scansion—how the strong beat was the window, and if you ignored the air conditioners, you'd have: wall WÍN(dow), wall WÍN(dow), wall WÍN(dow) . . . you saw iambic apartments! And you said that you felt your poems had to be graffiti across that row of windows: "handwritten, grounded, less organized, more like an ordinary human being talking to another." Do you still feel you're fighting the order of a lot of poetry?

SO Well, I wouldn't say "fighting." I see strong principles of order in my craft—in everyone's. I grew up hearing rhythms. I mean, I'm not going to do it again, but look at the fans.

AH Do it again! (*We look up at the six ceiling fans.*)

**SO** I could sit here happily for an hour and try to figure out which ones are going at the same speed, and what it means. There's a bit of compulsiveness in thinking that everything is going to mean something, but when you're raised in the church that I was raised in—

**AH** The Episcopal Church.

**SO** The church I went to was 1940s middle-class white Episcopalian, but the religion that I experienced was Calvinism. So I call it Hellfire Episcopalian. A male God had made and now owned every object and being, and everything meant something. Matter was God's speech. If this pillar is a message, what does it mean? And it's a message from someone who has Hell waiting there, ready, at every moment.

**AH** That's a terrifying thought for a young person.

**SO** A horrible way to live. A naturalist would be able to just look at the fans.

**AH** It's an interesting leap, to go from ceiling fans to a vision of hell. Back to the safety of craft, you're a master at finding a small way into a large subject. I've never taught a fiction writing class where I didn't use a poem from your new book—"The Lady Bug." A ladybug flies into a window where a woman has just learned that her daughter has gotten into college and will be leaving. You tell the whole story of loving, raising and letting go through the ladybug. And that poem where breaking the cow butter dish is the end of motherhood. You find an ordinary thing . . .

**SO** Or it finds you, maybe. The ladybug flies in the window. And then you remember, "Ladybug, ladybug, fly away home, Your house is on fire and your children are gone." So you start to write, and then the place of the will for the next half hour is not very certain. Or the cow butter dish is broken. And you sit and look at it. And you start to describe it, and it all seems so ordinary.

**AH** Are there poems that have eluded you, that you can't quite write?

**SO** I think that, sadly, that's not true of me.

**AH** Why "sadly"?

**SO** "Sadly" meaning I have a great admiration for people who are true to mysteriousness. True to the mysteriousness of perception, being, feeling. But my subjects—it's all simple, you know what I mean?

AH I think that what you call "simple," a reader finds *accessible*. We know what you're talking about, for starters . . . do you have to get yourself in the mood to write, or are you always "receiving"?

SO Well, if I'm depressed, probably a ladybug could fly in the window and I wouldn't focus on it. But there are things that help me to remain as little out of tune as possible. I did weightlifting for a number of years. That got me ready for the ladybugs. And what else helps the imagination? No drugs, as little alcohol as possible, no smoking, no coffee . . .

AH This sounds very ascetic.

SO I dance most days—not so ascetic. But as little sugar as possible (sometimes that's a lot of sugar!), and no TV. I stopped the newspaper and TV and drinking when I took the job as Director of the Creative Writing Program because I was so scared I would not be able to do that job. And I thought: Okay, I'm going to go into training, and cut off interference like a dedicated athlete. And then I didn't go back.

AH You've alluded to having had a vivid and literal sense of things as a child. So your image-making faculties didn't develop until later?

SO When I was two, it was explained to me, "This is how we will be eating now," and I was shown a book of ration stamps—I ate the book of ration stamps. I mean, plenty of things were *sort* of bizarre already. So this was food.

AH Paul Rudnick, writing about high culture a few years back, said, "Without poetry, high school girls in corduroy jumpers and black leotards might have to make some friends." All teenagers are sensitive and misunderstood, but did you feel more than usually so?

SO I'm not sure what that means—that poetry was born as a substitute for friendship? I thought the rhythms of poetry had to do with the rhythms of intense feeling about the most moving mortal experiences: birth, love, sex, death, grief, rage, joy. I thought that every group of people who ever existed have had poetry because passionate human life couldn't be led without it. As for teenagers, I see us at that age as people who are not able yet, some of us, to pretend not to be feeling what we're feeling. We forget what it's like to turn from a child into an adult. It felt to me almost like changing *species*. When we feel powerful feelings, we tend to speak in rhythm; we speak in more repetitive, forceful rhythm when we're upset. You hear people having a fight, it's not prose. People don't fight in prose: And if yóu do óne móre thing . . .

**AH** Writing about anger, and about sex—I also spoke to your friend Toi Derricotte—

**SO** Oh! It's like a surprise party!

**AH** She said you say an important thing about love in your poems, that it is possible to totally love a man and not be co-opted.

**SO** I'm thinking of how long it took us all to write about sexuality. I remember the night in Muriel Rukeyser's poetry appreciation course when, instead of reciting memorized poems to each other, we each read a poem of our own. And I read a love poem, and it had the word "creamy" in it twice and the word "milky" several times. And after I read it, someone said to Muriel, "I don't know, I don't know, it's too, too, it's too—" and Muriel said, "Too dairy?" (*laughter*) And we all laughed, and she said, "Yes, these words are too much from the same palette." But don't you think that most love poems, whether they're men to men, women to women, or other—I'm thinking of sexual poems—have equalness in them? Surely there is powerful, erotic work that is precisely about unevenness, that's a big theme in our culture. For some it's a part of the erotic, being equal, and for others it's a part of the erotic that it be extremely not equal.

**AH** One last thing. There is the famous T.S. Eliot precedent of "emotion which has its life in the poem, not in the history of the poet." Now, Galway Kinnell calls what you do in many of your poems, "going into the center of the intimate experience of a life, not just telling the story of a life." He says that to be daring in that area is to "open yourself to interpretation of the poems as expositions of your personal life." Does that come up anymore? Do readers still ask if a poem about a father is about your father?

**SO** Yes. But it has always seemed so obvious and powerfully true that art and life are incredibly different from each other. Flesh is flesh. A poem is breath in the air. Or it's ink and paper. It's *standing* for a heart and a mind. And I go to people's poems to learn about the heart and the mind, and to be less lonely as a human being, and to have fun. And maybe people go to poetry partly to find out what we're really like, to find out how bad we really are, how essential it is that we change while there's still time, maybe, to change. But a day in a life and a poem about that day, there's something profoundly different. Now, when I was a child, the bread was the flesh of Christ. I ate the ration stamps, I ate the communion wafer. And now, when I go to poems, I am hoping to be changed, to learn something about sexual love, or birth, or the joy or rage of some particular person or group—maybe very different from me or mine—while at the same time I am experiencing the physical pleasure of the beat, tone, music, shape, the whole intricate body of the poem and spirit of the speaker. So that, while one is still alive, one can feel, and know, as much as possible, so as to be fully alive.

# Dale Peck
# and Jim Lewis

DALE PECK was born on Long Island, New York, in 1967 and lived in Kansas for most of his childhood. He is the author of numerous works of fiction, nonfiction, and children's literature, including *Martin and John*, *The Law of Enclosures*, and *The Garden of Lost and Found*. His novel *Sprout* won the Lambda Literary Award for LGBT Children's/Young Adult Literature and was a finalist for the Stonewall Book Award. A Guggenheim Fellow, he teaches creative writing at The New School and lives in New York City.

JIM LEWIS was born in Cleveland, Ohio, in 1963. A graduate of Brown and Columbia University, he is the author of three novels: *Sister*, *Why the Tree Loves the Ax*, and *The King Is Dead*. His criticism has appeared in *Artforum*, *Harper's Bazaar*, *The New York Times*, *Slate*, *Rolling Stone*, *GQ*, and *Vanity Fair*. He has also contributed to many artist monographs for museums around the world, including Richard Prince at The Whitney Museum of American Art, Jeff Koons at The San Francisco Museum of Modern Art, and a Larry Clark retrospective at The Musée d'Art Moderne de la Ville de Paris. He lives in Austin, Texas.

**JIM LEWIS** I wanted to start with Henry James' essay, "The Art of Fiction." Because in it, James says, in response to some forgotten, pedantic piece about fiction writing, that the worst advice given to young writers is, "Write what you know."

**DALE PECK** Jesus, I must have gotten that advice fifty fucking times.

**JL** Well, there you go. James says, no, that's wrong. As a writer it's your job to be able to imagine any experience, whether you've had it directly or not. He says, "Try to be one of those people upon whom nothing is lost." I bring this up because both of us are coming out with books which are considerably removed from what anybody would think, on the face of it, was our own experience. I wonder if that was a conscious choice on your part.

**DP** It was. Specifically, one of the things I was trying to address was the idea of being a "gay writer." I don't have a problem with the label as much as its assumption that the work can only be about gay subject matter and only of interest to gay people. So in *Now It's Time to Say Goodbye* I used a spectrum of characters: gay and straight, black and white, male and female, young and old; but I also threw in a point character, a gay white man close to my age. This point character is closely allied with the narrator of my first novel, who is in turn allied with me. I wanted to make the process of writing outside my experience seem more self-conscious to readers, so that those characters who aren't gay white men could be seen as specifically not that, and could be compared with the point character for "clarification," if that's the right word. The result is that readers can look upon a character as a gay black man or a straight white female or whatever, or as nothing more than the projections of a gay white man and his vision of what these other identities and experiences are like.

Was it a conscious decision for you to make Caroline Harrison, the narrator of *Why the Tree Loves the Ax*, a woman?

**JL** Not really, not as such. I was looking for a story, and when I began it was the story of a love affair between a woman and a city. And then of course it grew, and she ended up telling it. Because when you write in the first person, there are gaps between what the narrator knows and what the audience knows, what the author knows and what the other characters know, and those gaps are a powerful place in which to play. You can twist things in there. In *Sister* I had an entire obverse plot hidden deep in the book. It was another picture of things, another story, another explanation. So when the narrator, Wilson, tells what happened to him, he also tells this other, buried story; but he doesn't realize it, himself. That was very hard to pull off—Wilson isn't stupid—and very few people noticed it. Or maybe no one cared. But I wanted to try again, on a much smaller scale; I wanted there to be moments of revelation in *Why the Tree Loves the Ax* that a reader might notice, even if the narrator (and again, she's not a fool) doesn't. So the reader is burdened with this secret, which they can't convey to the narrator—ever, even after the book is done. It's a kind of dirty knowledge. I had some friends from Dallas in a band called Killbilly, and once in the back room of a club in Kansas City I saw some graffiti they'd scrawled on the wall the week before: PUTTING THE 'PISS' BACK IN EPISTEMOLOGY. I wanted to do that. Then again, I wrote first person because the book is a love story, and "I loved him," "I didn't understand," "I started crying" are more powerful than "She loved him," and so on.

DP  I know it's a bit reductive, but I still think I should ask: Are you saying that the experience of gender is incidental to the story?

JL  I'm saying there's no such a thing as "the experience of gender." Maybe there is if you're reforming public policy, but certainly not when you're writing a novel. There's the experience of this character, who is, among other things, a woman. But she doesn't represent every woman in the world. She just represents herself. She's a character; she's not A Woman, she's Caroline; she doesn't have An Abortion, she has an abortion. So yeah, every so often I'd pass a sign that said, IF YOU LIVED HERE YOU'D BE HOME BY NOW. But I learned to ignore them—because if you go looking for archetypes, you lose. In the end, writing a character across that kind of boundary is . . . it's like having an orgasm: it's the sort of thing you can only do if you're not trying.

DP  What is it that makes a writer able to do that?

JL  Negative capability.

DP  Which you will define as . . .

JL  (*pause; laughter*) As far as I can remember this was Keats's idea, in a letter to his brother. For his purposes, it's the ability to suppress your ego and act as a medium when you're faced with something you don't understand. More generally, it's come to describe a kind of willful selflessness.

DP  And do you think that's possible?

JL Sure.

DP Do you think it's a complete suppression, or that your depiction of a woman, or whomever, is bound to be affected by your own experiences?

JL  I don't think it's a complete suppression, but I'd like to think that it's filtered through my writing style, rather than direct experiences. Of course, my writing style is ultimately a product of my experiences, but the distance between my own life (for example, the fact that I grew up, in part, overseas) and my book (say the fact that my narrator, Caroline, tends to ask rhetorical questions) is a very attenuated one, and I don't think much can be made of it.

DP  And that's where we differ. One of the tenets of identity politics that I do buy is the idea that an author's identity is inevitably a part of any character he creates. There are two issues here. The first is aesthetic, this idea of negative capability, which works for me as a metaphor but falls apart when you sit down and analyze it. The second issue, and for me the more important one, is political, and revolves around the historical problem of representation and power. To a certain extent the whole identity politics movement is a reaction against the tradition of certain groups, i.e., straight white men making art about other groups over whom they possess some level of socially or culturally ordained power, i.e., everyone else. And this results in all sorts of stereotypes and diminishing depictions, be it Shylock or Queequeg or even Uncle Tom.

JL  Fair enough. I don't know what good it does to describe either Shakespeare or Melville as a straight white man. They both seem a little bent to me. But okay; it would be ridiculous to claim that literature is untainted by prejudice. But when you abstract from that to a set of strictures, real or implicit, you lose me. I don't see the point in putting *a priori* limits on my imagination, nor can I waste time second-guessing myself. The alternative is to write only about myself, or stop writing, and I'm not going to do either of those things.

DP  No, no, no. Now you're being coy, or you're just wrong. I mean, one of the great tropes in literature, if not the great trope, is precisely what we're talking about here: the clash between one's notion of one's identity as it conflicts with some externally imposed notion, be it familial or societal or even physical. And it's pretty clear to me that you're working in that mode as much as I am. I mean, in your new book, Caroline's walked away from a life that wasn't hers before the novel even opens, and in many ways the book's action is a charting of her rediscovery of what it is that she ran from, which could be either a man or the state of being a wife. It looks to me like you're adopting a pose—a construction that allows you to deal with the same notions of identity that I do without slipping into the programmatic formulations advocated by the PC patrol—and all I'm doing is striking another pose, one that, if dissimilar to yours, nevertheless allows me to do exactly what yours does: think and write anything I want.

JL  If I'm posing, okay, that's all right. It wouldn't be the first time. But I don't think the great trope—and after all, it's only one of many—is about staking a claim to one's identity so much as it's about rejecting the very idea of identity—cultural identity, personal identity: they just don't exist. They don't. If you think they do, then you're just going to substitute one stereotype for another. I mean—as a Jew—I'll take Shakespeare's depiction of Jews over Philip Roth's any day. The proof is in the poetry: everything else is speculation. So I do what I want, I do what I can, and if I do it well, folks are happy with me, and if I don't, they're not. But I don't believe in prior restraint. I'll take my chances. Can we change the subject?

DP  Yeah, sure.

JL  I want to talk about story and character; we've talked about this before. Like the question of form and content, they're indissoluble in a lot of ways. I think you and I would agree on that. But with this book, as with my last, I started out with a situation I wanted to set up—or maybe a kind of language I want to use, which is after all a kind of plotting—and the characters came out of that. And it seems to me that this new book of yours is very elaborately plotted. Is that something you did deliberately?

DP  It is.

JL  Why?

DP  Because one of the issues I wanted to deal with in this book was the loss of interesting storytelling methods in literary fiction, and, even more importantly, the fact that interesting stories, elaborate stories have essentially been usurped by popular fictions. It's genre fiction that gets to offer up thrills and chills and heartache, whereas most contemporary literary fiction offers up interesting situations which seem to have been lifted from a newspaper headline, and which are then dissected and analyzed in a near-academic mode. And that's the supposedly innovative stuff. Most literary fiction is stuck in some pre-cinematic nineteenth-century Victorian mode, perhaps the least thrilling era in literature's history. I wanted to get away from all that, to write a story that was as exciting as an action movie or a Greek myth. So *Now It's Time* is a quest that takes the form of a detective story, and the object being searched for is a woman. And ultimately what's really being searched for are the identities of the various people who are looking, or not looking. Identity in this case not to be confused with the buzzword "identity," but meaning the notion of self.

JL   It's surprising, because under that description it sounds almost identical to my book, and yet they're so different.

DP   Actually, you started working on your book before I started writing mine, and when you first told me about it I remember being thrilled as you recounted the story to me. Hearing you describe your novel was in fact one of the things that nudged me along my own course, to really go for an intricate, suspenseful (dare I say it?) lowbrow plot in a literary novel. I mean, the story you were describing was almost racy, with money, criminality, sexual misadventure, and what it immediately reminded me of was the action-adventure stuff I read when I was a kid, and the gut thrill I got from reading it. And with the literary fiction I read today, I have to say I miss that. I wanted to bring it back.

JL   The question now becomes: how to do that? Say we both believe that one of the functions of literature is to provide stories that somehow mirror, or maybe even change, the way people structure the understanding of their lives. That's what Paul Bunyan stories do, and Br'er Rabbit stories, outlaw stories, good jokes, tall tales, and so on. *The Thousand and One Nights*—a book I love. Or story songs like *Frankie and Johnny*, or *Night of the Johnstown Flood*. There are these narratives that come up again and again that seem to have no origin. They're just there because people like to tell them, over and over again. It's not that they're universals . . . or whatever that Joseph Campbell nonsense is. They're very specific. It's just that certain people at certain times want to hear certain stories. So the question I asked myself was, how can we use that in a way that isn't merely reactionary? That isn't dopey, that acknowledges what literature has gone through for the past century?

DP   It's a funny question. I guess I want to ask one question before answering: Why should we do it in a way that isn't merely reactionary? If those old stories are so good and were so helpful, why can't they be helpful again?

JL   They can; but you can't pretend that Queneau never wrote *Exercises in Style*. Besides, there are new stories. 1998 becomes 1998, and not 1837, not 1971, and it becomes that in large part because we tell it that way. So with *Tree/Ax*, Caroline is something of a loner; a woman who moves from one society to another, alone; who has the strange, sidelong but very loaded relations with friends and family, with civic society, with her own restlessness, and fear, and desire. I don't think I could have told that story fifty years ago.

DP   Well, of course. As long as society keeps changing there will always be new things to write about.

JL   Bingo.

DP   I'm just not sure that those new things are new stories. I think they're simply our oldest stories, the stories that you find in most of the world's mythologies, in modern drag. In fact, I think there's really only one story: you're born and then you die. I look upon everything that comes after that as a kind of necessary incidental elaboration, because all that elaboration is the stuff that makes our time here bearable if not actually pleasurable.

JL   We were talking once some time ago, and I said, "I just keep writing the same book over and over again, and probably will until I die." And you agreed that you do that also. I would describe the book that I keep writing as "Looking for Home." How would you describe yours?

DP   "Looking for My Mother." (*laughter*) I qualify that by saying that my mother died when I was three, so I have an excuse to be looking for her. Look at the book I've just written: Here's a story in which a girl is kidnapped, and all of the characters in the book, including the characters who have absolutely no stake in whether she's found or lost, are obsessed with the idea of finding her. And while she's kidnapped her captor impregnates her, and then she's killed by her supposed rescuers in order to prevent her from giving birth to a monster, in essence to prevent her from becoming a mother, my mother, yet again. But birth or no birth, I think I'm still telling the same story.

JL   There's something we agree about. I'm obsessed with the idea of generations, of reproduction. To me, those are the oldest lessons. Being and begetting: pregnancy, abortion and miscarriage, parenthood, marriage, sex of course, siblinghood, fertility, the problems inherent in being fruitful and multiplying. And certainly in this new book, you have the same obsession.

DP I do, and yet I also abhor reproduction on some level. I just think that there are far too many people on the planet, overwhelmingly too many people on the planet, and that this urge to keep on producing more babies, it's just absolutely insane. But I am really fascinated by motherhood, fatherhood, childhood, you know, the condition of being a child.

JL You always cast yourself in the role of the child.

DP Well, no. I cast the narrator of *Martin and John* in the role of the child, but the two narrators of *The Law of Enclosures* were both conceived as parents, as, in fact, John's parents. And in *Now It's Time*, there are an assortment of parents and children. Only the point character is a child; I try to identify with all my characters.

JL Okay. So you'd say, when you're writing, you're looking for your mother; I would say I'm looking . . . for my children.

DP Looking for your children?

JL In some sense, yeah. I don't know what I am going to write about if and when I actually have them. By the way, we're going to have to cut all this out, because I don't think I want people to know this about me. Besides, you know, we've both just contradicted ourselves. You're now saying you identify with all your characters, and I'm now saying all my main characters are me. Which just goes to show you how fruitless it is to talk about this stuff. It's worth remembering that writers lie a lot when they talk about their own work. Lie all over the place. It can't be helped.

DP God, this is better than a session with my old psychiatrist, not to mention cheaper . . . So, um, where do you see yourself in the current panoply of American writers?

JL Oh God.

DP Do you feel allied with any, opposed to any?

JL In a word, no. How can I answer this? It's a question that appeals to my worst instincts. Let's just say that neither alliance nor overt opposition is quite my style. And anyway, one of the best things about being a writer is that a lot of your contemporaries have been dead for centuries. Among the living, there are some writers whose work I admire, and a few writers I like personally, and a very few writers I like to talk to about writing. Those are three different categories, which sometimes overlap and sometimes don't. In any case, I seem to have more to talk about with artists, and a few musicians. And then of course there's everything else in the world, everyone who does something else for a living.

DP One thing which I think does ally us, aesthetically I mean, is that you and I both have a utilitarian notion of fiction. We both believe people read novels in order to better understand their situation.

JL Yeah, I believe that, but then it's on such a subtle level, because literature is also about entertainment, and pleasure. I don't want to be giving people instructions or advice. I'll say this: To the extent that anything that's well made helps you appreciate God's glory, then I would agree with you. But I don't know if that's what you mean by utilitarian.

DP What I mean is that fiction should help readers understand something far greater than society or politics or the world in which they live. You can call that God's glory, which is a charming anachronism that probably a lot of people will find problematic (although I don't), or you can just say that fiction is supposed to help the reader understand his or her soul, which is just another anachronism.

JL I didn't mean it as a charming anachronism. I meant it quite literally. Somehow. I'm afraid that any way I try to explain it will sound glib. Here: Bach once dedicated a musical score, "To the glory of the most high God, and that my neighbor may be benefited thereby." I think that's a fine thing to strive for. And it has strange implications. One of the things, for example, that I find myself doing, I wonder if you do the same thing, is I put things into books that nobody will ever find. It's like making a chair, and up underneath where nobody's ever going to look, you make it especially beautiful. I mention this because it speaks to the question of utilitarianism.

DP I do sort of the same thing, but I think I do it for my own pleasure. I mean, I have such a Jesus complex when I write that I view the whole enterprise as this selfless act I'm offering to other people. And because a part of me knows that's not really the case, I do things to make the book purely my own. For example, there's a snippet in *The Law of Enclosures* where a sonnet is embedded within a paragraph. One or two people have caught it, most people have missed it.

**JL** I ever tell you this story? There's a sentence in *Sister* that I lifted, word for word, out of Proust, just because I liked it—a description of a church bell ringing. And then I got a review which cited that same sentence as an example of my fine way with language. (*laughter*)

**DP** There's a character in *Now It's Time* who is a painter who is commissioned to restore a mural of John Brown holding a Bible in the one hand and a gun in the other. When he's restoring the Bible he writes the words: "John Brown was right." Then he paints over them with the regular page of the Bible. So no one ever knows it's there until thirty years later, when he confides it to somebody. There are just ingenuous ways of concealing information and sometimes it just comes out. I sometimes wonder, even as I say this, if we do those little things so we can reveal them later.

**JL** I want to ask you about names and titles. Tags. *Martin and John* is the kind of book it is in large part because of this difficulty you had coming up with names for your characters—a brilliant move, a vice that you turned into a virtue. This new book of yours is so shaggy and at times sort of deliberately ridiculous, I thought. I mean, a man eaten alive by pigs . . . and you have a main character named Justin Time. When I started *Tree/Ax* my narrator was called Jane Doe; but then I chickened out. Probably wisely. But I put a lot of time into names. For example, I named Olivia in *Sister* for the letter O. Of course there's the sexual connotation; and the whole book was a circle, within which I made other circles. And then again she's named for Hamlet's Ophelia, and for a girl named Eliza whom I once met very briefly in a bar. In this new book, *Sugartown*, the name for an imaginary city in Texas was important to me; a contrast to the real city of New York. Billy was for Dollar Bill; Malcolm because I wanted this little white child to have the name of a black hero; Roy because I don't know anyone named Roy, so I could write the narrator's love for him without preconception. Sometimes I think names are about a third of the game. How much do you sweat over names; and do you ever worry that you won't get away with it?

**DP** I sweat names a lot—more and more with each book. With *Now* I went to town. Literally, actually: I operated on the principle that in a town of 350 people, everybody's name would be known by everyone else, and so I felt I had to name each and every person who passed a point of view character on the sidewalk.

But let's start with the town name: its black residents call it Galatia; its white residents call it Galatea. On the one hand, the reference is idiosyncratic: there's a real town in Kansas called Galatia, named after the Biblical land of plenty, but when I was a kid I pronounced it Galatea, as in the statue. I first realized my error in high school, and have wanted to use it in a book ever since. In those eight letters I managed to encapsulate the Bible, Greek mythology, and also the struggle between blacks and whites in my town. Character names followed from that. Some came from my earlier books; some were jokes the characters played on their readers—Justin Time is a pseudonym made up by a character who refuses to reveal his real name, but who wants to remind everyone that they don't know who he really is; and some were simply my jokes on the character—Portland Oregon Smith and his brother, Kissimee Florida Smith. Some names were imbued with symbolic meaning, for instance, Colin Nieman—Nieman means, literally, "No Man" in German, so the name was important symbolically and narratively.

JL   And how did you get the name of the book?

DP   *Now It's Time to Say Goodbye*? It's the closing theme song to *The Mickey Mouse Club*.

JL   But what made you use it as a title?

DP   I like the fact that it sounds so melancholy, but if you source it back it becomes maudlin. What seems to be tragic is really comic. Call it "irony." I have a tendency to just write down titles, lots and lots and lots of titles. In *Martin and John*, one of the stories is called "Given This and Everything," and it was simply thinking up the title that produced the story. Where'd you get your title?

JL   I didn't get mine until I was standing in my agent's office and she said, "All right, we're going to send the book out this afternoon. What's the title?" I'd had these horrible working titles. Just terrible. But Ellen [Levine] was sitting there waiting for me. And I kind of came out with, "Why the tree loves the ax." It's about sex, of course; it's a paraphrase of a line from the book, and I couldn't get it out of my head. It seems like the right question to propose. Why does the tree love the ax? It seemed like the question my narrator would ask. And Ellen said: That's the one. So that was the one. And now it's done, it's out, and yours is coming out. So here we go again. We have to start all over again. (*laughter*)

# Sapphire and Kelvin Christopher James

SAPPHIRE was born in Fort Ord, California, in 1950. She is the author of the poetry collections *American Dreams* and *Black Wings & Blind Angels* and the novels *The Kid* and *Push*, which was adapted into the film *Precious*. A graduate of Brooklyn College, where she received her MFA, Sapphire is the recipient of a United States Artists Fellowship in Literature. She lives in New York City.

KELVIN CHRISTOPHER JAMES was born in Port of Spain in Trinidad. He is the author of *Jumping Ship and Other Stories*, *A Fling with a Demon Lover*, and *Secrets*. He holds a BSc from the University of West Indies. For his work, James has been awarded a New York Foundation for the Arts Fellowship in Fiction and a National Endowment for the Arts Fellowship in Literature. He lives in Harlem, New York.

**KELVIN CHRISTOPHER JAMES** *Push* is a very dark, Dickensian book. It's mired in humanity. The characters do the worst to themselves and to each other. Its success surprises me, as recent writing seems to be moving towards the gothic. Did you consider this when writing *Push*: Be a winner by breaking the trend?

**SAPPHIRE** What I considered was that we were going to enter into a person's life who was being damaged, but was not intrinsically damaged. We're going to enter into and watch the growth of someone who has been emotionally crippled. That was the focal point of the novel. I wasn't interested in writing a dark, horrible story—a case history or a crime novel. I was interested in how, through all these impediments and all these trials, a human being could still grow. And why they could. I didn't get an answer in writing the book or in the people I encountered, but it has to do with human nature. It's human nature for young people to grow and learn. So we enter into *Push* with Precious doing a natural thing; it only seems bizarre because so many bad things have happened to her, but she just wants what any other kid wants. She wants to live. She wants a boyfriend, she wants to learn, she wants nice clothes . . .

**KCJ** That's why I said Dickensian. I see Oliver Twist and Nicholas Nickelby, but Precious goes through worse times than they did in every way.

**S** Part of what's so wrong in this story is that we're not in a Dickensian era. Those things shouldn't be happening in a post-industrial society.

**KCJ** Your character, Precious Jones, and her life could be said to be a caricature of white people's guilt in producing such disgusting social conditions. Are you turning this guilt against them? Is this a social-conscience novel?

**S** The novel definitely has areas of social commentary. I don't really see it as an indictment of white people, I see it as an indictment of American culture, which is both black and white.

**KCJ** What if it's white people who control the culture?

**S** This morning when I woke up to feed my cat, it was me that fed my cat. I had a choice of whether I was going to pet him or kick him. No white people were there. Even within slavery, in our most deprived state, we had choices. Yeah, we're looking at some people who are horribly, horribly oppressed. We can say that Precious's mother and father, and many of the people in the culture, find themselves in a steel box, that's how bad the oppression is. You can sit there in that steel box, you can kill yourself in that box, or you can turn on your young and kill yourself that way. Even when the choices are limited, you still have choices. To me, it is an indictment of the people who created the parents, but it's also an indictment of the parents. We can see in other circumstances where Precious interacts with people who have choices. The EMS man could have looked at her and said, "What the fuck?" and walked out. He chose to be a human being and say, "I don't understand this, I don't know about these people, but here is a child giving birth. Push." He saved her life.

**KCJ**  He's the only sympathetic male in the story. Other than Mr. Wicher, who is a wimp.

**S**  He's not a sympathetic male. He's a wimp who is terrified, like many inner-city teachers. He's using her to police other students.

**KCJ**  But he's the one she says she wants to marry . . .

**S**  Of course, she's in fantasyland, and she misunderstands his using her for love. She needs that misunderstanding, the conjecture of fantasy relationships. All this man wants is for her to keep beating up the other kids to keep them from bothering him.

**KCJ**  Am I on the mark when I find that most of the people who take care of Precious have dreadlocks and a West Indian quality?

**S**  I see Precious very much as an individual and as my creative child character: but she can also be a symbol of African Americans. And her first challenge towards growth is that her own xenophobia is called into question. Before the Hispanic man saves her life she says, "What is this spic doing here?" Even as ignorant as she is—she cannot read and write—she comments on him having an accent. Her narrowness, which is created by oppression, reinforces her own oppression. We see that if she is to grow, if she is to overcome her condition on any level, she will have to accept help from people who seem very different to her. Only to a very narrow minded, up-from-the-South black culture would a West Indian or an Hispanic person be so different. But to her it is. Any type of expansion of a human being's life has to do with expansion of consciousness. There are several points in the novel where Precious could have said "No." She could have said "No" to the man when he first came to help her. She could have said "No" when she found out Miss Blue Rain was gay. But she keeps saying "Yes." She keeps entertaining what I think is a very African mentality: she is able to embrace dual paradigms. Precious says, "I believe in Farrakhan, but I also believe in Alice Walker and Miss Rain." We see a multiple consciousness which is very different from a Western reality.

KCJ  Africans have many gods . . .

S  Yeah, in the same way you have Africans who believe in Yoruba and polytheism, and then say, "I'm Christian." We see the best of her roots come forward in being able to accept this consciousness.

KCJ  She doesn't accept the Jewish woman, her teacher Mrs. Lichenstein, the one who first comes to her house and challenges her.

S  Precious can't appreciate Mrs. Lichenstein, but the reader can. The reader can understand what it means for a white woman to leave her neighborhood and come stand on Lenox Avenue and ring that bell, and be polite while Precious is screaming, "Get out of here Mrs. Lichenstein . . ." Precious cannot understand that gift until much, much later. Precious has attitude, but that's what keeps her alive. Attitude.

KCJ  You have convincingly portrayed the more horrible experiences of Precious's life. Do you have an opposite moment that might not have been written into the book?

S  I think she has many happy moments in the book.

KCJ  She's going to die. She has HIV.

S  We're all going to die. Miss Rain might die before Precious dies. Precious just knows when and how she will die. Or, maybe she'll catch a bullet on the way home from school.

KCJ  And what will happen to Precious's baby boy, Abdul?

S  Well, we're all hoping that Newt Gingrich and Bob Dole don't get in, because then we know that Abdul will be slated for the orphanage. Now, we know that the white, middle-class and gay males with HIV are living twelve years after diagnosis. Precious is very healthy: she has no pre-existing conditions, no other STDs, she was diagnosed early . . . She may have been infected at sixteen. Add twelve years to that and what do you get?

**KCJ**  Okay, so she could live to her mid-twenties. Maybe until thirty.

**S**  Thirty years. And how old will Abdul be?

**KCJ**  He'd then be about ten.

**S**  Ten years with your mother is a lot of time to be infused with some deep love, and you know that she's a child who knows how to love. He would never forget that. So in the best world, Precious would live to be about thirty. That would mean that she would be able to see Abdul through elementary school, and have him recite his Langston Hughes, and be there. He may, if they had proper care, be part of her hospice experience and therapy, and learn what was happening to his mother. That would be the best thing. In the worst world, if she were to become homeless, and had to go back to the shelter, where the people have TB and stuff like that, she would get more sick and die in two or three years: and he would be put into foster care, where he would be raped and abused.

**KCJ**  Is Precious a child who never had anything? Not even sunshine, and the normal days of happiness?

**S**  Well, that's a lot. Have you ever been in prison and then you got out? You hear them talk about how they enjoy just walking. Here's someone who has had an almost parallel deprivation. Precious never had a friend, so just to go downtown with her schoolmates Rita and Rhonda is a high point. I imagine Rhonda will start taking her to church at some point.

**KCJ**  Let me tell you something. I read this book with a box of Kleenex next to me. It is so horrid where she lives. Every little touch of kindness that she feels breaks my heart. It's such a despairing happiness. I want her to have regular happiness.

**S**  Well, the novel is on us. People ask me stupid shit like, "What's going to happen to her?" You know what's going to happen to her! The literature program really existed—I used to teach there. Not anymore. The halfway-house really existed. Harlem Hospital—Koch wanted to close it. And they closed Sydenham Hospital. If you remove all the medical care, all the educational facilities, then you know what's going to happen to her. Part of my job as a citizen of America is to see that that doesn't happen. To see that the literature programs stand, to see that the Harlem hospital stays intact . . .

**KCJ**  So you write these stark stories . . .

**S**  That's part of it. And also, we're having to look at how black culture looks at women. I would like for her to have a boyfriend, but I couldn't just make one up. I would like for someone to love her for who she is. I would like for us to be able to look at somebody's soul and love them. I want that for her.

**KCJ**  When and why did you start writing, and what were your influences?

**S**  First I started writing in journals, and then I started writing poetry. My very early influences were people like Sonia Sanchez, Jayne Cortez, Don L. Lee—that whole Black Arts movement. Although I wasn't a part of it.

**KCJ**  They're predominantly straight people, is that deliberate?

**S**  That was San Francisco, where I was living when I first started to write. But I wasn't exposed to writers in real life until I started taking dance classes. One of the master dancers in the class was Ntozake Shange. I'm a young woman and I'm like, "Oh my God!" I never saw nothing like this before. It's much more a feminist woman's consciousness.

**KCJ**  And the women looked exciting and vigorous.

**S**  They were at the top then. They were doing with words what Tina Turner used to do with her body. And I saw Tina in her prime. She was the most sexually and physically assertive when she was in that Ike and Tina Turner thing. I saw her at the Five-Four Ballroom, in the early '70s with the Ikettes. I'd never in my life seen a human being move like that. And these women were doing that with words. Ntozake would come out there and do her thing, and that was a primal influence that freed me. But Don L. Lee and Sonia Sanchez—as a bisexual I didn't exist in their world. At that time Sonia Sanchez was in The Nation of Islam—I admired that, but I can't go there. I'm moving a bit more to the left.

**KCJ**  Beyond the physical geography of New York City or San Francisco, where are you from in America?

**S**  I'm from a secret world. I was born and literally spent the first years of my life on an army base. My mother and father met in World War II. My mother was born in 1920, a child of the depression who graduated from high school, which was a big thing in those days. Then in her twenties she ran away and joined the WACs, the colored WACs, it was a segregated unit.

**KCJ**  She ran away to war?

**S**  She wanted to escape poverty and working in a factory. She didn't do any combat. You know what I mean, they dated the soldiers. My father left the rural South, Texas, and joined the army. They met each other and married—all of my siblings were born on an army base. I didn't really leave the military life until I was twelve years old. It was another world that I have not yet seen in literature. It was not the ghetto or the rural South, and it definitely was not that fly-in-the-buttermilk, black-person-in-the-suburbs experience. This was raw. The white people there were in the Klan, and the black people there were escapees from poverty. And then you had years and years of war. My father was in World War II and Korea. It was the military. I was raised like that. And then we got into normal life. At twelve I moved to South Philadelphia, a large, urban black environment.

**KCJ**  Another life in the scene.

**S**  Exactly. Even as bad as life in the military was, and I can't describe how bad it was, under Truman's time they had desegregated the armed forces, so you couldn't overtly act out the racist stuff. Even when I was in Texas, the army base schools were integrated while schools outside—you know, they were using fire hoses and shit. They were going through a court order to integrate and they wouldn't do it, but at the base we were already doing that. So then I get to Philadelphia. I remember my first year there, 1963, they had a race riot. For the first time I was exposed to an urban situation . . . I already had internalized that as a black person I'm an outsider. On the army base, we never had a chance, as blacks, to divide into light-skinned or dark-skinned, or educated, or any kind of faction. We were under siege. But in Philadelphia, the black Northerners made fun of my accent. That's the most basic thing you have, your physical self and your speech.

**KCJ**  Nobody likes you. You're an outsider even when you're inside.

**S**  Exactly. But then from Philadelphia we moved to Los Angeles, another large, urban environment. And that became the rest of my life. Now, I can't be anywhere but a city.

KCJ  Would you now write a gentler, kinder novel, or do you still have material from this world that you want to explore?

S   I don't see things getting gentler and kinder. If I go forward, I will go more and more into depth. In this novel I made some big assumptions about my readers, that they would understand certain things. I feel comfortable with that. You can't write explaining something to the outsider.

KCJ  Yeah, some people have said that it is a negative version, right?

S   Yeah, but my next book will not be a response to that criticism. I feel that I gave a big picture. It's not my job as a writer to satisfy you. I'm not trying to jack you off. We're living in a culture where people are constantly screaming about family values, but I don't think we'll win the battle. The only time more children have been out of the control of their family was that Dickensian period of those orphanages. What does it mean in terms of the race and class that I come from—that large masses of my children, met-aphorically, are being raised by the state? In foster homes and in jails and in poor schools? That's something that intrigues me deeply. Even though I'm examining Precious, I'm also examining the family.

KCJ  How do you respond to skeptics, and how do you respond to envy at your success?

S   I have lived a very isolated life. I know people are envious of me, I can feel it. But I basically have kept myself away from people. I was upset that my life all of a sudden became so public. I'm used to my work being out there, but not me, literally. Now I'm starting to renegotiate my physical reality, trying to be and make myself safer. And if you're envious, I'm glad you're envious. I'm so glad I got something. Hey, I'm a black woman, and I'm forty-six years old, you know what I mean? I could write about scrub-bing floors because I've scrubbed floors; I could write about turning tricks because I've turned tricks. I did a lot to get where I am. But I'm glad for what I have and I'm not ashamed of it. I'm the type of person who, even when I had little, I put it to good use.

KCJ  So, now that you are well paid by publishers, lauded by the critics, and read by the masses, how do you feel to have arrived: satisfied, justified, or just impatient?

S   Number one, I'm real serious, and I've always been serious. And I've always been serious about my time, knowing that time equals life. I have a brother who is no longer here, my parents are dead, and I understand that one day I'll be dead too. I don't want to waste my time and I don't want to waste my life. I deserve to be paid for my work. I am a little skeptical of the critics, but I'm glad for the positive critical reception. I was on 125th Street on Saturday, and a young girl came up to me and said, "Are you Sapphire? I read your book. It's the best book I ever read." That meant something to me. I was in the Xerox shop xeroxing a manuscript, and there was this brother in there with his gold chains and his jeans and he looked like he was getting ready to do a rap concert instead of Xeroxing, like he was supposed to be doing. I was mad, and I said to myself, "Now if this was a white girl he'd be Xeroxing faster, why is this guy taking so long to Xerox my shit?" And then he turned around to me with tears in his eyes and he said, "Lady, did you write this here literature?" I said, "Yes, I did." He said, "This is some bad stuff." That was before the book was published, when I was Xeroxing the galley. Stuff like that, no one can take from me. The black middle class who are embarrassed because of the subject matter can't take that from me; the negative black journalist in the *Wall Street Journal* can't take it from me. That's something. And that has been holding me.

**KCJ** How does Precious learn to care for Abdul? Where would she learn care from? Nobody ever cared for her in a consistent way. I can see the possibility of a cycle of abuse happening.

**S** Two things happened, Precious got removed from her house when her mother attacked her and they sent her to a halfway house. We get some intimations that Precious has a positive relationship with the house mother. Often in these halfway houses the women literally go around and teach the girls how to nurture. Part of abuse, not sexual abuse but physical abuse, comes from not knowing what to do. So I see Precious as literally learning the things to do. Early childhood sexual abuse is, to me, like a car accident. We have, say, five people in a car that crashes: one person is killed, one person is paralyzed from the waist down, one person gets up and walks away, one person has psychic trauma for the rest of their life. Different people react differently to abuse. We see that one of the things Precious does, despite being abused, is fantasize about being loved. Some children who have been through that abuse fantasize about cutting the ears off a rabbit, or killing the family cat. So we see that she is pulled by a desire for love and affection. It's in her makeup to love. That's not to say that that love might not turn into something else, but it could be nurtured. She goes to a meeting of survivors. When I went to those meetings, women who were psychiatrists and therapists were not there to counsel people, they were actively seeking help on a peer level. We were examining some of the best literature on abuse and post-traumatic shock. That was the type of environment Precious goes to when she goes to that little tacky meeting. That's one of the first things she'll learn, that she, more than other people, is in danger of abusing her child. This is beyond social services. What you see here is the self-help network. The Body Positive meeting, and the Survivors of Incest Anonymous meetings are not funded by the state.

KCJ  What do you do when you're not writing?

S  I'm very obsessive about writing, so I do a lot of writing which is not writing: journal-taking, notes, and so on. I like to read, and I'm now taking myself back to African dance class, and I'm going to Haitian dance class tonight.

KCJ  With all of this love you have in you, what about adopting a child? Taking care of something other than a cat or a dog, another human being?

S  I have friends who have adopted, and this is the first time where I've felt psychologically healthy enough that I could do it. At a certain point you reach a lack of selfishness. I would like a baby but that's not the best thing for the world. The best thing would be for me to adopt a six- or a seven-year-old.

KCJ  It gives somebody a chance.

S  Yeah, and they have seven- and eight-year-olds, little Abduls, who nobody will ever take. That is definitely something that I'm letting in, it's part of my healing. Coming in from the outside. For the longest time I had an outsider mentality. My brother was a paranoid schizophrenic who was murdered. He manifested the outsider, and I identified with him deeply. He was all the way out there. But literally. I don't want to live out there. Part of the past twenty years has been about coming in and seeing myself as part of the human fabric, I'm not so different. Like when the nurse told Precious, "You're not so special. It's a lot of motherfuckers who are out there homeless. Get a grip, little girl . . ." So that's my thing too, everybody has been pained. When Precious learns to really read and starts reading about Bosnia, she'll understand that this is a world condition. It will either destroy or empower her. I could see her on television talking about HIV. I could see her doing the very best with what she's been dealt. And I can also see her going to her primary caretakers, her housemother, her teacher and saying, "How do I prepare for my death?" They had a beautiful article in *The New York Times* once, a young white woman with a terminal disease was trying to find adoptive parents for her child. This is what conscious people do. You don't run around on a train shaking a cup; that's not my girl. There's a way that we're all being dealt this shit, how are you going to deal with it? That's what this book is about.

KCJ  Do you love Precious?

S    I love her. I love everybody in the book, but I love her the most. Everyone says, "Well, the other people in the book aren't as developed." Okay, so what? I'm giving voice to the children that I saw.

KCJ  Has this book made you a stronger person?

S    It has made me stronger. No matter how strong you are, outside validation . . . I've watched black women, and I haven't seen the same thing in black men, but black women over and over will go to the mirror with positivity and say, "I am beautiful. I am strong." And then when they go down the street it's like, "You black bitch." It hurts them. Even though the females can't make her beautiful, Precious stops being ugly when she comes to Ms. Rain's class. In that world she gets to be with other women who are older than her, so they are able to embrace her. She's not competition, but she's also not the fat joke that she was with the little kids. She gets some sense of herself. I see them schooling her, telling her how to do her hair, taking her downtown . . .

KCJ  What about women in sports? I believe you get an advantage that men already know from playing sports, that feeling of support. You hit hard, but it's in the game. It's not you I'm trying to hurt, but the opponent.

S That's one of the early things that can be done to empower women. To learn how to kick ass, and to learn how to compete with other people without killing them. What women learn is that competition can kill you, but what you learn with team sports is that at the end of the game, we shake hands. At the end of the male-female competition, you've lost the man. But with team sports, there's something communal. When I teach writing, I teach everyone how to write. The Slave narratives are some of the most important American literature we have. Most of it is not high art, but it's part of what someone like Toni Morrison can read and make into high art. Most of the time when you listen to those Library of Congress folk recordings, they're not appealing, but when Muddy Waters listens to it, it goes farther. If those other people hadn't put their voices out there, our experiences wouldn't be documented. If we say that only a certain people can write, then we're left with less. For seven years I encouraged women to write their stories, so I've got an idea of the collective cosmic pain of women, as opposed to just my own story. As a teacher, you can't get by me without writing.

KCJ  It's important that you depersonalize your story. In the first book, *American Dreams*, most of the poems were your stories . . .

S   I needed to depersonalize, but I had no right to tell anyone's story until I told my own. I felt I could write about Precious's mother and father raping her because I talked about my mother and father raping me. I'm not making a class statement. I'm not saying that this is what the nigger parents in Harlem do, and what the Cosby parents or the army parents don't do. I felt that once I laid my things out, I could enter into other people's lives. I was not coming towards the book as God, I was coming as the wounded writer, and that gave me an authority that I wouldn't have had if I was not stating where I came from.

KCJ  You couldn't imagine this story of Precious, it would be cruel and wicked to put this upon a regular black family.

S   I don't think that this is what only black people do, you can't generalize. This is human behavior. This is something that has been going on since time began, and part of becoming conscious is attempting to root out the behavior that no longer serves us. In a society where it causes psychological and emotional breakdown, and the children end up crackheads, then I say stop fucking them. My friend works in homeless shelters and with all of them, over and over, it's the same story: the mother's boyfriend raped them. What we're dealing with is a nation of people in post-traumatic stress. We now know that when the men went to Vietnam and got shot up, they came back unable to cope. Part of what Precious describes and lives in is post-traumatic stress, a reaction to trauma, and you don't grow like that. It's warping us.

KCJ  I feel embarrassed by the black men in this story.

S   Well what about Precious's Mama? She abuses her too.

**KCJ** She's also victim of the black man. It's not a racist thing, but I prefer to see the white males in authority: the money holders, the buyers and sellers of culture and humanity, as the bad guys—the people who care about money and bottom-line profit before humanity. And now we have the black male who is usually a victim, who never had money or authority when he came to this country, as the guy who is fucking this whole family up.

**S** One of the myths we've been taught is that oppression creates moral superiority. I'm here to tell you that the more oppressed a person is, the more oppressive they will be. As a friend of mine, Black Magic Rainbow, a lawyer and writer explained, the white, sadistic master came to me and said, "Lay down, Sapphire. I'm gonna fuck you." Don't you know: That's what he did to Kelvin, and Michael, and John? Don't you know that part of the black male experience in slavery was repeated rape by white men? So this is what we enter in with, trying to make a family? This is our baggage?

**KCJ** How would you help a black man out of it? You're not against black men, are you?

**S** I'm not at all. Part of it is what we see at the end of the book, with Precious not being separated from her son. That's the most important thing, that early childhood development is nurturing. I was in Atlanta and a group of black men were reading and one of them started to cry. He talked about being abandoned by his father. A white person might ask me why Farrakhan is in the book. Well, to Precious he's a positive male role model of today. Twenty years ago I might have put in Malcolm X. A woman cannot give another woman, cannot give a man everything. Somewhere there has to be a positive male. Precious needs male interaction. We need to start thinking of how we can help children like Precious interact with their babies. We must begin to teach young men and women to begin to interact positively with each other. And not to let children be raised alone. Precious is not going to be able to give that boy a father. Where is the young black men's organization where Precious can take him to spend the day? Where can he learn how to be a man?

**KCJ** Do you mean like Big Brother stuff?

**S** Exactly. That's how I would start, to get black men and women involved. If push came to shove I wouldn't care if it was an Asian man or a white man that came up there to take Abdul out to play.

KCJ  So you see it as totally beyond race?

S  It's going to have to go beyond race. If we leave it there, then we're going to be lost. We're going to have to open up.

KCJ  Now what about sexism? What about the fact that we separate people into straight and gay?

S  I think some of that is being approached in New York. I think there has to be more interaction if possible. For whatever reasons, my gay characters, Jermaine and Ms. Rain, chose to be a part of their community . . . But if I was her mother and I saw Jermaine get beat up one more time, I would say, "Take off the necktie and go downtown. Don't stay up here and get killed." Just like I wouldn't go hold hands with a white boyfriend out in Howard Beach. We're talking about practical, life-saving things. I do think that any outsider has something to teach, and in the black community, the bisexuals and homosexuals have been the outsiders. Look what happened to James Baldwin—the oppression was so great he had to run. He didn't leave here because he was black, he left here because he was a gay man. He went away where he could be accepted and loved.

KCJ  He took France, and a white lover.

S  He took someone who could see him as beautiful. He said again and again that his own father used to look at him and say, "You're ugly."

KCJ  Something you said, that we should leave this culture in America, and go other places to see where we can be loved, and then come back. If we didn't come back, then all of the art, all of the feeling, all of the sensitivity would go away. We can't abandon this place.

S  There are a lot of different ways to leave. Precious only goes downtown; but she travels. Even by going to school, she's sitting with a West Indian woman, a Spanish woman, a gay woman, a bisexual woman, her world gets bigger.

KCJ  And she has to relate to all of them.

S  She better.

**KCJ**  Because they are her support group.

**S**  It's only white culture that can't see Precious as a child. I was being interviewed and I referred to Precious as a little girl, and this white woman said, "Who are you talking about?" I said, "Precious: she's a child." She's a baby.

**KCJ**  That's what I thought was so harrowing about the book. Because this is a child I'm reading about, and I am such a pussyfoot, I can't deal with that stuff.

**S**  I know that although I'm in the middle of my life, I'm just at the beginning of my life as a writer. I'm not being false and humble, I know that *Push* is not as well-written as *The Bluest Eye*, it's not as powerful as *The Color Purple*, but my girl doesn't die, you know what I mean? American solutions, the solution to rape and abuse used to be to go crazy and kill yourself. Now the American way is to go on television and embrace talking about it. We have to move forward. We can't stand still.

**KCJ**  We have the President's wife making this statement, "It takes a village." And so, in a way Hillary Clinton has gone out of American solutions. And whether we as Americans accept and employ this solution, that's another step. I think *Push* is a wonderful book. You're itching at us, and forcing us to scratch. I think that you're a wonderful person. And of course you would be, writing a book like that.

# Lore Segal
# and Han Ong

LORE SEGAL was born in Vienna, Austria, in 1928. She is the author of *Other People's Houses*, *Half the Kingdom*, and *Shakespeare's Kitchen*, which was a finalist for the Pulitzer Prize. For her work, she has been awarded the PEN/O. Henry Prize, the Carl Sandburg Award for Fiction, a National Endowment for the Arts Grant, a Guggenheim Fellowship, and a Dorothy and Lewis B. Cullman Center for Scholars and Writers Fellowship. Segal is a graduate of the University of London. She lives in New York City.

HAN ONG was born in the Philippines in 1968. He is a playwright and novelist whose work includes the novels *Fixer Chao*, which was nominated for the *Los Angeles Times* Best Book of the Year and the Stephen Crane First Fiction Award, and *The Disinherited*, which was nominated for the Lambda Literary Award; and the plays *Watcher*, *Middle Finger*, and *The Chang Fragments*. Ong is the recipient of a Guggenheim Fellowship, a MacArthur Fellowship, and the TCG/NEA Playwriting Award. He is also the recipient of the MacArthur Genius Grant.

**HAN ONG**  It has been more than twenty years between your last book, *Her First American*, and *Shakespeare's Kitchen*, which is coming out in a few months.

**LORE SEGAL**  I'm slow. It took me eighteen years to get where I was going with *Her First American*—and I stopped in the middle and wrote a book no one has heard of called *Lucinella*. That took me five years. I'm slow because I go back to the first sentence. Wherever I am in the book, I'm still working on that first sentence, even when I'm writing the last page. A very cumbersome business, but I don't know how one can change one's ingrained *modus operandi*. I have not even tried. One is a little scared of shaking the foundations of the system.

**HO**  During all those years between books, do you sometimes get nervous that you will not be writing another one because it's been so long?

**LS**  Yes! I regret that I have things I have to say that I'm not going to get to. There are many ways to screw oneself, if I may say so. I remember beginning *Her First American* and not being able to make up my mind if I had a married or a single protagonist. I couldn't get her situation right. I must think if you can't decide the situation of your main character, you're not ready to get going. I was holding myself up in some subterranean way.

**HO**  Your discovery phase is built into the writing process.

**LS**  There are people who write in response to their own writing. I put down a sentence, and that sentence makes it possible to make the next one. I don't have a usable plan. I have some notions and ideas but I don't have a skeleton. I don't experience my life as a plot and am not good at plotting my novel. A character opens a door, stands in the entrance and sees the room. His seeing the room creates the room. Saul Steinberg draws figures drawing themselves into existence. In the wonderful children's book *Harold and the Purple Crayon*, the little boy Harold draws a street for himself to walk on, the chair to sit on. I find that an extraordinarily accurate view of the writing process.

**HO**  In your introduction to *Shakespeare's Kitchen*, you said that you learn how to think by writing, and part of the process you find yourself embroiled in is to have a leading question around which to build a story.

**LS**  I can give you an example. Being an elderly person, I want to write about the loss or partial loss of memory, so I've got myself a character who remembers nothing—an amnesiac. She gets her memory back: a miracle! Now she can remember every one of her old rejections, hurts, and humiliations. This is the kind of thing that starts me on a story. Then I can have fun.

**HO** I imagine that although it took twenty-odd years for *Shakespeare's Kitchen* to appear, you were encouraged along the way. A lot of the stories appeared in *The New Yorker,* so you did get a sense of being a writer out in the world during those years. It wasn't pure incubation or isolation.

**LS** Seven of the *Shakespeare's Kitchen* stories were published by *The New Yorker* in the '80s and '90s, and Knopf said to me, Make these into a novel, but it wouldn't go—it wouldn't become a novel, though all the stories happen in the same place to the same cast of characters.

**HO** They all work at a place called the Concordance Institute, a think tank affiliated with a New England college.

**LS** Yes. I also had a theme: the need not only for friends but for a set of friends to belong to; how interesting—how comical—the creation of intimacies and the search for people with whom to exchange mind, how sadly and inexplicably some friendships fall apart.

**HO** Especially since the protagonist is an immigrant. She did not come up in this country with a given set of friends or extended family.

**LS** We all need friends. We all lose friends. I do not want to claim that immigrants experience what no one else knows, but perhaps the immigrant—the refugee—experience has an added hook.

**HO** What I find so marvelously original in *Shakespeare's Kitchen* and also in *Her First American* is this sense of appetite and avidity that Ilka, the protagonist in both books, has. She wants to surround herself with people and to become American. Usually that phrase "become American" is a little corny or cliché. But in your writing it takes an idiosyncratic, original turn. Ilka wants to have a sense of mastery over her environment, but it comes out of pure joy and not, as in most immigrant narratives, panic.

**LS** That's a lovely perception, and I recognize it.

**HO** It's stuff that I don't find in myself—this sense of joy. I'm conscious of writing more out of a sense of guardedness, a wariness, and a desire to have my isolation protected, whereas Ilka is so avid. She has such capaciousness in her for experience.

**LS** That's also a benefit in old age because the eagerness, that appetite, persists.

**HO** How old were you during the time you were writing *Her First American?*

**LS** It was published in '85, so I was fifty-plus years old and had, as I've said, been writing it for eighteen years. There wasn't much of it when I got started except the experience to build on. Everyone understands that this is partially autobiographical. So many of us, today, start with ourselves and write, to some degree, autobiographically.

One of my colleagues at the University of Illinois said, "You wrote a reverse Henry James. James introduces the simple American to the sophisticated European, and you do the opposite: You introduce a naïve European to a sophisticated black American." I didn't know that's what I had meant: That was mind-opening.

**HO** In *Her First American*, Ilka's surname is Weissnix, and in *Shakespeare's Kitchen*, it's Weiss.

**LS** Weissnix means "know-nothing." She no longer knows nothing. I'm using the method Kafka used with his "K." I don't want to pretend I'm creating a new character. The only character I know is my left rib, so let me face up to that. Ilka is Ilka. However, she's not the same Ilka.

**HO** Her lover from *Her First American*, Carter, makes a cameo in *Shakespeare's Kitchen*. He calls at a very inopportune moment.

**LS** We won't mention that Carter died at the end of *Her First American*. (*laughter*)

**HO** It felt emotionally right for Carter to be calling at that moment in the story, which is about Ilka's husband's sudden, accidental death.

**LS** When my husband died, an old boyfriend called just as we were leaving for the funeral and he said, "That's embarrassing," meaning, I'm embarrassed to have called you at this moment. But I understood "It's embarrassing to be dead." It's an example of how the autobiographical travels and transforms in fiction.

**HO** Going back to Ilka's husband's death in the story "Fatal Wish."

**LS** He's a character who comes out of a story I wrote about being a file clerk when I first came to New York. I dropped a file full of papers exactly the way Ilka's husband, Jimmy, does in the book. "Jimmy Gets the Creeps" was one of my earliest stories. See, there's an example of setting in motion a character—of putting an idea down on paper and the paper gives an idea back to you and then you give the paper back another idea . . . It's like playing ball with the paper. Jimmy is a character who has no skills, who could not even do a good job filing, but he has an almost tiresome sensibility about himself in the world.

**HO** You were born and raised in Vienna. You lived there until you were ten, when Germany annexed Austria. You were among the first wave of the Kindertransport.

**LS** I believe ours was the first experimental train; we were five hundred children. Between December '38 and the beginning of the war in '39, some ten thousand children were brought out of Hitler's Europe by these Kindertransports.

**HO** And in your case, you were taken to England.

**LS** All of us were taken to England from Germany, Austria, and Czechoslovakia, via Holland. We were meant to stay in England until we could go on to our final destinations, but many children stayed and made their home and had families in England.

**HO** Where was this final destination that you were en route to?

**LS** Wherever. The thing was to get out of Hitler's Europe and they wouldn't let us go. I've always compared the Nazis with the Biblical Egyptians who wouldn't let the Hebrews go. The Egyptians (in the King James Bible) experience the presence of all those Hebrew slaves as a "swarm." They are afraid of a possible fifth column in case of war, but they will not let them leave. Hitler wanted us gone, but wouldn't let us go. And, of course, the world did not want—refused, on the whole—to have us.

**HO** Your years in England as a young girl moving from foster home to foster home formed the basis of your first book called *Other People's Houses*. And as in *Shakespeare's Kitchen*, these started out first as stories that found their way into *The New Yorker*. Was it an editor at *The New Yorker* who suggested that you had a book of stories in you?

**LS** My first of these refugee stories was published in *Commentary*. *The New Yorker* had probably turned it down since all of us sent everything we ever wrote to *The New Yorker*. But I sent them my next story, which dealt with the Kindertransport—

**HO** Unsolicited, just through the transom.

**LS** Always. I once sent them a note saying, "Who's there at *The New Yorker*—I know there's a pencil that keeps writing sorry at the bottom of my rejection slip." I was at Yaddo when my mother called me and said, "There's a letter from *The New Yorker*. Do you want me to open it?" In those days magazines always sent your manuscript back—it was something you'd had to type or get typed. It would come back in a big self-addressed stamped envelope that you had included. But this letter came in a letter-sized envelope! They were taking the story; they had read the one in *Commentary*, and would I be interested in writing a series, something that had not occurred to me before.

**HO** And how far along were you?

**LS** I had only these two stories, the one in *Commentary* and the one *The New Yorker* accepted. There's a reason I write my novels as a series of stories: I don't have the long breath required to think in terms of a novel.

**HO** Earlier I referred to the marvelous avidity that Ilka exhibits in terms of wanting to fall in love with America. Between your first book, *Other People's Houses* (1964) and *Her First American* (1985), there seems to be a marked change in terms of temperament. *Other People's Houses* was very factual, what Cynthia Ozick referred to as "artless," and Alfred Kazin in a very laudatory review of your book called it a "document." The emotions in it are very tamped down.

**LS** I've changed some facts to make truer fiction. As for the emotion, it's an interesting issue.

**HO** The tone is almost afraid of feeling. When *Other People's Houses* was reissued in '94, you wrote an introduction in which you said, "It's the price a survivor has to pay—to detach oneself from feelings one cannot master." It had taken a toll on you that took several years to exorcise, when you went back to Vienna and afforded yourself the luxury of tears over your father, over your childhood. There's a closed-in-ness in *Other People's Houses*. I would even say mercilessness. Especially when the young girl, Lore, talks about her father, who has had a sequence of strokes and who has been demoted in the world from a banker in Vienna to a failed butler and then a gardener, and not a particularly competent one.

**LS** I have imagined that the child leaving her parents in Vienna transposed her grief into excitement, a form, surely, of denial.

*Shakespeare's Kitchen* continues to deal with this, though not explicitly. I think I relied too much on the reader recognizing this theme from *Other People's Houses*. The Ilka of *Shakespeare's Kitchen* does not respond adequately to the death of her husband or her lover: she is an inefficient mourner. Her tears don't come until the book's last sentence with the loss of a very secondary character, Bethy. Now Ilka is able to weep, and can't stop weeping.

**HO** She's ambushed into feeling.

**LS** Yes. The tears are not where they're supposed to be. I think there's certainly more heat in *Her First American*.

**HO** That's a good way of putting it: heat.

**LS** Vivian Gornick calls it "a terminal chill." I don't know whether you've seen her review of the re-issued books in *The Nation*, but her insights are wonderful.

**HO** It's a very apt phrase for *Other People's Houses*. The American tendency is to canonize childhood as a period of royal innocence, precocious wisdom, and saintliness, but the young girl Lore is so true to being is a young adolescent, that self-interest and snobbishness, aspiration and grasping.

**LS** My editor, Joel Ariaratnam, has said to me: You say all the things that other people hide. I believe in a community of rottenness and a community of goodness. There's nothing I can tell you about myself to which your understanding does not have access. I don't have that sense of shame. Or rather I have it, but don't pay much attention to it because I'm more interested in figuring out what is it that's being felt. I say to my writing students: The one thing you can rely on in any situation is that the feelings you're going to have are not the ones you think you're supposed to have. Look and see what's really going on. I might look back and think, I wish I hadn't written that, but not often.

HO The stories in *Other People's Houses* came about because you found yourself telling people what you referred to as your Hitler stories.

LS Yeah, my Hitler stories. It never occurred to me to go there; it seemed to me that people already knew and must be tired of these stories.

HO This was around what time?

LS After I came to New York in '51. Because all the people I knew knew all these stories, I thought they were common knowledge, which was a wonderful mistake. At a party once, someone asked me how I had come to the States and I began to tell stories and had, for the first time, the experience that you are giving me now—the experience of telling something and being listened to, and it was lovely. I thought—so bizarre!—this material is interesting! This is something to write. The fact is that I *had* written about these experiences in Liverpool, in German. That first act of writing came from a sense that my foster parents did not understand what was happening in Vienna. The questions they asked me were not relevant. They were simple-minded, I thought, as a ten-year-old, and so I began to write. It's what came to be called "bearing witness." The writing, of course, was utterly inadequate. I *felt* it to be inadequate and so I blew it up—kept adding sunsets and exclamation points. It occurs to me that my horror, now, of "blown-up" writing may give what you experience as "tamped-down." I don't want emotion to sit on the surface of the paper. I want it to happen in the reader's head.

HO The milestones in terms of your birth as a writer would include the very first piece of writing that you give importance to, the letter you wrote as soon as you got to London asking the review board to help your parents get out of Vienna.

LS I believe the letter was written to the cousins who had come to England earlier. Uncle Ernst had business connections in London. The cousins, I think, passed my letter on to Bloomsbury House, which found my parents work as a married couple—that means cook and butler—so that they could come to England.

**HO** Bloomsbury House was a relocation program?

**LS** A kind of clearinghouse for refugee matters.

**HO** And the second episode is the writing in your composition book for your foster family. But what strikes me about that episode is that you were already gauging, at age ten, the effect your writing had on other people. The scene is painted so that it is you looking at your audience.

**LS** Yes, and looking at sentences as sentences. I'd made up some similes that seemed to me very smart. Seem comically smart now. I remember enjoying my similes, enjoying writing them. I remember—I must have been around twelve in Guildford, when a favorite biology teacher went to the hospital for surgery. We were all encouraged to write her. I carried my sentences—the phrases of my own letter around and repeated them in my head. For days I went around with a sense of excitement at having created these sentences. You understand that because you're a writer, but "bearing witness" may be an easier concept for people who are not writers. It's that fascination, delight, and thrill with one's own capacity to make words hold an idea that, I think, is knowing you are a writer.

**HO** The third episode that strikes me is also in *Other People's Houses.* The constant moves from home to home had caught up with you, and you were starting to vomit a lot. One night as you were sick, your mother read *David Copperfield* out loud to you.

**LS** I never lived with my mother again—or not until I was twenty in the Dominican Republic. This reading and the vomiting happened on the night of our arrival in Guildford before the refugee committee had found a job for my mother and a new foster family for me to live with. (We'd had to leave Kent because it was too close to the Channel and my mother might have turned out to be a German spy.) What I recollect saying, at the phenomenal first meeting with Dickens, was, "That's what I want to do. I'm going to be a writer." It was the first time the words "to be a writer" came to me. The impassioned response to thought contained in language whether we make it ourselves or meet it in somebody else's writing.

**HO** Speaking of other writers, are you aware of yourself as a peer in a community of writers whose body of work parallels your own?

**LS** Actually, I'm looking backwards—way back. New York is full of reading groups: We read *Don Quixote*. The Bible. *Grimm's Fairytales*. Kafka. Is the zeitgeist telling us to go back to the big old stuff?

**HO** What are you currently reading?

**LS** Well, I have just given up on Dante. (*laughter*)

**HO** What was the verdict? What was the reason for giving him up?

**LS** This is the second time I have approached Dante. I may even do it again in the future. I cannot bear for there to be something of that stature and I don't get it. That bugs me. But the fact is I don't get it. I can't get over my disgust at this God who metes out his cruel and unusual punishments. *Don Quixote* was lovely. I'm doing Chaucer with some friends. We've organized a small group with the poet Rachel Hadas to help some of us who are wonderful readers of prose but don't really know how to read poetry. Then, there's the twenty-year-old Genesis Seminar.

**HO** I remember memorizing Genesis as a young boy because I was raised a Catholic.

**LS** I thought Catholics weren't allowed to read the Bible, because it's safer for you to be told what it says?

**HO** Where did you get that notion? I was raised in the Philippines as a Roman Catholic and we were taught the Old and the New Testament. And for some reason—it was not required of me—I sought to memorize it. Do you focus on both Old and New Testaments?

**LS** We focus on narrative. We did the book of Genesis verse by verse and it took us four years. I loved that.

**HO** Where do you do this?

**LS** At the Jewish Seminary on 122nd Street.

**HO** Speaking of the Upper West Side, how long have you been an Upper West Sider?

**LS** I came from the Dominican Republic to West 157th Street. From there I moved in with my husband, David Segal, at 72nd Street and West End Avenue. Before my second child was born we came here, to Riverside and 100th. Even the fourteen years I was teaching in Chicago, I kept this apartment and commuted for weekends. I couldn't bear to leave New York.

**HO** Did you raise your children in Chicago during that time, or did your mother take care of them?

**LS** Well, after my husband died, and even before that, my mother wanted nothing so much as to take care of us all. I moved the family to Chicago but we lasted only two years. Nobody liked it; everyone wanted to come back. The suburbs didn't suit us. I've been asking people where they would want their ashes spread, so that they will ask me, and I can say on Riverside Drive. My ashes, after I die.

**HO** This is home?

**LS** This is where I finally, finally got to be at home. Home was hard to come by.

**HO** Yes, it's been an arduous journey for you, out of which you've made a lovely body of work: the search for home. Let's talk about one of the outstanding stories in *Shakespeare's Kitchen*, which is "Reverse Bug." You have indicated that that story grew out of a question.

**LS** I'd been carrying the idea of a reverse bug around for a long time and didn't know what to do with it. It leans heavily on that movie called *The Conversation*.

**HO** The Francis Ford Coppola movie, with Gene Hackman? Where he eavesdrops on people and records them?

**LS** It had some marvelous music. In my story the taking down of the theater to look for the hidden bugging device comes straight out of that movie. I hoped it would be understood as a "quote" from the movie.

**HO** I didn't get that.

**LS** Well, it doesn't matter. I owe Coppola.

**HO** Is there such technology where you can have a reverse bug?

**LS** Not that I know of.

**HO** Let me read your question from the preface: "What if we were forced to hear the sound of torture we knew to be happening twenty-four hours a day out of our earshot?"

**LS** Being forced to know what we don't want to know.

**HO** The story involves an older Japanese gentleman, a sound engineer who sets up the sound system for a conference gathered by the Institute people about genocide and justice. He was also hired, decades earlier, to soundproof the extermination camps in Dachau.

**LS** That was my invention.

**HO** And he also had access to tapes that he or somebody made of Hiroshima victims. These are the rough, basic facts with which the story begins. He goes about setting a reverse bug in the auditorium in which the people there hear the howls funneled in from his Hiroshima and Auschwitz tapes. And so a lot of the story involves the idea of being literally, physically haunted. It's the one story in the book with this extra level. Whereas the other stories are lovingly wrought scenes of interdepartmental relations, friendships, and domestic dramas, this pops out. How do people feel this story fits in with the rest of the collection?

**LS** It doesn't fit, except that those ovens existed in the world from which Ilka had escaped and in which my grandmother's brothers and sisters died. My grandmother, one brother, and one sister came to the New World. One brother died during the First World War. All the others—eleven of them and their spouses—could have been the sounds on those tapes. So there's a different intensity in that story. There is, incidentally, one other "magical realist" element in *Shakespeare's Kitchen*—the little dog who barks at crimes, major and minor. But that's why the stories have not turned into a novel. That's what I tried to explain in the foreword. I meant: Don't tell me it doesn't fit; I'm telling you it doesn't fit. Be aware, everybody, that I'm aware that these are several stories that have not merged into one story. There is one sense in which the reverse bug impinges and that's on the love story:

It interests me that the love affair evolves to the sound of the howls from H-bombs and ovens.

**HO** The extramarital affair that Ilka Weiss conducts with Leslie Shakespeare.

**LS** I remember once seeing a B-movie where one of the bad guys sits eating a large, rich meal while somebody in the next room is screaming. We make love and eat and all the time someone is screaming. What, says the story, would happen if we were made to hear it? And no, I did not integrate that notion throughout the book.

**HO** Let's go back to *Her First American*. You were approached by a producer to turn *Her First American* into a script.

**LS** I did turn it into a script. I turned it into a really bad script. (*laughter*) Pippa Scott bought this movie and caused me to write a script very much against my expressed wishes. I like movies, but I *don't* know how they work. Because I *know* what it feels like to write a story, I know that I don't know how to write a script. However, nobody else would do it, so I went at it. Everyone knows those taped lectures on the craft of script writing—

**HO** Robert McKee.

**LS** Yes! I listened and learned something perfectly interesting. It's what every nineteenth-century novel knows and modern novels won't do—to the detriment in our pleasure of reading them. The "it" is that in a good plot there's no event that isn't the result of an event that went before and leads to the event to come.

**HO** Which is very pleasurable, especially since it's now so out of vogue.

**LS** I love reading nineteenth-century novels. I like watching the movies from the '40s and '50s that have nothing to do with my experience of life, and we can't write like that.

**HO** And she didn't get somebody else then, after you had given up?

**LS** She tried. Oh, indeed, she tried very hard. In fact they're still trying. But I have sold my option. I think the phrase is, "In perpetuity throughout the universe." My agent warned me not to sign this contract, and I said, "Oh, nobody's ever going to want this." So this is nobody's fault except mine. I would love to see this movie made, and I would hate to see this movie made.

**HO** It would provide such a wonderful role for an African American actor. The character's estrangement from society is treated as a given—it's not homiletic or sanctimonious—which makes the tragedy of his drinking and the tragedy of turning his destructive energies inward even more effective and devastating. It's a marvelous love story. You've really caught him.

**LS** I did do a good job, didn't I?

**HO** Not only did you catch him whole, but the openness of spirit with which you caught this world and with which you painted Ilka is fantastic. I'm assuming, Lore, that Ilka is some version of you? I was so heartened by the fact that this girl in *Other People's Houses*, who was so cold and shut off from the world, had flowered by the time of *Her First American*.

**LS** Indeed. I think it was this man who did it—the mix of thinking one was going to save an unhappy life, and of being loved and loving . . . That was the break. I'm talking now as myself.

**HO** Could we touch on the historical model for your character Carter, or is that off the—

**LS** Is that kosher? Are you allowed to do that?

**HO** It's completely up to you.

**LS** He did like the idea of my writing the book. His name was Horace Cayton. There's a fascinating book called *The Cayton Legacy* by Richard Hobbs that tells the story of this black family. Horace's maternal grandfather, Hiram Revels, was president of Alcorn University. Horace's father was born a slave and came to Seattle and ran a newspaper, the *Seattle Republican*—until the times and a bad lawsuit brought him down. They were a powerful, upright generation and, for a time, splendidly successful. It was Horace's generation—brilliant and charismatic, that could not fulfill their expectations of themselves. The dreams that dried like that raisin in the sun. The culture didn't allow them—or they didn't have the stamina for success. I'm in touch still with Horace's niece who runs a gallery of African American art in Chicago. Horace was a wit, a scholar-playboy, a star in America and in Europe. He knew everybody but he couldn't survive, he couldn't make it . . . I find a reluctance in myself to publicize the real Horace.

HO I think once enough time has passed, and if the portraiture in the book is—

LS Very friendly.

HO Friendly, yes. It is not a caricature, it is not an indictment.

LS Horace Cayton wrote a book called *Long Old Road*. He was a superb anecdotalist and talker; he was not a good writer. A sociologist. There is nobody in the black world of that generation who does not know him.

HO This was in the '30s, when he came up and was writing his books.

LS He was born in 1903, the year before my mother. My mother really liked him. My grandmother liked him.

HO Yeah, I'm gathering from those little episodes in the books where he comes and he offers flowers to Ilka's mother—

LS Ilka's grandmother.

HO Ilka's mother, I believe, in *Her First American*, Ilka's grandmother in *Other People's Houses*. See, it helps to have read the material!

LS (*laughter*) Yes, you're right.

HO A friend of mine, who is a big fan of your children's books, particularly *Tell Me a Mitzi*, remarked to me on the names in *Shakespeare's Kitchen*—the Ayes, the Zees, the Cohns, and the Stones. Are you aware of there being a crossover from your children's book writing in terms of that sort of pairing?

LS No, I'm not, but there was a purpose. I was saying to the reader, don't worry about keeping them apart. They are the chorus. In fact, I was going to say so *in* the story, but Bob Gottlieb, who was in those days my editor at *The New Yorker*, wouldn't let me. It was too meta-fictional for him.

HO Can you talk a little more about what you're currently working on?

LS Well, let me tell you one aspect of what I'm working on. Someone—a long time ago—asked me to work on a book of interviews with survivors and survivors' children, and I was fascinated, not by the stories so much as the non-communication between interviewer and interviewees. It has something to do with what we tell each other when we're not professional writers. Writers are in the business of explaining themselves. Most people are not. What interested me was how the interviewers didn't know where to go, and how to access the interviewees' truths. I am playing with that in the book I am writing now.

HO Are you aware of your standing in the American community of letters or is it an irrelevant consideration for you when you write?

LS Let me answer in terms of my other book, *Lucinella*, which you haven't read. In *Lucinella* there's a character called Lucinella, who appears in her twenties when, as she puts it, she doesn't have her hands on the rope. She doesn't know how to behave at parties; she doesn't know how to write her poetry; she doesn't know how to get herself published. Then in the middle there's the mature Lucinella who does have her hands on the ropes, who knows how to handle herself at parties, who gets published. At the end there's a third Lucinella—the three of them meet at parties—and the old one is out of the loop again, no longer has contacts, who goes to a party and everybody seems to be the age of her graduate students . . .

HO That's how you feel.

LS Oh well—that's one way of looking at it. Another thing to make a story out of.

# Charles Simic
# and Tomaž Šalamun

**CHARLES SIMIC** was born in Belgrade, Yugoslavia, in 1938. He is the author of many books of poetry, including *The World Doesn't End*, *Walking the Black Cat*, *Hotel Insomnia*, and *Sixty Poems*. He has received a MacArthur Fellowship, the Wallace Stevens Award, the Frost Medal, and the Pulitzer Prize. Simic was the fifteenth Poet Laureate, was the co-poetry editor of the *Paris Review*, and is Professor Emeritus of American Literature and Creative Writing at the University of New Hampshire. He lives in Stratford, New Hampshire.

**TOMAŽ ŠALAMUN** was born in Zagreb, Yugoslavia, in 1941. He is the author of *The Shepherd, the Hunter*; *The Four Questions of Melancholy*; *Feast*; *Poker*; *Row!*; and many other books. For his work he has won the Pushcart Prize, the European Prize for Poetry, and the Ovid Festival Prize. He has taught at the University of Iowa and the University of Pittsburgh. A graduate of the University of Ljubljana, he is a member of the Slovenian Academy of Sciences and Arts. He lives in Ljubljana, Slovenia.

# CHARLES SIMIC AND TOMAŽ ŠALAMUN

**TOMAŽ ŠALAMUN** How are you, Charlie?

**CHARLES SIMIC** Good. It's raining in New Hampshire. Finally, we're having a real good, solid summer rain.

**TŠ** Well, it's the opposite here in Slovenia. We had a lot of rain and today is better.

**CS** Speaking of weather, I had to introduce Charles Wright recently at a reading. I was rereading his poems, and what struck me is that almost every one is a weather report. It's sunny, it's cloudy, it's getting windy, it's winter, there are a few snowflakes . . . Have you ever been a writer obsessed with weather to that degree?

**TŠ** Not in writing. But I use weather, somehow, when I don't want to talk about other things. And this is kind of a form; a type of English way of establishing neutrality and distance. But Charles Wright, he puts himself into the weather, in his backyard, and that weather forms the whole picture.

**CS** It's really an old trick. Early poetry—Chaucer—or medieval Serbian folk songs often mentions weather in the beginning. Right? "In May, when birds are singing, I took a little girl with me for a walk," or something like that. After I read Charles, I began to notice it in my own old poems, as if the time of day and the condition of the sky was something inevitable in poetry. And yet, I'm a very different kind of poet than Charles Wright.

**TŠ** My instinct is to only be dependent upon my internal weather. I don't notice what is outside. When language wakes up, it just has its own weather. Then I don't even know what the weather is around me. In *your* poetry you do not talk about weather because everything is so clear. You can taste, even smell history, and then there's the presence of your mother, for example.

**CS** Yeah, my father used to haunt my early poetry, but as I grow older, it's more my mother. Anyway, the reason I mentioned weather, I guess, is because it's raining so hard. In the country, changes in weather are much more dramatic and important than in the city.

**TŠ** Several times you told me that you are now a New Hampshire poet. Your weathers are, for me, incredible. For example, your weather is what you told me about your father, how he studied Gurdjieff. Your weather is even connected to Paradjanov or Armenia. But strangely, I don't feel any New

Hampshire weather in you. I feel Paris, of course I feel Manhattan, and even Maribor, when you were in jail, about which you write, "I was lying on the floor when I was ten years old in jail in Maribor," which is in Slovenia, where I come from.

CS I haven't been in Maribor since 1948 (*laughter*), but I agree with you. I'm not really a New Hampshire poet because my imagination is elsewhere. My imagination is far busier with New York City than any other place. But when you live surrounded by trees and the woods, as I do, you can't help but write about trees and woods.

TŠ But your New York, this New York of the '50s has disappeared. Just like Paris from the '50s disappeared, and that was partly my Paris, too. To be able to read you, to experience how you carried some garment and escaped, how you slept with different women, how you sensed how this woman breathed and you were afraid and went away—this world doesn't exist anymore. Or when you went to that special occult bookstore; now I forget. I had a similar experience in Paris, when I went to a gathering of astrologers. Those people were very different but looked like a tribe. They had a totemistic basis somehow.

CS It's true. *That* particular New York: the esoteric circles, the people interested in Eastern religions, the occult and so forth—when I'm in the city nowadays I don't know anybody who is interested in any of that. When I write about the city, I often think back to the basement of the Wiser Bookstore, where I spent so much time.

TŠ Yes, I remember I couldn't even look at the books because the people were so special, so different.

CS Let me change the subject. How do you write? I know you like to isolate yourself and spend periods of time writing poem after poem.

TŠ Well, it was like this. Now I don't need isolation. I usually write while I'm traveling. I'm not writing when I'm a middle-class father, a grandfather, a husband. But as soon as I move, when I travel, I start to scribble something.

CS Can you write on a plane?

TŠ Yes, I can. But with the ups and downs and the pressure, maybe it's not the best for my heart. But yes, I do write on the plane. I write best when I'm anonymous: in a big city, in a café, looking around, losing myself. For the real intensity, I go to those Italian places: Civitella Ranieri, Bogliasco, Santa Maddalena Foundation. Only it's so beautiful that there's a danger that the poetry will become too aesthetic.

CS I can only write at home. I have to be in my room, close to my bed, because I love lying down when I write. It's my favorite spot. (*laughter*) A few years ago I was in a very beautiful place on the Mediterranean. I was thinking of lots of things I wanted to do that day, but it never occurred to me to start writing, because I associate writing with being home.

TŠ I can write at home, too, especially if I'm alone in my bed; the language just attacks me. Also, I cannot write anything else except what I then publish as poetry. Vasko Popa told me when I was a very young man, "Tomaž, you might be a good poet, but stop writing those small reviews, because you're from a very small culture. If you do this, you will never succeed as a true poet, you will become *kulturnik*." I listened to him. He crippled me! Now I am invalid. I have only my poetry, nothing else. But I still think it was good advice.

CS I started writing poetry in English, but of course English was not my first language. I had two languages in my head: English and Serbian. The good thing was that I then did not know Serbian poetry; I had studied some in school when I was in Yugoslavia, but not much.

TŠ But you knew French poetry, right?

CS I knew French poetry thanks to being in a school in Paris. They tortured us by making us memorize poems by Rimbaud, Verlaine, and Baudelaire. I hated it.

TŠ Me too, but I loved Rimbaud. We had a really good French professor, and the only real influence when I was a teenager was Rimbaud, especially Rimbaud and Lautréamont and not the other Slovenian poets, except Župančič who was the Whitman of Slovenia. So I was influenced by Whitman through Oton Župančič.

CS That's interesting.

TŠ When we met in 1972, in Iowa, I was reading you and I read you as a

French and a Serbian poet. And for me this was very strange and very different than other poetry I was reading, like Bob Perelman or Ashbery's *Three Poems*. Slowly, really slowly, I think you tectonically disrupted the continent. Like a stone falling in the center of the American heart. In three, four, five decades, you completely restructured not only American poetry now, but the history of American poetry. Would you agree?

CS  That's too high a praise for me to take seriously. Everything I ever did was kind of an accident. I really had no possibility of becoming a Serbian poet because I knew nothing about Serbian poetry when I started out. I was an immigrant kid who had an awful foreign accent, so reciting these poems in front of a class in Paris was humiliation; it was horrible. Only later did I realize, My God, I really love these poems and these poets. Once I started writing in English, I became curious about American poetry. The first poet that I loved was Hart Crane, which is kind of crazy because I didn't understand a thing he said; I just loved the way it sounded. (*laughter*) And then Wallace Stevens and Williams were influences. The moment I moved away from home, to Chicago, in 1956, I met people involved with literature and we argued about American poetry. I got so involved in American poetry, and kept changing my mind about how I wanted to write. It was only years later that I stopped and said to myself, Well, wait a minute, let's see what Serbian, Slovenian, and Croatian poetry looks like.

TŠ  But maybe we do carry something in our genetics. Because even if you didn't read Serbian poetry, you were somehow not that far away. Also, I want to ask about this 1957 picture in Oak Park, Illinois, with some paintings you did.

CS  (*laughter*)

TŠ  With these paintings you could practically finish academy in Europe.

CS  Well, I first started painting long before I wrote poetry, and I kind of imagined that I would be a painter. So that was the center of my attention until I was about twenty-five or twenty-six and I realized that poetry was more important to me.

TŠ  Amazing. We never talked about this and I didn't know this. You had to have studied Cézanne very carefully. I am formally an art historian, and I much preferred studying art than literature.

CS  Oh, yes, of course. I learned about modern literature and surrealism not through reading books about modern literature and surrealism, but reading books about Cubists and Dada and whatnot, by looking at visual arts.

TŠ  I had an episode of being a visual artist, and this is how I first came to America. I came into America in 1970 as an exhibitor in the Museum of Modern Art as a conceptual artist. As a member of the Slovenian OHO group.

CS  What was the work that you were exhibiting?

TŠ  There was a group called OHO and their leader Marko Pogačnik was in the army. When, as in a revelation, I saw a stack of hay from the bus, I knew. I said, I am one of yours; let's find the best gallery in Yugoslavia. And we'll do it differently! So we got the best gallery in Yugoslavia, a catalogue was printed, and it was seen by Kynaston McShine in Germany, a curator from MOMA who was preparing the first big international conceptual art show called *Information*. And in July of 1970 I was asked to be in the show and spent the whole month in New York, which turned my life around. Because New York was such an incredible explosion compared to what I knew in Europe during that time.

CS  So what was the piece you exhibited?

TŠ  It showed my foot above a fire on the snow and said "42 degrees." Or it showed one photo and it said "From here to here . . ." I forgot! It's so dull now after forty years of repeating such Duchampian salon work, but then it was pure fire. Without knowing it, I was very close to Michael Heizer and On Kawara. I measured myself every morning and sent a postcard to my younger brother Andraž, a painter, then one of five members of the OHO group every day for a month with the sentence: "Today I'm 180.3 cm high," or, "Today I'm 180.1 cm high." And I didn't know that On Kawara at the same time had written, "I'm still alive, I'm still alive, I'm still alive." But what stopped me from going on with this was that other artists like Heizer, Cristo, Sol LeWitt were all looking for $100,000 for their next projects. And I was a Slovenian, some pauper. I realized that this was not a cup for me. History had already chosen the heroes.

CS  Amazing. Didn't you also get in trouble over some political poem when you started writing poetry?

423

**TŠ** Yes, this was in '64. There was a very important cultural literary magazine called *Perspektive* in Ljubljana, which was battling with the official communist line. Heidegger was translated, Merleau-Ponty, Roland Barthes, *Tel Quel* authors. When they came to the border of being abolished, I was named editor-in-chief because they wanted to save the journal by putting an innocent young man in the position. And then I published a poem, which I thought was a kind poem, nothing special, but the government ideologues thought the poem itself and the gesture of me being put in charge as editor-in-chief was so transgressive that I found myself in jail. But the reaction from *Le Monde*, from *The New York Times*, from *Corriere della Sera* was so strong that they just pushed me out of jail after five days. I came out as a culture hero, and it was a very cheap glory. I realized, I have to become a really good poet to earn my fame. (*laughter*)

**CS** Was there anything in the poem?

**TŠ** It was a line: "Socialism à la Louis XIV." And in one line: "dead cat." But I had no idea that the interior minister was named Macheck (Maček), or "cat." So he took it personally. The really bad years were the mid-'70s, which I think were also the darkest political years in Europe; when Aldo Moro was killed, when Schleyer was kidnapped, when the Brezhnev doctrine was so strong. Coming back from America, from Iowa in 1973, I was annihilated. I couldn't make any money. The repression from Slovenia on me only stopped because of American PEN. So America really saved me several times.

**CS** You started out not wanting to be a political poet, right?

**TŠ** Yes. But because the system was very sophisticated then, when I came out of jail people from the Secret Service—the UDBA—said, "Oh, you lost your steam, you don't write any protest poems anymore." My second book, still published by myself, was about butterflies, about nothing. It was more subversive than if I would write protest poems, since the government needed to show its pluralism and democracy. One has to be very precise not to be corrupt or used.

**CS** Your poems since then, too, have had moments when they would be interpreted politically. Do you think of politics?

**TŠ** Well, I was fighting to be free within my writing. And just *this* was subversive, and therefore political. But, for example, during the Balkan wars, when Brodsky and Miłosz were able to write something, I was completely silent. I didn't write a line of anything from '89 to '94. I just stopped writing.

**CS** It was too depressing. I get upset on almost a daily basis about things going on in the world. But to say, "I'm going to write a poem about the injustice in whatever place in the world" isn't how it works with me.

**TŠ** And I think if you did intend to show that anger or depression, you wouldn't be able to write good poetry. But just being what you are, to be free within your writing, this is also the center of the real responsibility of the world. Therefore, your freedom is a political act.

**CS** I also think that for us who have a memory of communism, programmatic political poetry is an awful association. You think of all those terrible poets . . .

**TŠ** . . . or even great poets who have done great things, like Neruda or Éluard.

**CS** Right, who ended up writing shitty poems in support of some dictator or policy. Here's something that interests me: the experience of being a poet in the United States as compared to the rest of the world. What do you think about the notion that poets in the United States are marginalized and that poets elsewhere are more highly regarded?

**TŠ** Not true. So many people are studying poetry, there are so many new magazines and new daring authors. There's a very vibrant scene.

**CS** I agree. Look at all the writing programs, all the readings, all the websites. Being Poet Laureate this past year—it really surprised me how comfortable Americans have become with the idea of poetry. When I started out in the 1950s, people interested in contemporary poetry were like a cult.

**TŠ** Even what my undergraduate students at the University of Richmond discover on their own is incredible. Their motivation, competition, love for it, and admiration for older poets is incredible. You don't get this audience in Europe for poets, at all.

**CS** (*laughter*) When I became Poet Laureate, the first people to interview me were the big television stations: ABC, NBC, the usual places. The reporters would say, "How's it being a poet laureate in a country where nobody reads poetry?" I didn't say what I wanted to say: "You're full of shit." Instead, I would say, "In this country there isn't a college or a university that doesn't have a poetry reading series or hasn't had one for twenty or thirty years." I've been in the audience when you've given a reading, Tomaž, and your poems are original and not the easiest to follow and yet, I never had the impression that the audiences had any problem with them.

TŠ  Absolutely. But I'd be nowhere without my friends, specifically you, because you put me on the map. In 1984 I went to a seer with a young Slovenian poet, Aleš Debeljak, and the seer said to me, "The letter will come from the country where you already spent a lot of time. A friend will write you a letter that will change your life." And she started to describe you *exactly*. I knew who she was describing. And in 1986 you wrote me a letter: "I met Bob Hass and we talked about you, and we talked to Dan Halpern; he will do the book." And this book of my selected poems, published in 1988 by Ecco Press, changed my life.

CS  Well, you really have a huge following among younger poets.

TŠ  Because of this support. And I had another generation that was interested in my work. I am one of the luckiest European poets; I'm incredibly grateful for how I am treated in America. It's almost unbelievable.

CS  According to a mutual friend and editor, your books also sell well in this country.

TŠ  Well . . . relatively. (*laughter*) I'm looking at Amazon. You sell well and Bob Hass sells well, but translations don't sell well. But maybe enough that I can hope to go on. By now I have ten American books, and there are not many living European poets who have this.

CS  There's a question I'm very curious about: Do you think American poetry is changing?

TŠ  Yes, American poetry is *constantly* changing. So many poets disappear, the scene changes, yet it remains immensely strong. It's also much more healthy compared to visual arts, where curators are terrorizing artists. They don't allow paintings anymore. Poetry is much more honest, much more healthy.

**CS** What's happening in Slovenia?

**TŠ** In Slovenia I'm very lucky to be accepted by America and the world, translated a lot, so allowed to go on with my new books. I was lucky to be able to be a bridge. For example, Richard Jackson and his students have been coming to Slovenia and we have two international festivals: Vilenica and Medana. Slovenian poetry is very present in the United States, and American poetry is very present here, more so than in Germany, for example.

**CS** What of the European poetries, both East and West? Where do you think the most interesting poetry is being written?

**TŠ** Poland.

**CS** Still?

**TŠ** Yes. Irish poetry, Polish poetry, and then . . . I don't know enough about the Romanian basin, but it seems that Romania has very, very strong poets. They haven't had a lot of contact with the West in the last twenty years but there are great poets. Younger Polish poets are really strong. How would you judge?

**CS** I agree, Slovenian poetry is very, very strong. I think Serbian poetry is still very strong. I mean, you have Milan Djordjević, Dusan Novakovic, Radmila Lazic, Nina Zivancevic, and few others. Do you know Milan's work?

**TŠ** Oh, definitely. I adore him. Especially over the last fifteen years. He is a major world poet and also the best living Serbian poet at the moment.

**CS** I agree. The surprises are still to be found in the former Yugoslavia, or whatever you want to call the place. Russian poetry is interesting. I've seen a couple of anthologies with a great many poets that are very young who I've never heard of. Russian poetry seems to be much more intense, much more lively than what goes on in France and Italy, and Spain too. I was talking to a Spanish writer recently, and he said, "There's not much going on in Spanish poetry." Of course, one can never be sure about these things since often translations of recent poetry are not available.

Tell me about your own work as a translator. You translate your own poetry?

**TŠ** As a writer, I'm a moonwalker. I don't know what I'm doing. As a translator of my own poetry, I just do it like a lumberjack with a dictionary and try to be accurate and precise. I mostly have to translate myself, because I write only in Slovenian.

**CS** I've never translated myself. I'm always amazed that somebody actually makes the effort to translate me. I mean, I have translators in a number of places, people I've never met before, who translate me into Arabic, Spanish, Norwegian, Hungarian. A labor of love, I suppose.

**TŠ** Yeah. I remember I was very sad when I translated your selected poems into Slovenian and I was doing it slowly, slowly. It seemed easy, but it didn't really work—I was not satisfied until the end, and then I don't understand what happened. But after half a year of not working on your translation, I spent maybe ten days on it, made changes, and it worked. And I was very happy.

**CS** I think that has to be the way one works on these translations. I've had the same experience many, many times. There's a simple explanation for this. One is always looking for some equivalent, a language that, in some way, approximates what is being said in the original. And very often you just don't think of the right words or the right idiom at the time.

**TŠ** I try to be as direct as I can, as literal as I can. I still remember how Marguerite Yourcenar, for example, translated Catullus. It was as if she would read the page, and then she would do something else on her own. It's a French tradition of translation. German tradition is very different. Slovenians translate more like Germans. It all depends, but I am afraid of those translators who think that they can improve, or use the other language to do it another way. Usually it doesn't work.

**CS** I agree. I always begin humbly. I want to be as literal as possible. I don't want to impose myself, and I'm really afraid to take any liberties, even when it seems necessary. Even then, it's almost a blasphemy; it's a sacrilege to take freedoms to change something drastically in the translation. I try to be faithful. And, of course, sometimes it's not possible.

**TŠ** When will we see each other? Will you go to Bellinzona in Switzerland this year? I told them they should invite you, and they told me they would.

**CS** I wouldn't go now. I'm so happy to be home this summer after nine months of constant drama. I commuted every week between New Hampshire, New York, and Washington. It was exhausting.

TŠ  What is the situation? Being Poet Laureate, you have an office in Washington?

CS  Oh, I had a very nice office in the Library of Congress facing the Capitol, but I stepped down. I'm not gonna stay for the second year.

TŠ  Can you step down?

CS  Yeah, sure I can step down. It's a free country. (*laughter*)

TŠ  So you were there only one year?

CS  Yeah, I was Poet Laureate until the first of July. It was just too much. I had at least fifty or sixty interviews and *countless* number of other things I had to do. I would receive thirty emails every day relating to poetry. It's enough to make you hate poets and poetry. Enough! You know? I want to do other things.

TŠ  Yes, yes . . .

CS  Like, you know, sit quietly with a glass of wine and talk to my cat. (*laughter*)

# Justin Taylor and Ben Mirov

JUSTIN TAYLOR was born in Miami, Florida, in 1982. He is the author of the novel *The Gospel of Anarchy* and the story collections *Flings* and *Everything Here Is the Best Thing Ever*, which was named a *New York Times* Editors' Choice. He edited *The Apocalypse Reader* and co-edits the arts annual *The Agriculture Reader*. His work has appeared in *The New Yorker*, *Bookforum*, and *The Believer*, among other publications. He lives in Brooklyn, New York.

BEN MIROV was born in Santa Monica, California, in 1980. His books of poetry include *Ghost Machine* and *Hider Roser* and the chapbooks *Vortexts*, and *Collected Ghost*. He has contributed to HTMLGIANT, Diagram, BOMBlog, and *The Rumpus*. He lives in Oakland, California.

**BEN MIROV** While reading *Everything Here is the Best Thing Ever*, it occurred to me that you're the type of writer that is able to crystallize a lot of influences in your prose. I know you're a fan of Donald Barthelme, but I expected to see more of his influence in *BTE*. Were there specific writers that you drew from while writing *BTE*?

**JUSTIN TAYLOR** Absolutely. I think influence is a fascinating and powerful thing. I know some writers fear or are wary of it, but I'm an eager embracer of models and anti-models, both. Sometimes it's about saying "Okay, I love this, and it's monumental, but it's been accomplished already." I do love Barthelme enormously, and I've learned volumes from reading him, but I'm not going to match Barthelme at writing Barthelme stories, and even if I could, what would be the point? So I'm not worried about following in his footsteps, or appearing to, because my work is never going to look like his. It's about extrapolating a lesson, or picking up a technique, or having an idea of your own sparked by some idea you've encountered, and then putting those things to work in a wholly other context, the means to different ends of your own devising, where they may or may not even be recognizable anymore. I love the idea of building my nest from bits pinched from all over the place. If someone looks at my work and recognizes that this twig is from a birch tree, or that that bright red thing is a torn piece of label from a soda bottle—more power to that person for their good eye, but that doesn't make it any less my nest.

**BM** You have an admirable output. On top of your critical writing for places like *The Nation* and *The Believer* you also blog regularly for HTMLGIANT and write poetry. Do you feel it's important for writers to work across all genres, these days, in order to attain a reputable level of success?

**JT** I think that all the kinds of writing I've done—as well as my work editing anthologies, and a small magazine—inform each other in useful ways, some more obvious than others. I know that writing and reading poetry has taught me lessons about language that I couldn't have learned any other way. Which is not to say that they cannot be learned some other way, only that this was the right way for me. And I know that writing nonfiction—book reviews, journalism, essays—has given me a whole other set of perspectives and opportunities; it's a different skill-set, and one I'm glad to have. But I don't think it's "necessary" in any sense—artistic, commercial, or whatever. I think people do what feels right for them. I like to work with people, I like thinking up projects and executing them, and I like trying new things—but there's no denying that every thing you do is time spent not doing something else. You have to be able to prioritize, and more than that, to choose. I hardly ever write poetry anymore. I still read it, but I funnel my writing energy mostly into other projects—namely this novel I've been working on, which is almost due.

**BM** As an addendum to the last question, do you associate yourself or feel like you're part of an ever-burgeoning group of writers who actively work across genres and mediums, not because they are making some kind of overt aesthetic statement, but because it seems natural (I'm thinking of writers like Tao Lin or Blake Butler who seem content to work across genres or attempt to transcend them)?

**JT** Well, you're unlikely to confuse a page torn from my book with one torn from Blake Butler's *Scorch Atlas* or Tao Lin's *Shoplifting from American Apparel*, but yes, there are associations there, and not merely theoretical ones—they are really-existing personal and professional relationships. Blake is my editor at HTMLGIANT, as well as a friend. I've known Tao for years—I've published his work, we've lived together, etc. I don't know that we're "ever-burgeoning," but '09 was a pretty good year for us—each of us either put a book out or got a book deal, and I think we all have books coming out in '10. And it's not just about the three of us—Mathias Svalina's poetry collection, *Destruction Myth*, Joshua Cohen's monster novel, *Witz*, that Dalkey Archive is doing this spring, Shane Jones's *Light Boxes* getting picked up by Penguin—these are all examples off the top of my head. I'm sure there are more—I know there are. I don't think of us as a coterie or scene, but we're all aware of each other's work, and HTMLGIANT is the kind of nexus of that awareness, and it does feel like a critical mass is approaching, or has been obtained. A mass of what, I'm unsure, but here we all are.

As far as cross-genre goes, I can't speak for Blake or for Tao, but what are we really doing that Denis Johnson or Joyce Carol Oates or John Updike or John Ashbery haven't done already? Those guys all write in multiple disciplines—fiction, non-fiction, poetry; Ashbery also dabbles in the visual arts, as a critic and as a collagist, as did Donald Barthelme. Some writers specialize, others don't, and I think it's about what, as you put it, "seems natural." I think there's this urge to connect, say, blogging with age—something about "the kids are/n't all right" or "the way we live now." But my favorite blogger is Dennis Cooper, who is the same age as my dad. Dennis is more in touch with contemporary culture than I'll ever be, if I live to twice Harold Bloom's age.

BM I was thinking, and I'm not sure how to put this in question form, that your writing reminds me of John Hughes's movies in a number of ways, specifically the way you capture and articulate stereotypes of the '90s and the way your characters are often in periods of transition or liminality. Many of the characters in *BTE* are hybrid goth, raver, nerd types, or just simply outsiders that are struggling for acceptance or love or friendship. Am I way off base in making this comparison?

JT When I was growing up I was fascinated by people who seemed to fit snugly into their little sub-culture. They seemed like these great actors—not in the sense of being poseurs, but in the sense of knowing their lines, and their costumes, and being really comfortable in their roles, and expert at performing them. I never once felt that way in my whole life—I still don't. And I'm sure those people weren't really the way I imagined them; they were struggling to define themselves and live up to their own definitions as much as anyone else was—which is what I'm interested in exploring in the book. I hope I'm not just trading in stereotypes. But I think it would have been impossible to write about the '90s without making reference to that kind of pathological typing, because it was such a fundamental part of how the culture articulated itself during that era.

BM One of the things that struck me throughout *BTE* were the moments of violence strung throughout the collection. Characters often perpetrate violence, unwittingly or wittingly, upon each other with a disturbing complacency, almost as if they see violence as intrinsic to their lives. Do you feel like violence is a key aspect of the stories in the collection?

JT For me, the violence—in the stories where violence occurs, which is only some of them—has a feeling of inevitability. You don't necessarily see it coming, but in the instant of arrival it feels in some sense "right" or even (perversely) "proper." This seems close to your idea of its being "intrinsic," but it retains this sense of the violence coming from without, which is how I would prefer to think of it: a kind of necessary excess. By and large, in these stories, emotional violence is perpetrated unwittingly, whereas the instances of physical violence are mostly deliberate, though usually the result of some serious emotional miscalculating—the two things are hopelessly intertwined, of course. "Jewels Flashing in the Night of Time" is probably the darkest story in the whole book, but even that narrator's violence is essentially the result of his failure to negotiate a power-relationship, and even in the climactic moment of the story (which I don't want to spoil) he isn't sure whether his act is one of total control or total submission.

BOMB — THE AUTHOR INTERVIEWS

BM Do you have a favorite story in the collection, one that you're particularly attached to?

JT The one I'm most attached to is "The New Life." The setting is the South Florida suburbs where I grew up, and something about it just shakes me to my core. Writing that story, getting it right, was the apotheosis of something powerful and essential for me. Readers who have told me their favorites have tended not to pick that one, and I tried unsuccessfully to get it published before collecting it in the book, so it may not be objectively the "best" one, but it's my favorite. Apart from that, I love all the stories equally. I put everything I had into every single line. I wouldn't take a do-over on any of them.

BM I thought we should try some word association to wrap things up. I'm just going to say a few things and you write whatever pops into your head: Dennis Cooper

JT *My Loose Thread*

BM Harold Bloom

JT *Ruin the Sacred Truths*

BM Tao Lin

JT *Shoplifting from American Apparel*

BM Facebook

JT World's smallest megaphone

BM MFA

JT If the circumstances that led to your need for this deferment still exist, you may be eligible to extend the deferment, or there may be other types of deferment or forbearance for which you may qualify if you need to further postpone repayment on your loans.

BM David Berman

JT   I want to wander through the night / as a figure in the distance even to my own eye

BM New York

JT   Brooklyn

# John Edgar Wideman and Caryl Phillips

JOHN EDGAR WIDEMAN was born in Washington, DC, in 1941. He is the author of numerous books, including *A Glance Away, Hurry Home, The Lynchers, Philadelphia Fire, Brothers and Keepers,* and *Fanon.* Wideman, a Rhodes Scholar and graduate of the University of Pennsylvania and New College, Oxford University, has been awarded the PEN/Faulkner Award, the American Book Award, and the James Fenimore Cooper Prize for Best Historical Fiction. His work has been nominated for the National Book Critics Circle Award and the National Book Award. He is a professor at Brown University.

CARYL PHILLIPS was born in St. Kitts in 1958. He is a playwright, essayist, and novelist whose works include *Dancing in the Dark, The Final Passage,* and *Crossing the River.* Phillips has twice won the Commonwealth Writers Prize, as well as the Lannan Foundation Literary Award, the James Tait Black Memorial Prize, and the Martin Luther King Memorial Prize. He has been awarded a Fellowship of the Royal Society of Arts and a Guggenheim Fellowship. A graduate of Queen's College, Oxford University, Phillips has taught at Amherst College and Barnard College and is currently a professor of English at Yale University.

**CARYL PHILLIPS** I want to begin by asking you, John, about that moment, if there was such a moment, when you first decided that you wanted to write.

**JOHN EDGAR WIDEMAN** There are probably many moments. And what I'll do now is tell a story, hopefully slightly entertaining and with some bearing on the truth, although I wouldn't claim for it any veracity beyond that. My father was a reader and I have a very strong image of him right now: I remember him sitting in our living room, which was also our dining room, (*laughter*) which was also our kitchen, which was mostly the whole house. I remember him sitting in a chair, tired from work, and he would pick up these pulp novels, westerns mostly, like Zane Grey, and he'd read these things as a kind of sleeping pill. He was a big man, so these books were always small in his hands and his legs would be stretched out in front of him, and gradually, his eyes would start to drop and the legs would get more and more slack and then he'd fall off to sleep and I'd hear "plunk," the book would hit the floor. They were pretty trashy, tacky books, but I read them because that's what was around. And I began to see that there were certain formulas in these books which weren't too difficult to figure out. And I thought, Well, hell, I could do that. These things aren't hard to write: the guy rides into town, he sees a beautiful lady, something is at stake, he figures out a way to help her, etcetera, etcetera. And I thought, you know, this would be fun to do, easy to do. So, that's when I had this glimmer that I could, maybe, become a writer. The other part of it comes from another direction and has nothing to do with books and writing and reading but it has to do with listening. I was lucky enough to grow up in a family full of storytellers. It was particularly the women's province, and I grew up listening to women's voices tell stories—my aunts and my mother, my grandmother and their friends. And I loved to listen to these stories. And they created a world for me. Not only did they create a world, but they created a kind of sensibility—something to measure myself against. And the more I listened, the more the act of storytelling penetrated my consciousness. It was something I wanted to partake of. The reading was easy. Anybody could do the stuff that Zane Grey was doing, but telling the stories the way the women in my family told the stories was something that I could only wish I could do, hope I could do. That was the real comparison, that's what I wanted to be able to make—the kind of energy and eloquence, and the funny, crazy stuff that was in the stories women told. So those were my two models and as far back as I can remember, they were the models that I strove to emulate.

**CP** So, by the time you went to the University of Pennsylvania, did you embark on a degree in English with the notion that you wanted to write, or teach, or both?

JW Well, what I did was embark on a degree in Experimental Psychology. And I did that because I thought the idea of reading people's minds was kind of groovy. You know, to read people's minds and anticipate what they were going to say and do, that was a great power trip. And Penn was the center of Experimental Psychology. I lasted about a month, because I found out that, rather than reading Freud and getting into orgone boxes, what you do is count the number of times rats walk through this maze and pick up a pellet in an hour if you zap them with electricity.

CP We haven't talked about it, but did you know that I began in Experimental Psychology and (*laughter*) I switched after three months.

JW Well, there's something about it that has an appeal. But anyway. In college, I worked very hard to figure out a way that I could live the rest of my life and not have a job. To that end, I was a jock, I played basketball. I figured that I would play basketball and make a lot of money. Anything that I could do that would enable me to have my cake and eat it too, that is to have this sort of pseudo-job but have a good life, and have the good things, that's what I wanted to accomplish. So, basketball was the first thought. And then I didn't grow the extra foot I needed to grow as an undergraduate and so I decided well, what's the next best thing. I can't play ball, writing seems like a pretty good gig. Writers don't have bosses, they don't have to go and punch clocks. So that's the reason I thought to maybe try writing.

CP You ended up going across the water to Oxford. What influence did Oxford have on you as a writer, and as an American. And as a black person finding yourself at Oxford in the mid-1960s?

JW Yeah, (*laughter*) in any order. Well, going to Oxford, for me, was an exciting opportunity. In fact, I went there consciously because I had made the choice to be a writer. I had never been out of the country—and I knew, or I thought that, in order to be a writer, you had to be down-and-out in Paris or Rome. And since Mom and Dad were not going to send me to Paris or Rome, I had to figure a way to get there on my own, and the Rhodes seemed ideal. So, it was important in the sense that I had begun to identify with a kind of vocation and I was making big choices, major choices that would facilitate this writing business. What happened there? First of all, I heard the language spoken in a different way. People there take the language seriously in a way that we don't. You read a box of tea and it says, "Wait until the water boils furiously." (*laughter*) This is the kind of eloquence on a tea box that I didn't get from my professors at Penn. So that was exciting. And also the time at Oxford was an interesting time, because these were the early '60s. So, I left an America in tremendous ferment and found myself in a kind of catbird's seat across the water looking back on all this stuff that was happening. And that was, for me, a little frustrating. It's almost like the people you've heard about who never went to war and wondered, Well what kind of person would I be if I actually had that wartime experience? I didn't have the civil rights experience. The only march I ever went on was back in 1967 in Iowa City—a protest march—and by that time, it was no big deal. I still wonder—how my life would have changed if I were in America and had decided to go South during the Freedom Summer to ride the buses or join a radical organization. It would have been a different life. But I discovered that I liked that distance. I liked that angle, the oblique angle. The vantage point of seeing this business from England and having to put it together in my imagination on the basis of headlines and letters and spot visits back to the United States. So I found myself getting a lot of practice being an outsider. England was changing a lot at that time as well. The first wave of people from the so-called Third World were making their voices felt at Oxford. People who went back to Africa and became Prime Ministers of their countries, people who went back to the West Indies and became political powers, artists, etcetera. So, I had a firsthand look at this ferment: people of color who were unlike anybody I had ever known in the States. Now it may be hard for some of you to believe but, the degree to which black people—and all of us—were kept ignorant, and still are for that matter—but in the '60s it was appalling. Politically I was uneducated, unsophisticated, I could feel that race was a problem in the South, but as long as I kept my nose clean I could kind of make my own way in the North. I was very naive. So, England was a way of getting a perspective on a lot of these received attitudes. And in that sense, it was very important. It was a political renaissance. It was, for me, growing up.

CP  You began to write, pretty soon after you got back from Oxford.

JW  Well, I began to write there. I did do the tour of Europe and I began to keep notebooks. And by the time I got back, I had most of my first book finished.

CP  In 1988, you made this statement: "At a certain point in my writing career, after I had done three books, I made a decision, I wanted to reach out to readers that the earlier works had perhaps excluded. I wanted to get everybody's ear." Those three books were written in the late '60s and early '70s. Can you explain what it was about those first three books that you felt excluded certain people, and who were the people being excluded?

JW I would second-guess that statement. It's too simplistic because, for one thing, it served critics who have written about my work since, as a point of departure. And I think it's unfair. I believe if I look closely, objectively, at what I've done, the themes and the concerns and the centering in an African American world have been there from the beginning. What I sensed was a lack of fluidity in a vernacular voice that I wanted to change. We're talking shop, we're talking about a writer's ability to use various registers and communities of the language in a way that feels natural. I feel that in my first three books, as is the case with many writers, I had models, I had examples of eloquence, examples of people who I felt captured something special in their vision, in their themes, etcetera. And so, as I tried to get my own feet under me, I was imitating, I was enthralled, I had stars. And I realized, the more I wrote, that that kind of looking outside of myself for models was insufficient, that, as good as the stuff was that I had been reading, it missed whole levels, whole realms of experience that were personal, that were mine. I could not simply take my experience and put it in this language that I had received—as a graduate student and as an undergraduate—as the language of literature.

CP Who were the models and the stars?

JW Certainly, T.S. Eliot was one: his poetry, the blending of levels of language that's in his work, his concern with time, his concern with history, his use of classic sources, his ability to speak to, not only other writers, but other epochs, his sense . . . This was probably unconscious—but one thing that appealed to me was the West-African notion of "great time" that is part of Eliot's writing, that is not time as a linear flow but as a great sea. And if you read "Prufrock," Eliot is operating in "great time." People who lived a thousand years ago speak to people who live now. They bump up against each other: take a boat ride in the Thames and you might run into Queen Mary. All that appealed to me. I didn't know exactly why. Also, as a young writer particularly, anything that was strange, that I didn't quite understand, presented a challenge. So I had to go after it. I had to master it and figure it out.

CP Many writers have cited other art forms, perhaps most commonly painting and music, as influences upon them. When I was reading your second novel, *Hurry Home*, I was struck by the character Cecil who sees a relationship between his experience and what he sees when he looks at a painting by Hieronymus Bosch. Does one need some understanding of Bosch to get at the heart of this novel? And, to what extent, if at all, have other art forms influenced your writing?

JW  Hmm. What has been very useful to me—and simply fun for me—is to find that, through the medium of writing, I could think about things that were important to me. It's actually a means of thinking. I was very moved and excited by the paintings of Hieronymus Bosch. I didn't exactly know why, but then my handle on understanding him came intuitively. It wasn't a question of going out and reading a lot about Bosch. Although I did make it my business to travel to cities where there were Bosch paintings so I could see the originals. I had a kind of craziness about him, an obsession. On the other hand, it didn't drive me to the library. I began to see these black faces in Bosch, black people in his paintings, sometimes at the edges, sometimes at the center . . . Particularly the Bosch painting which contains the Annunciation and the Wise Men on the left-hand panel, the adoration of the Magi. And one of those Magi was a black person. I guess I can make this kind of simple. When you're traveling through Europe as an African American, and you see an image of yourself, it's rare, and you do get excited. I understood something very crucial about Bosch through the way that he depicted this African personality. Why was the African dressed so down, compared to these dowdy wise men? Why did he stand in a certain elegant way, with his limbs supported in a particular fashion? Why was his waist more narrow? Why was there a certain luxuriousness and splendor in his garments? What was this medieval Lowlander seeing in these African people? And why was what he saw so much of what people saw in Pittsburgh and in New York about contemporary African Americans? Why was there that kind of continuity? Jesus! And, through the character of Cecil, I sort of worked those thoughts out. So, Bosch comes into the novel. And no, you don't necessarily have to know a lot about Hieronymus Bosch, but if you listen to the questions I ask in the book then I would hope maybe you would become interested in Bosch and become interested in the whole idea of representation in Western art and where we fit in it and how we've influenced it from the very beginning.

CP  Okay, let's just go back to that quote of yours from '88. I picked it up from a piece you wrote for *The New York Times*. The title of the piece was, "The Black Writer and the Magic of the Word." Let me play devil's advocate for a minute and ask you: do you think of yourself as a black writer?

JW (*pause*) No, because the word, like so many words, has been totally . . . raped of meaning, it's been destroyed, it's a tool, it's a kind of tong, something to pick up people without touching them. And that aspect of the word, unfortunately, hits me when I hear it. I don't like it. And it has a very vexed history, that word. Those two words. On the other hand, in my own mind, there's something very much like the word "black" that resonates and is crucially important to me. I might lexify it with the term, African-American, but I have no doubt that I represent and am part of a very specific culture. And that culture has its roots in Africa and across the ocean; and some of you, fortunately, know the story of how African cultural traits were retained and transmogrified and met Europe. And so, I see myself in that cultural strain and it's crucial to me. And the more I understand about those roots, the closer I get to what's important in the voice that I have.

CP You mentioned, in a short interview in *The New York Times*, how over twenty years ago you were approached by students at Penn and asked to teach a black literature class. I quote from John Wideman, "I gave them the jive reply that it wasn't my field. I was one of the few black faculty members at Penn; they came to me for all kinds of soulful reasons and I gave them the stock academic reply, which was true. But I felt so ashamed that I got back in touch with some of them, then agreed to teach the course—and then began my second education." Can you characterize the nature of that second education?

JW Well, very specifically, I spent the summer in the Schomburg Library, reading books that had been written by people of African descent. Of course, we're all of African descent if we believe the latest anthropological bulletin. But, people of the African diaspora—I read those books, and then I made it my business to begin to interview and talk to and make a connection with other black writers. And I organized a course in Afro-American lit. And since that point, I've been reading everything I possibly can. As I learned more, I found out what I needed to understand, what African-American culture might be. It led me into linguistics, it led me into a study of the language. And that was a very fruitful part of it. I mean, once I was in Germany, giving a lecture on the black voice, of all things, black speech, and, at the end of the lecture—I was speaking English, I only know two German words—to an audience who supposedly understood English—and a fraulein raised her hand and said, (I had been talking for an hour about black speech) "Herr Professor Videman, vould you speak some of that black English for us?" (*laughter*) So, you're me up at the podium, what do you say? "Hey, baby, what's happenin'?" (*laughter*) I didn't know what to say. It stunned me. This was a nitty-gritty question. One answer is, "Hey, I'm an African American and I've been talking for the last hour. You've been listening to African-American speech." And I think that is something which is the beginning of the real answer: There is no single register of African-American speech. And it's not words and intonations, it's a whole attitude about speech that has historical rooting. It's not a phenomenon that you can isolate and reduce to linguistic characteristics. It has to do with the way a culture conceives of the people inside of that culture. It has to do with a whole, complicated protocol of silences and speech, and how you use speech in ways other than directly to communicate information. And it has to do with, certainly, the experiences that the people in the speech situation bring into the encounter. What's fascinating to me about African-American speech is its spontaneity, the requirement that you not simply have a repertoire of vocabulary or syntactical devices/constructions, but that you come prepared to do something with that repertoire, those structures, and do something in an attempt to meet the person on a level that both uses the language, mocks the language, and recreates the language. It's a very active exchange. But at the same time as I say that, the silences and the refusal to speak is just as much a part, in another way, of African-American speech.

CP Okay. I want to take a left turn now and ask you a few questions about your actual process of writing. You move with equal facility, it seems to me, between the short story form and the novel. What criteria, for you, defines whether an idea is better suited to a novel or a short story? Is there one?

JW Only the practical working-out of it. I still think the story, "Fever," is a novel. But one of the reasons it works well, and I'm happy with it as a short story is because, somehow, the novel is in there, and it's pushing to get out. And I think that gives it some of the resonance that it has. A novel is certainly not a single idea and sometimes a story can be. But I would hesitate to think that there are any absolute cues, because I know that things in my experience that have started as stories became novels. And vice-versa.

CP Let me ask you about the story form, specifically the short story, "Everybody Knew Bubba Riff" from your last collection, *All Stories Are True*. It reads as though it has been composed in one sitting. It is like a long modernist cry—almost like a long note blown by a jazz trumpeter—was it composed at one sitting?

JW About half of the body was composed in one sitting . . . But that particular text that came out of that one sitting, which is half the story . . . you'd probably have a hard time finding it in the published version, because the way I work is to work and work and to rewrite.

CP Which half-answers my next question. Are you a man who painstakingly revises loose drafts, or are you a man who crafts slowly and deliberately, almost chiseling into stone words, phrases, that are already finely tuned?

JW Well, I hate to cop out, but it's always a combination. Some things come easily.

CP Right.

JW And if some didn't come easily, I would change professions. (*laughter*) You have to have that gift every now and again. And when the gift comes, you open yourself to it and the words just flow and you love it and that's what the whole process is about. It's really a way of going outside of myself. The sculpting and the chiseling and the work is more of a different discipline altogether. And I get tired of myself. I'm too aware of my limitations there and I'm always working against my limitations. So it's claustrophobic for a while. And I wonder, Is it ever going to get any better, because it's me talking to me, what do I know? So you need that infusion from somewhere else, whether you call it the muse, or the unconscious, or whatever. It has to swing in, you have to be visited, I think. At least this writer does.

CP I want to ask you about your role as a teacher of writing. Two questions: Firstly, has teaching affected your writing in any disturbing way? And do you feel inspired when you read the work of students?

JW Hmm. (*pause*) This is not a commercial, I assure you. (*laughter*) Well unless you're a total hypocrite, if you sit around and your job is to tell people, "Hey, look at this, this isn't right, you can do better. Here's something, change this. Write something beautiful. Write something strong," if that's your job . . . I take those messages home with me. When I sit down at my own stuff that shrewish voice which I hope is not shrewish too often, but that voice talks to me about my own stuff. So that's one answer. Am I inspired?

CP Or encouraged by who is particularly good.

JW Bring it down a few pegs. (*laughter*)

CP Interested?

JW Alert. (*laughter*) I'm very lucky. Because we have an extraordinary group of writers at UMass. And I am in fact inspired by some of their work. Inspired that this whole activity of writing is still alive. Some people are still hooked into it, hooked on it, and willing to take the chances and willing to push themselves. And willing to go a little crazy and willing to confront demons. And I see that activity as absolutely rare and crucial because what it does is sustain the whole notion of imagination in the culture. If there is any threat to our humanity, it's the threat that somehow our imaginations will be squashed, will become obsolete. It will become redundant, useless. And writing is one way to keep that idea of imagination alive. In my best days I see that as the primary enterprise I'm involved in. Stimulating the imagination. Foregrounding it, saying that it counts. Saying that whatever is in your head has some meaning. And I think most of the messages in the culture are saying that it doesn't have meaning, that it doesn't matter what's inside your head. Fuck you, ya know. Get in line. So I welcome people who are on a different track. We're on our little boat, ship of fools, and there we are. It's nice to have company.

# Tobias Wolff
# and A.M. Homes

TOBIAS WOLFF was born in Birmingham, Alabama, in 1945. He is the author of the novels *The Barracks Thief* and *Old School*, the memoirs *This Boy's Life* and *In Pharaoh's Army*, and the short story collections *In the Garden of the North American Martyrs*, *Back in the World*, and *The Night in Question*. His most recent collection of short stories, *Our Story Begins*, won The Story Prize in 2008. Other honors include the PEN/Malamud Award and the Rea Award—both for excellence in the short story—the *Los Angeles Times* Book Prize, and the PEN/Faulkner Award. A graduate of Hertford College, Oxford and Stanford, Wolff is a professor of English and creative writing at Stanford University.

A.M. HOMES was born in Washington, DC, in 1961. Her fiction includes *The End of Alice*, *Jack*, *The Safety of Objects*, and *May We Be Forgiven*, which won the Women's Prize for Fiction. A graduate of Sarah Lawrence College and the University of Iowa Writers' Workshop, where she earned her MFA, Homes has been awarded a Guggenheim Fellowship and a National Endowment for the Arts Fellowship. Her work has been translated into twenty-two languages. She lectures in creative writing at Princeton and lives in New York City.

**A. M. HOMES** How has the process of writing changed for you over time?

**TOBIAS WOLFF** I'm not sure it has. No, it probably has. Let me say that I am now a little more reconciled to my peculiarities as a writer. When I first started writing, in my teens, I could write eight pages a day. And I believed that all eight pages were deathless prose. Now I am reconciled to writing a paragraph or two that I'll end up keeping.

**AMH** I wonder whether it gets harder and harder on some level.

**TW** Every successful piece of writing you do, I mean successful as art, illuminates even more greatly the difficulties of what you do. You're always trying to top yourself. You don't want to do what you did before again and again. You get tired of certain conventions. You want to do other things, so you're creating the difficulties as the very condition of your art. It's a way of keeping it exciting for yourself, but it also makes it increasingly harder.

**AMH** How do you know when you're finished with a story?

**TW** When everything necessary is done, and I feel as if even another word would be superfluous—would, in a manner of speaking, break the camel's back. That sense of completion comes about in different ways, and plot is only the most obvious of them. You should feel, when you've finished a story, that it has achieved a life independent of yours, that it has somehow gathered up the golden chain that connected you. This feeling is not always reliable. I often go back and revise endings that I was pretty sure about when I set the last period to the page. In writing, of course, everything is subject to revision. But I am guided, however roughly, by inexplicable instincts like the one I have just attempted to describe.

**AMH** In your story "The Chain" and in "Bullet in the Brain," events spiral and flip out of control, one bit of wrong thinking folds into the next in an effort to clarify or correct the last. Is this a recurring theme with you?

**TW** Some of my writing is about folly, and the capacity folly has for reproducing itself, how it multiplies. How a bad idea becomes ten bad ideas, becomes a hundred bad ideas. Stories are a good kind of theater for folly.

**AMH** A minute ago you mentioned your peculiarities as a writer—how would you characterize them?

TW  Oh, I'm not the best judge of that at all. I can say something about my intentions, though even those are finally beside the point when the work is finished. But I'm looking at the story or the book from inside, and I'm often unaware of what is plain as day to people regarding it from the outside. For example, a graduate student at SUNY Albany sent me an essay of hers concerning the terrible fate of dogs in my work, together with some speculations about my motives in writing about them in this way. She had plenty of evidence from my work—dogs shot, burned, even eaten. Yet in all honesty I'd never been aware of this . . . pattern, if you will, or peculiarity. I guess you'd be justified in calling it a peculiarity. And I'm glad I was unaware of it, because otherwise I might have avoided it and not written some things that I'm pleased to have written. That's the danger of excessive self-consciousness—it either becomes very constricting, or leads to self-parody of the worst kind. Like X. J. Kennedy's poem about the goose that laid the golden egg. She sticks her head up her rear end to observe the process, then gets stuck in that position. His poem concludes, "If you'd lay well, don't watch."

AMH  I'm interested in the idea of writing from a moral point of view. In one of the *In Pharaoh's Army* interviews you said, "It seemed to me that I was responsible for a moral accounting. A book like this has to be a personal moral inventory." Concepts of morality come up a lot in your work.

TW  When I talk about the "personal moral inventory" it's not so much about the immorality of the war itself, but the sense of how an ordinary person is complicit in the ongoing folly of his time. Even with honorable intentions and a certain measure of innocence, you can become a part of the very thing you fear and despise. And this shows up in my fiction. It isn't a question of the stories being moral fables: "Don't do this because something terrible will happen." It's more an exploration of the moral sense that dominates our lives for better or worse, the constant effort of trying to find the right thing to do in complex situations. I can't imagine not having that kind of reckoning in my work because it's at the center of our lives. Everyone I know is puzzling things out, trying to figure out the right thing to do. We're all in a web of connection to friends, family, community, and the moral sense is what determines how we honor those connections. To leave that out of one's fiction seems to me to be impossible. It's going to be there, so it's better that it not be there by default, but that you have some edge of consciousness about its workings.

AMH  We were talking before about how events in your stories spiral, how wrong-headed thinking multiplies, for instance, in your story "The Chain."

TW Here's a man who's trying to find the right thing to do. He isn't just trying to get even, he's trying to do what is right in this situation. He acts out of love for his daughter, through rage at the wrong done by the indifference of others, and from a sense of the wrong of being too timid in the face of evil. All these good motives are at work in what ends up being an absolutely catastrophic mistake.

AMH One of my favorite stories in the new collection is "Casualty." I was fascinated by the structure, the nurse who essentially ends the story isn't there at the beginning. This is very conservative of me, but I always think the people in the beginning of the story must be the same people around at the end of the story.

TW It does seem unfair, to spring a new character on you at the end. In the case of "Casualty," I had her in mind from the beginning. I didn't want too narrow an understanding of who gets hurt in this war. The word casualty usually refers to soldiers, but the damage ripples out in every direction, and touches all these people and harms them deeply . . . I had her in mind all the time I was writing that story, but how could any reader know that? Now if I had done that to evade the consequences of the story for the characters who were there at the beginning, B.D. and Ryan in particular, then I think her late appearance would be a mistake. But their stories are pretty well settled when she shows up.

AMH It's interesting that she was always in your mind—it works that she doesn't appear to us until later, it makes the story keep going.

TW She is very much a part of their story, but she isn't present until their circumstances compel her to enter. Then the story becomes as much hers as theirs. At one point I was thinking of calling it "The Nurse's Story." It would give people some sense that this was coming. I did realize that it was a gamble to introduce her so late, and give her so much weight. But her presence brings something essential. There's an almost romantic obsession with soldiers in most writing about war. It may not mean to be romantic, but it ends up that way because it views soldiers in isolation from the consequences of what they do and what is done to them. You don't see how they're situated in a web of relations, how one person's suffering bleeds into other lives. That is what is missing from so many of these war narratives, and why the nurse was so important to me.

**AMH**  I love the part when she slips the one dying guy's hand into the other's, that's just so lovely.

**TW**  Good.

**AMH**  How has the way you write about Vietnam changed over the years?

**TW**  I couldn't write very much about it in the beginning. I have one very short story in my first book which touches on it. I'm still hesitant to write about it.

**AMH**  Why do you think?

**TW**  It's one of those things you just don't want to get wrong. There's a way of writing about Vietnam that is extremely stale: the helicopters; the jazzed-up soldier lingo; all the acronyms; deadpan talk about killing. There's a strong pull exerted by the conventions of war fiction in particular. That's why I ended up writing about it in a memoir, because I thought I could resist those pressures more successfully by being faithful to my knowledge of my own situation, of the effect of that situation on my character and nature. I wouldn't just be writing about what everybody already knew about.

**AMH**  I've always been fascinated with the Vietnam War and I wonder where people who've been at war put the experience?

**TW**  What do you mean?

**AMH**  Where does it fit inside you? How do you reconcile it? Does everybody who has been in the war have side effects from it?

**TW**  I don't have post-traumatic stress syndrome. But I have no question that others do have it. It comes about through prolonged exposure to combat, which I did not have. I had some, but not very much, very little, compared to most of the people I knew. I got lucky—the place I was sent that year was quieter than many other places. The luck of the draw, really. It was bad enough for me. I had my stomach full of it and then some. But nothing like what happened to others. I was very lucky, and lucky not just in terms of surviving it, but lucky in that when I got home I was still healthy enough psychologically to have a reasonable life. But a lot of people weren't.

**AMH**  Are you by nature very aware?

TW  Cautious you mean?

AMH  I'm thinking about situations in which a person has to be aware of their surroundings, of their safety, and then about being a soldier, where something could happen at any moment, a sniper, something falling out of the sky, a land mine—and what that does to you.

TW  It had effects, there's no question about it. Nobody gets away scot-free from something like that. I certainly have a healthy sense of the dangers of this world. One way I do notice it is that I worry about my kids. One of my boys just started driving and the other will start driving in another month. I try not to think about it or else I'll go crazy. Nevertheless it's there. One of my boys likes to go for long walks at night, and although we live in a reasonably safe neighborhood, it's bordered by an unsafe neighborhood. I hear myself Mother Henning him all the time on this.

AMH  I have the feeling that you are a wonderful teacher and a good father. How have you transcended the experience of your own father?

TW  How do you learn to be a father without being your father?

AMH  Exactly.

TW  It has always come naturally to me to be affectionate with my kids and to enjoy them. They certainly make it easy. I have great kids. They're funny, they're good company. They always have been. It just hasn't seemed like hard work to me, to tell you the truth. One thing of course that makes it easy is that I have more time than other people do. I teach, and I work at home. When my kids come home I'm there. They can come up and talk to me. I'm not under the kind of pressures that make it hard for most people to be the kind of parents they want to be and just don't have the time to be.

AMH  But you also remade your experience of family.

TW  Oh, I was always pretty nervous about the whole idea. It's sort of like writing. You approach it very warily and then when you're in it, it teaches you what to do. But yeah, I had real doubts about my abilities to pull this thing off. But the moment children arrive, you're so busy with them, you find yourself doing the right things. Most of the time, anyway. I hope.

**AMH** I'm curious to hear your thoughts on the differences in your experience of writing nonfiction and fiction?

**TW** I hold myself to very different standards when I'm writing fiction and nonfiction. I have to be able, with a straight face, to tell myself that something is nonfiction if I say it's nonfiction. That's why, although there are autobiographical elements in some of my stories, I still call them fiction because that's what they are. Even though they may have been set into motion by some catalyst of memory.

**AMH** Why do you think people want everything to be true?

**TW** They're uncomfortable somehow with imaginative reality, which is a very powerful reality against which we have few defenses. They're perhaps unaccustomed to art and the assumptions of art. I'm not really sure.

**AMH** Do you think it's an American thing?

**TW** I think Americans are more accepting if they think it's nonfiction. Is it an American thing? No, my guess is it isn't. Writers and artists have always done what they could to seduce the audience into a sense that what they're looking at is genuine. That's the great power of movies, isn't it? They give you the feeling that what you are looking at is life happening before your eyes. Writers invite that kind of approach to their work. We want people to believe it while they're reading it—we want them to enter our world fully.

**AMH** I'm curious about how we grow up, the progression of things. You're fifty-one now—you seem incredibly stable—what about a midlife crisis? Are they inevitable? Do you have to have one? Do you feel one coming on?

**TW** I had mine when I was in my teens, that was my midlife crisis.

**AMH** Right, precocious.

**TW** I'm grateful to have had the life I've had. First of all, I feel lucky to be alive. I feel lucky to be sane and whole, to have a life as a writer. What a privilege that is, and one that for years and years I thought I would not have, that this would be something I would just do on my own all my life. That I would probably have to end up doing something else, and do this when I could. It still astonishes me that I've been able to have a life as a writer. I don't teach a lot, but I love the teaching that I do. And I meet people like you. What's to complain about?

AMH  I don't know.

TW  I do feel sometimes—which may be the kind of propellant for a lot of these absurd chapters in the lives of people my age—a sense of having become too comfortable, of being an old shoe and wanting to push myself to thinner air. But I find ways of getting around that. I drive too fast. I ski the black diamond slopes, and I play cutthroat softball. I'm being facetious. But that restlessness is still there. I don't think it's in a virulent state, I don't think I'm going to destroy my life in obedience to it. It isn't at its deepest level philosophical. I know I have found the ground on which I must make my peace, through these people I live with and not through change of circumstance or a dramatis personae.

AMH  In *In Pharaoh's Army* you write about joining the military to get at an experience. And I think about you having settled down, teaching and living this seemingly stable life; from where do you get experience now?

TW  In *The End of Alice* you write very powerfully and persuasively from the point of view of a pedophile. Am I to think therefore that you must have experience with pedophilia?

AMH  I actually know nothing about it, which is the funny thing. I did a lot of research.

TW  You know that old chestnut of Flannery O'Connor's, about anyone who survives adolescence has enough to write about for the rest of their lives. There's a strong, very early story of hers in *DoubleTake* magazine called "The Coat," written from the point of view of a black woman. She wrote it when she was in her twenties, at Iowa. How the hell did she know to do that? In the end, the writer's task is not to accumulate experience, but to develop a consciousness that can see the world with some accuracy and fitting sense of drama.

AMH  You went to boarding school, and then into the army, and then off to study in England; did you feel comfortable in all those settings or were you an outsider?

TW  I felt right at home when I went off to that boarding school because

I had wanted so much to go there. It was funny to be happy in this place where all the other kids wanted to be home. But it was much more peaceful than my home life. And it was intellectually alive, there were people talking about ideas and books in a way I'd never even known you could, except through my brother in the brief time we'd spent together before I went off to school. So I was quite happy and at home in that place. But God knows there were transitions to be made. I was aware of there being class tensions at Oxford, but as a Yank I was outside of those considerations. And I really felt as if I belonged to a community when I was there, an artistic and intellectual community. Those were the people I knew at Oxford, and they were not consumed by questions of class. Artists and intellectuals are their own class. These were people who were committed to writing, and reading, and understanding. And we talked incessantly. My real education came not so much through the classes and tutors, as through my time with my friends. The pubs closed at ten, so we'd buy some booze and sit around somebody's room and just talk, talk, talk, talk, and I've never forgotten that. The sharpening effect on the mind, the awakening, was so exhilarating that questions of class and economic status really didn't play much of a part. I started writing in a disciplined way, as soon as I got to Oxford, and that was very important to me. I was reading, making friends, traveling—it was a God-given time.

AMH  Were they amazed that you had been a soldier?

TW  We didn't talk about it very much. First of all, I did not have a way of talking about it that did not make other people extremely uncomfortable. I had this compulsion to rub people's noses in the horror of it, to tell them the worst things. But I would tell them in this cruel laughing way. Because the minute I started on that subject I'd go back to being a soldier, and that's the way soldiers handle it. I began to see how discordant a note this struck whenever we started talking. Most of my friends learned not to talk to me about it, and I never brought it up, I never brought it up.

AMH  But that in itself is fascinating. I'm always amazed by splits in people.

TW  Well, I still have plenty of those.